# RESEARCH METHODS

# RESEARCH METHODS

## Jack R. Nation

Prentice Hall, Upper Saddle River, N.J. 07458

*Library of Congress Cataloging-in-Publication Data*

Nation, Jack R.
   Research methods / Jack R. Nation.
      p.    cm.
   Includes bibliographical references and index.
   ISBN 0-02-386132-0
    1. Psychology—Research. 2. Psychology—Research—Methodolgy.
   3. Psychology, Experimental. I. Title.
   BF76.5.N27  1997
   150'.72—dc20                          96-41289
                                           CIP

*Editor-in-chief:* Pete Janzow
*Assistant editor:* Nicole Signoretti
*Director of production and manufacturing:* Barbara Kittle
*Managing editor:* Bonnie Biller
*Project manager:* Fran Russello
*Editorial/production supervision:* PublisherStudio
*Manufacturing manager:* Nick Sklitsis
*Prepress and manufacturing buyer:* Tricia Kenny
*Creative design director:* Leslie Osher
*Art director:* Anne Bonanno Nieglos
*Cover and interior design:* Levavi & Levavi
*Supervisor of production services:* Lori Clinton
*Line art coordinator:* Michele Giusti
*Electronic art creation:* PublisherStudio

This book was set in 10/12 Garamond Light by NK Graphics
and was printed and bound by R. R. Donnelley & Sons
Company. The cover was printed by Phoenix Color Corp.

 © 1997 by Prentice-Hall, Inc.
Simon & Schuster/A Viacom Company
Upper Saddle River, New Jersey 07458

Printed in the United States of America
10  9  8  7  6  5  4  3  2  1

ISBN 0-02-386132-0

Prentice-Hall International (UK) Limited, *London*
Prentice-Hall of Australia Pty. Limited, *Sydney*
Prentice-Hall Canada Inc., *Toronto*
Prentice-Hall Hispanoamericana, S.A., *Mexico*
Prentice-Hall of India Private Limited, *New Delhi*
Prentice-Hall of Japan, Inc., *Tokyo*
Simon & Schuster Asia Pte. Ltd., *Singapore*
Editora Prentice-Hall do Brasil, Ltda., *Rio de Janeiro*

This book is dedicated to Patricia and Derek Nation and Shannon, and Hunter Harris.

# Contents

# Preface

For more than 20 years, I have been intensively involved in research. My topics of interest have included learning models of human depression, sport psychology, and behavioral pharmacology and toxicology. The levels of analysis I have selected have varied from global behavioral measures to molecular mechanisms in neurochemical function. Despite my seemingly diverse research experiences, I have maintained a central theme—curiosity.

Grappling with an uncertain world and wanting to know more about how that world is fashioned is basic to human existence. People inherently just want to know. Consequently, it has been no surprise to me that the scores of undergraduate and graduate students that have assisted me in the laboratory over the years have demonstrated a keen intellectual and practical interest in our shared research. Indeed, I have never had a student in my laboratory who professed anything other than enthusiasm when it came to "finding out."

Research is vital, exciting, and fetches innovative thought, but it has to be brought to life in the same way as any other subject matter. Students will respond to any topic area if it is presented properly, and it is my aim to present research methods properly. To the extent that I am successful in this regard, my role as a teacher is enhanced and my commitment to research is expanded. Following are some features of this book I hope will assist in communicating the essence of research methodology and the thrill of scientific investigation.

## DISTINGUISHING FEATURES

A major objective of this book is to demonstrate the relevance of behavioral research. Working closely with the editorial staff at Prentice Hall, I have incorporated a number of features into the text that underscore the relevance of behavioral inquiry, while maintaining the needed balance between basic and applied research. In this final product, content and application are each given high priority. As we will see, they work in concert, not opposition.

## The Model Experiment

Over the chapters of this book, a model experiment is developed systematically. Commencing with the formulation of an original hypothesis, together we build an experimental framework that leads to a novel, programmatic project that is designed to assess the appropriateness of certain forms of cognitive therapy for treating pediatric oncology patients. Each chapter serves as a building block and vehicle for introducing new terms and concepts. As we see the model experiment unfold over the course of this text, we learn about the elements of research, how they are combined, and how they are related. To my knowledge, no other textbook has ever attempted such an undertaking. By the end of the course, you will see that, with our task accomplished and our journey ended, we will have proudly produced something that could advance our awareness of issues relating to chronically ill children in some small but meaningful way. After all, this is where the real thrill in research comes from—not from achieving a major breakthrough, but from participating.

## Thinking About Research

In this book you will find sections entitled "Thinking About Research." These sections pose questions about particular topics or issues in behavioral research and give you a chance to think about resolutions, alternatives, implications, and other aspects of research that present opportunities for creative thinking. In most cases, there are no clear-cut responses, but you will find the coverage provocative nonetheless. Ultimately, these sections ask you to reflect on current or timeless scholastic arguments or on approaches to conducting behavioral research.

## Spotlight on Research

Another feature presented in each chapter is a special section entitled "Spotlight on Research." These sections highlight some of the more interesting studies in behavioral research and address matters that are likely to be of general interest. These sections range from discussing ethics to potential confounds in the research of biological determinants of human homosexuality. These sections go beyond simple description and engage you on a more personal level.

## *Multiculturalism*

Cultural and ethnic diversity is increasing in North America, and behavioral researchers are becoming increasingly sensitive to the need to incorporate multicultural variables into mainstream activities. Where appropriate, this book discusses the unique ways that multiculturalism has changed the way we think about research and the implications some of these findings have on policy, decision making, and the growth of psychology and the social sciences.

I hope the discussion of cultural diversity in behavioral research elevates our collective consciousness of the need to examine all dimensions of human conduct. As the color and ambitions of the world change, we as investigators must also change and keep pace with the evolutionary phenomena that affect the way we all live.

## *Currency*

In the information age, each of us is obligated to remain current, and this textbook is no exception. I have integrated recent research examples, mentioned the latest computer search programs, and identified some of the more important changes in recording and analytical hardware. In addition, I used the fourth edition of the American Psychological Association (APA) (1994) *Publication Manual* to develop this text. Referencing, writing style, sensitivity to gender issues, and other matters relating to exposition follow the recommendations of APA.

# PEDAGOGICAL ELEMENTS

Several other features of this book are more directly related to the learning process and the accessibility of material.

## *Chapter Outlines*

Each chapter begins with a chapter outline that profiles the major headings and subheadings of the chapter. The objective of the outlines is to provide information on the overall organization of the chapters. These may help you as you read through your chapter assignments.

## *Graphs, Illustrations, and Tables*

The coverage is enhanced with graphic representations of selected data and tabular summaries and descriptions of important items or ideas. These elements highlight areas of focus and accent certain points in the discussion.

## *Key Terms*

In the margins of the pages of this book, you will find key terms and definitions. Give them special attention because they are important to understanding the chapters in which they appear, as well as later chapters.

## *Within Chapter Review and Study Questions*

At the end of each major section in each chapter, you will also find review statements and study questions. Your responses to these comments and questions can be used to identify areas of strength and weakness with respect to your understanding of the content of the chapter.

## *Index*

An alphabetized index of topics is at the end of the book. Refer to this index when you need information on a particular topic.

# Acknowledgments

The idea for this book grew out of several conversations I had with Chris Cardone, who was then an editor with Macmillan Publishing Company. She guided the development of the book in its early stages and continued to encourage the project until Macmillan and Prentice Hall merged in 1993. At that time, Peter Janzow and Nicole Signoretti assumed the editorial responsibilities for completing the book, and I am indebted to them for their many helpful suggestions regarding details of the final product.

In addition to the cooperative editorial staff at Prentice Hall, several reviewers of the original manuscript should be recognized. They are: Mike Knight, University of Central Oklahoma; Bernard Beins, Ithaca College; Diane Mello-Goldner, Pine Manor College.

These reviewers provided thoughtful, instructive comments on the suitability of the content and style of the book, and I greatly appreciate their willingness to work with me to complete this project. Surely, the quality of this book has been enhanced by their efforts.

Finally, I would like to express my appreciation to Patricia L. Nation for providing the research idea that forms the basis for the model experiment that integrates this book. My understanding of the boundaries for conducting research in an unfamiliar area has increased, and I have gained accordingly as a student of behavior. Once again, I am reminded of the teacher/student covenant—share.

Jack R. Nation

# Author Biography

Jack Nation is currently professor of psychology at Texas A&M University. He received his Ph.D. in psychology from the University of Oklahoma in 1974 and has written over 80 scientific papers on a variety of topics ranging from the personality profiles of college football players to the neurochemical determinants of drug abuse. Since 1995, Nation has contributed articles to such journals as *Brain Research, Experimental and Clinical Psychopharmacology,* and *Drug and Alcohol Dependence.* He recently received several grants from the National Institutes of Health (NIH) to support his research into the effects of environmental pollution on drug abuse. In 1995 Texas A&M University honored Nation with a Distinguished Achievement Award where he ranked first out of 2,500 faculty members in teaching performance.

# Introduction to Research Methodology

Through memory, each of us is able to fetch moments of our youth. For me, this process often involves recalling my time spent as a young boy growing up in rural Oklahoma and remembering languid summer days free of responsibility, each day buoyed by the promise of discovery. It is in this context that I can recount a childhood episode which I acted out in one form or another as a matter of routine.

My morning walk had taken me across an open pasture and toward a small pond that had been cast by a natural clay embankment. As I approached the pond, I noticed one of the all-too-familiar great-red-ant beds that pock the southwestern region of the United States. Looking down on the teeming center of the bed, I watched the worker ants move in and about the mound with considerable curiosity and soon discovered a pattern. Each insect would come off the mound and move a foot or so toward a second active mound not more than a couple of feet away. Invariably, the ant would then turn in a direction opposite the second mound and travel at least 20 yards toward a third mound along a trail that had been beaten into the land by low-impact ant treading.

I began to examine the activities of other ants in neighboring communities, and it seemed that much the same pattern would occur. Rather than do what would seem sensible to a nonant observer, the insects would forsake the local environment and hike cross-country to accomplish what could have been achieved closer to their home.

Now, this ant deal caused me considerable discomfort for a few days. In an orderly world, abiding ant phenomena that defy logic and reason can be a source of palpable anxiety. What on earth was going on here? What could produce such a strange behavior in a feral bug which, by definition, should be committed to a life of simplicity? There had to be an answer, and I was bent on getting it.

I read the meager materials on ant behavior from our unpretending home library, but they were of no help. In addition, I inquired among the local sages whom I felt might qualify as ant specialists, but they were equally uninformative. Finally, I placed a phone call to a legitimate entomologist at a nearby university and obtained an answer. The answer was ultimately a chemical one. The ants were responding to chemical tags that had been set down by the queen ant. Each ant in a colony is constrained by a biological imperative to serve only the queen that produces it. Thus the seemingly inappropriate behavior of the worker ants arose—the adjacent mounds I had observed were the beds of different queens; the distant mound was of a common origin.

The nuances of ant life may not be judged by most readers to be in the realm of high theater. However, this ant example illustrates a basic human quality. Each of us has an insatiable curiosity and an irrepressible desire to gather data. For some, the information search may focus on identifying the precise combination of ingredients that yields the ideal cheesecake. Another person may be concerned about recent market declines in pork belly futures and the impact such changes might have on other economic issues. Wrinkles in drug traffic, shifts in the geopolitical mosaic, housing sales, annual tallies of automobile deaths, preschools' efficiency, finding the address of the Selective Service System, or selecting an appropriate college or university might be prominent questions for certain people at given junctures in their lives. The point is that the most essential element of existence is the ability to collect and profit from information gained from the world about us.

As you will see later in this opening chapter, there are a variety of methods for collecting, compiling, and sorting data. It also becomes evident that the method recommended over all others is the scientific method. A word of caution is in order, however. Throughout this book, be aware that the scientific approach set forth in this work is convenient more than anything else. I am reminded of an insightful intellectual reprimand offered by the poet-scientist Loren Eiseley, former head of the Department of History and Philosophy of Science at the University of Pennsylvania.

Professor Eiseley had just had his first book, *The Immense Journey,* published in 1957. The manuscript, a delightful essay on the evolutionary development of humankind, was never intended to be a scholastic portrayal of selection and adaptation processes. It was, rather, an attempt to educate the general public about the absurdity inherent in the position many people take, which assumes evolution has stopped—people tend to project idealized versions of themselves into the future when the truth is humans as such will not be here in the world of tomorrow (Eiseley, 1957).

This admittedly nonscientific production so outraged an assistant professor in Eiseley's department that the assistant marched into Eiseley's office one afternoon and reproached Eiseley for his wasted effort. The assistant charged that Eiseley could have spent his time in scientific writing, rather than pandering to the public with a trade book. At this point Eiseley realized that because his colleague slavishly adhered to a scientific model, all the young assistant professor had accomplished was substituting the authority of science for the authority of religion (see Gerber & McFadden, 1990, for a biography on Eiseley).

The thrust of Eiseley's remarks, which I as a behavioral scientist support fully, is that science has never promised more than to offer a convenient framework for exploration. The scientific method prescribes a certain agenda, and events that fall outside this agenda are verboten. Science does not have all the answers, but through scientific investigation a more complete understanding of certain relations is possible.

Having offered this admonition, I feel equally compelled to note that once an individual chooses to work within a scientific framework, which is what is advanced in this book, that individual is obliged to remain within that framework. As a scientist, you cannot step outside the structure of your approach and make statements that are not scientifically credible. The scientific approach is a good system, but it requires discipline. The advantages of the scientific approach to data acquisition and examination can be appreciated more fully if we evaluate the approach in the context of the alternatives. Let's see what our options are.

# COMMON ATTEMPTS AT INTERPRETING INFORMATION

Belief systems have long been the focus of scholars in the philosophy of science area (see Cohen & Nagel, 1934). Much of the academic discussion along these lines has centered on how people evaluate and interpret new information. In essence, **the acquisition of knowledge** emerged as a distinct subject matter which attracted the attention of writers, artists, and scientists alike (Helmstadter, 1970). The coverage of different approaches to accepting a belief begins here with one of the most basic methods for assessing new information: tenacity.

## *Tenacity*

The term *truism* refers to a belief or position that is so self-evident that it renders review of the accuracy of the viewpoint unnecessary. Some phenomena are so conspicuous in their meanings and causes that it seems like a waste of time to discuss the authenticity of statements that derive from these events. Everyone knows that "As you grow older you need to slow down and get more rest," and that "There is a fine line between genius and mental illness." With such truisms, an evaluation and examination of the true facts rarely takes place because such things are "givens" in a predictable and certain environment.

In point of fact, however, truisms are often accepted inappropriately, and the beliefs, held however firmly, are in place merely because someone has proclaimed a doctrine or dogma to be true. Should an individual accepting an idea make an effort to examine further the legitimacy of the issue, it may become apparent that a position is incorrect despite the fact that "it has always been this way." Our examples agree with this assertion. Scientific evidence indicates that as you grow older you actually need less sleep (refer to Benjamin, Hopkins, & Nation, 1994), and that the more intelligent you are, the more satisfactory your level of emotional adjustment (see Carson, Burcher, & Mincka, 1996).

When a person accepts information just because it is repeatedly presented as authentic, that person's approach to knowledge acquisition and understanding can be said to result from **tenacity.** In its simplest form, tenacity means that people will believe virtually anything you tell them if you say it often enough and with conviction.

For example, one of the darkest periods in American political history was in the early 1950s when Senator Joseph McCarthy persecuted innocent U.S. citizens, ostensibly because they were Communists (for further reading see Vedlitz, 1988). Using the authority of the U.S. Senate as his cudgel, "Tailgunner Joe," as he was called, forcefully sold the American public a script which told them any person even remotely associated with socialism was a threat to national security. The fact that many of the accused were not Communists is incidental; what is important is that for a brief period the Constitution of the United States was thrown out the window because of belief systems which had been built on tenacity. McCarthy's line had been carefully and deliberately restated in the same way so often and so confidently that the public willfully endorsed censorship, job dismissal, and even imprisonment simply because a person was alleged to be a Communist.

When people arrive at such conclusions, they build a knowledge base that suffers from two fundamental weaknesses. First, the method of tenacity is often flawed by reality—the position advanced as true may be false. In the case of the "Red Scare" period of the 1950s, as the McCarthy era was called, it may or may not have been the case that Communists operating in the United States posed a discernable threat to national security. Even in instances where Communist party members worked in government operations, several factors (i.e., a low number of Communist employees) might have discredited the argument that Communists were a menacing and potentially lethal element in society. The second weakness of tenacity is that there is no vehicle for correcting false assumptions. Because the original position is arrived at in the absence of data, marshaling evidence against an erroneous doctrine is not likely to have much impact.

Accepting information through tenacity is in many ways infantile. We blindly accept reports as gospel, in the same manner that we blindly do what we are told as children. This orientation, whereby individuals adopt a stance or interpret information based on a perceived discrepancy between themselves and another person or outside force, addresses matters relating to authority.

## Authority

In the absence of information about the relation between and among various environmental events, we may look to another source for explanations. Rather than grope in the dark, looking for clues to understand specific phenomena, it is often easier, and surely quicker, to accept the position that is set forth by **fiat.** Fiat refers to an authoritative order

**the acquisition of knowledge—** academic subject matter concerned with determining how beliefs are accepted

**tenacity**—the quality of accepting information because the information is repeatedly and forcefully presented

**fiat**—an authoritative order or decree

or decree, and it may come in the form of an institutional command or a personal prejudice.

In cases of uncertainty about practical and organizational matters that are either beyond our level of understanding or that fall into an unfamiliar realm, we rely on the recommendations of some external structure. Because it is not possible for us to answer questions such as, "What is the true origin of humankind?" or "What purpose is there in existence?" we must turn to something we view as more powerful than ourselves for resolution. This may involve embracing a persuasive religious ideology, a compelling philosophical orientation, or an organizational code. A military officer who renders judgments about battle tactics based on an accepted strategic manual or a corporate vice president who carries out the policies of her parent company acts according to prescribed rules. In such contexts, there really are no judgments to be made; one just follows the guidelines of an authority—a fiat.

Submission to authority similarly is revealed in our reactions to individuals deemed to be experts, leaders, or simply more knowledgeable about an area. Certainly, when we as a matter of faith swallow pharmacological products prescribed by a physician, which at some concentrations are toxic, we accept the authority of medical practice. You take the product because you are told to take the product and because you don't know any better. In much the same way, you accept the information on research methods set forth in this book. The belief is that I am an experienced investigator and as such am a reliable source of information about a new and unfamiliar topic.

As a general rule, the greater the perception of the authority figure's credibility, the more dramatic the figure's impact on decision making. In a classic series of psychological experiments on authority and obedience conducted by Stanley Milgram (1974), it was discovered that people were more obedient to authoritative demands when the fiat came from what seemed to be a more sophisticated source. That is, it was found that people were more inclined to go against their values and respond with hostility toward other people when the instructions to do so came from someone who was alleged to be a famous scientist, as opposed to someone of lesser rank and reputation. When the source of our information is judged to be exceptionally knowledgeable or otherwise in control, we feel more comfortable letting the source direct our behavior.

Although responding on the basis of authority may sound mindless and even reprehensible, it should be understood that as a method for interpreting and accepting information, doing so has certain advantages. First, there is no deliberation, so we can proceed toward a conclusion. Also, because we know less about the issues than does the perceived authority, the information will likely improve our chances for understanding. However, you have to be careful about stating that any information is better than none at all. If the authority is flagrantly wrong, and you accept the fiat anyway, you are worse off than before.

Consider *The Malleus Maleficarum,* or The Witches' Hammer, which was published in 1484 and sanctioned by the Roman Catholic Church as an inquisitional manual. With this manual, mysterious events could be understood as incidents of witchcraft, and clear recommendations about remediation were detailed by an omnipotent institutional authority. As a result, thousands of innocent women were burned at the stake because an authority (the Church) mistakenly promulgated an erroneous doctrine.

Because of the potential for misguided beliefs stemming from incorrect authorities, claims have been made that decisions should rest more squarely on observation. As we shall see, however, what we see is not always what is real.

## Empiricism

**Empiricism** refers to the practice of relying on observation. While empiricism may involve an objective analysis of events outside our sensory world, it often involves an approach to understanding events that is based on experience. Having just experienced the softness of an October snowflake, American author Henry David Thoreau once remarked, "Winter, with its inwardness, is upon us. A man is constrained to sit down and to think" (Thoreau's Journal, Oct. 27, 1851).

We all respond to such signals in our environment. The re-creation of life in a spring blossom, the effects of economic recession on unemployment, the consequences of flipping on a light switch in a dark room, and arriving late for an early morning class are all events we know something about because we have experienced them. We have gathered the data, and under the conditions imposed by the environment we feel confident the pattern of results will be the same again.

To be sure, experience is a master teacher, but it is sometimes a teacher who strays from the lesson plan or instructs us in the art of deception. This point was cleverly made by Professor Vincent Dethier in his informative and amusing classic, *To Know a Fly* (1962):

> One day in the laboratory I astounded my students by showing them a fly so well educated that he could write my name in fine Spencerian script (an accomplishment beyond the capability of many of my students). To accomplish this I first removed the wings from a hungry fly so that he could not stray from the sheet of paper on which I planned to turn him loose. Before class I traced my name on paper with a fine camel's hair brush dipped in dilute sugar. As soon as the trace dried it became invisible. When the time came for the demonstration, I attached to the tail of the fly a minute wick dipped in ink and then released him in the vicinity of the invisible trail. After wandering a bit, his feet encountered the sugar deposited on the paper. The rest is history.

**empiricism**—a method for gathering information through normal sensory channels

Now, based on empirical evidence gained through experience, Dethier's students had no choice but to accept the fact that the intellectual apparatus of the common housefly includes the ability to spell. Of course, experience in such cases is insufficient because what is evident through observation fails to accurately characterize the situation. Actually, this failure to accurately characterize happens frequently when one relies on personal experience for understanding. It is not enough to see that something is repeatable and verifiable by consensual validation. Uniform descriptive accounts provided by equally deceived observers do not further our understanding of behavioral phenomena. All of Dethier's students reported the same fact—the fly wrote in cursive and spelled Dethier's name. However, more important than the fact is, "How did this happen?" How does one go about determining the true reasons for a relationship? Empirical accounts are integral to answering such questions, but a much more elaborate organizational structure is required. Such a structure is available in the framework of the scientific method.

# UNDERSTANDING PSYCHOLOGY: THE SCIENTIFIC APPROACH

Although the coverage in this text is appropriate for any subject area in which research and experimental analyses are of interest, the focus of the discussion is on matters most relevant to psychological research. Because of the broad nature of the study of behavior and mental processes, any attempt to address psychological issues from a research vantage must include a variety of examples and illustrations. Accordingly, you will see how the basic principles of research methodology are applied in social psychology, life-span development, animal behavior, assessment, psychobiology, clinical treatment, and other specialty areas in the field. As a foil for demonstrating the application of principles covered in each chapter, a particular topic is selected for building a model experiment. Realize the topic is chosen more out of convenience than anything else.

Over the last few decades, psychology has shifted sharply away from a philosophical posture and toward a more scientific position. Psychological research in the 1990s is characterized by laboratories equipped with sophisticated data-collection systems, computers, monitoring devices, automated scoring packages, and so on. As a result, based simply on face validity, psychology would seem to have made real movement toward full enfranchisement in the scientific community. What has taken place in post-World War II Western academic environments, however, is much more than a face-lift. *The way in which questions are being asked is different*. Unwilling to accept interpretations based on common sense, reason, or personal experience, psychology has gravitated toward more traditional scientific expression. For a more complete understanding of this method of analysis, some appreciation of the overall community of social scientists must be realized.

## *The Scientific Community*

Regardless of one's bias with respect to how best collect data (naturalistic versus laboratory research is discussed later in this chapter), investigators of psychological phenomena work within a common social/scholastic framework. Borrowing from a concept introduced in *Constructing the Subject: Historical Origins of Psychological Research* (Danziger, 1990), the community of psychological scientists can be portrayed graphically as operating within the three concentric circles in Figure 1–1.

Note that each circle has an increasingly greater radius. This is intended to reflect the fact that as we move from one context to the next, more members of the scientific community are brought into the picture. Basic and applied research findings are shared first with specialists who have directly overlapping interests, and then with other professionals who may benefit from the research results more tangentially. Also apparent from this image of the scientific community is the idea that each level of investigative practice is embedded in a broader

**FIGURE 1–1 The scientific community in psychological research**

**research report**—the central document that serves as the core of the scientific process; the center of the scientific community

**research community**—specialists within the scientific community who are qualified to challenge the research report on scientific grounds

context that extends beyond local research concerns. As Dethier (1962) put it, "All knowledge, however small, however irrelevant to progress and well-being, is part of the whole" (p. 118). From this perspective, the scientific community is viewed as an intact organizational setting in which everyone contributes and in which each element of the process is integral to the success of the whole.

**The Research Report.** At the core of the scientific community, which is the innermost circle in Figure 1–1, is the **research report.** This aspect of the process of scientific inquiry involves direct contact with the research setting. The investigator working at this level is responsible for collecting data, analyzing the findings, drafting a report, and distributing the results to the rest of the scientific community.

The critical nature of this process is evident from the central position the research report occupies in the series of concentric circles which define the scientific community (Figure 1–1). If an inappropriate test is used, an error is made in recording, or the investigator chooses to ignore some seemingly obscure but ultimately exceedingly important aspect of the data, the flawed result will ripple through the rest of the scientific community. The credibility of the entire investigative process rests squarely on the validity of the research report. If personnel closest to the project are too casual in their scientific demeanor and in the manner in which they conduct themselves in the research setting, a likely consequence is a corrupt and misleading report that at best creates confusion and more malignantly perpetuates a false belief. Because the research report is extremely important, the bulk of the coverage in this text is concerned with the basics of proper data collection, analyses, and reporting.

**The Research Community.** Assuming that the research report has been prepared scientifically, the next step is to present the findings to the **research community.** The research community is comprised of recognized authorities in the specialty area. Although the research community cannot detect flaws in the report due to recording errors, lack of attentiveness, and so on, it can question the interpretive remarks in the report. If alternative accounts of the results exist, it is incumbent on the research community to step forward and point them out. More importantly, it is the research community's responsibility to show that the findings of the research report are replicable.

Replication is one of the most important aspects of scientific research. Used here, *replication* means that if a particular finding occurs in one setting under prescribed conditions, that finding should be reproducible in a second setting given the same set of conditions. Demanding replication in scientific research accomplishes several things. First, it further establishes the robustness of the phenomenon under investigation. Next, it underscores the strength of the effect.

Finally, should an untrue finding occur due to chance or errors in the basic research process, the true pattern of results ultimately can be made evident by independent investigators in the research community who attempt to replicate the effects.

**The Professional Community.** The outermost circle in Figure 1–1 encompasses the **professional community.** The professional community is comprised of scientists and other interested people who are not sophisticated evaluators of the research report but who nonetheless may be able to use the information contained in the report in their own research or even in their own practices. For example, a life-span psychologist concerned with the effects of maturational processes on cognitive development may be unappreciative of the importance of developmental psychobiology on the whole but acutely thankful for a recent neuroscience report which clarifies the role age plays in hippocampal memory formation. Similarly, a private practitioner providing services to the homeless may benefit from a published report on feelings of alienation and detachment among outgroups. In cases like these, the consumers (the readers) are not required to assess the scientific credibility of the research findings—they can rely on the research community to provide that assurance. Members of the professional community simply use what is relevant and what works. With respect to applied issues, the professional community serves science by documenting the utilitarian value of discoveries made in a scientific arena. In this sense, the professional community is responsible for taking the information from the test tube to the vat. Ideas are thereby translated into real-world applications.

With this perception of the overall scientific community in mind, it would be useful to examine science in psychology more directly. In the following section, the characteristics of the scientific approach as they relate to psychological research are delineated more clearly.

## *Characteristics of Scientific Psychology*

As mentioned earlier, what is unique about the scientific approach to making judgments about the information given us is the manner in which questions are asked. The scientific method prescribes an agenda all investigators must follow. What may at first appear to be a system that imposes unnecessary constraints is actually a framework that offers certain assurances about the authenticity of a chosen position. While numerous characteristics of the scientific method in psychological research exist, among the most important are the formation of the hypothesis, empirical observation, acceptance or rejection of the hypothesis, and replication. Figure 1–2 shows how each of these features of scientific research are connected.

**professional community**—the larger community of interested scientists and practitioners who may benefit in some way from the results of the research report

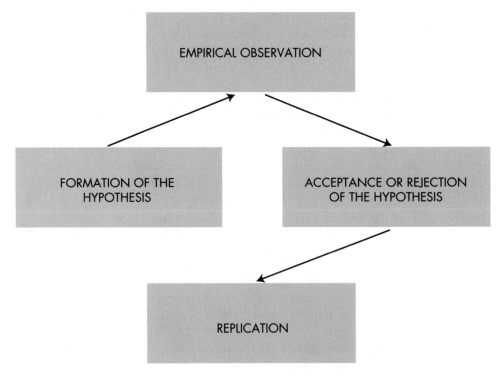

**FIGURE 1–2** Once a hypothesis is formed, it is subjected to empirical testing, from which the results either support or refute the idea. At this point, the research may be repeated (replicated).

**Hypothesis Formation.** The launch sites for scientific research projects in psychology are as varied as the scientists who choose to conduct them. For example, an environmental psychologist concerned about facilitating human needs in the workplace may overhear employees complaining about inadequate space and noisy distractions from other offices, and may launch a research program, or a pediatric psychologist attempting to alleviate the suffering of terminally ill oncology patients may notice that a particular child seems especially responsive when talking with older children who have the same affliction and may investigate further. Elsewhere, a social psychologist living in Manhattan may informally keep a record of the reluctance of people on the street to having their pictures taken.

Despite their different starting points, research projects aimed at exploring these issues have a common characteristic: interest in the topics is based on observation. Every scientific research effort has begun with an awareness that something deserved more scrutiny. This youthful element in scientific research makes the research sparkle. It is that "I wonder what would happen if" feeling we enjoyed as children.

In more formal terms, formulating an idea based on preliminary observations refers to the development of a **hypothesis.** A hypothesis is a statement that proposes an explanation which can be tested through further observation or experimentation (see Hurlburt, 1994). For instance, the following hypothesis might be formed regarding the observation by the pediatric psychologist in the previous example:

> Chronically ill young children suffering from an incurable and intractable cancer may achieve some measure of anxiety relief by discussing their feelings about their illness with older children who have the same disorder.

Notice that no statement about a relation between events or variables is made. Rather, an idea or expectation is simply acknowledged and expressed in more formal terms.

It should be understood that hypothesis testing is based profoundly on inductive reasoning (Deese, 1972). Induction involves producing and compiling specific facts to prove a more general statement. Philosophers such as 18th-century Scottish scholar David Hume invoked the concept of induction to challenge rationalism, inasmuch as inductive reasoning defies rational decision making and substitutes factual accumulation. In fact, this issue is what distinguishes science from mathematics. Unlike mathematics, which attempts to identify laws that have generality and to explain orderly events, science expresses the need to generalize from facts to universal laws. In this sense science is not rational. Scientific psychologists accept the following basic proposition as a matter of faith: Knowledge may be increased through induction.

Because the remaining research activities rest so squarely on the hypothesis to be tested, formulating the hypothesis may be the most critical stage of research. Bad ideas lead to poor results, regardless of the degree of scientific rigor exercised in data collection and analysis. A false perspective on the importance of racial characteristics for altruistic (helping) behavior, for instance, will yield useless data if the notion for conducting the investigation is flawed from the beginning. Because such misguided projects are costly, both in terms of human and nonhuman resources, every effort must be made to work within the framework of a believable hypothesis.

I was once involved with a behavioral toxicology study which hypothesized that inorganic lead contamination would cause greater conditioned taste aversion in animals because the metal would increase sensitivity to aversive stimulation (see Domjan, 1996, for a detailed discussion of the phenomenon of taste aversion). Lead did cause increased taste aversion, but not because of an enhanced reactivity to an aversive event—it simply

**hypothesis**—a hypothetical statement or idea about why something occurs the way it does, which can be tested through experimentation

made the animals sick so they could not eat! The point is that had there been greater deliberation about the wisdom of conducting the experiment, the working hypothesis would have been abandoned early on and considerable time and effort would have been saved.

Accordingly, before a hypothesis can be stated, a great deal of groundwork must be completed. Personal observations, information from published journal articles or books, and anything else you can find should help in formulating a legitimate hypothesis. The extra effort at the beginning of the study can spare you later unpleasantness.

**Empirical Observation.** Once a working hypothesis has been formulated, the task of the investigator shifts to securing empirical documentation and support for the rationale underlying the study. As noted, empiricism means relying on observation to gather information. Contemporary scientific investigations in psychology often benefit from well-equipped laboratories in which data collection procedures are automated. A neuropsychologist interested in brain mapping, for instance, is likely to have a digital converter that reads brain wave patterns from an electroencephalograph (EEG) and reconfigures the results as color images on a monitor. Different color codes would be associated with different levels of central nervous system activity. An advantage of this sort of recording procedure is that the researcher is not involved directly in data collection. Instead, the results are obtained via an automated process which ensures no human bias or error contributes to the findings. Empirical measures are recorded and maintained through sophisticated machinery, and in some sense the scientific credibility of the operation is bolstered.

However, this is not to say that empirical recording requires expensive electronic devices, computers, monitors, and so on. Indeed, it is quite common in psychological research to see a pencil and a sheet of paper employed as the sole recording apparatus. Moreover, records obtained with these tools may be as scientifically valid as those gathered with more elaborate equipment. For example, when a child psychologist observes that a 2-year-old is more likely to play with another child when his or her mother is present, an empirical measure is taken. Similarly, empirical accounts of animal behavior in natural settings are possible and add to a scientific database which either supports or refutes a particular hypothesis. So, although automated recording systems may offer certain conveniences, the ultimate value of the information collected in a research project is determined by the empirical nature of the result.

The use of empirical observations in hypothesis verification derives in many respects from the tie between psychology and the physical sciences, as well as the tie with elementary mathematics. All sciences accept only what can be observed, and all require that observations be quantified in classic mathematical form. In the same manner that a mathematical argument or theorem can be tested, empirical tests of hypotheses can be conducted. Individual data points can be converted to numbers, and numbers can be analyzed and their true meanings interpreted. This essential element of the scientific method, which is discussed in great detail in this text, is the basis on which a given hypothesis is accepted or rejected.

**Acceptance or Rejection of the Hypothesis.** Once the quantification of empirical results has been completed, the next step in the scientific investigation is to decipher the meaning of the numerical pattern. What is the true story behind the numbers? Is the story consistent with the hypothesis that formed the basis for the study? How strong is the degree of agreement or disagreement?

Research psychologists answer these questions by judiciously using **statistical analysis.** The use of statistics in psychological research permits confirmation or refutation of the working hypothesis (Gravetter & Wallnau, 1995). Although considerable attention is given to this topic in Chapter 12, for now it is sufficient to note that we can make better judgments about the reliability, acceptability, and meaning of our findings with the use of appropriate statistical techniques. For example, when eye-witnesses improve their recall of the specifics of a crime by returning to the scene, there is a need to know if this enhanced recall is a general result or one that is specific to the case. Is it chance? How predictable is this finding? Psychological statistics can help us unravel such intricacies and clear up an otherwise confusing picture.

Of course, a clear picture is attainable only in situations where the hypothesis is stated unambiguously. A fuzzy hypothesis results in fuzzy interpretation, regardless of the extent of the statistical treatment of the issue. We can feel confident about accepting or rejecting a hypothesis only when we have a firm grasp of what is being tested. This goes back to the statement made earlier about hypothesis formulation being the most critical stage of research. If the scientist fails to state explicitly what is under investigation, the empirical recording may not be corrupted, and inferences about the meaning of the data may even be drawn from quantified observations. *However, the test of the idea will be lost.* If the reason for conducting the study is gone, we cannot add systematically to a knowledge base. The fate of this type of research is the accumulation of unrelated facts. Nothing is tied together, and understanding at a broader level is not possible. Accordingly, it is not enough to merely accept or reject hypotheses. We must accept or reject *relevant* hypotheses.

**Replication.** As acknowledged in the earlier section on the scientific community, reproducibility of results is one of the most important aspects of scientific research. For psychology, this means that every aspect of the research must be specified in such detail that another investigator could install the same procedures and come up with the same findings.

**statistical analysis**—the use of statistics to confirm or refute a hypothesis

**partial-replication design**—design in which part of an investigation includes a previous design as part of its experimental framework; used to confirm earlier findings

Replication in psychology is especially important because of the complexity of the issues under study and the vast number of factors that may influence the measures being recorded. If the test can be repeated and the earlier report confirmed, we can feel more confident asserting that our position on the subject is correct.

Perhaps the most significant service replication provides is that it prevents us from perpetuating myths. Although it is rare, an untruthful and false position may be published as factual. The fundamental issue in what is undoubtedly one of the most controversial, and potentially even scandalous, cases in the history of psychological research, is the inability to replicate.

As a committed eugenicist, British researcher Cyril Burt was dedicated to showing that intelligence quotient (IQ) has a strong hereditary component. A number of Burt's publications expressed extremely strong correlations for the intelligence profiles of identical twins, and many other statistics which supported a genetic conclusion were reported (Burt, 1940). However, Leon Kamin of Princeton University and others later argued that Burt's data were unreliable (cf. Kamin, 1974). The findings Burt presented could not be reproduced, and indeed there was considerable evidence to indicate that Burt may have faked much of his data. Burt may have even invented coauthors and scientific colleagues to create the illusion of an impressive research team (Joynson, 1990). Had there been no attempt to replicate Burt's original report, the scientific community would have continued to accept his data, and an exceedingly important issue would have gone uncontested.

Unfortunately, the incidence of absolute replication in psychological research is low (Campbell & Jackson, 1979). Journal editors are disinclined to publish replications that confirm earlier findings because they view the replications as redundant and because they have no page space for this type of material. Practically speaking, the best we can hope for is that some element of a previous study is integrated into the design of a second investigation. This procedure, which is known as a **partial-replication design,** is helpful over the long term. Certainly some form of replication is essential for psychology research to gain and maintain respectability in the scientific community.

# NATURALISTIC OBSERVATION

Once an investigator identifies a subject area and formulates an idea, formal testing of the idea begins with a selection of available methods for collecting data. In many instances, the decision to choose one research method over another is based on the types of questions being asked. When someone is interested in characterizing behavioral patterns that occur in wild animals, for example, it would seem reasonable to study the animal's behavior in its habitat. Similarly, should a person be interested in the effects structural layout of an office has on personnel efficiency, it would make sense to take records while people were doing their work. These sorts of investigations require that the subjects be observed naturally. **Naturalistic observation** is a research method that permits the investigator to collect information in a naturally occurring environment.

In some respects, it is appropriate to argue that naturalistic observation as a recording technique dates to Paleolithic times. Hieroglyphs beaten into cave walls with stone implements and highlighted with dyes show ancestral records of the behavior of animals, hunters, warriors, and the like. However, a key distinction to be made here is that these recordings were unsystematic. In contrast, naturalistic observation requires that detailed accounts of behavior be made systematically. This systematic recording may take the form of a journal, time sampling (after a set amount of time passes, the investigator records whether or not the behavior is occurring), or some other organized data collection procedure. In all cases, the investigator looks for consistency, both within a given subject and across members of the sample.

One of the most celebrated examples of naturalistic observation comes to us in the popular book, *In the Shadow of Man,* written by primate expert Jane Goodall in 1971. This fascinating account of the routine activities of chimpanzees living wild in the Gombe Stream Research Centre in southeastern Africa offers astonishing insights into how infrahuman primates care for their young, establish territories, and even how they deal with the death of a parent or an infant. The contribution Goodall made was not realized by a curious woman who informally watched a troupe of cute simians and later recollected their playful habits. Rather, Goodall maintained a detailed diary on each animal, noting peculiarities such as grooming habits, reactions to intruders, food searches, and so on. Naturalistic observation conforms to the scientific rule that reliable, empirical records are essential for understanding psychologically relevant phenomena.

The Goodall example illustrates other fundamental characteristics of the method of naturalistic observation, as well. First, the chimpanzees were observed without bias. That is, the observer's familiar presence in no way influenced the behavioral patterns the subjects being studied displayed. This ensured a more genuine description of the behavior of the chimpanzees in their natural environment. Also, naturalistic observations allow us to get a feel for the broader scheme of events which define the context against which isolated responses can be compared. For example, aggression between two male chimpanzees may take on added meaning when it is realized that the victor assumes greater breeding rights. Because it is helpful to

**naturalistic observation**—a method that allows for recording in a natural or "wild" setting

understand how one behavior is tied to another, naturalistic observations that permit an array of behaviors to be measured simultaneously can be extremely useful.

It should be understood that naturalistic observation is not the exclusive province of animal behaviorists. A developmental psychologist observing the activities of preschool children on the playground, a social psychologist studying the behavior of guards at a maximum security facility, or a courtroom conduct analyst may all employ naturalistic techniques. The essential feature in such projects is that the investigator wants a glimpse of typical behaviors in a real-world setting, unencumbered by the contaminating influence of experimental trappings.

Despite the many advantages of naturalistic observation, this approach does possess some features which detract from its otherwise attractive veneer. For example, while the method allows for a *description* of a particular event or phenomenon, it says nothing about the *causes* for such behavioral occurrences. In addition, the naturalistic approach is often slow and costly, both financially and in terms of time. Goodall's records mentioned previously were the result of more than a decade of living among wild chimpanzees. Because of such constraints, many investigators opt for more controlled laboratory situations.

# LABORATORY RESEARCH

Often an investigator is concerned with why an event occurred and not just that it occurred. To better appreciate the forces that determine the direction and frequency of responding, it is sometimes necessary to create an arbitrary environment in which the investigator can control the degree of involvement of selected elements of that environment. This may appear sterile to some, and in certain respects it is—you prune the inessentials, leaving only a few items to investigate. However, strict control permits greater explanation of the causes underlying psychological phenomena. The contrived environment, or laboratory, has served psychology well for over a century. It all began in Leipzig, Germany.

## *Historical Roots of the Psychological Laboratory*

It has often been said that the birthdate of modern psychology can be placed toward the end of 1879 when Wilhelm Wundt designated some space at the University of Leipzig to be used for conducting psychological experiments

(Danziger, 1990). Much of the work completed at the Leipzig laboratory involved studies of human sensation and perception. Included in these studies were experiments on reaction time.

Reaction time was believed to be an index of mental acuity and quickness. In a typical study, for instance, a subject might be presented with a simple task which required that a single button be pressed when a red light was illuminated. The individual's average speed in responding would then be compared to the more complicated choice reaction time situation in which different buttons had to be pressed depending on the presence of a particular color selected from a stimulus array. In the simple case, limited mental processing would be necessary, but in the more difficult case, appreciably greater mental activity would be required. Precisely how much more mental activity was involved could be determined from the discrepant reaction time values.

One unique historical feature of the Wundt laboratory is that several students conducted the experiments. Whereas other classic investigations into sensory physiology, those conducted by E. H. Weber, H. Helmholtz, and G. T. Fechner, had been carried out by a single person, Wundt's used groups. His purpose was to teach as well as to enlighten. By establishing the teacher/scholar model in

**FIGURE 1–3** Wilhelm Wundt established the teacher/scholar model in psychology.

psychology, Wundt set the scientific agenda for psychologists for the next 100 years.

Other psychological laboratories emerged in Germany. Hermann Ebbinghaus conducted classic memory studies at the University of Berlin. The Gestalt psychology group, which originated with Max Wertheimer, Kurt Koffka, and Wolfgang Kohler, provided students with an alternative to the introspective position Wundt took. Ultimately, one of Wundt's students, E. B. Titchener, would bring laboratory psychology to the United States. Since Titchener first set up his lab at Cornell University in Ithaca, New York, in 1893, scientific psychology has relied on controlled experimentation for understanding and interpreting.

## The Structure of the Psychological Laboratory

Modern psychological laboratories have changed considerably since the early days of Wundt, Titchener, and other pioneer investigators. The same scientific orientation exists, but the level of sophistication and the quality of the instrumentation has increased dramatically. There are several distinguishing features in the laboratory environment of the 1990s. Among the more important aspects of laboratory operations are the resources available for research design, the research setting, the apparatus, and the recording techniques.

**Resources.** Traditionally, ideas about particular issues and ways to explore these issues have led psychology researchers to the library. For some larger laboratories, this has involved searching a topic area in a specialized library in the research suite or building. In most cases, however, it has meant trekking to the campus library or to some other central facility. In any event, the library has been long considered an integral part of the overall laboratory environment.

Today, "library work" is changing. The Internet and other emerging computer systems are redefining our lives. With software such as Netscape and *Windows95,* we can immediately access a worldwide information base which includes information on virtually any topic, however obscure. Consequently, conventional library searches and material storage are becoming out of date. Should you want to know something about "the reproductive habits of gophers" or "the percentage of incoming first-year college students who are women," all you have to do is punch the information in on your home computer. The same is becoming true for psychology researchers—anything you can imagine and a lot you cannot is readily available on "the Net" (the Internet).

Along with network offerings, a number of more specialized computer searches exist. One example of such a system is Psyclit. Psyclit indexes recent books, journal articles, and other publications and permits access by individual terms and conjunctions. For instance, if you want to review all articles on cocaine since 1988, you would just enter *cocaine* at the appropriate prompt. This option, however, would yield thousands of entries, and it probably would be so unfocused that it would be useless. An alternative would be to use a conjunction where only those articles that were related to several key terms would show up in the search. For example, you could restrict the number of reports that would appear in the search by entering *cocaine * human * intravenous*. Consequently, you could quickly sift through the relevant articles on the self-administration of the drug in human subjects.

If your computer search is not successful, or if such services are not available, you can always go back to the shelves of the library for the original materials. Many times, there is simply no substitute for this approach. Because of the diverse nature of psychology, materials are likely to be scattered throughout the library. The classification systems presented in Table 1–1 can help organize your search and at least get you to the general area where you may find individual items of interest.

**The Research Setting.** The physical makeup of the psychological laboratory is as varied as the topics under investigation. Different phenomena require the inclusion of different environmental features. For example, a well-equipped psychopharmacology laboratory includes an animal holding area, a surgery room, a biochemistry room, an electronics and shop suite, a supply store, and various other support subunits. Someone interested in the effects of crowding and space on logical problem solving may use a social laboratory in which moveable walls can determine space and density coefficients for human subjects working on selected tasks. Similarly, a clinical psychologist concerned with monitoring the effectiveness of a particular intervention strategy may monitor the progress of acutely depressed clients via a remote audio-visual tracking system which permits tapes/films of the sessions to be reviewed. In both of these cases, the layout of the research setting is dictated by the precise nature of the rationale for conducting the study.

Of course, not all psychological research projects are carried out within the confines of four walls. In many instances the laboratory is defined by real-life environmental features. Such a research setting is employed in what is known as a **field study.** A field study is literally conducted in the field, that is, in the setting where the behavior normally takes place. Naturalistic observations, discussed previously, represent one type of field study. Goodall would be quick to tell you that the forested valley of the Gombe Stream Research Centre is her laboratory. Another kind of field study is the method of unobtrusive observation. In an unobtrusive observation study, the investigator remains outside the sphere of behavior, permitting the responses to occur naturally. Unaware that they are being watched and records are being made, the subjects are free to respond the way they would ordinarily.

**field study**—a research project conducted in the environment in which the studied behavior normally occurs; naturalistic observation is one example

| LIBRARY OF CONGRESS CLASSIFICATION | SUBJECT AREA | DEWEY DECIMAL CLASSIFICATION |
|---|---|---|
| RC512–571 | Abnormal psychology and psychiatric disorders | 616.852–616.89 |
| BF636–637 | Applied psychology | 158 |
| Q334–336 | Artificial intelligence | 006.3 |
| BF721–723 | Child psychology | 155.4 |
| BF311 | Cognition | 153.4 |
| BF660–678 | Comparative psychology | 156 |
| LB1051–1091 | Educational psychology | 370.15 |
| HQ503–1064 | Family (social groups) | 306.8 |
| IA167 | Human factors | 620.82 |
| HF5548.8 | Industrial psychology | 158.7 |
| BF501–504 | Motivation | 153.8 |
| BF1001–1999 | Parapsychology and the occult | 133 |
| BF231–299 | Perception | 153.7 |
| BF698 | Personality | 155.2 |
| HF5549 | Personnel management | 658.3 |
| QP351–495 | Physiological psychology | 152 |
| HV689 | Psychiatric social work | 362.2 |
| BF455–463 | Psycholinguistics (psychology of language) | 401.9 |
| RC475–510 | Psychotherapy | 616.89 |
| RC435–510 | Psychotherapy and psychiatry | 616.89 |
| BF231–299 | Sensory perception | 152.1 |
| HM251–291 | Social psychology | 302 |
| LC4601–4803 | Special education (mentally handicapped and learning disabled children) | 371.92 |
| QA278 | Statistics (correlation) | 519.5 |
| BF39–39.2 | psychometrics | 150.151 |
| BF237 | psychophysics | 152.8 |
| HQ1206–1216 | Women, psychology of | 155.633 |

**TABLE 1–1** Distribution of psychology-related materials in the library (Library of Congress and Dewey Decimal systems). (Adapted from Reed & Baxter, 1992.) Copyright © 1992 by the American Psychological Association. Reprinted with permission.

This is exactly what social psychologist Lauren Wispe accomplished years ago in his studies on helping behavior (see Wispe, 1991).

The "Broken Bag Capers," as Wispe's project was called, involved studying the reactions of people outside a food market to a controlled event. A confederate (a member of the research team working for the principal investigator) ripped the bottom of a bag of groceries, allowing the groceries to spill onto the sidewalk. Filming secretly from a van parked nearby, the researchers were able to index the likelihood that other shoppers would assist the confederate. Detailed records were made about gender, race, and other variables that contributed to the probability that innocent, and unwitting, shoppers would offer to help pick up groceries they thought had fallen out of a defective paper bag accidently. Had the "subjects" known they were being observed, their helping behavior may have been greatly changed.

Unobtrusive observations provide untainted data—we can feel more secure that what we see is genuine. Of course, there are some serious ethical issues here, considering that people are being studied without being aware. However, I postpone comments along these lines until Chapter 4.

**The Research Apparatus.** As is true for the research setting, the research **apparatus** is determined largely by the hypothesis being tested. An apparatus is defined as "the functional machinery by means of which a systematized activity is carried out" (*Webster's New Collegiate Dictionary,* 9th edition). The functional machinery element is critical in that the apparatus must work; it must be appropriate for the task at hand. If a psychologist who is interested in animal learning and behavior aims to explore the relation between novelty and general activity, it makes sense that the apparatus used in the research would include a novel environment as well as a familiar one, and that both environments would allow locomotion, grooming, and rearing measures to be taken. Someone studying human memory might require some method for projecting word lists onto a screen. The apparatus the investigator uses does not have to be elaborate, but it must meet the minimal criteria of yielding data which have bearing on the questions the researcher asks.

In sciences such as chemistry, physics, and molecular biology, the hardware that constitutes the research apparatus is conspicuous. Scintillation counters; high-pressure liquid chromatography (HPLC) units; and lab shelves loaded with test tubes, beakers, graduated cylinders, and other familiar equipment items lend a certain face validity to the scientific character of so-called "hard-science" laboratories.

To be sure, many research settings in psychology are outfitted similarly with a degree of ornate instrumentation which would rival Dr. Frankenstein's laboratory (still the most fascinating scientific setup I have seen). In the social sciences, however, often the apparatus employed is not visible or impressive to the uninitiated. A psychotherapy tape on assertiveness training, a block-design problem, or a target of a human face used to study the orienting reaction of 1-month-old infants may lack the credible veneer of equipment in other sciences. However, it would be a mistake to assume that the

**apparatus**—the equipment or tools the investigator uses to collect data

research laboratories of psychology are any less scientific than those in low-temperature physics laboratories or any other arena. The same degree of rigor is maintained in social sciences laboratories, and the scientific flavor of the experiments that use paper-and-pencil tasks is as compelling as it is in the laboratories of the physical and biological sciences.

In this regard, it should be acknowledged that interviews and questionnaires serve as the apparatus for many scientific studies in psychology, both in contrived and field laboratory situations. When a volunteer human subject responds to the statement, "I am in favor of the death penalty for capital offenses," by circling a value ranging from *1* to *5* where *1* is "strongly agree" and *5* is "strongly disagree," the attitude questionnaire functions as the apparatus. That is, the questionnaire is the "functional machinery" which permits the research to be carried out. In its absence, data collection would not be possible.

Many of the most intriguing findings in the history of psychology have come from such attitude surveys. The point is that the structure of the experimental design prevails, and the apparatus is a tool that contributes to the overall process. The apparatus is an important tool, but it is not an end in itself.

**Recording Techniques.** For our purposes, we can classify recording procedures as either automated or manual. In automated techniques the investigator plays no role in the data collection process. For example, in an operant conditioning laboratory where pigeons peck a key to receive a food reward, individual key pecks register automatically on a cumulative record (a rotating drum that graphically depicts response rate) or on a computer file. Alternatively, in a study on auditory sensitivity in humans, males and females may react to sounds of different tonal frequency (Hz) and intensity (decibels) by pressing a handheld lever that stops a digital clock. In these examples, the information that will be used for later analysis is stored automatically.

In contrast to automated records, manual records are produced and maintained by the investigator and the research staff. When someone scores a self-report for suicidal ideation or keeps a frequency tabulation of the number of overt acts of aggression in a socially competitive situation, the results are determined manually. Because manual recording requires human involvement, the chances for error and prejudicial reporting necessarily increase. Nonetheless, careful attention to detail can produce an unblemished record that is accurate and reliable. As with most every aspect of the research project, the quality of the study results ultimately is determined by the skill of the personnel in the laboratory. There is a great deal more to say about the world of laboratory research, and much of the remainder of this text is devoted to this methodology.

# BASIC AND APPLIED RESEARCH

Large research projects aimed at answering several interrelated questions in an in-depth fashion often require sizeable budgets. Personnel costs, equipment, supply items, subject costs, and miscellaneous other expenses can drive a budget up to several hundred thousand dollars, or even millions. Because of the enormous expense that is inherent in conducting some research, many countries set aside funding that is allocated by a ministry, a foundation, or some other administrative agency. In the United States, two of the chief funding sources are the National Science Foundation (NSF) and the National Institutes of Health (NIH). While the two agencies may express some overlapping interests, on the whole NSF is concerned with more **basic research** issues, and NIH funds more **applied research.**

Basic research projects focus on fundamental informational issues with minimal regard for the utilitarian value of the results. That is, in basic research the sole object is to explore, find out, and communicate the findings to those interested in the theoretical and academic implications of the data. There is nothing practical about this sort of study. In contrast, the findings obtained from applied research projects often impact directly important real-world issues that affect all of us. Applied results offer solutions to problems that extend far beyond the scientific community.

An example of basic research is available from a report by Davis and Smith (1992). In this report it was discovered that the licking patterns of rats that were presented different sugars were organized into bursts of licks rather than being distributed uniformly throughout the test interval. Clearly, one would be hard pressed to identify the direct application of these results. Although the information is not useless, the practical significance of such findings is not readily apparent.

Compare this basic research example to an article published by Harford, Parker, Grant, and Dawson (1992). This report details the drinking patterns of different types of workers. The researchers found that more white-collar workers than blue-collar workers drink alcohol, but that when blue-collar workers drink, they consume significantly greater amounts than do their white-collar counterparts. Such findings can have a direct effect on alcoholism treatment strategies, and they can even dictate factors such as life insurance premiums. These results deal with a practical social problem and may impact each of us in some small way.

**basic research**—research that focuses on academic issues with no direct concern for the applicability of the results

**applied research**—research that is intended to produce results that may have practical significance

It is easy to misjudge the relative importance of basic and applied research. Even though basic research findings may have no apparent applications, the yields from such studies may enhance the quality of human life. For instance, in the Davis and Smith (1992) article cited earlier, the findings regarding tongue movements in rats actually tell us a great deal about the central nervous system's control of eating. By systematically building a larger and more complete database, we may eventually be in a better position to correct eating disorders such as obesity or bulimia nervosa. Basic research findings can actually function as a scientific well from which investigators can draw buckets of information that help them solve real-world problems.

This imagery raises a serious issue, however. The basic research well is not inexhaustible. As depicted in Figure 1–4, normally information flows from basic to applied research. As the basic research pool is depleted, the base on which many applied studies are built dwindles. Should the basic research pool not be replenished, the fate of the transfer process is obvious—applied research will

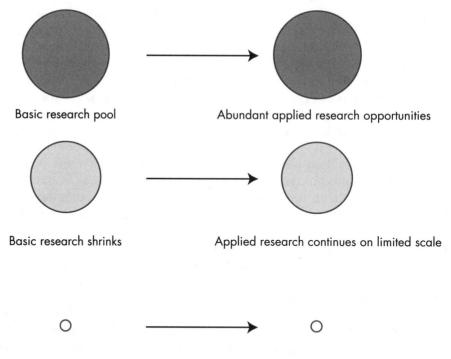

Basic research pool                     Abundant applied research opportunities

Basic research shrinks                  Applied research continues on limited scale

Basic research pool exhausted           Applied research stops

**FIGURE 1–4** The relation between basic and applied research. As the pool of basic information shrinks, applied research opportunities also shrink.

suffer because investigators will be working with limited understanding of more fundamental operations. For this reason many scientists argue fiercely for increased funding for basic research. New practical problems cannot be resolved with obsolete scientific technologies. In the final analysis, basic and applied research must work in concert.

# THEORY AND RESEARCH

Regardless of the basic or applied flavor of a research project, the overall strategic framework for conducting the investigations in the first place must be specified. To an extent, this issue was addressed earlier in this chapter in the discussion of hypothesis formation. A carefully thought out idea is essential to a successful research venture, but for many psychologists it may not be enough. A more comprehensive picture is required for a more complete understanding of the meaning of the results. Often, this broader perspective is achieved through theoretical formulation.

A **theory**, as the term is used here, is a set of structured and testable principles which guide and direct research. This means that the various tenets which comprise the theory offer investigators clues about the direction in which to go with their research. A historical example of one of the most elegant theories ever developed in psychology is the "drive-reduction theory" advanced by Yale psychologist Clark Hull and colleagues (cf. Hull, 1943). Based on the notion that the psychological states of arousal arising from underlying physiological need states impels an organism to respond, this elaborate system of postulates and corollaries permitted specific predictions to be made along systematic lines. The key is that such directed research produced an organized, coherent body of information that could be interpreted on a global scale. One idea proceeds logically from another. In the absence of theoretical guidelines, the investigator risks gathering unrelated facts, the result of which is a lot of information, none of which is tied together.

Note that the preceding reference to Hullian theory is historical. Although some contemporary theories might be appropriately called neo-Hullian, virtually no one today accepts the model as it was originally formulated. This leads us to one of the most distinguishing features of a good theory—it must be disconfirmable. This means that the theory must make explicit predictions which can be tested empirically and disproved. When a theory is so circular or so poorly defined that you can neither support it nor refute it, the model is of limited value. In dealing with theory, we do not talk

**theory**—a set of structured and testable principles which guide and direct research about truth. We talk instead about a convenient framework which helps us make sense of the commonalities that exist between and among our data. Theories generate separate informational sets that can be organized into a meaningful whole.

Because students and faculty alike sometimes confuse predictive relationships, it is useful to distinguish between hypotheses, theories, and laws. Although these terms are often used interchangeably, technically it is wrong to do so. The principal differences here rest with the complexity and reliability of the statements being made. As a rule, the hypothesis is the simplest proposition; it deals with only one relationship. For example, an investigator might hypothesize that during the summer months in the United States, violent crime increases as the ambient (outside) temperature increases (this phenomenon has been observed; see Anderson & Anderson, 1984). In this statement, there is no attempt to speculate about the various environmental events which might produce the result. Conversely, a theoretical statement might assert that heat-induced frustration combined with inappropriate socialization processes would be expected to trigger hostility and aggression. In contrast to the simple hypothesis, theory addresses the integrated nature of effects that are produced by several, interrelated events. A theory may become a law if the outcome is invariant. That is, should a prediction based on related events be verified to the extent that it is apparent the results will always be the same, then the relationship is characterized as lawful. Unlike theories, laws cannot be disconfirmed; they can be demonstrated empirically and established through testing, but they are not subject to disproof. In the context of the illustration employed here, the fact that ambient temperature rises in the summer months in the United States is a lawful statement.

It should be apparent that theory and related predictive scientific components of the research process are important in psychological research. On occasion, the instructive features of theory will be used in this book to accent a point or to clarify a fundamental concept in research methodology. Additional learning and instructional aids also are incorporated into this text.

## OVERVIEW OF THE TEXT

Many of the pedagogical features of this book are standard and common in other college textbooks on research methodology. Key terms, end-of-chapter summaries, glossary items, and so on are considered by many to be lethal in their absence. Perhaps this is as it should be given that it has been demonstrated that these features aid students in their efforts to understand methodology. However, my experience has shown that other techniques can improve a student's grasp of the exciting world of research. In this vein, this book offers a few opportunities to learn about methodology in ways that make the material more relevant, more interesting, and frankly more like what you will encounter when you launch your research career.

## *Building an Experiment*

Clearly, no single experiment can incorporate all aspects of research methodology and experimentation in psychology. You cannot, for instance, speak directly to issues of between-subjects analysis (see Chapter 8) when you talk about a totally repeated-measures design (see Chapter 9). However, it is safe to assert that the overall topic being discussed is relevant to virtually any experimental research operation. Surely, the topic of variability is as important for studies where the same subjects are used for several different experimental treatments (repeated-measures design) as it is for studies where different subjects show up in different treatment manipulations (between-subjects design). With this in mind, this text has been designed to build an experiment as we move through the chapters. In some chapters, the relevance of the contents is more conspicuous than in others. In all cases, however, some aspect of the chapter material applies to the development of our "model experiment." To assist you in detecting when the coverage shifts to the model experiment, the symbol ( ✦ ) and a special font will be used to introduce these sections.

As you see the experiment unfold and the research process work over the course of this book, be aware that the design, subject sampling procedure, suggested data analysis, and other elements of the research approach are in many ways arbitrary. A different topic could have been chosen, a more elaborate design may have been employed, and so on. The crucial lesson is that you are covering research methodology in an all-encompassing sense. Regardless of your scholastic orientation, you can benefit from appreciating the issues central to conducting meaningful experiments. This can best be accomplished by a gradual, thoughtful introduction to the research. Simply stated, you must walk before you run. The format of this book reflects this bias.

## *Thinking About Research*

It is possible, even likely, that ultimately you will find yourself in a position in which you will have to make decisions about research events for which you have no formal training. For example, you may find yourself conducting an investigation of laboratory-induced depression and discover through an initial interview that one of your subjects is acutely depressed, even suicidal. What will you do? What are your options? Oftentimes, your options are those you deem fair and reasonable. There is no manual, no authority who can provide an on-the-spot recommendation. A decision must be made, and it is yours alone to make.

No experiment has ever been conducted where something did not go wrong. Human subjects become ill, animals develop upper respiratory dysfunctions and have to be sacrificed after months of observation. Again, it is your move. A critical appraisal of the situation is required. This is just one part of any research operation. To give you a better feel for this aspect of research, sections of each chapter labeled "Thinking About Research" will present real as well as hypothetical events and ask you to think of ways in which the problems might be resolved. The answers for these sections have to come from you. That is the whole point, isn't it? You will get a chance to glimpse a dimension of research that is as critical as good data collection—the chance to think for yourself.

## *Spotlight on Research*

An added feature of this book is the "Spotlight on Research" sections which appear in most chapters. These sections focus on a phenomenon, a story, a case history, or an issue that relates directly to the content of the chapter. These entries may be classics or more contemporary pieces that have meaning in this day and age. In all cases these sections are intended to highlight the vitality and animation of the research game. Make no mistake, research is a game, an awesome, stimulating game played according to prescribed rules. In the pages that follow you will learn a great deal about these rules.

# The Development of the Hypothesis

**hypothesis—a hypothetical statement about an idea that can be tested through observation or experimentation**

The bulk of the coverage thus far has been concerned with characterizing the research environment. We have seen that there are different ways to collect information and to make observations about events in our world. In addition, we have seen that there are stark differences in the settings in which research is conducted. However, despite the varied nature of research activities, all research projects have a common point of inception. That is, every research study ever undertaken began at the same point—the hypothesis.

A **hypothesis,** as noted in Chapter 1, is a hypothetical statement which proposes an explanation that can be tested through further observation or experimentation. In effect, the hypothesis is, as Plato describes, a "likely story." It makes sense that the hypothesis defines the starting point for a research project, because you can only investigate once you suspect. One is not likely to be inclined to gather unrelated facts simply because there is nothing else to do. When a systematic study commences, and this is what research is all about, there is a reason for it. Some biological or environmental event has caused us to wonder, and in wondering we have come up with a hunch about why the event happened the way it did. The hunch, or hypothesis, can now be used to guide our thinking and to direct further inquiry.

In psychology, hypotheses about behavior and mental processes are in no shortage, partly because of the intriguing nature of the subject matter, but also because of the complexity of the events. Everyone has ideas about why we act the way we do, say the things we say, or live the way we live. In most instances, however, an individual's perspective on a particular issue has not been arrived at easily or in an informational void. More likely than not, the development of hypotheses occurred systematically. The next section examines the structure of hypothesis formation.

# THE STRUCTURE OF THE HYPOTHESIS

While the hypothesis serves as the "launching pad" for experimental and non-experimental research, "liftoff" actually occurs in stages. The countdown to a successful launch begins with an interest in a particular topic, then moves to exploration, and ultimately goes to the compilation of facts (Figure 2–1).

## Topic Interests

People become interested in topics for many reasons. An Inupiat Eskimo fisherman may notice that fish are more readily available in shallow streams when the water is very clear and slow moving. Does the fish see the bait? Is feeding more

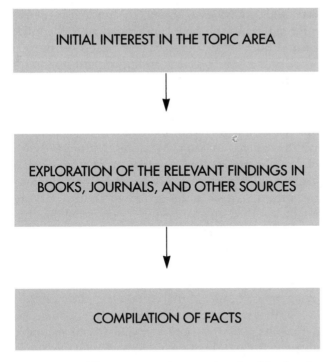

FIGURE 2–1 **The sequential stages involved in the development of a hypothesis**

likely when the animal is forced near the surface? Such questions interest the Inupiat for obvious reasons—answers to the questions may affect the Inupiat's food supply and survival.

Fascination with other topics may emerge along very different lines. Consider the art historian who closely examines Rembrandt's classic *Man in the Golden Helmet.* Questions arise about the authenticity of the painting (the authenticity of the work was challenged recently; see Hughes, 1992). Is this the work of the master, the product of Aert de Gelder and Nicolas Maes, or the collaboration of several other very skilled apprentices to Rembrandt? Why do the color combinations and stroke patterns appear to be at odds with other Rembrandt paintings? Of course, the answers to these questions may not bear directly on life or death, as did those in the previous Inupiat example, but they are interesting questions nonetheless. Interest in a topic sometimes occurs spontaneously and sometimes after careful deliberation. Whatever the path, the interest always leads to further reflection.

Of course, interest in a particular topic area is not always the result of inherent curiosity or even practical concerns. Much of the research conducted in the

United States and other countries is driven by funding sources. In Chapter 1, I mentioned that the NIH and the NSF fund much of the applied and basic research that is carried out in the United States. Based on program needs, these agencies and other public and private funding organizations send requests for proposals (RFPs). An RFP may solicit applications for research on the differences in psychological profiles of depressed women and men or on the effects of offshore drilling operations on the behavior of shrimp.

Because of the expense involved in maintaining a scientific laboratory, many investigators find themselves making decisions that favor their chances of obtaining outside financial support. This may mean that a particular research agenda is determined more by the practicalities of getting funds than anything else. In such circumstances, the "interest" in the project is stimulated more by realistic assessment of what it takes to keep a laboratory operational than by inquisitiveness.

It should be understood that when investigators respond to RFPs, they do not "sell out." The questions posed in the planned research area are valid, important questions, and the findings should provide information about meaningful issues. The danger, however, is that an entire national scientific research program may be prescribed by agency officials who are not necessarily on the cutting edge of a given topic area or that political biases may dictate a course that will not yield the most creative results. Perhaps there is some way to reconcile the legitimate needs of funding agencies and the demand for originality in the laboratory. What do you think?

## ⚛ Thinking About Research

**N**obel laureate Julius Axelrod is perhaps best known for his discoveries, which detail the kinetics of catecholamines. Catecholamines, or brain chemicals, are critical to a number of behavioral activities in the human organism, including motor responding and ambulation (walking). Dopamine is one of the neurotransmitters in the human brain that falls into this class of brain chemicals. When dopamine systems are impaired, as they are in Parkinson's disease, a conspicuous loss of coordination results. Movements are awkward and difficult to execute and, as the disease progresses, the symptoms get more severe, eventually imprisoning the person in a dysfunctional body.

Axelrod's basic research findings regarding catecholamine biosynthesis and metabolism led eventually to the development of L-DOPA, a chemical treatment that promotes dopamine activity in key brain regions and ameliorates the symptoms of Parkinson's disease. As a result of Axelrod's early laboratory efforts, many Parkinson's victims today can lead more normal lives. It is in this context that Axelrod expressed his delight that humanity benefitted so directly from his work, and that some forms of human suffering were being alleviated. However, Axelrod also indicated that had this been the purpose of the research from the outset, he likely never would have undertaken the project to begin with.

Clearly, Axelrod conducted his investigations in transmitter kinetics because of basic rather than applied interests. To be sure, the scientific community has achieved a significantly enhanced awareness of neurochemical functioning because of Axelrod's preliminary findings, and the world outside science also reaped rewards. In this case, both basic and applied areas were served by a common research agenda.

Perhaps rather than thinking about "basic" or "applied" research, we should think about "basic-applied" research (the reader is encouraged to reexamine the coverage of basic and applied issues in Chapter 1). Is it possible to establish programs which generate data that is meaningful along both lines? Obviously it is possible because it has been done, but the question is, "How can this be accomplished by design?" What has happened in the past is largely fortuitous—one fact stumbles out of one area into another, and fortunately there has been someone there to catch it. How can we program this to happen, however? Perhaps professional "liaison investigators" could be trained to identify common areas of concern, or maybe institutes commissioned with the joint responsibility of conducting basic-applied research could be created. What else? Are there other ways of accomplishing this consortium?

Whatever the solution, the system cannot undercut curiosity. In the final analysis, the investigator must be free to explore and upon discovering an interesting phenomenon, drop everything and pursue it. Imagination is the mother's milk of successful research, regardless of the research's applicability.  ▪

## *Exploration*

Regardless of the forces underlying an emergent interest in a topic, once the topic has been identified, the researcher needs additional information on the subject. The ability to ask the right questions in an area depends on a grasp of what has been done previously and on an understanding of how the parts of the literature fit together in a more complete and larger framework.

In the opening chapter of this book, I stated that my desire was to write a research methods book that built an experiment, chapter by chapter. Because the development of the hypothesis is the starting point for any research project, it is appropriate that we begin laying the foundation for our experimental project at this juncture. The following description of the topic area sets the stage for our entry into research:

> I recently visited a pediatric oncology ward at M. D. Anderson Hospital at the University of Texas Health Sciences Center in Houston, Texas. Recoiling from the initial shock and emotional devastation that goes with the awareness that many of these beautiful children on the ward would die from their afflictions within a matter of months, I soon realized that extremely important medical and psychological services were being carried out by staff professionals.
>
> Regarding psychological support, separate intervention programs were available for the clients and their parents. On closer inspection of the types of psychological treatment programs that were being implemented, I discerned that the

**working hypothesis**—a preliminary statement about an idea which is based on limited information

dominant theme in treating patients was cognitive in nature. That is, the attempts to control stress and pain were based on coping strategies which required the use of mental imagery, thought reorganization, and other types of uniquely cognitive techniques. I was aware of the success these procedures had had at the adult level, but I was a bit surprised such strategies were being used with young children ranging between 6 and 9 years old.

Because the effectiveness of cognitively oriented intervention strategies is constrained by the ability of the client to use an elaborate mental apparatus, I wondered about the wisdom of using such techniques at all, at least with children so young. Are children capable of generating the imagery and thought processes the treatment regimen demands? Is this a case where we have assumed that a therapeutic procedure is appropriate for all ages, when actually there are no data to support such a position? Are we as a professional community inadvertently denying treatment by offering a package that is contraindicated for this particular age range?

We have now an expressed interest in a topic and are in the early stages of developing a hypothesis. Our hypothesis in this instance grew out of routine observations that were made in an everyday life circumstance. Each of us visits a hospital setting from time to time, but on this occasion a responsive chord was struck which triggered the idea that, "Cognitive strategies may be more effective in older rather than younger age ranges."

Although this poses an interesting question, we are still a long way from a fully formulated hypothesis. What exists at the moment is a **working hypothesis.** A working hypothesis is a preliminary idea about something that is based on limited information and is subject to modification. The possibility that age variables may affect the efficacy of a given treatment outcome is reasonable, but it is mostly conjectural at this point. What is needed is a much more convincing reason for suspecting that a relation really does exist between age and the therapeutic efficiency of cognitive interventions for treating the terminally ill.

In effect, the next step in the research process is exploration. We will seek information on the chosen topic from a variety of sources, including Psyclit and other computer-based searches, as is mentioned in Chapter 1. Now let us see how some of these materials will aid us in hypothesis development.

**Books.** A convenient starting place for the uninitiated is often a book that is related directly or indirectly to the topic area. The advantage a book has over some other sources of information is that it is likely to provide more summary information. Only in a book does an author have the space to discuss the theoretical factors and ancillary issues that form the underpinnings of a specific concept area. As a result, someone who is unfamiliar with the subject matter can be brought to a reasonable level of sophistication relatively quickly. The global coverage of a book also ensures that the central features of the subject matter are addressed along with more incidental, but potentially important, facts. For the rapid reader, a book's table of contents allows selected subtopics to be identified quickly. The table of contents also moves the reader to a more focused examination of the material. In a book, much of the review work that is essential to the research project has been done for you.

An investigator's initial inquiries may be facilitated by a publication called *Books in Print,* which is a source catalog of all currently available books. In our case, we are interested in how young children handle the psychological and physical stress that goes with an extended or even terminal illness. In our instance, a computerized listing of books is available, so we can enter the words *stress* and *coping* into a computer that has stored information on published books. Because we find that there are 2,345 entries in the area of stress and coping since 1983, which is obviously an unmanageable number of books, we add other identifying words like *chronically ill* and *children.* Eventually, only a few books on the subject remain on our list. The information on one of the books, a volume edited by La Greca, Siegel, Wallander, and Walker in 1992, looks especially promising (see Figure 2–2). The book includes chapters on psychological approaches to treating chronically ill patients.

After locating the book, we notice that there is a chapter by Miller, Sherman, Combs, and Kruus (1992) which examines coping patterns in children who face medical stressors. Turning to this chapter, we find that there is evidence that simply providing children with information about how the medical treatment is likely to feel, how long the treatment will last, and so on actually has a beneficial effect with respect to alleviating tension and anxiety levels.

More importantly, we find that in this chapter is a **secondary reference** to a report by Curry and Russ (1985), which shows that information is used differently by older and younger children. A secondary reference is obtained from a **primary reference,** which is an original and complete article or a book chapter like the one we have in hand. You may not need the complete report in the case of a secondary reference because the summary remarks contained in the primary work tell you what you need to know. Be careful here, however, because reckless secondary reporting can steer you wrong.

In the Miller et al. (1992) chapter we find information which is compatible with our idea that cognitive processes are more acute, and consequently more effective as agents of therapeutic change, in older children. Cognitive integration is more probable in older children because older children have the intellectual apparatus to reconcile what treatment really means, whereas the younger children may just be confused.

**secondary reference**—a reference to a report which appears in an original publication such as a journal article or a book chapter

**primary reference**—an original and complete publication, such as a scientific report in a journal or a book chapter

**FIGURE 2–2** Edited volume of *Advances in Pediatric Psychology,* which includes chapters on approaches to treating chronically ill children. Copyright © 1992 The Guilford Press. Reprinted with permission.

Additional chapters in the La Greca et al. book (1992), and a couple of others we eventually locate, offer helpful clues about the nature of cognitive functioning. Moreover, this book provides a theoretical structure within which such a pattern of results can be understood. Although all of this information is congruent with our original idea about the relation between age and the therapeutic effectiveness of cognitively based intervention strategies, it is still not enough. We need information that is more directly relevant to the use of cognitive coping mechanisms of differently aged children. For such detailed analyses, we likely will have to turn to scientific journals.

**Journals.** Scientific journals publish the detailed reports investigators submit for consideration by the scientific community (refer to Chapter 1 for a description of the hierarchical connection between the original research report and the broader research community). Journal articles may be published as full-length papers, which usually present the findings of several, interconnected experiments, or they may be published in the form of brief reports. In the brief report, the author usually concentrates on a narrowly defined effect that can be tied to a large database. For example, someone interested in the effects of physical attractiveness on interpersonal attraction may find that high and low scores on an ad hoc moral judgments scale differentially dictate an individual's position on the importance of physical attractiveness in establishing close relationships. In such a report, the vast literature on interpersonal attraction is acknowledged, and the limited impact of the new findings is recognized. Still, the information can be quite useful to certain scientific investigators. The brief report provides a rapid communication vehicle for getting the word out.

In psychology, journals typically publish "specialty reports" or articles of a more general flavor. Journals such as the *Journal of Experimental Psychology: Animal Behavior Processes,* the *Journal of Consulting and Clinical Psychology,* and *Psychopharmacology* are examples of specialty journals that are likely to appeal to experts in selective subareas of psychology. In truth, the level of sophistication expressed in these papers, coupled with the prohibitive terminology inherent in technical areas, often means that it is difficult for psychologists outside the specialty area to glean much from reading the reports. On the other hand, articles written for a general audience, such as those traditionally published in journals such as the *American Psychologist,* are of interest to the entire profession. Here, issues are addressed in a nonthreatening format, which makes the information accessible to the inexperienced reader. The combination of specialty and general-orientation journals in psychology permits investigators with the most esoteric interests to satisfy their needs for up-to-date information on selected topics and yet maintain an awareness of what the rest of the field is doing. Table 2–1 presents a list of the journals published by the American Psychological Association (APA).

Many of you, even as undergraduate students, will be part of research projects that are written and submitted to high-quality journals for editorial consideration. Indeed, some of you will take the lead in drafting the papers and will share

American Psychologist
APA Monitor
Behavioral Neuroscience
Clinician's Research Digest
Contemporary Psychology
Developmental Psychology
Experimental and Clinical Psychopharmacology
Health Psychology
Journal of Abnormal Psychology
Journal of Applied Psychology
Journal of Comparative Psychology
Journal of Consulting and Clinical Psychology
Journal of Counseling Psychology
Journal of Educational Psychology
Journal of Experimental Psychology: Animal Behavior Processes
Journal of Experimental Psychology: Applied
Journal of Experimental Psychology: General
Journal of Experimental Psychology: Human Perception and Performance
Journal of Experimental Psychology: Learning, Memory, and Cognition
Journal of Family Psychology
Journal of Personality and Social Psychology
Neuropsychology
Professional Psychology: Research and Practice
Psychoanalytic Abstracts
Psychological Abstracts
Psychological Assessment
Psychological Bulletin
Psychological Review
Psychology and Aging
Psychology, Public Policy, and Law
PsycSCAN: Applied Experimental and Engineering Psychology
PsycSCAN: Applied Psychology
PsycSCAN: Behavior Analysis & Therapy
PsycSCAN: Clinical Psychology
PsycSCAN: Developmental Psychology
PsycSCAN: LD/MR
PsycSCAN: Neuropsychology

**TABLE 2–1 Journals of the American Psychological Association (APA)**

---

authorship on articles that contribute prominently to the scientific information base in psychology. To the extent that this textbook assists you in that regard, I feel that something of immense value has been achieved.

In any event, most of the top-tier journals in psychology are **refereed journals.** In refereed journals, manuscripts are first submitted to the journal editor.

The editor then identifies reviewers (referees) who must evaluate the scientific credibility of the research papers and render judgments about the importance of the information in the reports. Typically, a completed manuscript is submitted to three or more outside reviewers who remain anonymous to the author. These reviewers independently evaluate the suitability of the paper for publication in the journal. Ultimately, the journal editor must decide whether or not the research report is acceptable for publication. Because all journals have limited page space, only the best articles merit inclusion in the journals, which may be published monthly, bimonthly, or quarterly. The fierceness of the competition along these lines is reflected in the fact that some of the better journals have rejection rates as high as 80% (four out of five submitted manuscripts are not published).

This brings me to an extremely important point. Getting started in research can be scary. As a beginning student, it is easy to be intimidated by the demonstrated expertise of established investigators in an area. I know from dealing with my own students that there is an endemic belief that "If I thought of it, then it must have already been done." This sort of attitude preemptively kills many solid ideas. I am reminded of Ralph Waldo Emerson's essay, "Self-Reliance" (1868), in which he remarks:

> A man should learn to detect and watch that gleam of light which flashes across his mind from within, more than the lustre of the firmament of bards and sages. Yet, he dismisses without notice his thought, because it is his. In every work of genius we recognize our own rejected thoughts. (p. 145)

In "Intellect" (1868) Emerson again admonishes the timid:

> Men say, Where did he get this? and think there is something divine in his life. But no; they have myriads of facts just as good, would they only get a lamp to ransack their attics withal. (p. 296)

The message here is one I believe in and one that is commonly affirmed. Good ideas come from all quarters, and your thoughts and guesses about scientific issues can yield publishable reports. Do not assume that journal publications are the exclusive province of "bards and sages."

Like intimidation, the fragile status of the neophyte researcher can also lead to premature abandonment of a project. Unhappily, the review process can sometimes (although not often) be a capricious process. If you are not prepared for it, the impact of a negative decision can be ruinous, as the following case history (of me) shows.

**refereed journal**—a journal where the decision to publish or not to publish is made largely by outside reviewers who are specialists in the field

## Spotlight on Research: SUBMITTING A MANUSCRIPT

In the spring of 1972, I was nearing completion of my first year of graduate school in the Department of Psychology at the University of Oklahoma. At the time, my major professor and my mentor, Roger Mellgren, was actively pursuing empirical and theoretical issues related to a phenomenon known as "incentive contrast." Contrast effects are said to occur when an organism that is suddenly shifted to a higher or lower reward value performs dramatically different than controls that were maintained at that higher or lower reward value throughout training. This typically involves an "overshooting" effect when there is an upward shift and an "undershooting" effect when there is a downward shift.

Using rats, I had designed several experiments which addressed issues of contrast in an aversive conditioning setting (where reduction of electric foot shock serves as the reinforcer). I was granted the opportunity to write the report and, under the supervision of Professor Mellgren, I thought I had put together a pretty convincing scientific article. I submitted the manuscript to a reputable journal for consideration.

I anxiously awaited the editorial response to my first effort at publishing a research report. After a couple of months the original paper was returned through the mail, complete with detailed comments from the editor. I was absolutely crushed. Not only was my paper deemed unworthy of publication, the editor expressed serious reservations about whether or not someone like me, who was given to ". . . serious confounds and a striking inability to design projects that yield unambiguous results . . . ," should even be permitted to work in a laboratory. I was so thoroughly embarrassed by this vituperative review I was disinclined to show Mellgren what had happened.

Finally, I summoned the courage to go to Professor Mellgren's office and expose myself as unworthy, a sham scientist of questionable ability and demonstrated incompetence in the writing market. When Mellgren read the reviews and listened to my interminable whimpering and self-effacement, he rolled with laughter. He said, "You must understand that the editor of this particular journal is of a theoretical persuasion that is virtually opposite the position you have taken in your manuscript. There is nothing wrong with what you have done, just resubmit the article elsewhere."

Pulled back from the abyss, I did resubmit my article, this time to the top journal in the field—the *Journal of Comparative and Physiological Psychology* (now called *Behavioral Neuroscience*; see Table 2–1). All I did was remove the old cover letter and attach a new one—the manuscript was unaltered. This time when the reviews came back, the editor stated, "This manuscript is in fine shape. We are simply adding the words "with rats" to the title and sending it on to the printer." [Note: This is the only time in my career, after more than 80 published journal articles, that this has happened; all the remaining reports have required at least some minor changes prior to publication.] Thus it was that my first research report was published (Nation, Wrather, & Mellgren, 1974). ▮

I benefitted early from this type of experience. Most of the time, of course, the review process is smooth, unbiased, and constructive. Comments are intended to help, and a higher quality manuscript results. However, you do need to be persistent and, occasionally, a little thick skinned. Scientific writing is an acquirable skill. Give yourself time, and do not be too quick to dismiss your talent.

Now that we know more about journals and the publishing process, we are in a better position to show how journal publications can assist us in developing our hypothesis. Continuing with our working hypothesis that age may affect the therapeutic effectiveness of cognitive interventions in chronically ill children, let us see how we can use some of the sources that are available to us.

**Psyclit.** Psyclit was mentioned previously as a frequently used tool for searching a given topic area. Although this computerized searching technique has the advantages of being quick and comprehensive, the usefulness of the information you get from Psyclit is determined by judiciously selecting key terms for the search. When too broad a field is specified, the result is that so much information is generated that it serves no purpose. You cannot possibly assimilate all findings from a vast database, so you really gain very little. Conversely, too narrow a search misses key articles and books.

Continuing in our effort to formalize a hypothesis, we begin our computer search on Psyclit by entering the term *coping* at the prompt. Within a couple of seconds, a message projects on the screen that 4,314 articles dealing with coping were found. It goes without saying that this result falls into the range of "too broad a field." Next, we enter the term *children* into the search. Not surprisingly, 31,519 entries are reported. At this juncture, we enter the conjunctive phrase *coping and children,* and the computer indicates that 313 articles on the subject were found. These articles are more appropriate for our research plan because they deal only with coping strategies in children of different age ranges. Still, over 300 reports is likely too great a literature base to realistically comprehend. Additionally, many of these papers are likely to be of marginal interest to our purpose. In response, we enter the more complete conjunctive phrase *coping and children and chronic illness*. Now the computer searches only for those articles on coping strategies in children of different age ranges where the stressor is a chronic disease or ailment. Our list of entries now numbers 23, which is a very manageable figure. At this time it is appropriate to scroll through the abstracts on the list and determine the relevancy of the reports to our developing project.

The Psyclit search yields several useful finds, including a paper by Sargent and Liebman published in 1985 in *Community Mental Health Journal* (see Figure 2–3). After carefully reading the abstract, it is apparent that this paper addresses a number of issues of potential importance regarding the effectiveness of intervention strategies in children. Various models of psychotherapeutic intervention in the treatment of chronic illness are discussed, and some of this information could be incorporated into the project we are planning. Of course, the real value of the report will become evident only once we have had an opportunity to read the complete paper. As the reproduction of the Psyclit

TI: Childhood *chronic illness:* Issues for psychotherapists.
AU: Sargent, -John; Liebman, -Ronald
IN: Philadelphia Child Guidance Clinic, PA
JN: Community-Mental-Health-Journal; 1985 Win Vol 21(4) 294–311
IS: 00103853
LA: English
PY: 1985
AB:Outlines the stresses inherent for child and family in the care of *children* with *chronic illness* or physical handicap and presents models for effective psychotherapeutic intervention. Active *coping* styles in which family members draw on experiences, consider multiple alternatives for handling problems, take positive action, and seek out information in an active fashion have been identified as reducing emotional and physical symptoms for the child and his/her parents; the need for consistent support, understanding, and reinforcement for the child from his/her family is emphasized. Five characteristics of family interaction have been found to be more prevalent in families with a child in whom illness has become repeatedly symptomatic: enmeshment, overprotectiveness, rigidity, lack of conflict resolution, and involvement of the *children* in parental conflict. Two cases are included as examples of these principles. It is suggested that psychotherapists, with knowledge of the child's illness and the tasks to be accomplished by the child and his/her family, can collaborate with the child's physician to carry out goal-directed therapy that would manage the illness and promote the growth and development of all family members. (22 ref) (PsycLIT Database Copyright 1987 American Psychological Assn, all rights reserved)
KP: psychotherapeutic intervention & active *coping* techniques; family functioning & symptom management; families with chronically ill or physically handicapped child
DE: CHRONICITY-DISORDERS; PSYCHOTHERAPEUTIC-TECHNIQUES; *COPING-BEHAVIOR;* ADJUSTMENT-; PHYSICALLY-HANDICAPPED; FAMILY-THERAPY; PSYCHOTHERAPY-; FAMILY-RELATIONS; SYMPTOMS-
CC: 3313; 33
PO: HUMAN
UD: 8702
AN: 74–04872
JC: 1178

**FIGURE 2–3 An abstract from a computerized search of Psyclit**

printout in Figure 2–3 shows, all the information we need to track down the primary source is available.

**Medline.** Because our topic relates to the treatment intervention of a medical disorder, a computer search called Medline is relevant to our task. Medline can be accessed through the Internet. Consequently, you never have to leave your home or office to conduct the search. On your personal computer, you simply type the appropriate words or phrase and follow the logic outlined previously for the Psyclit search. Figure 2–4 profiles a relevant abstract from our Medline search.


I
UI —QE399–0005
AU —Weekes DP
TI —ADOLESCENTS GROWING UP CHRONICALLY ILL—A LIFE-SPAN DEVEL-
OPMENTAL VIEW
SO—Family & Community Health 1995 Jan; 17(4):22–34
MH —Childhood. Illness. Cancer
AB —More than 7.5 million children and adolescents experience a chronic ill-ness between birth and 18 years of age. Because of technologic advances, in-creasing numbers of adolescents are living and growing up chronically ill. As a result, the attention of health care professionals has shifted to supporting these adolescents in coping with the day-to-day realities of growing and developing within the context of a life characterized by the demands of chronic illness and its treatment. The challenge, then, is to gain insight into how development oc-curs within the chronic illness context and in so doing to explicate coping ap-proaches that facilitate enhanced quality of life for chronically ill adolescents. This article focuses on the life-span period of adolescence, which encompasses the period beginning at 11 or 12 and ending around 19 to 21 years of age. The life-span developmental perspective is identified as a particularly useful theo-retic approach for viewing this period in the life cycle. This article includes a general overview of the life-span developmental perspective, application of the life-span perspective to adolescent development, application of the perspective to adolescents growing up chronically ill, and discussion of the research and practice implications inherent in viewing chronically ill adolescents from a life-span developmental perspective. [References: 38]
LG —English
PT —Article
IN —Reprint available from:
Weekes DP
BOSTON COLL
SCH NURSING
GRAD PROGRAM
CHESTNUT HILL, MA 02167
USA

**FIGURE 2–4 An abstract from a computerized search of Medline**

**Specialized Retrieval Systems.** In addition to comprehensive databases such as Psyclit and Medline, many subject areas in psychology offer highly specialized searches. An example is ETOH (ETOH is the chemical designation for ethyl alcohol), which is a large collection of reports on alcohol and alcohol-related problems. Made available by the Office of Scientific Affairs, the National Institute on Alcohol Abuse and Alcoholism (NIAAA), this retrieval system includes records, which are complete with abstracts, covering journal articles, books, conference papers and proceedings, workshops, dissertations, and chapters in edited works. The system is located in Rockville, Maryland, and it can be accessed from anywhere with a telephone and a modem. Researchers, clinicians, and anyone else interested in alcohol-related phenomena can transfer files to their computer banks and systematically build information networks.

The advantage the specialized retrieval systems have over the more general databases is the diverse character of sources they include in their searches. Most general computer searches are restricted to publications in major journals and books. The more specialized coverage permits the inclusion of more obscure reports, such as unpublished doctoral dissertations, which may be immensely valuable to an investigator. Together, general and specialized computer searches afford a fast and efficient method of information access.

**Index Medicus.** Because our topic is concerned with medical issues, *Index Medicus* may be useful as we expand our search. Unlike Psyclit, Medline, and many other computer-based searches, *Index Medicus* does not present an abstract or summary of a journal article. Instead it provides a listing of references which have been published recently in a given area, so in this respect *Index Medicus* is truly an index only. Each listing begins with the title of a journal article, the authors, an abbreviated title of the journal, and the volume and page where the article can be found. Figure 2–5 shows a page from the April 1995 volume of *Index Medicus* which presents recent publications in the area of "Chronic Disease." A paper written by Garralda and several others is listed under the "Psychology" subheading. Even though we have only title information, it is reasonable to suspect that this report may be an additional source of information on the topic of chronic illness and coping in children, and we will want to obtain a copy of it.

**Science Citation Index and Social Science Citation Index.** Two additional sources that have been popular reference materials in psychology are the *Science Citation Index (SCI)* and the *Social Science Citation Index (SSCI)*. Both of these sources are published by the same company (The Institute for Scientific Information in Philadelphia), and while there is some overlap between the two

arriers. Breast Cancer Linkage Consortium. Easton DF, et al. **Am J Hum Genet** 1995 Jan;56(1):265-71
An evaluation of genetic heterogeneity in 145 breast-ovarian cancer families. Breast Cancer Linkage Consortium. Narod SA, et al. **Am J Hum Genet** 1995 Jan;56(1):254-64
Acute promyelocytic leukemia with t(15;17) abnormality after chemotherapy containing etoposide for Langerhans cell histiocytosis [letter] Egeler RM. **Cancer** 1995 Jan 1; 75(1):134-6
Detailed deletion mapping of chromosome segment 17q12-21 in sporadic breast tumours. Nagai MA, et al. **Genes Chromosom Cancer** 1994 Sep;11(1):58-62
Neurofibromatosis type 1. Legius E, et al. **Genet Couns** 1994; 5(3):225-41 (132 ref.)
Chromosome mapping of the human arrestin (SAG), beta-arrestin 2 (ARRB2), and beta-adrenergic receptor kinase 2 (ADRBK2) genes. Calabrese G, et al. **Genomics** 1994 Sep 1;23(1):286-8
Chromosome locations of genes encoding human signal transduction adapter proteins, Nck (NCK), Shc (SHC1), and Grb2 (GRB2). Huebner K, et al. **Genomics** 1994 Jul 15;22(2):281-7
Localization of the VHR phosphatase gene and its analysis as a candidate for BRCA1. Kamb A, et al. **Genomics** 1994 Sep 1;23(1):163-7
Physical mapping of chromosome 17p13.3 in the region of a putative tumor suppressor gene important in medulloblastoma. McDonald JD, et al. **Genomics** 1994 Sep 1;23(1):229-32
Human retinal guanylate cyclase (GUC2D) maps to chromosome 17p13.1. Oliveira L, et al. **Genomics** 1994 Jul 15;22(2):478-81
A point mutation in the putative TATA box, detected in nondiseased individuals and patients with hereditary breast cancer, decreases promoter activity of the 17 beta-hydroxysteroid dehydrogenase type 1 gene 2 (EDH17B2) in vitro. Peltoketo H, et al. **Genomics** 1994 Sep 1;23(1):250-2
Mapping GRB2, a signal transduction gene in the human and the mouse. Yulug IG, et al. **Genomics** 1994 Jul 15; 22(2):313-8
Human breast and colon cancers exhibit alterations of DNA methylation patterns at several DNA segments on chromosomes 11p and 17p. Ribieras S, et al. **J Cell Biochem** 1994 Sep;56(1):86-96
Prenatal diagnosis of lissencephaly: Miller-Dieker syndrome. McGahan JP, et al. **J Clin Ultrasound** 1994 Nov-Dec; 22(9):560-3
Familial half cryptic translocation t(9;17). Köhler A, et al. **J Med Genet** 1994 Sep;31(9):712-4
A gene for pachyonychia congenita is closely linked to the keratin gene cluster on 17q12-q21. Munro CS, et al. **J Med Genet** 1994 Sep;31(9):675-8
Alterations at chromosome 17 loci in peripheral nerve sheath tumors. Lothe RA, et al. **J Neuropathol Exp Neurol** 1995 Jan;54(1):65-73
Inactivation of the p53 gene in leukemias and myelodysplastic syndrome (MDS) with 17p monosomy .[letter] Preudhomme C, et al. **Leukemia** 1994 Dec;8(12):2241-2

GENETICS

8;21 and 15;17 translocations: abnormalities in a single cell lineage in acute myeloid leukemia. Knuutila S, et al. **Acta Haematol** 1994;92(2):88-90
Breast cancer incidence, penetrance and survival in probable carriers of BRCA1 gene mutation in families linked to BRCA1 on chromosome 17q12-21. Porter DE, et al. **Br J Surg** 1994 Oct;81(10):1512-5

ULTRASTRUCTURE

A 1.5-Mb deletion in 17p11.2-p12 is frequently observed in Italian families with hereditary neuropathy with liability to pressure palsies. Lorenzetti D, et al. **Am J Hum Genet** 1995 Jan;56(1):91-8
Detection of residual leukemic cells in patients with acute promyelocytic leukemia by the fluorescence in situ hybridization method: potential for predicting relapse. Zhao L, et al. **Blood** 1995 Jan 15;85(2):495-9

## CHROMOSOMES, HUMAN, PAIR 18

Social preferences by and for pigtailed macaques (Macaca nemestrina) with trisomy 18. Swartz KB, et al. **Am J Ment Retard** 1994 Sep;99(2):141-50
Lymphomas with testicular localisation show a consistent BCL-2 expression without a translocation (14;18): a molecular and immunohistochemical study. Lambrechts AC, et al. **Br J Cancer** 1995 Jan;71(1):73-7
Genetic alterations in localized prostate cancer: identification of a common region of deletion on chromosome arm 18q. Latil A, et al. **Genes Chromosom Cancer** 1994 Oct; 11(2):119-25
Molecular analysis of the expression of transthyretin in intestine and liver from trisomy 18 fetuses. Loughna S, et al. **Hum Genet** 1995 Jan;95(1):89-95

GENETICS

Tumor progression and loss of heterozygosity at 5q and 18q in non-small cell lung cancer. Fong KM, et al. **Cancer Res** 1995 Jan 15;55(2):220-3

## CHROMOSOMES, HUMAN, PAIR 19

Structural and functional studies of the intracellular tyrosine kinase MATK gene and its translated product. Avraham S, et al. **J Biol Chem** 1995 Jan 27;270(4):1833-42
Shared allelic losses on chromosomes 1p and 19q suggest a common origin of oligodendroglioma and oligoastrocytoma. Kraus JA, et al. **J Neuropathol Exp Neurol** 1995 Jan;54(1):91-5
[Isolation and characteristics of an ordered library of transcribed sequences of human chromosome 19 from hybrid human-hamster cells] Obradovich D, et al. **Bioorg Khim** 1994 Aug-Sep;20(8-9):919-31 (Eng. Abstr.) (Rus)

## CHROMOSOMES, HUMAN, PAIR 20

Refinement of the localization of the gene for neuronal nicotinic acetylcholine receptor alpha 4 subunit (CHRNA4) to human chromosome 20q13.2-q13.3. Steinlein O, et al. **Genomics** 1994 Jul 15;22(2):493-5

ULTRASTRUCTURE

Molecular heterogeneity at the breakpoints of smaller 20q deletions. Hollings PE. **Genes Chromosom Cancer** 1994 Sep; 11(1):21-8

## CHROMOSOMES, HUMAN, PAIR 21

Use of the polymerase chain reaction in the detection of AML1/ETO fusion transcript in t(8;21). Kwong YL, et al. **Cancer** 1995 Feb 1;75(3):821-5
Congenital cardiac defect in a patient with mosaic 45,X/46,XX,i(21q) karyotype. Digilio MC, et al. **Clin Genet** 1994 Sep;46(3):268-70
Isolation and mapping of human chromosome 21 cDNA: progress in constructing a chromosome 21 expression map. Cheng JF, et al. **Genomics** 1994 Sep 1;23(1):75-84
Cloning and characterization of a 135- to 500-kb region of homology on the long arm of human chromosome 21. Dutriaux A, et al. **Genomics** 1994 Jul 15;22(2):472-7
Five new microsatellite polymorphisms at the q21 region of human chromosome 21. Bosch A, et al. **Hum Genet** 1995 Jan;95(1):119-22
Identification of flanking markers for the familial amyotrophic lateral sclerosis gene ALS1 on chromosome 21. Figlewicz DA, et al. **J Neurol Sci** 1994 Jul;124 Suppl:90-5
The AML1 and ETO genes in acute myeloid leukemia with a t(8;21). Nucifora G, et al. **Leuk Lymphoma** 1994 Aug; 14(5-6):353-62 (47 ref.)
[Jarcho-Levin syndrome. Description of a clinical case with familial 14;21 translocation] Sellitto F, et al. **Minerva Pediatr** 1994 Oct;46(10):451-7 (Eng. Abstr.) (Ita)

GENETICS

8;21 and 15;17 translocations: abnormalities in a single cell lineage in acute myeloid leukemia. Knuutila S, et al. **Acta Haematol** 1994;92(2):88-90

## CHROMOSOMES, HUMAN, PAIR 22

see related
PHILADELPHIA CHROMOSOME

Interstitial deletion of 22q11 in DiGeorge syndrome detected by high resolution and molecular analysis. Franke UC, et al. **Clin Genet** 1994 Aug;46(2):187-92
Chromosome mapping of the human arrestin (SAG), beta-arrestin 2 (ARRB2), and beta-adrenergic receptor kinase 2 (ADRBK2) genes. Calabrese G, et al. **Genomics** 1994 Sep 1;23(1):286-8
Selection of chromosome 22-specific clones from human genomic BAC library using a chromosome-specific cosmid library pool. Kim UJ, et al. **Genomics** 1994 Jul 15; 22(2):336-9
The fibulin-1 gene (FBLN1) is located on human chromosome 22 and on mouse chromosome 15. Mattei MG, et al. **Genomics** 1994 Jul 15;22(2):437-8
Deletion mapping of the long arm of chromosome 22 in human meningiomas. Akagi K, et al. **Int J Cancer** 1995 Jan 17;60(2):178-82
Frequent loss of heterozygosity at telomeric loci on 22q in sporadic colorectal cancers. Yana I, et al. **Int J Cancer** 1995 Jan 17;60(2):174-7
Extra marker chromosome, dic(22)(q11), associated with gonadal dysgenesis and multiple malformations [letter] Imai A, et al. **Int J Gynaecol Obstet** 1994 Oct;47(1):63-4
"CATCH 22" sans cardiac anomaly, thymic hypoplasia, cleft palate, and hypocalcaemia: cAtch 22. A common result of 22q11 deficiency? [letter] Lipson A, et al. **J Med Genet** 1994 Sep;31(9):741
Cloning and comparative mapping of recently evolved human chromosome 22-specific alpha satellite DNA. Rocchi M, et al. **Somat Cell Mol Genet** 1994 Sep; 20(5):443-8

GENETICS

Analysis of the NF2 tumor-suppressor gene and of chromosome 22 deletions in gliomas. Hoang-Xuan K, et al. **Int J Cancer** 1995 Feb 8;60(4):478-81

CHROMOSOMES, RING see RING CHROMOSOMES

## CHROMOSOMES, YEAST ARTIFICIAL

Large-scale screening of yeast artificial chromosome libraries using PCR. Khristich JV, et al. **Biotechniques** 1994 Sep; 17(3):498-501
Simple and robust screening of pooled yeast artificial chromosome libraries by the restriction enzyme digestion of polymerase chain reaction products. Wang X, et al. **Genet Anal Tech Appl** 1994;11(3):63-8
Regional localization of 725 human chromosome 7-specific yeast artificial chromosome clones. Kunz J, et al. **Genomics** 1994 Jul 15;22(2):439-48
A YAC contig spanning the nevoid basal cell carcinoma syndrome, Fanconi anaemia group C, and xeroderma pigmentosum group A loci on chromosome 9q. Morris DJ, et al. **Genomics** 1994 Sep 1;23(1):23-9
A YAC contig in 6p23 based on sequence tagged sites. Nemani M, et al. **Genomics** 1994 Jul 15;22(2):388-96
A YAC contig spanning a cluster of human type III receptor protein tyrosine kinase genes (PDGFRA-KIT-KDR) in chromosome segment 4q12. Spritz RA, et al. **Genomics** 1994 Jul 15;22(2):431-6
Multicolor FISH mapping of YAC clones in 3p14 and identification of a YAC spanning both FRA3B and the t(3;8) associated with hereditary renal cell carcinoma. Wilke CM, et al. **Genomics** 1994 Jul 15;22(2):319-26

## CHRONIC DISEASE

Revisiting our ideas about health. Golub ES. **Hosp Health Netw** 1995 Jan 20;69(2):78

EPIDEMIOLOGY

Damp housing and adult health: results from a lifestyle study in Worcester, England. Packer CN, et al. **J Epidemiol Community Health** 1994 Dec;48(6):555-9
Patterns of sedentary lifestyle in Missouri. Pruitt JL, et al. **Mo Med** 1994 Nov;91(11):675-9
[Chronic diseases in immigrants from Russia (CIS) at a primary care clinic and their sociodemographic characteristics] Ben-Noun L. **Harefuah** 1994 Dec 1; 127(11):441-5, 504-5 (Eng. Abstr.) (Heb)

NURSING

The stages of the prediagnostic period in chronic, life-threatening childhood illness: a process analysis. Cohen MH. **Res Nurs Health** 1995 Feb;18(1):39-48

PSYCHOLOGY

Psychiatric adjustment in children with chronic physical illness. Garralda ME, et al. **Br J Hosp Med** 1994 Sep 7-20; 52(5):230-4 (19 ref.)

REHABILITATION

[Current legal principles for geriatric rehabilitation] Igl G. **Z Gerontol** 1994 Sep-Oct;27(5):319-23 (0 ref.) (Ger)

THERAPY

Functioning and well-being outcomes of patients with depression compared with chronic general medical illnesses. Hays RD, et al. **Arch Gen Psychiatry** 1995 Jan; 52(1):11-9
A model for symptom management. The University of California, San Francisco School of Nursing Symptom Management Faculty Group. **Image J Nurs Sch** 1994 Winter;26(4):272-6
[To the hospital or not? A dilemma in nursing home medicine] Konings JW, et al. **Ned Tijdschr Geneeskd** 1994 Dec 31;138(53):2633-6 (Dut)

CHRONIC FATIGUE SYNDROME see FATIGUE SYNDROME, CHRONIC

CHRONIC ILLNESS see CHRONIC DISEASE

CHRONIC LIMITATION OF ACTIVITY see ACTIVITIES OF DAILY LIVING

CHRONIC OBSTRUCTIVE PULMONARY DISEASE see LUNG DISEASES, OBSTRUCTIVE

## CHRONOBIOLOGY

From circadians of the fifties to chronomes in vitro as in vivo. Halberg F, et al. **Arch Med Res** 1994 Autumn; 25(3):287-96
Proceedings of the 8th Workshop for the Clinical Research on Chronobiology. Kyoto, September 30-October 1, 1993. **Jpn J Psychiatry Neurol** 1994 Jun;48(2):449-509
Cronobiologic analysis of abortions in two related populations of teenager girls during two decades. Mikulechý M, et al. **Panminerva Med** 1994 Jun;36(2):66-70

PHYSIOLOGY

The period clock gene is expressed in central nervous system neurons which also produce a neuropeptide that reveals the projections of circadian pacemaker cells within the brain of Drosophila melanogaster. Helfrich-Förster C.

Index Medicus Apr 1995 333

**FIGURE 2–5** Listings under the subject heading "Chronic Disease" from *Index Medicus* (April 1995)

depending on the subject area, as a rule information in the *SCI* is more likely to be of concern to biopsychology or other more molecular approaches to understanding behavior. The material referenced in the *SSCI* is a more complete representation of the so-called "softside" of psychology.

Regardless of which index you select, you will find that there are three types of volumes for each year. First, there is the Subject Index. The Subject Index lists articles for a specific topic which have been published during that year. In this sense the index information is similar to what we have reviewed for the other search procedures. For instance, by looking under the topic "Chronic Illness" we could find many of the same articles we uncovered in our earlier searches. The second of the three volumes, called the Source Index, lists all published works of a particular author during the year. Previously, it was noted that J. Sargent coauthored a paper on chronically ill children in 1985 (refer to Figure 2–3). Perhaps this investigator has done something more recently along the same lines. Using the Source Index it is possible to track Sargent's scientific contributions over successive years and see if other related materials have been published. Finally, the *SCI* and the *SSCI* offer an additional organizational scheme, the Citation Index volume, which other reference sources do not. The Citation Index references a particular article and lists how many other articles include it in their reference lists. In a separate listing for each year, the Citation Index gauges the frequency with which a journal publication has been cited recently. Accordingly, the index is often used as a sort of national Richter scale for the scientific impact of a given publication. That is, the more articles listed which cite the key paper, the greater the perceived significance of the report.

In addition to telling us something about the relative impact of a selected article, the Citation Index can be useful in determining what follow-up work has been done along the same lines. It makes sense that when a key paper opens a new line of inquiry, other programmatically related articles on the subject cite the seminal paper. The Citation Index permits you to systematically trace the development of a literature. In our case, because we have identified a relatively new subject field, no particular report stands out. Should something emerge, however, we will be able to turn to the Citation Index of *SCI* or *SSCI* to appraise the recognized interest in the published article.

**Knowledge of Related Concepts.** To be sure, the information gained from searching book and journal publications in a particular area or by a particular author is essential to the process of hypothesis formulation. However, the investigator cannot rely on such narrowly defined material. A much broader grasp of psychology is required, and frankly this can only be achieved through experience.

Previously, I have made several comments about the diversity of psychological research, and there is no denying that the field is broad. Even with this breadth, however, there is often a common thread or theme across topic areas, and events that are the focus of attention in one domain are sometimes relevant in another. This feature of psychological research dictates that the individual investigator read widely, and gain at least a nominal understanding of several different lines of research. There is simply no substitute for a knowledge base which is acquired systematically over a period of years by carefully examining more general literature.

With respect to the development of our hypothesis, it would make sense that the available literature on the changing cognitive capacity of children as a function of age would be of interest. That is, because our working hypothesis is tied to the idea that the cognitive apparatus of younger children limits the relative effectiveness of cognitively oriented interventions, it would seem reasonable to see if there is information to suggest that younger and older children differ in terms of their cognitive processing. In this regard, the information need not come from studies on psychotherapy. Reports on basic research issues are valuable to our cause insofar as the findings address the basic issue of cognition in children of different ages.

The following summary of established patterns of performance in a developmental learning paradigm illustrates the importance of knowing something about the broader literature which pertains to the research topic under investigation:

> In studies of discrimination learning, a reversal shift occurs when there is a change in the designation of the correct value within the same dimension (cf. Baddeley, 1993). For example, in a discrimination study involving stimuli of different colors and shapes, if red has been rewarded over blue in the dimension of color, but then blue is rewarded over red, a reversal shift has been introduced.  Alternatively, a nonreversal shift is said to occur when you reward some value on the previously irrelevant dimension. Had we been rewarding red in the dimension of color, for instance, we might shift to the dimension of shape and begin rewarding triangle over square, regardless of color.
>
> The literature on children's performance on such discrimination problems reveals a counterintuitive result. Younger children (5- or 6-year-olds) perform better on the nonreversal shift than on the reversal shift (Kendler & Kendler, 1967). This pattern, which is opposite that evident in older children (11- or 12-year-olds) and adults, has confused developmental researchers because the reversal shift on face value seems easier to effect. That is, switching to "the opposite of what was rewarded before" is one of the first problem-solving strategies you would think someone would invoke, and certainly this is simpler than searching outside the rewarded dimension. Indeed, debriefing sessions with the older children and adults confirms that this "cognitive shortcut" is precisely why the reversal shift is accom-

plished so readily in the older age ranges. Why then do the younger children perform as they do? What renders a nonreversal shift easier to deal with than a reversal shift?

While many accounts of these findings have been suggested, the most compelling has centered on the differences in cognitive functioning across age ranges (refer to Reese & Lipsitt, 1970, for a detailed review). More than younger children, older children should be able to conduct more sophisticated cognitive searches for a solution. Invoking abstract decisions rules, applying a problem-solving strategy such as "choose opposite," and so on would be more probable in older children who would presumably possess a more elaborate mental framework than their younger counterparts. In fact, it is possible, perhaps even likely, that 5- and 6-year-olds may not be responding "mentally" at all. With limited cognitive skills, children in this age range may rely on simple conditioning. That is, they determine decisions by the algebraic summation of accrued excitatory and inhibitory tendencies, independent of thought. While the theoretical details are not important here, it is sufficient to note that when an organism responds within the controlling influence of simple stimulus-response (S-R) conditioning, the clear prediction is that nonreversal shifts will be more easily accomplished than reversal shifts. This point is buttressed by findings that show white rats perform like younger children, i.e., the rats learn nonreversal shifts faster than reversal shifts, ostensibly because they must respond based on their conditioning histories and nothing else (see Reese & Lipsitt, 1970).

These findings support the contention that the cognitive and intellectual processes of younger and older children are sufficiently discrepant to produce markedly different patterns of responding on concept identification (discrimination learning) tasks. In effect, the state of mental complexity defines the manner in which problems are solved.

Nowhere in this discussion do we find a reference to treatment, chronic illness, or anything of an applied nature. The research findings summarized previously come from basic research laboratories that are concerned with fundamental issues in human learning. Still, these results are exceedingly important to the development of our hypothesis. The evidence favors the position that older children are more likely to employ cognitive mechanisms in dealing with a changing environment and in this sense supports our basic contention that cognitively based forms of therapeutic intervention may be of limited use to younger children. If 5- or 6-year-olds are disinclined to invoke cognitive strategies or are incapable of abstracting such strategies, it makes sense that treatment approaches which rest squarely on such processes would be of limited value to children in this age range. Specifically, younger children who suffer from chronic maladies will not benefit from cognitive therapy because they do not approach the world from a cognitive perspective. In effect, attempts to get these children to do something they do not want to do or are not able to do will be wasted.

As a result, we see it is immensely important that the investigator have some knowledge of events outside the specific literature defining a narrow topic area. As indicated, this awareness is not achieved easily. Experience, years of covering broadly defined materials, and interaction with colleagues contribute indirectly to hypothesis formation. It is a tough assignment and in some instances may be unrealistic. You may have to call for help.

**Collaboration.** In happier times, when the research world was simpler and the information flow was a freshet instead of a white water river, it was more common for an investigator to work in relative isolation. The literature was manageable, the number of relevant issues was reasonable, and there were only a few other researchers in the field, so their work was tracked easily.

Today, it is virtually impossible to keep up with all developments in a given concept area. Different levels of analysis, specializations within the field, and numerous other demands make it difficult for one person to stay abreast of everything that impacts her research. Consequently, more people are turning to **collaborators** for assistance. A collaborator may be a departmental colleague, a research specialist in another department on campus, or a scientist from some other institution. For instance, someone interested in the effects of early childhood physical abuse on later social behavior may be aware of the possible contaminating influence that socioeconomic status (SES) may have on the findings, but he may not know how to measure it. What is needed in this case is a consultant who can assess SES and statistically control for its influence. Similarly, someone interested in the effect of phencyclidine (angel dust) on learning and memory may have to engage an electrophysiologist to record brain wave patterns to determine if the behavioral impairment is secondary to some form of physiological dysfunction. In these sorts of consortia, each member of the research team plays a specific role; everyone performs a job and the result is a more thorough and sophisticated treatment of the subject matter.

Considering the advantages of collaboration, it is not surprising that many major research funding agencies explicitly solicit research applications from interdisciplinary teams of investigators. By involving specialists from separate disciplines, a greater range of questions can be answered and resource allocation is more equitable. You can expect to see more collaborative arrangements in the future, particularly in highly technical areas. In any event, along with books, journals, and your understanding of related material, the knowledge and skill of a collaborator can be considered an important source of information.

**collaborator**—a colleague or research specialist who agrees to work with an investigator and provide specialized input on selected aspects of a research project

## Compilation: Bringing It Together

Obviously, a great deal of work must be completed before we can be in a position to formally express a hypothesis. Even after the original idea is formulated and information is gathered from the literature and other sources, we are still not finished. At this juncture, we have assembled an impressive array of factual accounts of phenomena related to the topic, but what does it all mean? What is the overall picture?

Integrating findings from books, journals, and other people is crucial to effective hypothesis formulation. This often is a tedious and difficult task. In our case, the original idea began with a suspicion that some of the attempts used in a hospital setting to control pain and discomfort might be ineffective because of the limited cognitive capabilities of younger children. This suspicion was borne out of observation and a recognition that many cognitively oriented intervention strategies were being used in a pediatric oncology ward. In ordinary parlance, this is a matter of "keeping your eyes open."

Exploration efforts aimed at collecting information from the literature yielded data on the effectiveness of existing approaches to alleviating stress in children undergoing medical treatment. For example, we find that just keeping children informed about the nature of their treatment and telling them ahead of time what is going to happen to them produces real benefits. Moreover, the impact of providing such information may be different in older children than in younger children (Curry & Russ, 1985). This tells us something about the wisdom of our original idea. Obviously, if children of different ages respond differently to some types of interventions, it is not unreasonable to think that age might also affect the efficacy of cognitive therapy.

Given that age is a factor that has been shown to determine the effectiveness of treatment, what about cognition and age? Our search reveals that cognitive attempts at problem solving do change as children grow older (Kendler & Kendler, 1967). Combined with evidence which shows that younger and older children receiving stressful medical treatments respond differently to other types of psychotherapy, the report on changing cognitions takes on even greater meaning. Age affects both psychotherapy and cognition. It is a logical fallacy, of course, to draw any direct relation between psychotherapy (B) and cognition (C) as a function of age (A) from this statement (A is linked to B, A is linked to C, B and C are not necessarily linked). However, the possibility that age may be an important determinant of the effectiveness of cognitive treatment is enhanced by the awareness that a common variable alters both cognition and therapy. Insofar as one is integral to the other, mutual differences due to age manipulations would be expected. Of course, our uncertain predicament here defines the explicit purpose for doing the research in the first place: We do not know for sure whether or not a relation between B and C exists. We must formally test this hypothesis.

Other information on the relative effectiveness of different intervention strategies, assessment instruments, and so forth was obtained in our search. All of these findings are useful because they will help set up the appropriate design and procedures for testing our hypothesis. It goes without saying that exploring the literature on age, cognition, and psychotherapy would produce considerably more reports than have been mentioned here. In the interest of space, I have omitted most of what would be found from this search. What I have attempted to communicate in this section is the manner by which the investigator goes about polishing an idea. You start with a crude concept or rudimentary notion, you gather information with bearing on the issue, and you compile evidence and place yourself in a position to state a hypothesis. The next step is to formally describe the hypothesis to be analyzed experimentally. Now we must exercise extreme care.

## WITHIN CHAPTER REVIEW AND STUDY QUESTIONS

### THE STRUCTURE OF THE HYPOTHESIS

1. What is a hypothesis and what role does it serve in an investigation?
2. The concept of a "working hypothesis," which was introduced, implies that formulating the hypothesis is accomplished in stages, changing the hypothesis as you go. What sources of information are available during the period the working hypothesis is being considered?
3. I find a chapter directly relevant to what I am interested in studying, and it cites a published journal article which provides additional, useful information. The journal article is called a:
   a. primary reference
   b. secondary reference
4. If a computer search is unavailable, where can you turn for information about a particular topic?
5. In today's research environment, why is it important to work with other members of a research team? Do you see this situation changing in the future? In what ways do you expect the role of collaboration in research to change?
6. You go to Psyclit and look up "pediatric oncology," but find no listings under this heading. What is your next step?

# The Formal Hypothesis

Until now, we have dealt with a working hypothesis that provides a general framework for gathering information about an idea. Such a hypothesis is a convenient guideline; it is subject to amendment based on what we discover during our search for related findings in the area. However, there comes a time when the research idea must take on a definite, unalterable character and thereby set the rest of the research program in motion. This is when we present the formal hypothesis.

The **formal hypothesis** is the precise expression of a predicted relation between or among events which is capable of being tested. Unlike the working hypothesis, the formal hypothesis is not subject to change. It is fixed before the investigator begins to collect data and, regardless of what the results show, remains as originally stated. As the true anchoring element in any research project, the statement of the formal hypothesis represents what is perhaps the most crucial step in the entire investigatory enterprise. All the activities that follow are tied to the formal hypothesis. Accordingly, should an investigator present a flawed formal hypothesis, the probability is that the research will be doomed from the outset. Bad ideas give birth to bad results and waste time and resources.

Some features in my definition of the formal hypothesis deserve more attention. Inspection of some key points in the definition unveils a subtle but sophisticated rationale which is integral to any formal hypothesis. Simply stated, some things are "musts" when you formally lay out your final research idea.

## The Issue of "Precise Expression"

In the definition of a formal hypothesis presented here, it was noted that the hypothesis is a precise expression of some suspected relation. Central to this position is the notion that there can be no uncertainty regarding what is under investigation. A death knell for hypothesis formation is a vague expression of why you are conducting the research. If you are unclear about the issues at hand, how can you expect to make meaningful comments about a topic area?

A useful analog for ensuring precision in the expression of a hypothesis is the funnel approach to hypothesis development. Think of the initial stages of developing a hypothesis as parallel to the top of a funnel. There is a wide region which keeps the material within a boundary and guarantees you do not spill over inappropriately. It is difficult to make a mistake during this period because breadth is on our side. As events proceed, however, the flow of material becomes more restricted and a narrowing process permits greater focus, which makes it possible to deal with events within a small space. Finally, with pinpoint accuracy, we are able define a region or an application that has been built on precision. We are at the point of expressing the formal hypothesis in singular, unambiguous terms, and we leave no doubt that we are interested in only this specific idea. Nothing else is an issue in our research agenda.

This approach to hypothesis development, which is based on a rationale of going from a broad subject matter to an extremely narrow concern, is helpful when we begin writing our report. There is a logical progression of thought, with one finding leading to another, which tells the reader how we pruned inessentials and came up with our formal hypothesis. I will have a great deal more to say about this in Chapter 12—The Scientific Report.

With respect to the hypothesis we are formulating, this precision issue is addressed in our psychology literature search of treatment of chronically ill children, an awareness of related findings in other subject areas, and all the other sources of information we looked at in the section on exploration. We see that there is a large information base on chronic illness, and we see that within this context a number of reports on intervention strategies are available. Getting even more specific, it becomes apparent that some of these intervention techniques either are exclusively cognitive in nature or they include cognitive elements as major components of the treatment regimen. Consistent with the funnel approach, we are systematically paring the subject field so that we are left with one concern or idea.

## Is It Capable of Being Tested?

Also included in the aforementioned definition of a formal hypothesis is the requirement that the predicted relation be capable of being tested. As with lack of precision, presenting a hypothesis that is disconfirmable assures failure from the outset.

One of the chief problems associated with an untestable hypothesis is that it is not possible to make any scientific conclusions. Indeed, it is not possible to reach a conclusion of any sort when the hypothesis

**formal hypothesis**—the precise expression of a predicted relation between or among events; a testable idea

under consideration is neither capable of being supported nor refutable. Anything you say has no impact one way or the other. Because your hypothesis is couched in such a fashion that it cannot be challenged, there is little reason for pursuing the project.

Recognizing the enormous value of the psychoanalytic perspective on personality in terms of its setting the foundations for more contemporary models of psychotherapy (see Benjamin et al., 1994), it is fair to argue that most of the principles in classical Freudian theory are untestable. For instance, the notion that in-depth analysis promotes unconscious growth which leads to a more balanced and fully integrated life sounds wonderful. This idea contains the elements of intellectual elegance and personal enrichment which give it instant appeal. However, is the position scientifically credible? How could you test such a hypothesis? Because we cannot directly measure unconscious processes, it is impossible to identify a starting place. In the absence of a designated beginning, it seems unwise to make comments about movement. Even if there were growth, how would you know it? By definition unconscious events fall outside the realm of objectivity. Anyone making predictions about the relation between psycho-analysis and unconscious growth, then, must do so fully aware that this idea is not testable. It cannot be confirmed or rejected.

Given the expressed importance of presenting a testable formal hypothesis, it follows that we should be in a position to meet this criterion with our own hypothesis. Can we subject the idea that cognitively oriented intervention strategies are more suitable for some age ranges than others to scientific confirmation or disconfirmation? Because the beneficial effects of psychotherapy on the behavior of children undergoing medical intervention for a chronic disorder can be objectively measured, we would seem to be on safe ground. That is, insofar as the reactions of a child to an anxiety-eliciting circumstance can be determined by empirical means, it would seem that the criterion "capable of being tested" has been met.

## WITHIN CHAPTER REVIEW AND STUDY QUESTIONS

### THE FORMAL HYPOTHESIS

1. What is the difference between a working hypothesis and a formal hypothesis?
2. Explain why each of the following characteristics of a formal hypothesis is important:
   a. The hypothesis must be expressed precisely.
   b. The hypothesis must be testable.

## STATING THE NULL

I have devoted considerable space here to characterizing the formal hypothesis that forms the basis for a research project. It would seem reasonable to think that any test of a relation between or among psychologically relevant events would have to include at least some version of the formal hypothesis. This is not the case, however. The formal hypothesis, which defines the concern of the research, is not part of the testing process. Rather, the hypothesis that is actually tested in a research project is the **null hypothesis.** The null hypothesis, developed by Sir Ronald Fisher, states that there is no relation between the events under consideration.

Why do we approach our research topic this way? If we are interested in the association between age and the effectiveness of cognitive therapy in chronically ill children, then what is wrong with just putting forth the idea that such a relation does exist, and then testing this proposition? The answer has to do with the inability to prove a hypothesis.

### *The Nature of Proof*

Although it is possible to gather evidence favoring a particular position or hypothesis, you can never declare the idea "true." That is, you may conduct 50 experiments all showing the same result, and all supporting the same thing, but you are never really sure what experiment number 51 will reveal. Perhaps number 51 will be consistent with what has been done previously, but it is also possible that number 51 will be the exception and render a pattern of results that reveals a hypothesis invalid for all cases. The point is that although you can always add evidence in support of an idea, unless you can test all possible cases (which you cannot), you can never prove anything. The following illustration should help you understand what I mean.

I have a rule which permits me to express a relation between any three numbers. Consistent with the rule are the three following values:

6 7 9

What do you think the rule is? See if you can discover the rule behind the expression of these three numbers.

Perhaps you are thinking in terms of any three numbers of increasing value, so you say *2, 3,* and *4.* When I reply that this is not the rule, you look more closely and see that it may be a more restrictive case of the same idea: the first two numbers must be consecutive, and then you

**null hypothesis**—the statement on the lack of differences between or among events which is actually subjected to testing and, ultimately, confirmation or disconfirmation

must skip a number. As a result, you try *5, 6,* and *8.* I respond that you are correct. Now, because you may feel you are on to something, you say *10, 11,* and *13.* Again, I inform you that you are correct. You further suggest *14, 15,* and *17,* and as before I tell you that this series is consistent with the rule.

Now you are fairly convinced that you have the rule. You have accumulated a great deal of data which agrees with the position that the rule is "consecutively increasing values followed by a number that skips the last value." In your search for the rule, you systematically eliminated some alternatives while bolstering your position with tests of new possibilities which time after time agree with your idea about the rule. Although you may feel secure in your judgment, the truth is you are no further along than when you first started. Here is why.

Confident after making all the aforementioned tests, as one last display of your idea you suggest *21, 22,* and *24.* However, I indicate, "This is wrong. This is inconsistent with the rule." What? Why? Everything you have done up to this point agrees with your position, so what happened? This is the issue: Up to this point you have been right, but you have not tried every possibility. You can never try every possibility. There is always one more relation that may defy the rule, so it follows that you can never truly know the rule unless I give it to you. The rule is, "Any three numbers increasing in value which fall in a range between *5* and *20.*"

It should be apparent from this example that you can prove what the unknown rule is not, but you can never prove what the unknown rule is. The same is true for hypothesis testing. We can arrange our tests of ideas so that we can tell which hypotheses are incorrect, and in so doing we narrow the range of possible alternatives. Ultimately, we may narrow the alternatives to such an extent that we achieve a good sense of knowing what relation really does exist—we can feel more comfortable that our formal hypothesis is correct. We can never be totally sure, however.

As a result, we are left with stating the null hypothesis. We must test the idea that a particular relation between or among events does not exist. In Chapter 11—Drawing Inferences About Results, we return to issues related to rejecting the null hypothesis. For now, however, it is sufficient to understand that sometimes it is as useful to know what "it" is not, as what "it" is.

## WITHIN CHAPTER REVIEW AND STUDY QUESTIONS

### STATING THE NULL

1. Define the null hypothesis.
2. Why is it impossible to prove a hypothesis? What advantage is there to disproving a specific hypothesis?

---

 ## The Model Experiment

In this chapter, we have seen that formulating the working hypothesis requires synthesizing information which is gathered from a variety of sources. Moving to the formal hypothesis must be accomplished carefully and with an understanding of the precision and quantifiability that is essential to that statement. Finally, we accept that we cannot prove our formal hypothesis, but we can gain confidence in our idea by eliminating alternatives through rejecting the null.

The formal hypothesis that will be used as a guide for the remainder of this text predicts that chronically ill younger children will derive fewer benefits from a cognitively oriented therapeutic intervention than will older chronically ill children. Accordingly, we are in a position to state the null for our model experiment as:

> There are no significant differences between chronically ill children of younger ages, and chronically ill children of older ages, regarding the effectiveness of cognitive treatment.

As you shall see, we will design an experiment that is aimed at rejecting this null statement, therein indirectly affirming our belief that such a relation does exist.

# The Experiment

> A properly conducted experiment is a beautiful thing. It is an adventure, an expedition, a conquest. It commences with an act of faith, faith that the world is real, that our senses generally can be trusted, that effects have causes, and that we can discover meaning by reason.

This quote is by Professor Vincent Dethier, who was acknowledged in Chapter 1 as the author of the delightful *To Know a Fly* (1962). In that chapter, I discussed briefly several alternative methods for conducting inquiry into points of interest. Included in that discussion were naturalistic observation, field research, and other nonlaboratory approaches. As was noted, the scientific method affords some advantages not present in the other approaches. These advantages are simply but eloquently expressed in Dethier's quote.

# WHAT IS AN EXPERIMENT?

I agree with Deither that beauty, adventure, faith, cause-effect, and discovery are essential elements of an experiment. Let's take a closer look at each of these dimensions.

## *A Beautiful Thing*

Beauty is a dimension to life that is often attributed to crystalline October mornings, the expanse of the open prairie, a forest cathedral, physical appearance, or numerous other visually pleasing scenes. To a scientist, a well-designed experiment is no less fetching. Like a Raphael fresco, a carefully designed experiment that is free of flawed ideas and conduct is an artistic achievement that at once inspires and evokes further questioning. Unfortunately, the canvas of science sometimes turns out to be blemished.

I am reminded of a story that is commonly told in the southwestern part of the United States. The subject of the tale is a species of bullfrog, *Rana catesbeiana*, which is indigenous to this part of North America. As the story goes, Seth and Hannibal were two ordinary retired gentlemen of moderate intelligence who had an almost unnatural curiosity about animal behavior. Daily arguments over the determinants of various aspects of animal foraging, reproduction, aggression, and so on were common, as were attempts to resolve certain other issues. On one occasion, the topic moved to jumping behavior in *Rana catesbeiana.*

"You must understand that the bullfrog has tiny audio sensors embedded in its hind legs which pick up even the slightest noise," Seth said in a clever disclosure of the nuances of animal behavior. "When these sensors detect any sound, the frog jumps reflexively."

"The bull around here is not restricted to frogs, I see," Hannibal replied. "True to form, your latest contention is decidedly more preposterous than the one that preceded it."

"But it's true," Seth responded. "I'll prove it."

Seth collected a respectable number of bullfrogs and divided them into three groups. The first group was left untouched and, sure enough, when Seth yelled "Jump frog!" each amphibian became airborne. In the second group, the frogs' right hind legs were carefully amputated under anesthesia. When the frogs recovered, Seth again yelled "Jump frog!" Although you couldn't really label them full-scale leaps, there were some semblances of launches, or at least the frogs pushed off the ground. Finally, the frogs in the third group had both of their hind legs removed. When Seth again registered the vocal stimulus to jump, the frogs remained immobile.

"Told you so," Seth said smugly. "Cutting off the frogs' hind legs makes 'em deaf because you remove their audio sensors."

Although it may have not been apparent to Hannibal, my guess is that you will immediately detect that Seth's experiment falls somewhat short of the beauty and elegance mark, at least with respect to scientific criteria. True, the bullfrog project did rely on empirical observation, and the experimental manipulations were carried out systematically and logically. However, there are some serious questions about the interpretation of the experimental findings. The difficulty seems to rest with **confounding variables.** As we shall see in Chapter 7—Experimental Control and the Research Setting, confounding variables are uncontrolled sources of influence which affect results. Confounding variables create a transmogrification: Something that was once beautiful becomes ugly; something that was once elegant is rendered shabby.

The idea I wish to convey is that just because you meet the minimum requirements for the experimental method, you in no way ensure that anything useful will result from your investigation. You must fashion the experiment such that the outcome of the research can be interpreted within narrow limits and the causes of the results can be determined. It may not be possible in all cases, but what you should strive for is an experimental procedure that yields meaningful results, regardless of the direction or pattern of the data. When this is achieved, a genuinely beautiful experiment is conducted. The following example will give you a feel for what I mean.

**confounding variables**—uncontrolled sources of influence which can lead to misinterpretation of experimental findings

# Spotlight on Research: LAWRENCE AND DERIVERA (1954)

In the field of psychology, as in many other disciplines, it is uncommon for a given theoretical formulation to dominate a research area for several decades. It is even more unusual for opposing theories to survive and to control the thinking in a specific area for such extended time spans. However, this is very much the case in the research literature associated with discrimination training in animals.

In the 1950s, two competing accounts of discrimination learning emerged, and fundamentally these positions remain intact today (see Domjan, 1996). On one hand is the absolute model. This model assumes that performance on a task which requires the organism to discriminate between or among stimuli is determined by reinforcement history. That is, the absolute model contends that an excitatory tendency builds to a stimulus value when that value is associated with reinforcement, and an inhibitory value builds to a stimulus value when that value is associated with nonreinforcement. The total tendency to respond to a given stimulus, then, is determined by algebraically combining excitation and inhibition. Ultimately, the organism responds to the stimulus that has greater net excitation (greater reinforcement).

The other model of discrimination is the relational model. Unlike the conditioning interpretation of animal discrimination proposed by the absolute model, the relational model assumes that cognitive and mental operations determine response patterns. Specifically, this position asserts that the organism learns a relationship exists for the stimuli being compared, and it responds based on the acquired relationship. For example, in a size discrimination task, an animal may learn that "the larger stimulus is correct." In a novel test situation, this decision rule should translate as responding to the "larger" stimulus, independent of the reinforcement history of that particular stimulus event.

In 1954, Lawrence and DeRivera provided a formal test of the predictions the absolute and relational models made. Rats were trained on a modified Lashley Jumping Stand to respond to cards that differed in color (brightness actually—rats have no color vision). Where a numerical value of 1 corresponded to white, and 7 corresponded to black, several different cards of varying numerical values were presented to the rats during discrimination training. In all cases the bottom half of the card was a 4 (a neutral gray). On some of the cards the top half was darker (7/4, 6/4, 5/4), and on some of the cards the top half was lighter (3/4, 2/4, 1/4). When a 7/4, 6/4, or 5/4 stimulus was presented, the rat was required to "jump right" and through a hinged gate. When a 3/4, 2/4, or 1/4 stimulus was presented, the animal was required to "jump left."

All of the rats learned the discrimination easily. The real test came when Lawrence and DeRivera began presenting test stimuli after the original discrimination training was completed. Specific test stimuli which would lead to diametrically opposite predictions by the absolute model and the relational model were selected.

For instance, a stimulus card of 3/1 was used as one of the test stimuli (recall that the numbers refer to "whiteness" rather than numerical values). Because both 3 and 1 had been reinforced when a left jump was executed, an absolute account of discrimination training would predict that the animal would jump left. Conversely, the relational model would predict that the animal would jump right because the rule "darker than on top" still applies and 3 is darker than 1. In the latter case, reinforcement history is incidental to abstracting a decision rule and responding based on an acquired relationship. The results: On twelve test stimuli where opposite predictions would be made, the rats responded relationally 65% of the time.

Clearly, the authors of this classic study in animal discrimination designed an experiment that was likely to produce positive results. Regardless of the results, they would favor one theoretical orientation over the other. In such circumstances, the investigators can be confident that they will have something meaningful to say at the end of the project, and they know this before the experiment is ever conducted. ∎

In the Lawrence and DeRivera illustration, we see the beauty of experimentation. The form of the research idea, the manner in which the investigation was carried out, and the indisputable outcome contribute to a product that is as polished and complete as any Rodin sculpture. As with any great work, however, such achievements in science are not accomplished without considerable deliberation, planning, and insight. Take the time to design your experiment carefully and avoid an ill-fated ending.

## Adventure, Expedition, and Conquest

If we return to Dethier's quote which opened this chapter, we see that an experiment is characterized as ". . . an adventure, an expedition, a conquest." Ironically, one of the most important dimensions of experimental research addresses an issue where I can be of no instructive force. I speak of the sheer excitement that comes from "finding out." There are many parallels between the attitude of the research scientist and the attitude of a child. For both, there is the relentless process of manipulation, examination, and discovery. The child who turns over a rock just to see what is beneath it is on a common plane with the scientist who introduces an experimental variable to see what effect it may have on the outcome of a study. The fascination that goes with either enterprise cannot be taught. It is either there, or it is not.

When childlike curiosity prevails, experimentation truly does become an adventure. There is always the element of the unknown, of not being sure what will happen. In addition, there is the feeling that you are searching for something hidden, that you are cutting your way through a thicket that is reluctant to give up some secret. When you finally reach a clearing, the experience can be exhilarating. Your triumph is that you have contributed to an information base. Your conquest is not measured by the external impact of your findings as much as by the internal gratification you derive from uncovering a new principle.

Perhaps the most important thing to retain concerning this part of Dethier's quote is that you should have fun conducting research. Your efforts should never be a drudge. If they seem so, perhaps it is time to move to something else.

## *An Act of Faith*

In Chapter 2, much of the discussion centered on the importance of asking the right questions. As indicated, no experiment, however elaborate and methodologically sound, will yield a positive outcome if the appropriate questions are not tested. In this regard, I am reminded of a recent comment by Peter Milner of McGill University (1991):

> During most of the first half of this century, psychologists knew what they wanted to do but had no idea how to do it, and during the second half they have, for the most part, been so preoccupied with how to do it that they have forgotten what they wanted to do. (p.1)

Milner suggests that you can become so enamored of the instrumentation and precision of the laboratory that you lose sight of why you are conducting the study in the first place. We must always maintain the perspective that "the idea" is the most sacred component of any experimental project. Sophisticated procedures for dealing with the idea are simply convenient vehicles for getting to the issues and coming up with believable solutions.

Speaking of beliefs, Dethier's remark that an experiment is ". . . an act of faith, faith that the world is real . . ." underscores the importance of asking the right kind of questions. Clearly, there must be some basis for your suspicions or you wouldn't be conducting the research. There is more to it than this, however. You must believe in what you are doing. In many instances this means you must operate from a position of faith. Around the turn of the century, when Edward Thorndike began his now classic experiments on instrumental conditioning, he built his program of research mostly on an abiding commitment that behavior is orderly, reliable, and predictable (cf. Thorndike, 1898). At the time there was no empirical support for the position. In such cases, the researcher finds herself in *terra incognita,* in an unexplored field of knowledge. It is easy to be dissuaded by setbacks and unforeseen events which cast obstacles to successfully completing the experiment, but persistence ultimately pays, as Thorndike, having run numerous experiments with different species before finally devising the famous "cat in the puzzle box" preparations, shows us. If you have a good idea, and you believe in what you are doing, stay with it until you get it right. In the final analysis, your conviction that "the world is real" will be confirmed, and your questions will be suitably answered.

## *Effects Have Causes*

Again returning to Dethier's quote, we see further that an essential aspect of experimentation is a cause-effect relation. **Causation** is defined in Webster's Dictionary as "the act or agency by which an effect is produced." Implicit in this definition is the notion that one event is responsible for another. That is, had the initial event never occurred, the second event would not have happened.

The logical position that A causes B requires the specification of **antecedent conditions.** Antecedent conditions are the events, circumstances, and points of influence which precede some consequence or behavior. Examples of antecedent conditions are dialing a telephone number before speaking, placing coins in a vending machine prior to selecting a soft drink, picking up a book before reading, clouds building prior to a rain storm, or tasting wine to render a judgment on its bouquet. In all cases, one event precedes the other.

Although causal relations require that certain antecedents be present, it is not true that all antecedent events are causative. Some antecedent conditions reliably precede other events that are in no way tied to the antecedents. The sun's coming up and your rolling out of bed is one example. Arguing that the rising sun causes you to get out of bed and go to work or to school is not likely to be convincing in the face of evidence which points to other controlling circumstances. However, you may predictably and reliably get up each morning as the sun rises. Similarly, it would be difficult to make anyone believe that moving your elbow makes your mouth fly open. It happens and it is invariant—just watch someone at the dinner table. Surely something other than your bending elbow causes your mouth to open. In these situations, antecedent conditions do occur before other events, but they do not cause the events.

**The Nature of Causation.** Long before issues of causation were discussed in psychological quarters, matters relating to cause-effect concepts were debated in the realm of philosophy. Classical and medieval philosophers placed "cause" and "effect" events in distinctive, nonoverlapping categories. According to them, there were simply things in the world that caused other things to happen, and the consequences and the triggering events defined separate categories (Deese, 1972). By the 18th century, David Hume began to question the reality of cause-effect phenomena. Do such operations actually exist, or do they exist only in the mind of the observer? Hume argued that cause and effect were merely the result of **temporal covariation**—when two or more events occur together, one thing *seems* to cause another. From this perspective, there is really

**causation**—when one event is responsible for the occurrence of another event

**antecedent conditions**—the events, circumstances, and points of influence preceding some consequence

**temporal covariation**—when two or more events occur together in time and space

**logical positivism**—a philosophy of science which focuses on objectively determinable events

**necessary condition**—the minimum circumstances necessary for an effect to occur

**sufficient condition**—a condition that always produces an effect

no such thing as causality. Rather, the perception of a causal relation in the human experience defines causation in nature. The venerated German philosopher Immanuel Kant stated the position even more forcefully. He said that the human mind imposes a cause-and-effect relation on the world, and the illusion of causality is an artifact of the peculiar properties of an observing, thinking being.

Of course, the philosophical stance Hume and Kant take is at odds with modern psychological theory. More recent philosophical orientations, most conspicuously **logical positivism,** offer precise descriptions of cause-and-effect relations based on sophisticated analyses of the physical universe. Logical positivism is a view of science that is largely associated with philosophers in Vienna around the time of World War I (cf. Benjamin, 1988; Hanfling, 1981). As positivists, these philosophers emphasized objectivity and empirical observation. Their position was that theoretical developments should be grounded to observables instead of to assumptions based on reason. For psychology, reliance on objectively determinable events was a persuasive argument, and it shifted the focus of the field from arts and religion to science.

> Science has proven to be humankind's most powerful means of understanding reality, of producing knowledge, so that the task of epistemology should be to explicate and formalize the scientific method, making it available to new disciplines and improving its practice among working scientists. Thus the logical positivists purported to provide a formal recipe for doing science, offering exactly what psychologists thought they needed. (Leahey, 1987, p. 312)

So, while logical positivism was originally presented as an account of physical concepts such as time, space, motion, and so on, it had a profound impact on the discipline of psychology. Arguments rooted in insight and rational thought were replaced by arguments predicated on empirical demonstrations. Formulations such as William James's "stream of consciousness" gave way to John Watson's "behaviorism." For James, psychology was philosophy. For Watson, psychology was science.

One precept of logical positivism is that evidence favoring the objective existence of cause and effect can be provided. That is, it can be scientifically determined that Event A causes Event B. This process of determination requires that certain criteria be met. Included prominently on the list is the notion that the cause must be necessary and sufficient to the effect.

**Necessary and Sufficient Conditions.** It makes sense that before a cause-and-effect relation can be identified, it must be demonstrated that one event must be present for the other to occur. This is what is referred to in the philosophy of science as a **necessary condition.** Necessary conditions define the minimum circumstances under which an effect is observed. An example of a necessary condition is hitting a home run in the Little League World Series championship game played annually in Williamsport, Pennsylvania. For this to happen, your team must first win the appropriate number of preliminary games to make you eligible to play in the championship game. This qualifies as a necessary condition because you cannot hit a home run in a game in which you never participate. There is also another requirement. For the home run to occur, you must strike the ball with sufficient force to drive it out of the ballpark. Because this event may or may not occur, it is labeled a **sufficient condition.**

A sufficient condition is one in which one event always occurs when another event happens. You hit the ball hard enough and it will leave the ballpark. Still, sufficient conditions require that the necessary conditions are in place. You may hit a home run (sufficient condition), but if it is not in the championship game of the Little League World Series (necessary condition), the desired effect will not be observed. Figure 3–1 graphically depicts the relation between necessary and sufficient conditions.

Regarding the concept of causality, a reasonable position philosophers of science take is that both the necessary and sufficient conditions must be satisfied before we can say that Event A causes Event B. That is, in the absence of A, B never happens, but B occurs every time A is present. This renders the issue of causality cumbersome for empirical investigators. The problem, duly shouted from the halls of academe, is that it is unlikely to identify all the necessary and

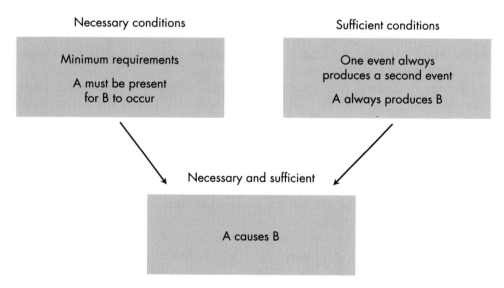

FIGURE 3–1 Necessary and sufficient conditions must combine before causality can be assumed.

sufficient conditions that would produce a given psychological effect. The analysis of behavior and mental processes is immensely complex, and in all probability you will never see a result that cannot be interpreted in more than one way. As Popper (1968) noted, all causal assertions based on empirical observation are just ". . . waiting to be disconfirmed."

Consider a line of research where it has been demonstrated reliably that acceptance and agreement make people feel better about themselves. Study after study, experiments unfold in a uniform pattern which shows that approval from others causes a person to feel greater self-esteem and enhanced perceptions of self-worth. Indeed, a thousand experiments document this apparent cause-and-effect relation. Finally, a conscientious observer runs across actor-comedian Woody Allen. Allen makes it clear that, "When more than half the public likes something I have done, I know I have made a mistake and it is time for wholesale change." Now we have an exception to our pattern. With this one observation, we have invalidated the view that acceptance and agreement cause people to feel better about themselves.

The point here is that regardless of how much evidence you marshal in support of defining the complete list of necessary and sufficient conditions, you can never be sure that one additional, undefined condition is not out there. In Popper's terms, the disconfirmation process is still underway and can never end.

Because psychologists accept that the necessary and sufficient conditions can never be exclusively determined, psychological investigators are inclined to accept a less rigorous definition of causality. In other words, when two events occur together reliably, a cause-and-effect relation is often assumed. This takes us back to Hume's principle of temporal covariation—we say that events seem to be causally related because when one occurs, the other also occurs. Implicit in this definition of causality is the idea that over a number of replications, the reinstatement of Event A brings forth Event B. Although it is true that we are defining only an approximation to a cause-and-effect arrangement, we are on relatively safe ground when we argue that the essential character of causality is evident when two events occur repeatedly.

**Antecedents as Treatments.** For the bulk of psychological experiments, if not all, it is not only impossible to specify *all* the necessary and sufficient conditions, it is also hazardous to attempt to identify *a single* necessary and sufficient condition. Because psychological phenomena are multiply determined for the most part, a behavioral or mental event is rarely considered to be caused by a single antecedent. Nonetheless, it is possible to focus on a cluster of antecedents that appears to be causally linked to a specific outcome. When several antecedent conditions are manipulated at once in an effort to establish the cause of a particular event, the set of conditions is called a **treatment.** A treatment condition is the array of events the scientific investigator introduces into the experimental setting.

An example of a treatment condition is available from a study conducted by Stanford psychologist Albert Bandura. Bandura was interested in the role naturally occurring opiate-like chemicals in the body had in determining the effectiveness of a technique designed to mentally alleviate pain (Bandura, O'Leary, Taylor, Gauthier, & Gossard, 1987). In one treatment condition, people suffering from an earache were told to concentrate and tell themselves things such as, "The pain is going away. My ear is no longer hurting." Under these conditions, the amount of pain reported was actually reduced. However, in a second treatment condition, where earache sufferers were instructed to make the same self-statements but were also administered a drug called naloxone which blocks the naturally occurring opiates in the body (such as the beta-endorphins), the self-statements were less effective. This tells us this particular mental technique is in some way mediated by endogenous (naturally occurring) opiates in the body. More important to the present discussion, it illustrates two different treatment manipulations. One treatment was restricted to the various mental manipulations necessary to produce benefits with respect to pain control. A second treatment contained all of the elements of the first, plus an added feature—the presence of naloxone. By systematically changing the treatments (the antecedents), we are in a better position to assess the causal connection between mental operations and the control of pain.

As a result, we see that issues relating to cause-and-effect determination are difficult to grapple with, and yet they are exceedingly important to psychological research. Ultimately, good decisions about the experimental process will permit us to make sense of a world that might otherwise appear to be nonsensical.

## We Can Discover Meaning by Reason

The final part of Dethier's quote says that the experiment permits us to ". . . discover meaning by reason." As noted in Chapter 1, empiricism and careful observation are insufficient approaches to understanding the relation between and among events in the world. Although empirical observation is essential to scientific research, it is only part of the story. To gain real meaning from our empirical recordings, we must formulate a rationale based on reasonable interpretation of the results.

**treatment**—all of the antecedent conditions that are manipulated or otherwise introduced by an experimenter into the experimental situation

In this instance, "reasonable interpretation" does not mean interpretation that falls within a range of respectability or justifiable belief. Rather, it is interpretation based on reason: reason grounded on logic, reason evolving from intelligent deliberation, reason stemming from persuasive and orderly inference. The thrust of Dethier's statement is that after all is complete, after the experiment is conducted and the findings are analyzed, there remains the pressing question, "What does this really mean?"

Deciphering experimental findings is facilitated by converging patterns which point to a narrow interpretation of the results. In some cases alternative interpretations can be dismissed logically, but in others additional experimentation is required. In the next section, I chronicle a personal scientific tale in which my colleagues and I were able to reach a conclusion through reason and further experimental investigation.

## WITHIN CHAPTER REVIEW AND STUDY QUESTIONS

### WHAT IS AN EXPERIMENT?

1. Why would a scientific investigator interpret a well-designed and properly executed study as "elegant?" Does such a description fit with a conception of science as a realm apart from art? Why or why not?
2. The concept of causation was discussed, and it was noted that in a rigorous sense, psychological studies are not likely to ever establish cause-and-effect relations. Why not? Does a less rigorous definition of causation have a place in psychology? Why or why not?
3. When two or more events appear to be causally related simply because they occur together, we invoke Hume's concept of:
   a. contiguity
   b. temporal covariation
4. The philosophical position that interpretive comments should be based on observables and objectively determinable events is known as:
   a. logical positivism
   b. determinism
5. What is a necessary condition? What is a sufficient condition? Why must both the necessary and sufficient conditions of a relation be specified before cause and effect can be determined?

# SHIFTING INTERPRETATIONS: A PERSONAL STORY

During the mid-1980s, I was pursuing a research agenda that concentrated on the effects of environmental pollutants on aversively motivated behavior. Using laboratory rats as subjects, I observed, as did others in Germany and elsewhere, that chronic low-level exposure to inorganic lead heightened a rat's sensitivity to mild electric footshock. I began to consider the possibility that other response systems that are influenced by elevated stress reactivity might be similarly affected. In this regard, I entertained the notion that this metallic pollutant might alter patterns of alcohol ingestion.

My hypothesis about lead/alcohol interactions was grounded to the syllogism, "Lead toxicity increases anxiety and anxiety increases alcohol consumption. Therefore, lead toxicity should increase alcohol consumption." With the assistance of several graduate and undergraduate students, I proceeded to explore this possibility.

## *Now I've Got It*

The seminal experiment involved two groups of rats. One group (Group Lead) was exposed to an adulterated food supply which contained lead. A control group was given ordinary rat chow with no lead. After a lengthy period of exposure to their respective feeding regimens, all rats were presented with the option of drinking tap water or a 10% alcohol solution. Because the rats had been housed in isolation, which is moderately stressful for them, I knew they would consume alcohol. The question was how much.

Over a 10-day test period, we observed that the lead-treated rats ingested significantly greater amounts of alcohol than did the controls. In 1986, our laboratory published the first study demonstrating a behavioral link between the Number 1 pollution problem in the United States (lead contamination) and the nation's Number 1 drug problem (excessive alcohol consumption) (Nation, Baker, Taylor, & Clark, 1986).

## *No, I Don't*

It seemed my suspicions about lead/alcohol interactions had merit. With financial support from the NIAAA, I explored the issue in greater detail. To the extent that alcohol did possess greater anxiety-alleviating properties in lead-exposed animals, it followed logically that alcohol would have greater rewarding effects in an operant context. Consequently, we trained lead-exposed and control rats to press a lever to receive an alcohol reinforcer.

To my surprise, the lead-exposed rats responded for the alcohol reward at significantly lower rates than did the controls (Nation, Dugger, Dwyer, Bratton, & Grover, 1991). Now I was really confused. How could this be? If lead exposure increases the desire for alcohol because higher anxiety levels in exposed rats make the drug more attractive, then why isn't alcohol a more effective reinforcer for these rats?

Then came my epiphany—perhaps my reasoning was upside down. If the lead-exposed rats were not more sensitive to alcohol, perhaps they were less sensitive. That is, decreased responsiveness to the drug would render the drug less reinforcing in an operant setting (Nation et al., 1991). In a free-access situation such as we had in 1986, animals would consume more of the drug to compensate for its reduced impact. Simply stated, lead-exposed animals may drink more alcohol to realize the same subjective effect as their control counterparts.

### Yes, I Do

The NIAAA was as interested in the interpretive issues as we were, so support for the lead/alcohol research was continued. Over a period of several years, our laboratory established that chronic dietary exposure to inorganic forms of lead results in diminished responsiveness to alcohol (Burkey, Nation, & Bratton, 1994; Davis, Nation, & Mayleben, 1993; Grover, Nation, Burkey, McClure, & Bratton, 1993; Nation, Burkey, & Grover, 1993). The implications remained—lead may augment alcohol consumption by inducing compensatory drinking—but our interpretation had shifted markedly from our original position. Logic, an orderly examination of the possibilities, and persistence were the keys to increasing our understanding of an interesting environmental issue.

## WITHIN CHAPTER REVIEW AND STUDY QUESTION

### SHIFTING INTERPRETATIONS: A PERSONAL STORY

1. What advantage is there to conducting additional investigations into the cause of an earlier finding? Does decreasing the range of alternative explanations of the findings through further exploration ensure that you have identified the real cause of the results?

# THE STRUCTURE OF THE EXPERIMENT

In this chapter, several of the characteristics of scientific experimentation are discussed. An appreciation of experimental operations is essential for the beginning student, as it is for the veteran investigator, but it is equally important to understand the structure of the experiment. "Structure" means the basic components that define the overall composition of the experiment.

Central to any scientific research project is the question of what is to be changed or manipulated and what is to be recorded. In research methodology terminology, we are talking about independent and dependent variables.

## *Independent Variables*

A common dictionary definition of **variable** is "a quantity that may assume any one of a set of values." In psychological research, this mathematical description of *variable* is amended only slightly to include events, features, or phenomena that may take on different values or occupy points along some psychological continuum.

In a psychological experiment, investigators make deliberate decisions about which variables they would like to manipulate. Such variables are called **independent variables** and are defined as "those events that the experimenter changes or calls into question." The term *independent variable* tells you something about the nature of the concept, for each factor that is manipulated is indeed independent of any other factor in the experiment. To the extent that the rule of independence is violated, interpretation of the results is compromised. Simply stated, when two or more events are introduced simultaneously as a compound, and some consequence is noted, it is impossible to ferret out how much of the effect is produced by each element of the compound. In order to distinguish the precise nature of a relation between any two variables, the effects of one variable must be examined independent of the influences of other variables.

The position adopted in experimental research where only one event can be changed is often referred to as **the single variable rule.** The single variable rule does not prevent the investigator from simultaneously examining the influence of two variables that are wholly independent of each other, however (I discuss this situation in greater detail in the chapters dealing with design considerations, Chapters 8 and 9).

**variable**—an event, feature, or phenomenon that may take on one of several values

**independent variables**—the variables the experimenter manipulates or changes

**the single variable rule**—the position that only one factor can be manipulated at one time

**presence/absence technique—** when an independent variable is manipulated such that it is present in one condition and not present in a second

What is restricted is the manner in which a given independent variable can be introduced into the experiment. All potential sources of influence, other than the one that is being changed or manipulated must be held constant.

To illustrate, assume we are interested in the effects IQ has on learning to speak a foreign language. Do people with higher IQs acquire a second language faster than people with lower IQs? A great number of things could affect the rate at which a person learns a new language. Age, native language, number of other languages spoken, number of years in a formal educational setting, and a host of other factors may determine how quickly a person picks up a second language, but we are interested in none of these. We are interested only in the effect of a single variable, IQ. Accordingly, we must create conditions that vary in terms of IQ, but are of the same age, native language, and so on. Everything, other than the one variable of interest, must be constant across conditions.

It goes without saying that the minimum requirement for an independent variable is that the variable exists in at least two forms or takes on at least two values. If you have only one of something, you obviously cannot manipulate that something because it is by definition a constant. When varying the independent variable is possible, it commonly is accomplished in one of three ways: presence/absence, quantity, and quality (see Figure 3–2).

**Presence or Absence of the Independent Variable.** One of the most common methods of introducing an independent variable into an experimental setting is to include it as a treatment effect in one condition (refer to previous discussion in this chapter) and exclude it in the other. This comparatively simple approach, which is often referred to as the **presence/absence technique,** defines an economical model that is especially useful for preliminary investiga-

1. PRESENCE/ABSENCE
   A given value of the independent variable is present in one condition, and it is not included in a second condition that is neutral, or has a zero value of the independent variable.
2. QUANTITATIVE INDEPENDENT VARIABLE
   The amount of a variable is manipulated. Typically, this involves three or more conditions where two of the conditions have nonzero values that are distinctively different.
3. QUALITATIVE INDEPENDENT VARIABLE
   The type or kind of variable is varied across conditions. There is no attempt to specify how much the variables differ.

FIGURE 3–2 Three different ways an independent variable may be manipulated or changed in an experiment

tions in a subject area. In the initial phases of a research project, it is sometimes necessary to determine whether or not an independent variable even has an effect on psychological events before you start considering something more sophisticated or in depth.

An example of the presence/absence technique in psychological research is a study where an investigator is interested in the effects of a noisy distracting stimulus on some measure of cognitive processing. It is reasonable to expect that a loud beeping sound may negatively affect a memory-based event such as digit span (digit span is tested by presenting a series of numbers, such as 3-7-4-8-1, to a subject and asking the subject to recite the numbers). Figure 3–3 is a graphic profile of a hypothetical experiment comparing "noise" and "no noise" conditions on a digit-span task. Notice that in one condition the value of the independent variable is present (the beeping sound is present with the series of numbers), while in the other the value of the independent variable is absent (only the series of numbers is present).

As mentioned earlier, procedures that employ the presence/absence technique are simple demonstrations of whether or not the independent variable is of concern or impacts the behavior under investigation. In our "noisy distractor" illustration, for example, we are not concerned with issues such as the effects different noise intensities have on digit-span performance. Rather, our preliminary question is, "Does noise, when present, affect cognitive functioning?" When

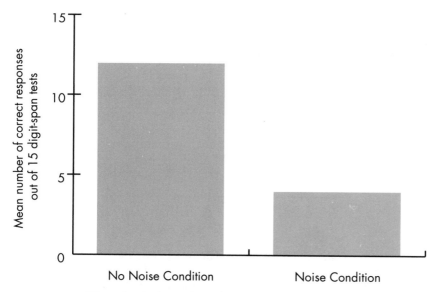

FIGURE 3–3 Hypothetical results of a study on the effects of noise on short-term memory (digit span)

such straightforward questions form the rationale for conducting a study, presence/absence techniques are appropriate. Other techniques for manipulating the independent variable are available when more extensive information is needed.

**Quantitative Independent Variables.** Had we been interested in the relation between the level of noise and cognitive functioning in the hypothetical experiment depicted in Figure 3-3, it would have been possible to systematically manipulate the volume of the beeping. Employing a device to measure decibel readings, we could have increased or decreased the noise stimulus. For instance, we might want to present beeping sounds of 30, 60, and 90 decibels to three different groups of subjects. Each of these conditions could then be compared on the digit-span task. This type of experimental paradigm, in which the amount of the independent variable is varied, is known as **quantitative variation.**

Another example of quantitative variation is shown in Figure 3–4. In this study by McNamara, Davidson, and Schenk (1993), adult male rats that had been exposed to amphetamine (a psychoactive drug) were placed in activity chambers and their overall levels of activity were recorded. As Figure 3–4 shows, approximately 1,000 activity counts were recorded when the rats received intraperitoneal (ip) injections of physiological saline (a drug dose of 0). This figure was almost doubled by ip injections of 1 milligram (mg) of ampheta-

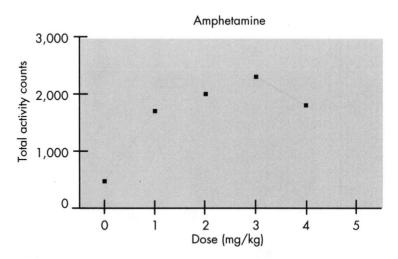

**FIGURE 3–4 Activity for adult male rats following different doses of amphetamine (Point 0 is a control condition where no drug was given). (Adapted from McNamara, Davidson, & Schenk, 1993). Copyright © 1993 by Elsevier Science Inc. Reprinted with permission.**

mine/kilogram (kg) of body weight. Higher drug doses resulted in even greater increases in behavioral activation.

The study by McNamara, Davidson, and Schenk manipulates an independent variable quantitatively by changing the amount or quantity of the drug (amphetamine) across different conditions. Notice that if only Group 0 (no drug) and Group 1 (1 mg/kg drug) had been in the study, the experiment would qualify as a "presence/absence" study. With more values of the independent variable included, however, the character of the experiment changes.

**Qualitative Independent Variables.** When an independent variable is manipulated qualitatively, changes in kind or type are introduced. Once again, when there are only two values, the experiment takes on many of the same features as the presence/absence technique. As is often the case, however, several qualitative variables may be presented in a single experiment. Consider a human study on the effects stress has on aggression, where physical stress (strenuous exercise), emotional stress (watching a disturbing film clip), and cognitive stress (working unsolvable problems) are compared. Here, our questions concern differences in kind rather than amount.

We have several choices regarding types of independent variables. In addition to deciding which type of variable to manipulate, we must determine how many independent variables to include in the experiment. Occasionally, this issue becomes hydra headed.

# ⚛ Thinking About Research

**H**ow many independent variables should you include in a psychological experiment? In research involving human subjects, should gender (male versus female) be a variable? In animal learning studies, how important are developmental parameters such as age, and should different strains of animals be used to test for genetic variation? Should the experiment involve a single test trial, or should multiple trials be included as a repeated factor?

I could keep going with this topic, but there is no need. It should be apparent that the number of possibilities for complicating an experimental design is enormous. There are so many different things that *might* make a difference, one may be left in a quandary. What goes, and what stays? Is there some sort of rule that can be invoked to get out of this predicament? Unfortunately, no rule is available.

Given that there are no explicit guidelines about how many independent variables should be included in a psychological experiment, investigators are left to their own devices. In addition, investigators must ask certain questions. Place yourself in the situation of deciding on the number of variables that should be incorporated into the design of the model experiment we are constructing in this book. We have decided to test chronically ill children, so do we need to think about subject availability? Geographically, how many settings can we realistically expect to get to if the hospitals, parents, and medical professionals cooperate? Based on these and other considerations, perhaps we should keep our number of variables down, to just a couple. We could look at therapeutic effectiveness across different illnesses, of course. Perhaps the pattern of pediatric oncology patients differs from that of children suffering from juvenile diabetes? It is an interesting possibility, but not one we can afford in terms of time and resources.

Although no rule exists for determining the number of independent variables, one recommendation can be made from this sort of deliberation: Always follow the principle of **parsimony.** Parsimony means being frugal, stingy, and employing "economy in the use of a means to an end." Use the minimum number of variables to examine the relations of interest. Include what you absolutely must and nothing more. Careful planning and reflection pay off in time and money. Before turning to the next section, take a while to think about what you would include as independent variables in our model experiment. Let's see how closely we match up.    ■

Now we can return to the experiment that we aim to build over the course of this book. Recall that the topic area selected for investigation deals with the effectiveness of cognitively based intervention strategies employed in the treatment of chronically ill children.

Based on the literature search we conducted, we have been able to establish that the degree of cognitive functioning evident in younger children is appreciably less than that observed in older children. It is reasonable, then, to assume that the relative success or impact of a cognitively oriented treatment rationale may be diminished for younger children.

Given the apparent importance of age differences as determinants of cognitive processing, it follows that age should be incorporated into the design of the experiment as one independent variable. A critical next step is specifying values of this particular independent variable. How many age ranges do we include? Which ages are most likely to yield a fair test of the hypothesis under consideration?

To answer the first question, we must include at least two age ranges (i.e., a younger condition and an older condition). Because the type of research we are about to undertake is constrained by subject availability (obtaining permission to conduct research on a chronically ill population may prove difficult) and financial concerns (we will have to travel to a hospital setting, pay research assistants, and so on), we must be content with just two age ranges.

The literature helps us regarding the issue of selecting the age ranges. Several reports (Brown, O'Keeffe, Sanders, & Baker, 1986; Curry & Russ, 1985; Worchel, Copeland, & Barker, 1987) have shown that children in the age range 4–6 make fewer spontaneous cognitions about how to control stressful situations than children in the age range 10–12. Although these findings do not address directly the effectiveness of treatment outcomes in the different age groups, they do provide clues about suitable age conditions. Accordingly, within the independent variable "age," values of 4–6 and 10–12 years of age will be employed.

In addition to the issue of the effect of age on cognitively oriented treatment strategies, there is the broader issue of the importance of developmental parameters to other forms of therapy. That is, because age variables could affect the efficacy of several different styles of treatment, it would be appropriate to qualitatively vary "type of treatment" as an independent variable. Along these lines, it is noted that simply providing information about the nature of stressful medical treatments helps people cope with situational anxiety (Miller, Sherman, Combs, & Kruus, 1992). Moreover, there is some indication that these benefits may be different for older children than for younger children. Consequently, it is appropriate to include an "information" condition with a cognitively oriented condition in our study. To complete the "type of treatment" manipulation, we would need to include a control condition that receives no formal therapeutic treatment. (Note: There are some ethical issues associated with this sort of control procedure. I have more to say about this in Chapter 4.)

In summary, two independent variables have been identified: (1) age, with two levels (4–6 years and 10–12 years), and (2) type of treatment, with three levels (cognitive therapy, information only condition, and control). Because of the number of variables we have chosen to manipulate, this experiment is called a two-way design.

To use terms mentioned in the earlier discussion, the independent variables to be used in the model experiment represent examples of *quantitative* and *qualitative variation*. The age variable is quantitative in that two nonzero levels of the dimension "number of years old" were chosen. In comparison, the decision to use different treatment styles is a variation in kind, not amount. It is not uncommon in psychological research to see quantitative and qualitative variables manipulated in a single experiment. In our discussion of design features in Chapter 8 (Between-Subjects Designs) and Chapter 9 (Within-Subjects, Mixed, and Single-Subject Designs), we explore some of the advantages of a rationale of incorporating multiple independent variables into the design of an experiment.

## *Dependent Variables*

Along with selecting the appropriate independent variable or variables, the investigator must choose a **dependent variable.** A dependent variable is defined here as what the experimenter actually measures. It is so named because its value depends on some value of the independent variable. That is, when researchers manipulate X, they must carefully monitor Y in order to assess the possible relation between the two variables. If Y changes as the investigators systematically change the value of X, then they can infer a causal relation.

**parsimony**—the act of taking the simplest approach to arrive at a goal

**dependent variable**—the variable the experimenter measures

**Sensitivity and the Range of Dependent Variables.** It goes without saying that designating the dependent variable is a critical step in the experimental process. A reckless decision to include an inadequate dependent measure may obscure genuine effects and mislead the scientific community. In this regard, it is essential to select a measure that is sufficiently sensitive to pick up the subtle effects the independent variable produces.

For instance, a biopsychology researcher hoping to examine the effects of an experimental drug on pupil size would be ill advised to make decisions about the drug's effect merely by looking at pupillary dilation. Greater precision is needed; perhaps a sophisticated optical monitoring system which measures on a scale of nanometers could be used. Similarly, a social psychologist interested in the effects of persuasion on attitude change would be disinclined to use a measure of attitudes based on a 3-point scale where a value of *1* corresponds to "agree," *2* means "cannot say," and *3* means "disagree." There is no room on the scale to permit subjects to indicate the strength of their feelings and, because the scale arbitrarily restricts the response options, slight but reliable differences may go unwitnessed.

So, when selecting a dependent variable, make it sensitive, or at least sensitive enough to get at the issues at hand. Also make sure that the distribution of scores permitted by the dependent variable is of sufficient range to allow for differences to be observed. A well-known example of a violation of this rule is available from the literature on positive contrast effects. Positive contrast effects are said to occur when an organism that is shifted from a small magnitude reinforcer to a large magnitude reinforcer performs at a higher level than a control condition that has been maintained on the higher magnitude variable throughout training (Domjan, 1996). In effect, we are talking about an overshooting effect that is associated with reward shifts.

Years ago, in the animal learning literature, there was an enduring debate over the reliability of positive contrast effects. The typical experiment on positive contrast effects involved placing rats in a straight-alley maze and rewarding them when they ran to the goal box at the end of the maze. Positive contrast was evident when a rat ran faster when shifted from low to high reward (reinforcer) relative to the case where the high reward was given throughout training. Some investigators could usually get the positive contrast effect, but they could not get it every time. Even when the positive contrast effect was present, it was weak. Finally, it was shown that the trouble was not with the reliability of the positive contrast effect, but with the method of recording. Speed down a maze was the dependent measure, and at certain reinforcer (food) levels, it was discovered that a "ceiling effect" had been imposed. That is, the high reinforcer controls were already responding at such a high level that it was impossible for the animals shifted from low to high reward to run any faster. Accordingly, Mellgren (1972) slowed both the control and the shifted conditions by introducing a constant 20-second delay in the delivery of the reinforcement outcome (food). With the values of the dependent variable (speed) falling within a range that permitted contrast effects to be observed, the phenomenon could be reliably demonstrated.

**Types of Dependent Variables.** Along with sensitivity and range, the type of dependent variable that is to be used in the project must be considered. Although several different kinds of measures could be mentioned, I shall mention three distinctively different types of dependent variable: behavioral, cognitive, and biological.

**Behavioral Measures.** When investigators record movements or empirically observable responses the subject makes, they measure **behavioral dependent variables.** Examples include the frequency with which a pigeon pecks an illuminated disc to receive food, the magnitude of a conditioned salivation response in a dog measured in milliliters of saliva, the number of times a person lights a cigarette during a 1-hour observation session, or how often a person responds to threats with assertive reactions during a group therapy session. In all examples, the researcher measures something that is observable and indexes the strength of responding either by the frequency or the amount of the behavior.

The use of behavioral measures in psychological research has a long and distinguished history. Indeed, John Watson's 1913 manifesto *Psychology as the Behaviorist Views It* was a bold statement which argued that no other form of dependent variable is appropriate for psychological research. Watson contended that if you cannot see it, feel it, hear it, and so on, then you should not attempt to study the phenomenon within a scientific framework. Today, many psychologists claim that such a doctrinaire position is shortsighted and ignores more subtle, nonbehavioral events which are also predictable. In any event, a bias favoring behavioral measures in psychological research persists among many human and animal investigators, and this situation is not likely to change any time soon.

Although the strength and quickness (latency to respond) of the behavioral measure are commonly reported records, it should be understood that other indices of behavioral responding may be derived from these basic measures. For instance, Figure 3–5 shows conditioned eyeblink data in albino rabbits in terms of "mean percent responding" (from Canli, Detmer, & Donegan, 1992). In this case, the data show the relative number of eyeblinks (conditioned responses [CRs]) which occur to a conditioned stimulus (the CS+) that predicts the unconditioned stimulus (a mild electric shock to the orbit of the eye), and a CS− that predicts the absence of the unconditioned stimulus. In this experiment on simple discrimination, the dependent variable is

**behavioral dependent variables**—variables that are empirically observable

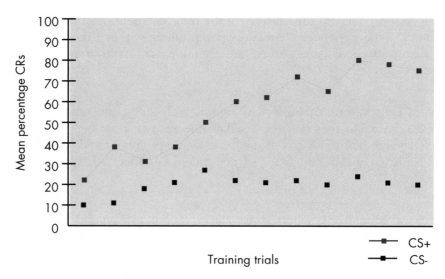

**FIGURE 3–5** Mean percentage conditioned responses (CRs) in a conditioned eyeblink study for a group of rabbits where one conditioned stimulus was paired with the unconditioned stimulus (CS+) and another conditioned stimulus was paired with the absence of the unconditioned stimulus (CS−). (Adapted from Canli, Detmer, and Donegan, 1992.) Copyright © 1992 by the American Psychological Association. Reprinted with permission.

**cognitive dependent variables**—mental or cognitive events that can be measured indirectly

based on the frequency of conditioned responses, but it is expressed according to a ratio of how many responses occurred relative to how many could have occurred (percentage).

Behavioral measures have an appeal in that the researcher is very clear about what is being recorded, and thus the reader is very clear on what was measured in the study. However, for some topics, behavioral measures are not only not possible, they are inappropriate.

**Cognitive Measures.** Cognitive psychology deals with events such as thinking, reasoning, and problem solving. Insofar as a thought is not an observable process, it follows that it would be senseless to try to measure thought directly. It is perfectly reasonable to assume, however, that cognitive events can be measured indirectly with the use of **cognitive dependent variables.** To the extent that mental or cognitive processes alter measurable responses, inferences can be drawn about the existence of underlying, unobservable determinants of behavior.

In a classic memory experiment by Endel Tulving (1962), human subjects were given a 16-item list of words to remember. A free-recall procedure was employed in the test phase of this study. In this technique, subjects are permitted to recall as many words as they can, in whatever order they can. Central to the rationale of the study is the belief that individual subjects tend to arrange the words they recall according to whether the words can be placed in a common category. For example, *sheep* and *hay* might be recalled together in a free-recall task because they are consistent with a farm scene. To the extent that subjects cluster recalled items according to overlapping characteristics, the subjects can be said to engage in the process of subjective organization. As Figure 3–6 indicates, the more people rely on subjective organization, the better their overall memory performance.

Obviously, it is not possible to measure an organizational scheme directly. That is, the cognitive patterns that are integral to arranging items by similar features do not lend themselves to scientific measurement per se. As we see with the Tulving experiment, however, we can gain some index of the degree to which such organizational operations have been carried out by looking at parallel changes in observable events. Consequently, legitimate statements can be made about the involvement of cognitive processes in the experimental setting. In many respects, cognitive dependent variables make use of behavioral

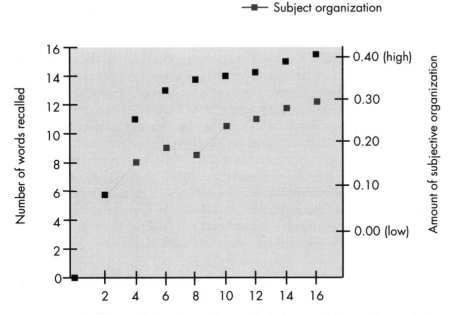

FIGURE 3–6 The number of words recalled from a 16-item list and the amount of subjective organization over trials in a free-recall task. (Adapted from Tulving, 1962.)

**biological dependent variables—measures of body function or morphology**

dependent variables and then go a step further with respect to gaining insight into the controlling forces of psychological phenomena.

**Biological Measures. Biological dependent variables** refer to measures that are obtained from physiological recordings or from changes in body function or morphology. Sophisticated monitoring instruments may record such things as shifts in brain wave pattern, galvanic skin resistance, blood pressure, core body temperature, cortisol amounts released from the adrenal glands, or necrosis (cell death) in the brain stem. Regardless of the index, a general feature of biological dependent measures is that they require no assumption that there is anything psychological going on. Given this, why do psychologists select biological measures?

The answer is that while biological events may be examined apart from any psychological manipulation, unique psychological events cause biological changes. Consider the findings by Squire, Amaral, and Press (1990) regarding the size of the human brain structure called the hippocampus in controls, alcoholics (Korsakoff patients who suffer alcohol-related memory loss), and psychogenic amnesiacs (see Figure 3–7). Psychogenic amnesia, unlike organic dysfunctional syndromes such as Korsakoff's, is a form of forgetting where memory loss is purely psychological. That is, there is no disturbance in the genetic compliment, no tissue deterioration due to disease or physical insult, and no evidence of congenital or developmental retardation. However, it is clear that psychogenic amnesia but not Korsakoff's is associated with a decrease in the size of the hippocampus. Here is an instance where biological markers reveal some very important information about the broader consequences of a psychological disorder.

As with statements about other dependent variables, statements about the effects of psychological events on observable biological changes must be made with some degree of caution, because inferences must be drawn. This means that some other factor may be responsible for the observed change. Still, the topic of interest often dictates the selection of variables, and so the list of possible dependent variables must include these types of measurements.

Keeping the issues discussed here in mind, it is appropriate at this point to specify the dependent variables we intend to include in the experiment we are building. The variables selected for our study are as follows:

As indicated, two different age groups of chronically ill children will receive one of three psychotherapeutic interventions for dealing with the stress associated with medical treatments. In order to gauge the effectiveness of the different intervention strategies, it is desirable to have some overt indicators of stress reactivity. This means that a behavioral dependent variable is needed for this study.

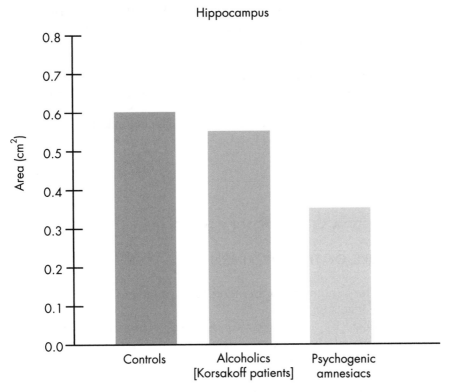

**FIGURE 3–7** The size of the hippocampus for controls, alcoholics (Korsakoff patients), and psychogenic amnesiacs. (Adapted from Squire, Amaral, and Press, 1990.) Copyright © 1990 by Elsevier Science Inc. Reprinted with permission.

One such measure is the Observational Scale of Behavioral Distress (OSBD). This scale (refer to Smith, Ackerson, & Blotcky, 1989) requires that trained observers record behaviors in 11 categories (e.g., crying, nervous behavior, verbal resistance) in 15-second intervals for 2 minutes to obtain a total distress score. The scale has good reliability and validity and has been described in detail (Jay, Elliott, Ozolins, Olson, & Pruitt, 1985). For our experiment, the overt behaviors that are obtained from the scale should permit us to determine the relative effectiveness of the different interventions at each age range.

Another dependent measure that we can include is the Self-Report Measure of Fear and Pain developed by Katz, Kellerman, & Siegel, 1982 (refer to Chapter 5 for a discussion of self-report measures). In this procedure three visual analog thermometers are used to assess the child's perception of fear and expectancy of pain. The child simply points to a location on the thermometers that best describes how he or she feels (*0* = no fear; *100* = maximum fear). This self-report measure has also been shown to be reliable in experiments similar to the one that we are building (Katz, Kellerman, & Siegel, 1982).

Along with these measures, a biological marker of stress and anxiety is needed. Accordingly, heart rate (HR) will be measured. Heart rate can be monitored using an electrocardiograph (EKG), which is a device that attaches chest electrodes to the participants.

So, for our experiment, we have settled on three dependent measures: the OSBD, a self-report of pain, and the physiological measure HR.

## WITHIN CHAPTER REVIEW AND STUDY QUESTIONS

### THE STRUCTURE OF THE EXPERIMENT

1. What are the minimum requirements for a variable? List five variables, each with three levels or values.
2. What is meant by "the single variable rule"? Why is this rule important in an experimental investigation?
3. Two conditions are compared. One condition receives Drug A, another condition receives a placebo. This describes the:
   a. presence/absence technique
   b. qualitative independent variable approach
   c. quantitative independent variable approach
4. When one condition receives 30 training trials, another receives 60 training trials, and still another receives 90 training trials, the manipulation of the independent variable is:
   a. quantitative
   b. qualitative
5. How does the principle of parsimony relate to selecting the number of independent variables? Is there a guideline for selecting how many variables should be included in an experiment?
6. Give three examples of dependent variables. For each example create two or more values of an appropriate independent variable that might be expected to affect the dependent variable(s).
7. Define each of the following terms:
   a. behavioral dependent variable
   b. cognitive dependent variable
   c. biological dependent variable

# The Model Experiment

In this chapter, we discussed the importance of selecting the appropriate independent and dependent variables for an experiment. The number, type, and arrangement of variables impacts directly on the likelihood of completing a successful study. If solid decisions on these issues are not made, some findings may be uninterpretable, and important relations may be obscured.

Two independent variables were selected for the experiment we are developing. One factor is age, which has two levels (4–6 years and 10–12 years). The second factor is the type of intervention. This will consist of three levels (cognitive therapy, information only condition, and control). In addition, three dependent variables were selected: scores from the OSBD, scores from the Self-Report Measure of Fear and Pain, and HR. Having identified what we want to change (the independent variables) and what we want to record (the dependent variables), we are now in a position to move to other important issues in psychological research. The next chapter is on ethics.

# Ethics

**ethics—a moral framework that determines what is right and wrong**

The very nature of psychological research raises questions about the treatment of subjects in an experimental setting. In research people are observed under a variety of conditions. Because the true nature of research often cannot be revealed to these people beforehand, they must rely on the integrity of the experimenter to protect their interests. Make no mistake about it, the experimenter will protect their interests.

In this chapter, I discuss **ethics.** Ethics is the discipline of dealing with what is right and wrong within a moral framework that is built on obligation and duty. In psychological research where humans are used as subjects, ethics is more than a perceived responsibility. It is a systematized procedure that governs the conduct of each person even remotely linked to the study. Every move, every manipulation, every facet of the experimental operation must be carried out according to a script that ensures decency, sensitivity, and openness. While we shall see there have been a few violations of the rights of individuals, on the whole psychologists work very hard to guarantee the safety and comfort of human subjects who choose to participate in their experiments. The concern over the welfare of the human subject has more recently been extended to animals. Although psychological investigators have always attempted to deal with animals humanely, it has only been in the last couple of decades that a "consciousness of animal rights" has arisen (see discussion later in this chapter in the section entitled "The Animal Rights Movement").

Before commencing our discussion of ethics in human and animal research, it is appropriate to address an issue that is corruptive in either camp—scientific fraud. For human and animal experiments alike, professional dishonesty defines an ethical violation of the highest order. True, the subjects may not be at risk in such situations, but the scientific community is. When experimental findings are misrepresented, the essence of inquiry is compromised. Why even do research? Why bother? Why cheat?

# Truth in Reporting: Scientific Fraud

In a world of fierce competition, it is not uncommon to hear about deception, subterfuge, and illicit conduct. In the 1992 Olympic games in Barcelona, the unexpected domination of women's swimming by athletes from China evoked a chorus of complaints about "doping" with steroids and other performance-enhancing drugs. In the wake of the established drug usage by the East German women in the 1988 games in Seoul, perhaps such suspicions were not really that surprising. Elsewhere, insider trade deals in the stock exchange, theft of an examination at a prominent military academy, false claims about product safety, attempts to cover up covert government operations in the Middle East, and a host of other acts of misconduct have been paraded out before us. While we see these violations as distasteful and a breach of proper behavior, they are not likely to grate on us to the point where we rise up in personal protest or question the moral fiber of contemporary society. Then why is it such an outrage when a scientist is found guilty of fraudulent reporting? Why should one profession be held to such an exacting standard when the currents of the broader social environment are so strikingly asynchronous?

Perhaps the extreme pressures on scientists to maintain accuracy and fairness in reporting their findings stems from an inherent belief in the value of a factual portrayal of the world of which we are a part. Science does not pretend to promote a spiritual covenant. What it does promise is an unbiased account of relations between and among events in our environment. Scientists know going in that they must conform to an accepted, almost sacrosanct code. When scientists take on the enterprise of research they agree that honesty is the most important rule. Thus, when fraud occurs in science, it is especially reprehensible. A scientist who strays from the truth suffers the opprobrium of society because a promise was broken—a promise to each of us to be credible.

Over the years, there have been some rather sensational cases of scientific misconduct, each with fiery debate about the degree of the ethical violation. In Chapter 1 the scandal associated with the possibility that British scientist Cyril Burt may have fabricated his data on the genetic basis for IQ was mentioned (refer to Joynson, 1990). In this instance, the inability to replicate Burt's findings over a period of years led to greater scrutiny of Burt's original findings. Although some contemporary writers have attempted to rescue Burt's reputation (e.g., Samuelson, 1992), at the time a sufficient number of discrepancies in the data were noted to cause a furor in the scientific community. The magnitude of the problem was increased by the realization that educational and vocational-training policies were installed by government agencies that had been persuaded by Burt's earlier reports. If indeed there was a lie, the lie rippled throughout the nonscientific population.

Fraud in its current form may be less conspicuous than the flagrant fabrications of which Burt has been accused. An investigator who conveniently throws out an outlier from the data set may be guilty of fraudulent activity. Similarly, reporting only those aspects of the data that are consistent with a prejudiced position can be considered a type of scientific misconduct, at least insofar as the researcher knowingly and willfully slants the report. The notion that, "If the data are inconsistent with the theory, there must be something wrong with the data," hardly characterizes a legitimate scientific doctrine. However, this is a berth occupied by some investigators who fall into the "true believer" category and assume that theoretical inconsistencies derive solely from experimental error.

Of course, very few scientists really cheat. My experience, if anything, reveals an almost opposite profile. Most of the scientific professionals I have dealt with are so careful and so vigilant to ethical issues and valid recording that they might even be accused of being excessively cautious. Still, fakers do exist, and many academics and researchers privately fear that the number of frauds in the industry is on the rise. Why? What would cause an increase of this kind?

One circumstance that may contribute to scientific misconduct is the competition for jobs (Knight, 1984). For an established investigator with a secure position, a failed experiment is a disappointment, but events may turn more favorably next time. In comparison, a failure can be devastating for an untenured assistant professor facing a review during a probationary period. The academic climate today demands production, and scholarship is often gauged by quantity rather than quality. It follows that pressures to produce something publishable are enormous. A colleague of mine once used the expression "least publishable unit" in reference to the target for many young scientists. The idea is to complete as many publishable pieces as possible. Within this competitive and production-oriented context, it is easy to see how fraud might escalate.

Apart from job security, there is the issue of "who gets there first." In science, there is no prize for coming in second. When a breakthrough occurs, the recognition goes to the individual who achieved it first. The person who arrives later offers a mere replication of the pioneer's finding. Considering the sense of urgency that surrounds the scientific chase, it is easy to see why an investigator would want to do everything possible to gain a competitive edge. Unfortunately, this may include inventing subjects or data sets that fall into the phantom category. As I said, it is extremely rare, but it has and will continue to happen.

Ultimately, it is up to the scientists to police their disciplines. I feel that the system for conducting high-quality research works. Many comments have been made in the popular press recently about the increase in the number of cases of scientific misconduct, but these comments actually may support the system. After all, the violators were caught. The fact that fakers eventually will be found out via such tools as the inability to replicate seems to validate the scientific method. In the final analysis, the system cleanses itself.

Before moving to the next section, it should be noted that there is another side to the scientific misconduct issue. What happens when someone is falsely accused? What protection does the individual have against reckless accusation? Ask Herbert Needleman of the University of Pittsburgh.

# Spotlight on Research: THE NEEDLEMAN CONTROVERSY

In 1979, Herbert Needleman, then associated with Harvard Medical School, published a paper with his colleagues demonstrating that low levels of lead in the body are associated with lower intelligence, even though there are no obvious physical symptoms of lead poisoning. In this report, which was published in the *New England Journal of Medicine,* the IQs of 58 children with high concentrations of lead in their teeth were compared to 100 children who showed only slight traces of the metal in the teeth they had shed. Along with a drop in intelligence scores, increased conduct disorders in the classroom were evident among the children in the high-lead sample.

Largely because of Needleman's findings, the Centers for Disease Control (CDC) lowered its threshold definition of dangerous levels of lead over the next several years, and by October 1991 the maximal allowable concentration was set at 10 $\mu$g/dl in blood, which was less than half the amount allowable only a couple of years earlier. Because of the widespread presence of lead in the environment, this placed 1 out of 2 children living in the inner cities at risk (Centers for Disease Control [CDC], 1991). Needless to say, the potential costs for industry and government, at least with respect to correcting the problem, would be substantial.

In 1991, something unexpected happened. Two researchers concerned with the toxic effects of lead exposure filed a complaint with the National Institutes of Health (NIH) that Needleman was guilty of scientific misconduct. They charged that Needleman failed to consider the contaminating influence of variables other than lead, including age, and that he discarded data that was not consistent with the theme that lead causes a decrease in IQ.

Having moved to the University of Pittsburgh, Needleman would have to withstand the scrutiny of the University of Pittsburgh panel that would determine his guilt or innocence. After almost a year of expert testimony, reanalysis of the data, grueling defenses, and attorney fees, Needleman was exonerated. There was no indication of scientific fraud, and it was revealed that the accusers had ties to the lead industry. This is not to say that the charges were trumped up in the interest of furthering an industrial franchise, but clearly some elements of the proceedings left many scientists feeling vulnerable (cf. Putka, 1991).

What protection does a scientist have against flimsy assertions of misconduct? Not much, it seems. After being cleared of all charges, Needleman remarked, "For the last year, I have accomplished nothing scientifically. All of my intellectual and financial resources have been committed to defending myself against unfounded claims by only two people." The frightening part of this, of course, is that it could happen to anyone. Allegations of misconduct from an individual could disrupt someone's entire research agenda. It creates what some have referred to as "a scientific filibuster." The bulk of the scientist's time is devoted to nonscientific activities, so the result is that the accuser keeps potentially damaging findings from the scientific community.

Cases such as Needleman's are very unusual, but this sort of tussle in the academic world no doubt will recur, and perhaps it should. However, as members of a body that prides itself on objectivity and fairness, maybe we need to remind ourselves of the fundamental rights of the accused in any arena. ∎

## WITHIN CHAPTER REVIEW AND STUDY QUESTIONS

### TRUTH IN REPORTING: SCIENTIFIC FRAUD

1. How common is scientific fraud? What conditions are likely to promote faking?
2. What defense does a scientific investigator have against charges of scientific misconduct? What is the disadvantage of a system that permits an individual to challenge the credibility of a research scientist? What are the advantages of such a system?

## IN THE ABSENCE OF GUIDELINES

As we shall see later in this chapter, psychological researchers have been provided with explicit guidelines about how to conduct experiments within an ethical context, and these rules and recommendations are very helpful in most situations. As any veteran researcher will tell you, however, events could unfold during the course of an experiment that could not have been anticipated, and there is no manual, no agency publication, and often no advice on how best to handle the problem. In such situations, you as the investigator call the shots. On occasion, this can be unsettling.

Consider the following laboratory example. You are using college students who are completing research requirements for course credit. The focus of the study is on the effects of an acutely negative affective state (depression) on spontaneous social interaction. Confederates (people who work for the experimenter but are pretending to be subjects) and the real subject are placed in a waiting room under the guise of waiting to participate in a second study. During this waiting period, the frequency with which conversations are initiated is recorded. Inasmuch as the experiment centers on mood and depression, it follows that some measure of the negative mood state must be taken and subjects assigned high and low depression conditions accordingly. On your depression inventory, there is an item, "I have thought of committing suicide frequently in the last week." A subject responds "True." What do you do with this information? Do you go about business as usual and assign this person to the high depression condition? Do you intervene and suggest that the person seek help from the personal counseling center on campus? Or should you just let it go and dismiss the subject?

The answers here are not as simple as they may first appear. The tendency is to intervene, forget the experiment, and adopt the noble position of possibly saving a life. Technically, however, this is an invasion of privacy. The student has not come to you for help, and it would be presumptuous of you to offer to help someone who may be offended that you have used laboratory data to judge her or his life. Of course, if you do nothing, your lack of caring may be interpreted as indifference and therefore exacerbate the problem. Doing nothing doesn't leave one feeling good about the situation either. Ultimately, you must decide. You have to do what is right from your frame of reference. These type of cases are hard calls, but someone has to make them, and that responsibility typically goes to the senior investigator.

Now let's take another example. You are conducting an animal learning study on the effects of brightness cues on lever-press rates where food deliveries serve as the reinforcer. Ten rats are in a "dim" condition and 10 are in a "bright" condition. Except for one bright animal that responds at a lower rate than any animal in the dim condition, the distinct separation in animal intelligence produces higher rates in the "bright" group. This outlier in the bright group creates havoc with conventional parametric statistical assays, and yet such tests are needed for a number of reasons which need not concern us here. What do you do with this aberrant subject? Do you throw the rat out of the experiment? Do you keep the rat and scrap the project? Do you rerun the whole study? Basically, it is up to you. If you discard the subject according to some set criteria (a 2 standard deviation [SD] difference from the group average [mean]), you must so indicate in your report and let the reader decide about biases in your findings. Starting over is expensive in terms of time and money, but your results may be more convincing. Whatever you decide, recognize that your behavior is arbitrary but probably appropriate. Just be honest with yourself and your readership.

Numerous other unforeseen problems may also arise in the course of a study. Human subjects may become ill in the middle of a test, an animal may die from a respiratory infection, equipment may fail, someone may drop a trashcan lid in the hall and startle a rat during a testing session, data sheets may be misplaced, and on it goes. Decisions are one of the most difficult parts of completing a research project, but they have to be made moment to moment and often decisions are visceral, seat-of-the-pants calls. My advice is to just do the best you can.

## WITHIN CHAPTER REVIEW AND STUDY QUESTION

### IN THE ABSENCE OF GUIDELINES

1. A participant in a research project performs in a manner strikingly unlike any of the other subjects in the same control group. Do you include the subject's data? What criteria might you use for discarding these data?

# WHEN GUIDELINES ARE AVAILABLE: ETHICAL PRINCIPLES OF PSYCHOLOGISTS AND CODE OF CONDUCT (APA)

In the United States, the 1960s and 1970s were decades of dramatic social and moral change. With a redefinition of personal rights and obligations came a review of the appropriate conduct of institutions and government agencies. Caught up in the spirit of moral responsibility, the American Psychological Association (APA) set out to formulate a code of ethical practices to govern research involving human participants (Blank, Bellack, Rosnow, Rotheran-Borus, & Schooler, 1992).

The APA's initial effort involved forming a committee that was charged with developing a document to provide research guidelines for psychologists. This committee rendered a set of ethical regulations that APA published in 1973, called *Ethical Principles in the Conduct of Research with Human Participants*. A separate committee revised this document a decade later (American Psychological Association [APA], 1982).

The most recent development in establishing ethical standards for psychologists has been the publication of the *Ethical Principles of Psychologists and Code of Conduct* (APA, 1992). This lengthy document consists of a preamble, six general principles, and several specific ethical standards. Much of the *Ethics Code,* as the document is called, deals with the ethical responsibilities of health-service providers. While this is an exceedingly important part of the document, this information is not directly relevant here. What is pertinent to our coverage of ethical guidelines for conducting human research is Section 6 under "Ethical Standards," which is labeled "Teaching, Training Supervision, Research, and Publishing." Figure 4-1 lists in capsule format each of the areas covered in this section. For our purposes, I at this time include only those subsections that address issues in human research. Consistent with the theme of this book, applications to the experiment we are building throughout the text are made when appropriate.

## Planning Research (6.06)

This section of the *Ethics Code* has the four following components (presented verbatim from the code).

  a. Psychologists design, conduct, and report research in accordance with recognized standards of scientific competence and ethical research.

6.     *Teaching, Training Supervision, Research, and Publishing*
6.01   Design of Education and Training Programs
6.02   Descriptions of Education and Training Programs
6.03   Accuracy and Objectivity Teaching
6.04   Limitation on Teaching
6.05   Assessing Student and Supervisee Performance
6.06   Planning Research
6.07   Responsibility
6.08   Compliance with Law and Standards
6.09   Institutional Approval
6.10   Research Responsibilities
6.11   Informed Consent to Research
6.12   Dispensing with Informed Consent
6.13   Informed Consent in Research Filming or Recording
6.14   Offering Inducements for Research Participants
6.15   Deception in Research
6.16   Sharing and Utilizing Data
6.17   Minimizing Invasiveness
6.18   Providing Participants with Information about the Study
6.19   Honoring Commitments
6.20   Care and Use of Animals in Research
6.21   Reporting of Results
6.22   Plagiarism
6.23   Publication Credit
6.24   Duplicate Publication of Data
6.25   Sharing Data
6.26   Professional Reviewers

**FIGURE 4–1** Section 6 of *Ethical Principles of Psychologists and Code of Ethics,* "Teaching, Training Supervision, Research, and Publishing" (APA, 1992)

---

b. Psychologists plan their research so as to minimize the possibility that results will be misleading.
c. In planning research, psychologists consider its ethical acceptability under the *Ethics Code.* If an ethical issue is unclear, psychologists seek to resolve the issue through consultation with institutional review boards, animal care and use committees, peer consultations, or other proper mechanisms.
d. Psychologists take reasonable steps to implement appropriate protection for the rights and welfare of human participants, other persons affected by the research, and animal subjects.

The thrust of this section relates to design decisions on the part of psychology researchers. From the preliminary stages of a project, every effort must be made to maintain professional responsibility, to protect the rights of everyone associated with the research, and to work within an established ethical framework. In virtually all experiments involving human participants, the investigator can design the study in such a fashion as to minimize risks and respect basic rights. In our case, planning operations are especially critical because our subjects are chronically ill patients who are suffering pain and discomfort, and we have the added ethical responsibility to treat all participants as effectively as possible. Accordingly, for our model experiment we install the following design considerations:

For this experiment, which involves evaluating different treatment strategies (cognitive therapy, information only condition, and control) at two different age ranges (4–6 years, 10–12 years), every effort will be made to minimize the discomfort of the participants. Patients will be evaluated within the context of their daily routines, they will remain in the hospital setting, visitations will continue as before, and all other aspects of their lives in the medical environment will remain as before.

Should the research findings indicate that one intervention strategy produces more favorable results than another for a particular condition, at the conclusion of the study patients in that condition will have the opportunity to undergo the more desirable form of treatment, regardless of their prior role in the research.

Of course, other considerations would be necessary during the planning stages of our model experiment, as they would be for any study. We cannot address every issue that would need attention here, but it is important to recognize that from the very beginning there are ethical concerns you must resolve. Solid planning prevents unnecessary problems.

## Responsibility (6.07)

The four following subsections are listed in this section:

a. Psychologists conduct research competently and with due concern for the dignity and welfare of the participants.
b. Psychologists are responsible for the ethical conduct of research conducted by them or by others under their supervision or control.
c. Researchers and assistants are permitted to perform only those tasks for which they are appropriately trained and prepared.
d. As part of the process of development and implementation of research projects, psychologists consult those with expertise concerning any special population under investigation or most likely to be affected.

As relates to the construction of our model experiment, item c is of particular interest. In psychological research, it is common for undergraduates and other workers with limited training backgrounds to assist in the conduct and analysis of experiments. However, in our case, this is not an option. Because the model experiment we propose to conduct involves therapeutic intervention with chronically ill children in a hospital setting, only highly skilled professionals will be permitted to take part in the various research operations.

The experimenters will include graduate students and postdoctoral students who have received extensive training in psychotherapeutic intervention. All personnel will have a minimum of 100 practica (therapy) hours of supervised experience with children.

Each experimenter involved in the treatment phase of the proposed project will be supervised by a licensed clinical psychologist, certified by the state Board of Examiners of Psychologists as a health-service provider in the state of Texas. During the data collection phase of the experiment, it will be the responsibility of each experimenter to monitor the psychological welfare of the participant (patient) and determine whether or not the participant is at risk.

Respecting the dignity of human subjects is essential, and while violations of this basic principle have occurred, overall psychology researchers have an excellent record in this regard. The experimenter is trained to be sensitive to subject issues because in many ways the subject is a guest and deserves to be treated accordingly.

## *Institutional Approval (6.09)*

Psychologists obtain from host institutions or organizations appropriate approval prior to conducting research, and they provide accurate information about their research proposals. They conduct the research in accordance with the approved research protocol.

This section of the APA *Ethics Code* relates to what has become known as the **institutional review board (IRB).** The IRB is a standing panel of qualified professionals who make decisions about the ethical treatment of human subjects. The board is comprised of mostly psychologists, but it may include physicians and other specialists from the

**institutional review board (IRB)**—a review panel of professionals who ensure that human subjects are treated ethically host institution. The IRB has the authority to approve, require modifications to, or disapprove proposed research.

For the model experiment we are building, we will use the proposal forms from Texas A&M University. These forms, which are shown in Figure 4–2, are uniform documents used by all investigators at this institution who include human subjects in their research.

Submitting a proposal to the IRB requires a great deal of effort. A hastily prepared proposal that fails to specify the basic elements of the experimental protocol in sufficient detail is kicked back to the principal investigator, and permission to conduct the research is denied. Stiff penalties are imposed for conducting human subject research without an approved protocol. For institutions that have agreements with federal funding agencies such as the NIH and the NSF, violations can lead to bans on access to human subject populations (Sieber, 1992).

Included in the list of items which must be incorporated into the proposal that is submitted to the IRB are a consent form (see following section), a statement on the exact experimental procedures that will be followed, and an acknowledgment of any risks to the subject. The latter is one of the most important ethical concerns with which the IRB must wrestle. It is easy to define risks in certain situations, such as in a study on stress-induced changes in memory function or in an experiment on the fear response to boa constrictors among snake-phobics, but in some cases the risks to subjects may not be so obvious. Take a proposed experiment on the effects of context on eyewitness testimony, for example.

It is well established that people retrieve information more efficiently when they are placed back in the environment where they originally acquired the information (cf. Smith, 1988). Accordingly, someone may propose to show a videotape of a staged bank heist in a given room (context) to determine the accuracy of recognition memory (identification of the robber) when the subject is in the same or a different room. This approach seems reasonable, and there should be minimal risks to the subject, but what if the subject is a recent robbery victim or has had a relative who has been involved in a violent crime? The risks here are insidious but real. The IRB must, in good faith, do the best it can with respect to considering aspects of the proposal that may negatively affect the subject. For this reason, the review of proposals often takes a good bit of time, and although some investigators see it as a slowdown, everyone agrees that the review must be deliberate and carefully conducted.

Form I
Protocol for Human Subjects
in Research

TAMU _____
Scott & White # _____
Other # _____

Please check off or provide details of the following (enter N/A if not applicable):

Principal Investigator _____ Faculty _____ Graduate Student*_____

College/Dept _____ Phone_____

Project Title _____

PI's Subjective Estimate of Risk to Subject: __ Low __ Moderate __High __ None

Gender of subjects: _ Male _ Female _ Both  Age(s):_____ Total Participants (est.) ____

Source of Subjects:
__ Psychology Subject Pool          Subject Recruitment:
__ Other TAMU Students          __ Direct Person-to-person contact    Compensation*** Yes__ No__
__ Community               __ Telephone Solicitation     Deception      Yes__ No__
__ Public Schools            __ Newspaper Ad**      Debriefing Form* Yes__ No__
__ Hospitals/Nursing Homes       __ Letter**          (If yes attach a debriefing
__ Prisons               __ Posted Notices**      form)
__ Other (Please specify)_____ __ Other (Please describe) _____
Location of Experiment _____

Invasion of Sensitive Procedures              Sensitive Subject Matter  Yes __ No __

__ Blood Samples          __ Urine Samples          __ Alcohol, Drugs, Sex
__ Physical Measurements     __ Stress Exercise        __ Depression/Suicide
   (electrodes, etc.)        __ Review of Medical Records   __ Learning Disability
__ Depression Inventory      __ Other (Please describe) _____

Use of Video/Audio Tapes      Provisions for Confidentiality

Retained  Yes __  No __           __ Replies Coded
Length of Time _____           __ Secure Storage
Destroy/Erase Yes __ No __         __ Anonymous Response
Other (Explain) _____
Use specified in consent form? Yes __  No __
Use/Access to tapes

Exact Location Where Signed Consent Forms Will Be Filed _____

* Must include signature of committee chair on protocol.
** Please attach
*** Please attach conditions, schedule of payment.

_____  _____  _____
Principal Investigator    Graduate Committee Chair   Department Head
Date _____      Date _____       Date _____

Date Approved:                    _____
                           Chair
                           Institutional Review Board

Form II
Protocol Format for use of Human
Subjects in Research

Instructions

In addition to the attached summary sheet (Form I), please prepare a brief (2-3 page) research protocol which provides the information requested in the numbered items below for review by the Institutional Review Board, plus a copy of each consent form to be used in the study. The format for your protocol is described below; please do not return or sign this form with your material.

PART I.

Please list (1) Project Title; (2) Principal Investigator; (3) Department, (4) College; (5) Phone; (6) Sponsor or Source of Funds.

PART II.

Please include the following statement:

I have read the Belmont Report, "Ethical Principles and Guidelines for the Protection of Human Subjects of Research* and subscribe to the principals it contains. In light of this Declaration, I present for the Board's consideration the following information which will be explained to the subject about the proposed research:

PART III. Experimental Procedure

A.  Physical/Behavioral Aspects. Describe in order exactly what is to be done to the subject(s), and what the subject is expected to do. Be specific. For example, specify volume of blood to be drawn, tissues collected, in terms of amounts, dosages, frequency (use common measurement terms, eg. teaspoons), how long they will be expected to participate.

B.  Deception or Coercion. If the experiment involves coercion or deception please describe in lay terms how and why coercion or deception is required and how this explanation will be provided to the subjects at the end of the experiment (eg. in person, written form, telephone).

PART IV. Risks and Benefits to Subjects:

Please provide a concise, clear description understandable to non-specialists which includes:

A.  A description of risks that may include risk or discomfort to the subject. Risk refers to possible physical, psychological, or social injury from participating in the study over and above the ordinary risks of daily life and chosen occupation. Common discomforts include for example, bruising from venipuncture, slight abrasion from electrode placement, or fatigue associated with physical activity.

B.  Benefits or alternatives for the subjects.

PART V. Source of Subjects:

Describe (a) source; number (b) method of recruitment; (c) ages; (d) compensation (if any); (e) location and duration of experiment; (f) specific steps to ensure confidentiality of responses or results; (g) special physical or psychological conditions.

Please attach copies of notices or advertisements used to recruit subjects. These must contain the name, phone, address of investigator; purpose of the study; eligibility of the subject(s); description of benefits; compensation; and location of the study.

PART VI. Signatures of:
• Principal Investigator/Graduate Student
• Department Head
• Chair, Graduate Committee
• Date

**FIGURE 4–2** Proposal forms from Texas A&M University. Copyright © 1996 by Texas A&M University. Reprinted with permission.

What risks do you feel might be present in the kind of experiment we are building in this book? Because we are dealing with chronically ill children who are undergoing stressful medical treatments, fear and anxiety are unavoidable. Is it possible that as agents of intervention (therapists) working for the experimenter, you may unwittingly make events even more difficult for the patient? How might the psychotherapeutic procedures impact the medical status of the patient? The suppression of immune function under conditions of stress is well established in humans (Dyck, Greenberg, & Osachuck, 1986; Shavit et al., 1985), so is it possible, and even likely, that an experimental presence may compromise an already fragile immune system. Are the anticipated gains from the proposed experiment worth these risks? Fortunately, you do not have to make these judgments in isolation. The IRB, which has no vested interest in the project, works as an impartial advisor on such matters and as such reassures the subject and the investigator that the proper resource course is taken.

Many psychology departments or divisions have their own in-house review committees work in tandem with the IRB. This additional set of eyes offers even further guarantees that the rights of human subjects will not be violated.

## *Informed Consent to Research (6.11)*

This section from the APA *Ethics Code* has the five following subsections:

a. Psychologists use language that is reasonably understandable to research participants in obtaining their appropriate informed consent (except as provided in Standard 6.12, Dispensing with Informed Consent). Such informed consent is appropriately documented.

b. Using language that is reasonably understandable to participants, psychologists inform participants of the nature of the research; they inform participants that they are free to participate or to decline to participate or to withdraw from the research; they explain the foreseeable consequences of declining or withdrawing; they inform participants of significant factors that may be expected to influence their willingness to participate (such as risks, discomfort, adverse effects, or limitations on confidentiality, except as provided in Standard 6.15, Deception in Research); and they explain other aspects about which the prospective participants inquire.

c. When psychologists conduct research with individuals such as students or subordinates, psychologists take special care to protect the prospective participants from adverse consequences of declining or withdrawing from participation.

d. When research participation is a course requirement or opportunity for extra credit, the prospective participant is given the choice of equitable alternative activities.

e. For persons who are legally incapable of giving informed consent, psychologists nevertheless (1) provide an appropriate explanation, (2) obtain the participant's assent, and (3) obtain appropriate permission from a legal authorized person, if such substitute consent is permitted by law.

Regarding subsection a, **informed consent** refers to an agreement by the subject to participate in the research *after* the details of the experiment have been made clear to him or her. This agreement is typically signed and dated by the subject. Obviously, the psychological investigator cannot explain every behavioral result to the subject, because the hopes and expectancies of the experimenter have been shown to bias the performance of participants. However, the researcher can and should provide full disclosure of those aspects of the experiment that relate directly to the safety and welfare of the subject.

In addition to explaining the procedural elements of the study, the informed consent document should clearly outline the ultimate purpose of the experiment. The subjects have a right to know what their role in the project is going to be, and they deserve to know how the results will benefit them and others.

In some instances, the subject may not be in a position to fully grasp the meaning of the research. To an extent, this is the situation we have in the experiment we are constructing in this book. It is unlikely that children 4–6 years old possess the cognitive apparatus to follow the logic that led us to formally state the hypothesis (see Chapter 2). Nonetheless, the investigator is obligated to explain the purpose of the experiment as simply as possible and to obtain the subject's agreement (in our case, a chronically ill pediatric patient) that he or she is willing to participate in the research. The consent form for our model experiment is reproduced in Figure 4–3.

Some of the darkest moments in the history of psychological research are linked to failures to obtain informed consent and to an unwillingness on the part of the investigators to share all aspects of the research with the participants. The Tuskegee syphilis study conducted from 1932 through 1972, although technically a medical experiment, illustrates what can happen when human subject research ignores the rights of individuals.

**informed consent**—a signed agreement between the experimenter and the subject in which the subject agrees to participate in the experiment after having been told of the procedural details of the research

## INFORMED CONSENT

This study is about the benefits of different kinds of psychological treatment for children of different ages who have been ill for a long time. The study may last several weeks and will be conducted in this hospital. Participants in the study will experience one of three treatments: (1) a treatment that asks you to think about and imagine certain things, (2) a treatment that tells you more about what exactly is happening to you when you receive medical treatment, and (3) a treatment that involves reading a short story. It is possible that one or all three of these treatments may make it easier for you to get through the medical treatments you must have for your illness. If you are not in the group that benefits most, you will be given the opportunity to have that treatment at the end of the study.

Your participation is voluntary, and you can withdraw at any time with no penalty. If you like, at the end of the study you can still receive any treatment that proves helpful. No added discomfort or stress is expected, and all of your responses will be kept secret.

"This research study has been reviewed and approved by the Institutional Review Board—Human Subjects in Research, Texas A&M University. For research-related problems or questions regarding subjects' rights, the Institutional Review Board may be contacted through the Office of University Research."

I have read and understand the explanation provided me and voluntarily agree to participate in this study.

_____                    _____
Signature of Subject                               Date

**FIGURE 4–3** Informed consent document that will be used in the model experiment built in this text.

## Spotlight on Research: THE TUSKEGEE SYPHILIS STUDY

In 1928, the Julius Rosenwald Fund, a philanthropic organization dedicated to promoting the welfare of blacks in the United States, approached the Public Health Service (PHS) in an effort to help rural Southern blacks. Ultimately, the PHS collaborated with the Rosenwald Fund and conducted a control demonstration program in five predominantly black counties in the rural South.

Unfortunately, with the Depression of 1929, the financial resources of the Rosenwald Fund were devastated. Without financial backing from the Rosenwald Fund, the PHS determined that it would be impossible to fund treatment programs.

Still, numerous syphilis cases had been identified (in Macon County, Alabama, 40% of all black males tested were found to have syphilis), and it seemed to make sense to glean as much from the project as possible. The PHS judged that the best chance for salvaging anything of value from the project would be to conduct a well-controlled experiment (Thomas, 1991).

Historian James Jones has provided a detailed account of what happened after 1929 in his 1981 book, *Bad Blood: The Tuskegee Syphilis Experiment—A Tragedy of Race and Medicine.* The original population consisted of 399 black men, of which 201 had been diagnosed as having syphilis. Partly because the Tuskegee Institute had a history of service to blacks in Macon County, but also because PHS wanted to facilitate the co-operation of the subjects, black physicians from the Institute participated in the data collection part of the study.

Incredibly, a decision was made by the PHS to deliberately provide ineffective treatment for "an experimental group." Initially, the study was to last for 6 to 9 months, but it continued for 40 years and now ranks as the longest nontherapeu-tic experiment in medical history (Jones, 1981). The staff of the PHS, the Alabama state health of-ficer, employees of the Macon County Board of Health, and virtually everyone except the subjects knew that the treatment was insufficient to cure "the bad blood." Not only did the PHS not effec-tively arrange for the treatment of the syphilitic subjects, it actively prevented anyone else from treating those in the experimental condition. For instance, during World War II when the syphilitic cases were being screened by the local draft board, letters from the board telling the subjects in the "experimental group" to seek treatment were withdrawn, at the behest of the PHS (Thomas, 1991).

Various reviews of the Tuskegee study were un-dertaken over the years, including one by the CDC in 1969. In each instance, however, the study continued and a decision was made to fol-low the subject to "end point [death]" (Thomas, 1991). The experimental subjects with syphilis who were never treated never knew they were not receiving adequate health care. Finally, a vene-real disease investigator named Peter Buxtun broke the story, and on July 25, 1972, the *Wash-ington Star* ran a front-page story on the project. On that day, the study was still being conducted by the PHS.

The American public and black political lead-ers throughout the country were outraged. How could such a travesty be perpetrated over so many years? Why were the subjects never told? Perhaps only a small group of men in the PHS were even aware of what was happening. Cer-tainly Dr. John Heller, director of Venereal Dis-eases at the PHS from 1943 to 1948, endorsed it. In an interview in 1976, Heller stated, "The men's status did not warrant ethical debate. They were subjects, not patients; clinical material, not sick people" (Jones, 1981, p. 179). So, although only a few staff members of the PHS may have known about what was going on in the Tuskegee study, they should have been sensitive to the rights of the subjects. Obviously, no one was looking out for the interests of the subjects in this slice of human misery.    ■

The Tuskegee study represents a flagrant violation of trust. It is essential that participants in any research project be adequately informed about what risks they are likely to incur and what their role in the research is going to be. This is as true for studies on language acquisition as it is for studies on syphilis. Every participant has a right to know, and this is what signed informed consent forms accomplish.

Another important section of section 6.11 relates to informing participants that " . . . they are free to decline to participate (6.11)." Although this idea has been underscored by the APA *Ethics Code* since the 1970s, and although it is at-tractive on purely ethical grounds, problems remain. First, the freedom of choice issue is often hazy (Sieber & Sorensen, 1991). When an investigator offers sub-jects money or other inducements to participate, what kind of choice are we

**volunteer participants**—subjects who enter into experimental research of their own volition

**confidentiality**—an agreement between the participant and the experimenter to protect the identity of the subject

really talking about? Also, when subjects are genuinely permitted to select the experiments in which they will participate, what is the effect on the sample? Does the "freedom to choose" bias the sample and limit our ability to make general statements about other populations? To add to the complexity of the problem, one must question the wisdom of conducting research with only college students, which is the most common population from which experimental samples are drawn (Blanck et al., 1992). When lower-income people are induced to participate, their behavior is often much different from that of college students who are tested under the same set of conditions (Rosenthal & Rosnow, 1975). How, then, do we justify continuing to draft a psychology of human behavior based on experiments that use an exclusive, and somewhat elite, segment of the population? Does this not call for more coercive recruitment procedures?

The prickly issue of **volunteer participants** is a part of the subject selection bias question, of course. With volunteers, the question is not "In which experiments will they continue?" or "From which experiment will they resign?" but rather, "Will they arrive to participate?" Volunteers go to the experimental setting because they want to: they have a vested interest in the outcome of the study, they see the research as important, or they are just curious. Any one of these concerns can prejudice the outcome of an experiment, however. For example, Strohmetz, Alterman, and Walter (1990) have shown that volunteering for a study on alcoholism is directly related to the severity of the disorder. The more extreme the condition, the greater the chance of participation. Virtually identical results have been obtained with Vietnam veterans (King & King, 1991). Such findings question the validity of data from studies which use only volunteers. How meaningful are these studies when the behavior patterns do not parallel those of nonvolunteers?

As a result, we see in the "freedom to choose" clause of the APA *Ethics Code* the creation of a thin gray line. This line is formed by the realization that representation often requires pressure to participate and the commitment to respond ethically. While the IRB may be of some help here, negotiating this gray area really relies on the integrity of the experimenter in charge.

Still another issue covered (created) by Section 6.11 is the position on **confidentiality.** Confidentiality is an agreement between the participant and the investigator to keep the identity of the subject anonymous and to ensure that no traceable record of the individual's data will be disclosed. Figure 4–4 lists several reasons that have been used to justify the inclusion of statements of confidentiality in informed consent forms.

Regarding the "enhanced credibility" assertion in Figure 4–4 (number 3), it should be noted that while there is some evidence to support the views that a written or verbal assurance of confidentiality increases honesty in responding, the results in this area are sometimes at odds. For instance, an experiment by

1. Researchers have a professional right to keep a subject's disclosures secret.
2. Fairness on the part of the experimenter requires respecting the privacy of the participants and their desire to remain anonymous.
3. The credibility and validity of the research findings is likely to be enhanced when the experimenter has promised to keep disclosures confidential.

**FIGURE 4–4** Justification for maintaining confidentiality in human subject research. (Adapted from Blanck et al., 1992.)

Esposito, Agard, and Rosnow (1984) favors the idea that ensuring participants of confidentiality increases the likelihood that the participants will be honest and open in their responses. In this experiment, participants were administered two questionnaires under two different conditions. The Trait-State Personality Inventory and the Social Desirability Scale were administered in a "confidential" context and in a "control" context where confidentiality was not ensured. The results showed that when confidentiality was guaranteed, people were less evasive when answering questions on the questionnaires. In comparison, in an interview study of young people previously arrested for criminal behavior, Reamer (1979) failed to find any evidence that honesty in responding is increased by assurances of confidentiality.

One of the possible reasons for conflicting findings in this area is that participants in research sense that the ethical climate is shifting (Bayer & Toomey, 1992). People often do not feel secure about their personal anonymity, which can lead to inconsistent reactions to statements of confidentiality. There have been several instances where the anonymous status of the subject has not been maintained, and in some cases, such as in AIDS studies where positive diagnoses are made, you can see why the investigator feels ethically obliged to violate the agreement of anonymity. The HIV-positive people need to know their condition, but technically the experimenter should remain blind and respect the participants' privacy. Such dilemmas are inherent in conducting research with human subjects. Ultimately, the researcher must be trusted to make the right decision.

Finally, I would like to comment about subsection d of ethical standard 6.11. As undergraduate college students with an interest in psychology, many of you have been asked to participate in experiments conducted at your respective campuses. In most instances, students receive credit for participation, which can help fulfill a course requirement. When you were recruited to participate in the research project, it should have been made clear to you that the course requirement could have been satisfied in some other way. That is, no one should be coerced into taking part in an experiment. In truth, most psychology students find the experience enjoyable. Also, participating in psychological experiments is a credible way to learn how research in the field is carried out. Nonetheless,

**demand characteristics**—the tendency on the part of a subject to respond in a fashion that is consistent with the perceived expectancies of the experimenter

prospective investigators are obligated to provide an alternative and "equitable" learning opportunity, such as writing a review of a published report or some other research-related activity. The essential element is that the student not feel pressured to participate.

## Offering Inducements for Research Participants (6.14)

a. In offering professional services as an inducement to obtain research participants, psychologists make clear the nature of the services, as well as the risks, obligations, and limitations.
b. Psychologists do not offer excessive or inappropriate financial or other inducements to obtain research participants, particularly when it might tend to coerce participation.

Section 6.14 of the APA *Ethics Code* addresses the issue of professional enticements, and it is especially important for research projects such as the model experiment we are building. In our experiment, we have made it apparent that we aim to use different psychotherapeutic intervention strategies for ameliorating stress in chronically ill children undergoing painful medical treatments. In this regard, we offer a professional service that is designed to benefit the participants in the study. It is appropriate, then, to make it clear to each patient (participant) exactly what we hope to accomplish during the course of therapy. The patients need to be informed of the likelihood that the intervention will help them handle stress and whether or not they are receiving or will receive the best treatment available. In addition, they need to be told what is expected of them if they agree to participate in the experiment. Section 6.14 is included in the ethical guidelines to protect participants from exploitation. As in our model experiment, all subjects need to understand that the benefits of the project are available, whether or not they choose to participate. This way no one feels compromised or bought.

## Deception in Research (6.15)

a. Psychologists do not conduct a study involving deception unless they have determined that the use of deceptive techniques is justified by the study's prospective scientific, educational, or applied value and that equally effective alternative procedures that do not use deception are not feasible.
b. Psychologists never deceive research participants about significant aspects that would affect their willingness to participate, such as physical risks, discomfort, or unpleasant emotional experiences.

c. Any other deception that is an integral feature of the design and conduct of an experiment must be explained to participants as early as is feasible, preferably at the conclusion of their participation, but no later than the conclusion of the research.

Regarding subsection a of section 6.15, it should be acknowledged that the debate over the use of deception in psychological research has a stormy history, and that even today psychologists disagree on the practice. Proponents justify the use of deceptive techniques on the grounds of **demand characteristics.** In psychological research, *demand* refers to a cuing process in the experiment which insidiously instructs the subject about what is expected (Orne, 1962). That is, if the participants determine that they are expected to respond with compassion, then they will tend to behave compassionately, commensurate with the perceived wishes of the experimenter. Alternatively, if a participant perceives that the experimental situation calls for aggression, then the participant may respond aggressively. Of course, if the real purpose of the experiment is disguised, then systematic subject bias arising out of demand should not occur. Within this context, deception must be used to ensure that the overall response profile is valid.

On the other side of the issue, those favoring full disclosure argue that any form of deception is lying and as such is not permissible (Bok, 1978). The belief is that any scientific gain is offset by unethical misconduct and that alternative research methods must be pursued. At any rate, for the moment deception is common in psychological laboratories that conduct human subject research, and this situation will likely persist for some time.

Perhaps of greater concern than the issue of whether or not deceptive practices should be used is how far the deception should go. As subsection b of section 6.15 states, the investigator must never deceive the participant about such things as " . . . physical risks, discomfort, or unpleasant emotional experiences." The spirit of this rule is that subjects should never be in the dark about events that may harm them or put them ill-at-ease. Unfortunately, some of the most famous psychological experiments have employed procedures that fundamentally violate this principle.

## Spotlight on Research: THE MILGRAM STUDIES

In 1963, psychologist Stanley Milgram published a study entitled *Behavioral Study of Obedience,* which still ranks as one of the most controversial research projects ever undertaken.

Milgram recruited human volunteers to participate in a study on the effects of authority on obedience. The experimenter ordered the subjects to deliver severe electric shocks to a victim in what was claimed to be a study on the effects of punishment on learning. The shocks were to be delivered by activating 30 different switches that were labeled as increasing in current from a low point of "Slight Shock" to "Danger: Severe Shock." In actuality, the shocks were delivered to a confederate of the experimenter (no electric current was actually applied, but the confederate was cued to flinch when the true subject delivered what he or she thought was a genuine electrical jolt).

The primary dependent variable in this experiment was the maximum shock level the subject was willing to administer before he or she refused to go further. When subjects expressed concern over the welfare of the "learner" (the confederate), they were simply reminded that they had volunteered for the experiment and that the experimenter would assume responsibility for anything that happened.

Astonishingly, 25 out of 40 subjects obeyed the experimenter's commands fully and activated the "Danger: Severe Shock" switch. Milgram (1963) described the subjects' reactions to delivering the shocks as follows:

> The procedure created extreme levels of nervous tension in some [subjects]. Profuse sweating, trembling, and stuttering were typical expressions of this emotional disturbance. One unexpected sign of tension— yet to be explained—was the regular occurrence of nervous laughter, which in some [subjects] developed into uncontrollable seizures. (p. 371)

To be sure, the results of the Milgram experiment offer valuable insights into understanding obedience and the human posture of compliance. No one, certainly not Milgram, expected these data. That people would go so far just because they were told to do so was an astounding finding, and even in the 1990s this project impacts the way psychologists approach the study of social behavior. The underlying, and perhaps more important, issue rests with the fact that the research was done at all. Participants in this experiment were not told that the shock deliveries were being faked, they were not warned about the stress they would feel from participating, and they were encouraged by the experimenter to continue in the experiment when they reported emotional discomfort. Indeed, some subjects were pushed to go on after pressing a fist to their forehead and muttering statements such as, "Oh God, let's stop it" (p. 377). The subjects did continue—all the way to the end. Obviously, Milgram and his colleagues violated the rights of the subjects in this classic study, and many members of the scientific community were appalled (cf. Baumrind, 1964).

Some defended Milgram because prior to commencing the 1963 experiment Milgram sought input from psychiatric specialists regarding the likelihood that people selected from a volunteer pool would really comply with the expressed wishes of the experimenter. The predicted number of "fully obedient" subjects was less than 1%. However, the violation here stems not from an unanticipated statistic, but rather from the ethical misconduct derived from the flagrant deception carried out throughout the experiment. Milgram's case is not helped by the fact that many additional obedience experiments were conducted over the next few years. The extent of deception in this instance was just too much, and as useful as the results have been to the present generation of social psychologists, the risks were not justified. ▪

There are other sensational accounts of ethical violations involving the use of deception in psychological research, including researchers posing as "watch queens" while recording homosexual behavior in public places and faking impending airplane crashes to observe the panic responses of innocent passengers. Frankly, however, these examples are few and old. Today, more than ever, psychologists are careful to protect the dignity and welfare of research participants.

For our model experiment, concerns over deceptive practices are nominal. Because all patients (participants) in the study will be informed of the procedures that will be used in the project, there is no need to deceive anyone.

## *Providing Participants with Information About the Study (6.18)*

a. Psychologists provide a prompt opportunity for participants to obtain appropriate information about the nature, results, and conclusions of the research, and psychologists attempt to correct any misconceptions that participants may have.
b. If scientific or humane values justify delaying or withholding this information, psychologists take reasonable measures to reduce the risk of harm.

This section of the APA *Ethics Code* makes it clear that it is the responsibility of every psychological investigator to explain in detail what the experiment was all about. For reasons I have already mentioned, on occasion the researcher may be disinclined to divulge the specifics of an experiment prior to participation because that information may prejudice the subject's performance. However, all subjects can and should be told about the ultimate aim of the project once they have completed their participation.

The term psychologists use for the information disclosure that takes place upon completion of the study is **debriefing.** The word *debriefing* has its roots in the military, originating during World War II (Blanck et al., 1992). When World War II fighter pilots returned from combat missions, they were "debriefed" to find out what they had observed, and the information they divulged was used accordingly. As currently employed in psychological research, the term *debriefing* refers to the information exchange that goes in the opposite direction. The explicit purpose of debriefing is to reassure participants that their time was not wasted and to remove any fears or apprehensions the participants may have about the project (Harris, 1988).

Another important role debriefing plays is that of instructional aid. Many people volunteer for psychological experiments because they

**debriefing**—an explanation given after the experiment is completed of the details of the experiment and the participant's role in the research

want to know more about human behavior, especially their own. For instance, a participant in a clinical experiment on the effects of assertiveness training on marital satisfaction may have a very personal interest in the results of the study. Indeed, in such cases knowing the outcome of the research may have acute benefits for the participant's interpersonal relationships. Similarly, people who are involved in a study on the advantages of mnemonic formations (tricks that improve recall) for encoding events into long-term memory may find the results from the experiment help them improve their ability to retrieve information from selected memory stores.

Debriefing also can be of value to the experimenter. During a debriefing session, information often comes out that clarifies why subjects responded the way they did. In fact, debriefing can lead investigators to completely reorient their thinking about a topic. For example, Rotheram-Borus, Koopman, and Bradley (1989) conducted a study on AIDS in adolescents, and only during the intensive debriefing sessions did it become clear that these young people had been routinely engaging in group sex (sexual intercourse with several different partners during a single encounter). Although previous questionnaires, interviews, and so forth failed to pick up this information, the debriefing sessions unveiled this important variable as it relates to the development and potentially the prevention of AIDS.

As a result, we see that the debriefing phase of the research project is an exceedingly important part of the experiment. The participant and the investigator mutually benefit from a complete disclosure of the purpose of the experiment and the specific role the individual plays in executing that experiment. It often helps to provide the participants with a written account of this information so that they can refer to it later. Such a document prepared for the model experiment we are building in this book is shown in Figure 4–5.

Finally, before leaving this section on debriefing, it should be acknowledged that debriefing may not always be successful. Consider the following situation.

# ⚛ Thinking About Research

*L*earned helplessness is a behavioral phenomenon that refers to the performance deficits observed in animals and humans following a period of exposure to an uncontrollable situation (Overmier & Seligman, 1967; Seligman, 1975). When an organism is presented with unpredictable, un-controllable aversive events, it fails to respond in a subsequent situation, even when the environment is controllable. It's like a "What difference does it make" reaction in which the experimental participant just gives up.

The learned helplessness concept has been

DEBRIEFING FORM

Name of experiment:

Name of participant:

Summary of results:

Role of participant:

Signature of principal investigator_____

**FIGURE 4-5** The debriefing form to be used in preparing a complete disclosure statement for the model experiment. The completed form will include a summary of results and an explanation of the role of the individual in the project.

invoked as a theoretical model for human depression (cf. Abramson, Seligman, & Teasdale, 1978). The belief is that depressed persons feel they cannot control their world, so they don't even try, even when they are in a position to take charge of their lives. Numerous experimental demonstrations of learned helplessness in a laboratory setting confirm the parallels between the experimental phenomenon and human psychopathology.

One problem with conducting learned helplessness research relates to the effectiveness of debriefing. The explicit aim of a learned helplessness manipulation is to induce a negative affective state. I know, because I have published several articles on this topic (Jones, Nation, & Massad, 1977; Nation, Cooney, & Gartrell, 1979; Nation & Woods, 1980). Typically, the induction phase consists of misleading the subjects during a learning task and convincing them that their failures (on unsolvable problems) are due to their own incompetencies. In many instances, the

investigator ensures that the subjects blame themselves by making statements such as "O.K. You did not do very well on those problems. These new problems are easier than the previous ones, and most people get these correct" (Nation et al., 1979, p. 125). The procedure clearly works. People really do "get down" on themselves and report increased dysphoria.

The subjects are then debriefed. The subjects are pulled aside after their participation is complete and the truth is revealed. "The experiment was rigged. The problems were not solvable. You shouldn't feel badly because you were in a 'guaranteed to fail' condition." This is the testimony of a known liar, however. At the beginning of the experiment the experimenter stated that all problems were solvable. Now the experimenter is asking the subject to trust and accept a reversal of the original statement. Do you see the problem? What is shortsighted about the experimenter's debriefing tactic? Is there anything that could be done to enhance the credibility of the seemingly untrustworthy investigator? What would you recommend in such experiments?

To date, little is known about the long-term effects produced by inducing negative mood states such as learned helplessness. Should you ever participate in such a project, give some serious and deliberate thought to ways the effectiveness of the debriefing phase of the experiment might be improved.  ▮

## WITHIN CHAPTER REVIEW AND STUDY QUESTIONS

### WHEN GUIDELINES ARE AVAILABLE: ETHICAL PRINCIPLES OF PSYCHOLOGISTS AND CODE OF CONDUCT (APA)

1. When designing an experiment, it is important at the outset to establish ethical guidelines. Identify some of the reasons the planning stage of an experiment is so important with respect to preventing ethical violations.
2. A panel of experts who make judgments about the ethical treatment of human subjects is called:
   a. a review committee
   b. an institutional review board
   c. an oversight committee
3. Why is informed consent essential for human subject research? Was informed consent obtained in the infamous Tuskegee study? Could it have been?
4. Define the following terms: volunteer participants, confidentiality, demand characteristics, debriefing.

## RESEARCH USING ANIMALS AS SUBJECTS

If you look back at ethical standard 6 of the APA *Ethics Code* (Figure 4–1), you will see that section 6.20 deals with the "Care and Use of Animals in Research." Figure 4–6 lists the individual subsections of this very important ethical commitment.

Many people wonder why psychologists use animals in research. This is a reasonable question which has several reasonable answers. Among them is the fact there are many psychologically relevant issues that require invasive procedures. When I use the term *invasive* I refer to events such as surgery, chemical injections, and neuroanatomical lesions, each of which may bring discomfort and produce irreversible tissue damage. Of course, it can and has been argued

6.20  Care and Use of Animals in Research

(a) Psychologists who conduct research involving animals treat them humanely.

(b) Psychologists acquire, care for, use, and dispose of animals in compliance with current federal, state, and local laws and regulations, and with professional standards.

(c) Psychchologists trained in research methods and experienced in the care of laboratory animals supervise all procedures involving animals and are responsible for ensuring appropriate consideration of their comfort, health, and humane treatment.

(d) Psychologists ensure that all individuals using animals under their supervision have received instruction in research methods and in the care, maintenance, and handling of the species being used, to the extent appropriate to their role.

(e) Responsibilities and activities of individuals assisting in a research project are consistent with their respective competencies.

(f) Psychologists make reasonable efforts to minimize the discomfort, infection, illness, and pain of animal subjects.

(g) A procedure subjecting animals to pain, stress, or privation is used only when an alternative procedure is unavailable and the goal is justified by its prospective scientific, educational, or applied value.

(h) Surgical procedures are performed under appropriate anesthesia; techniques to avoid infection and minimize pain are followed during and after surgery.

(i) When it is appropriate that the animal's life be terminated, it is done rapidly, with an effort to minimize pain, and in accordance with accepted procedures.

**FIGURE 4–6** The subsections of section 6.20 of the APA *Ethics Code* dealing with the "Care and Use of Animals in Research"

---

that animals deserve the same consideration as their human counterparts and that exploiting animals is a form of speciesism. Every investigator who uses animals as subjects must reconcile this dilemma, and ultimately it becomes a question of risk/gain. Are the expected scientific, educational, or applied implications of the research sufficiently great that they justify the use of the procedures (subsection g in Figure 4–6)? Are there any alternatives? In many instances there are no alternatives to the use of animals as subjects, and yet there is a clear demand for information in the area.

For instance, consider the exciting work that is being done in the area of psychoimmunology. It is now apparent that under conditions of prolonged stress that animals and humans become more vulnerable to disease because of emotionally based disturbances in immune function (see Ballieux, 1995). Biopsychologists have determined one mechanism central to this curious relation involves the body's endogenous opiates. When a person grieves over the death of a spouse, for example, the body releases internal pain-controllers such as beta-endorphins. This is an adaptive response because it helps a person get through rough times. However, the endorphins also bind to the natural killer (NK) cells in the immune system, rendering them inactive (Shavit et al., 1984). Consequently, elevated stress levels put an individual at risk because the body's defense system is compromised.

**animal use protocol**—an approved account of all aspects of a given study involving animal subjects that is on record with an oversight committee

For this line of research, animals simply must be used. Researchers must track the biochemical changes that occur during periods of apprehension and anxiety and determine the impact of these changes on survival. With an increased understanding of the interactive relation between psychological stress and immune function, lives can be saved, and I refer to animal as well as human lives. If we better understand the kind of environmental events that threaten animal populations, we can move to install buffers against those events. In the final analysis, all organisms benefit from this type of invasive work, which can only be accomplished using animals as subjects.

In addition to the issues associated with mandated surgical or chemical manipulations, animals may be used in psychological research because of time considerations. Where longitudinal issues are a concern, the investigator may want to follow the development of the individual subject over the course of a lifetime. With human subjects, monitoring long-term behaviors is expensive and the data are slow in coming (Benjamin et al., 1994). With the relatively more compressed lifespan of an animal, for example the standard laboratory rat, more information is available quickly. Studies on reproductive habits, maternal behavior, reactions to aversive situations such as intruders or predators, feeding, drug self-administration, pollution, and crowding are other cases where animal use is recommended.

The balance of coverage here indicates that psychologists justify using animals because findings from animal research can help improve the quality of life for humans and animals alike. However, it should be recognized that many researchers study animals simply because they are interested in animal behavior. That is, these investigators are not concerned about the applied implications of their experiments or whether or not their results will help anyone, and they attempt to provide nothing more than a descriptive account of what a given animal does under a set of established conditions (see Gould, 1991, for a more expansive treatment of the value of research in the dynamics of animal behavior). This relates to my comments on basic versus applied research in Chapter 1. There is considerable gain just from knowing more about the world around us. Knowing the intricacies of animal behavior is sufficient unto itself and need not be justified on the basis of "meaningfulness."

Whether or not animals are observed in a laboratory or field setting, be assured that an approved **animal use protocol** is on record. The animal use protocol is a detailed description of the procedures to be used, the number of animals that will be needed, the housing arrangements that have been made, and a statement of assurance that animals rights will be respected. While each of the issues covered in ethical standard 6.20 of the APA *Ethics Code* (refer to Figure 4–6) is likely to be addressed in the animal use protocol, technically speaking APA does not govern animal treatment in the United States. This responsibility belongs with the American Association for Accreditation of Laboratory Animal Care (AAALAC). This national organization works with the institutional review group such as the University Laboratory Animal Care Committee at my university, Texas A&M University, and performs the same function and services as the IRB discussed in the earlier section on human subject research. AAALAC accreditation is extremely difficult to get and equally hard to keep. Its standards include such items as daily records of room temperature, weekly microbial assays of housing areas, maintenance of a viral-free atmosphere, routine training courses for caretakers responsible for the welfare of the animals, and a detailed specification of what constitutes appropriate laboratory attire. Although AAALAC approval is not required presently for NIH or NSF funding, these latter agencies are moving in that direction, and it is virtually certain that in the future only accredited laboratories will be able to compete for federal grant dollars. The product will be an even better research environment that protects the rights of animals.

## The Animal Rights Movement

I would be remiss if I failed to say something about the impact of the animal rights movement in North America. Beginning several decades ago and peaking in the 1980s, a collective voice expressing concern and outright horror over the treatment of laboratory animals was heard in the United States and Canada. Animal rights activists who were sensitive to the documented abuse of animals in certain facilities launched an aggressive and focused campaign that forever changed the climate of laboratory research. Many of these people who took part in the demonstrations and "liberation exercises" were, and are, malcontents who have little awareness of the more central issues in this arena. However, many are caring, dedicated participants who have channeled their energies into a worthwhile cause.

The downside of the animal rights movement is that a few of the more radical elements have corrupted the peaceful policies of change that form the agenda for the more general group. It is one thing to insist on improved living conditions and more humane treatment of all laboratory animals, but something else again to charge into a facility releasing animals into the wild (many of which have no chance of surviving outside the laboratory), destroying thousands of dollars worth of equipment, and physically attacking employees. These acts accomplish nothing positive and only drive more moderate types from the fold.

Largely because of these extremists, in 1992 the United States Congress approved a bill (H.R. 2407) which provides tough penalties for criminal acts against animal research facilities. Perpetrators are subject to fines, imprisonment up to 1 year, or both when the economic damage exceeds $10,000. If there is bodily harm to another individual, the consequences become even more dire (e.g., life imprisonment). Of course, this legislation is designed to preempt assaults on laboratory facilities that comply with federal regulations and therein permit scientists to conduct important investigations in an unencumbered atmosphere.

Unfortunately, all of this obscures the positive achievements of the animal rights movement. Without a doubt, there is a greater consciousness today and more respect for animal subjects on the part of research personnel. The outcry from a concerned public has caused scientists to review more carefully what they do. However, when an investigator who has spent 7 years scrutinizing retinal deterioration in an aging primate loses a subject to an uninformed vigilante group, it is a travesty. The public and scientific communities must work together and define a responsible treatment policy that protects animal rights and permits high-quality research.

## WITHIN CHAPTER REVIEW AND STUDY QUESTIONS

### RESEARCH USING ANIMALS AS SUBJECTS

1. Why do psychologists feel it necessary to use animals in experimental research? What is your position on this topic?
2. What is the animal research counterpart to the IRB in human research?
   a. the animal use protocol
   b. AAALAC
   c. the institutional review committee
   d. b and c collectively perform the functions of the IRB

## The Model Experiment

The content of this chapter makes it clear that the rights of participants are foremost in the minds of psychology researchers. In the model experiment we are constructing in this book, the following applications were made: a plan was implemented to minimize risks for participants, professional training parameters for therapists involved with the treatment manipulations were established, an informed consent document was developed, and a form for debriefing at the completion of the project was identified.

It is appropriate to take care of these matters early in the research project. The welfare of subjects is a top priority. Before proceeding with the experiment proper, we must feel secure that we have done all we can to protect our participants (in this case, chronically ill pediatric patients). Next, we consider measurement and description.

# Measurement and Description

At this stage of the model experiment we are systematically building as we move through this text. We have accomplished the following. An appreciation of the scientific approach to conducting research is evident, and the traditional experimental methodology that is tied to this framework has been set forth. Additionally, a hypothesis concerning the anticipated relation between chronological age and the therapeutic effectiveness of a cognitive intervention strategy has been developed. Finally, several ethical issues inherent in any research project involving human subjects have been addressed.

With this foundation, we begin the "hands on" tasks of preparing materials for data collection, making decisions about what equipment items are needed, and selecting the most favorable vehicles for characterizing the data. Measurement and description are essential elements of any successful experiment. Studied choices of the tools of research protect against folly and waste. As with any building project, if the inappropriate tools are chosen, the work becomes more cumbersome and the product less compelling.

In the next section, I cover four standard scales of measurement: nominal, ordinal, interval, and ratio. Each of these scales is important to psychological research, and some understanding of the differences between and among them is necessary before we can make informed judgments about which measurement devices are most suited to be included in our model experiment. Keep in mind as we review measurement scales that we are not dealing with qualitative issues. That is, one type of scale is not necessarily better than another, even though there may be profound differences in their respective levels of sophistication. Rather, it is a matter of selecting the scale, or combination of scales, that best suits the needs of the research.

## SCALES OF MEASUREMENT

In all cases, scaling involves a level of transformation. When an industrial/organizational psychologist observes cooperation among team members of a work station, the psychologist must have some way to transform the information. You can talk about cooperation, you can even describe events that promote it, but you cannot subject cooperation to analysis—not directly. Similarly, when an investigator studies the foraging practices of the Sandhill crane in a natural setting, not much of a systematic nature can be made of simple visual observations. However, cooperative behavior on the job and food selection in cranes can be converted to numbers. By quantitatively representing the behavior, a greater understanding of the phenomena under investigation can be achieved. Scaling permits this quantitative transformation (Roberts, 1979). Let's begin with the most elementary scale and proceed to the most elaborate.

## *Nominal Scales*

**Nominal scales** of measurement use numbers or symbols to identify distinct categories. In essence, nominal measurements "name" mutually exclusive objects, events, people, or any other collective stimulus category in which differences can be detected. With this most basic scale of measurement, there is no attempt to specify directional differences or even to say *how* the items differ. You cannot say that one event or object is better, harder, more accommodating, or more anything. What you can say is that the objects or events are not the same; they fall into separate categories.

Examples of nominal scales are the uniform numbers of the Boston Bruin ice hockey team, military occupational status, or taxonomy in biology. I assert that each of us can distinguish between a Bombardier beetle and a Graylag goose. Given a dozen of each, I bet we would have no difficulty clustering the organisms by physical appearance and disposition. However, we could say nothing at this point other than one is a bug and the other a bird. At least this is true if we adopt only a nominal measurement scale. You name only and make no statements about how the objects may differ along some dimension.

Think for a moment about including a nominal scale in the model experiment we are putting together. Is there such a scale that is either overtly or tacitly operational in our age/intervention study? Have we used a nominal scale in designating participants? Indeed we have. Recall that ours is an experiment on the relative effectiveness of cognitive-based therapy on very young and older children who are chronically ill. The label *chronically ill,* which identifies the patient as a prospective subject in the experiment, illustrates a nominal scale. There is no attempt to characterize the degree or severity of the affliction, no attempt to classify the children according to the amount of pain they are experiencing, no attempt at all to say how the children differ. We simply place the children in a category of *chronically ill* based on set criteria. So, as with our model experiment, nominal scales in psychological research are often employed in inconspicuous but important ways.

## *Ordinal Scales*

In addition to assigning a name to an object or event, **ordinal scales** specify differences along some dimension. For example, if two rocks clash with sufficient force, one of the rocks will break the other. Invoking an

**nominal scales**—measurement scales that name events and place them in distinct categories

**ordinal scales**—measurement scales that name events and specify differences along some continuum

**interval scale**—measurement scale that names events, specifies differences along some continuum, expresses how much difference exists between scores, but has no absolute zero point

ordinal scale of measurement, it is appropriate to say that one rock is "harder" than the other. Similarly, when a public official declares that "community health services are better than they have been in recent years," a statement about ordinal events is made.

One of the distinguishing features of ordinal scales is that while differences along some dimension are indicated, there is no attempt to specify how much difference exists between the items being compared. For example, when someone pronounces the summer "hotter than I can remember," there is no suggestion of just how much warmer the summer may be. A counterpart laboratory example is the degree of impairment caused by applying a toxic chemical agent. When a biopsychologist administers kainic acid to the rat brain and examines the extent of hippocampal tissue damage, often no claims are made about how much damage the brain sustains (Kasof et al., 1995). The presence or absence of a lesion (tissue damage) is simply proclaimed. In this sense an ordinal scale of measurement is used.

Another characteristic of ordinal scales is that the distances between values are unequal. Consider the rankings of the top tennis professionals in the world. The Number 1 player is believed to be superior to the Number 2 player, the Number 2 is judged to be better than the Number 3 player, and on it goes. No one is likely to argue that the qualitative differences separating Number 1 and Number 2 are the same as those separating Number 2 and Number 3. The top two players in the world may be very close in terms of skill, and no one else can touch either of them. In such a situation you have ordinal assignment because you can specify directional differences, but you cannot go any further.

Because of the unequal distances between scale values, ordinal scales are most useful when the data are separated by dramatic differences. For an investigator interested in the effects of noise pollution on stress, for example, it may suffice to identify people as "high stress" or "low stress." By discarding people in the mid-range from the sample, the experimenter can feel secure about the ordinal classification scheme.

## Interval Scales

When the data have all the properties of the previously mentioned scales, and the distances between scale values are equal, the data conform to an **interval scale.** Interval scales name events, specify differences along some dimension, and express how much difference exists between any two values on the scale. Regardless of where you are on the scale, a constant separation between scale values occurs as you move from one point to the next. Accordingly, as an animal's core body temperature drops toward room temperature as a result of receiving a heavy dose of alcohol (Hirvonen & Huttunen, 1995), each 1° C decrease is equivalent in magnitude.

Traditionally, one of the distinguishing features of ordinal scales is that they possess no absolute zero point. This means it is impossible to have a nonscore on the test or measurement scale. It is easy to see that many psychometric instruments psychologists use fall into this category. Consider the social introversion subscale of the popular Minnesota Multiphasic Personality Inventory (MMPI), for example. You may not describe yourself as a "social lion," but you will not register a *0* on the social introversion dimension of the MMPI, because a value of *0* is a theoretical point which cannot occur. On such scales the zero point simply provides a convenient anchor for successively increasing values which take on genuine meaning.

As noted elsewhere (Benjamin, Hopkins, & Nation, 1994), psychologists often face tests where it is unclear what type of scale is being used. Return to the MMPI and the social introversion scale. Let's say Jamail completes the test and obtains a score corresponding to the 90th percentile. Kalita takes the identical test and scores in the 70th percentile. Despite arguments that the MMPI achieves an interval scale of measurement, it is difficult to accept that the 20 percentile points separating Jamail and Kalita equal the 20 percentile points separating Kalita from the median (the 50th percentile), because higher percentiles mean increasing greater distinction.

Extreme scores carry added baggage, and this is true for many other psychological tests. Certainly, the 50-point separation between *550* and *600* on the quantitative component of the Graduate Record Exam (GRE) carries more distinction than the comparable point spread between *500* and *550*. It seems, then, that the scores on such tests are unequal. Therefore, one of the key assumptions of interval scaling is violated. Still, we can say how much difference exists between two scores on such tests, so it is not really an ordinal data set either. As a rule, when the situation is uncertain, most psychologists assume that the more sophisticated scale applies because more elaborate statistical manipulations are possible. Nevertheless, the investigator needs to be aware of the ambiguity here.

## *Ratio Scales*

The most sophisticated form of measurement is the **ratio scale.** The ratio scale has all the features of an interval scale, but it has an absolute zero point. Typically, ratio scales apply only in physical measurement. The distance of a discus throw, the height of a building, or the volume of fluid in a container are all examples of ratio scales. Psychologists, for example, use ratio scales to measure motor impairment in the "righting

**ratio scale**—measurement scale that names events, specifies differences in direction along some continuum, expresses how much difference exists between scores, and has an absolute zero point

reflex" where animals are dropped upside down from increasing heights. Similarly, researchers who record heart rate as a dependent measure employ a ratio scale. (Recall from Chapter 3 that heart rate is one of the dependent variables we have opted to use in our model experiment.) Much of the time, however, psychological investigators use measurement mechanisms that do not assume absolute zero points. It is nonsensical to talk about someone having "no intelligence" or to suggest that an individual's degree of social competency is *0*. In these cases, it is more appropriate to think in terms of interval measurement, which is what most psychologists are likely to deal with.

Even though the bulk of psychological data are based on interval scaling, inappropriate claims of ratio characteristics are often made. For instance, a pain specialist may report that a technique can reduce headache by one half. This, of course, is a statement predicated on ratio values, and it assumes that headache measurements have the properties of metric data or other physical records. Because pain is a psychological dimension that involves perception, attention-related phenomena, cultural and emotional elements, and a host of other factors, it is probably a mistake to make such an assertion. Although it is acceptable to casually refer to ratio measurement in such cases, technically it is not correct to do so.

## WITHIN CHAPTER REVIEW AND STUDY QUESTIONS

### SCALES OF MEASUREMENT

1. Define each of the following items and give an example of a dependent measure on which the scale would be used.
   a. nominal scale
   b. ordinal scale
   c. interval scale
   d. ratio scale
2. Which scale of measurement do psychology researchers employ most commonly?

# TYPES OF MEASUREMENT

As discussed in Chapter 3, there are several different types of dependent measures, and selecting a measurement technique for recording these measures is an essential part of the data collection process. I cover three types of measurement approaches: covert measurement, empirical measurement, and self-report measurement (see Figure 5–1 for a summary).

## Covert Measurement

As scientists, psychologists sometimes face the awkward predicament of attempting to characterize unobservable phenomena in tangible terms. This means they must label something they cannot see or hear, measure it, and report on it as if it corresponded to an established reality. Obviously, this presents a challenge to the psychological investigator.

**covert measures**—measurements of events that cannot be observed directly

Measurements of events we cannot observe directly are referred to as **covert measures**. When covert phenomena are measured, an indirect estimate of a change in the value of the dependent variable must be made. This concept can be illustrated by mental imagery studies. Imagery is often described as something akin to "pictures in the head." Actually, this description is somewhat misleading because sensory modalities other than vision can be used to form images. In any event, although we cannot measure image formation, we know it occurs and we can index it covertly.

For instance, Shepard and Metzger (1988) were able to measure people's ability to rotate visual objects in a three-dimensional space by having them look at pictures and then match those pictures to rotated patterns. Note that in such experiments the phenomenon under investigation is not the ability to select the matched pattern per se. Rather, the aim is to get at the underlying cognitive operation on which the match is based. A simpler test of a covert process is determining "object permanence" in a 10-month-old child. When rolling a ball to the child, you suddenly roll it under a sofa. If the child attempts to retrieve the ball that is hidden from view, he or she must have some mental representation of the

| | |
|---|---|
| **Covert measurement** | This measurement gauges events that cannot be observed directly. Because the events cannot be measured directly, an indirect estimate of the event must be obtained from some other dependent variable believed to be linked to the covert event. |
| **Empirical measurement** | This measurement is based on experience and is taken from events that are directly observable. |
| **Self-report measurement** | An individual measurement provides this measurement based on the way she or he is feeling or what he or she may be thinking. Self-report data sometimes reveal information other measurement techniques are likely to miss. |

**FIGURE 5–1** Three types of measurement

empirical measures—measurements of directly observable changes in behavior that permit recordings

object (i.e., object permanence has been achieved). Once again, the objective is to measure a cognitive event (the image of the ball) that cannot be observed directly. Thus, a covert measurement is made via indirect recording.

Covert measurements are also useful in monitoring the effectiveness of certain psychotherapy techniques and other procedures where internal (cognitive) manipulations are performed (Speigler & Guevremont, 1993). Because so many psychological events fall into the unobservable category, covert measures are integral to the overall research picture in psychology.

## *Empirical Measurement*

Unlike covert procedures, **empirical measures** refer to records that are made from directly observable changes in behavior. Although covert measures have yielded some of the most interesting and credible scientific results in psychological research, many psychologists are prejudiced to favor empirical recordings that are based on what you can feel, see, hear, and so forth. This is not to say that one type of measure is better than the other, but rather that the historical bias in science is to put faith in direct observation.

There are many forms of empirical measurement. Recording the number of times a rat retraces an alley in a maze or tracking the number of correct word pairs recalled in a verbal learning task are examples of empirical measures. Similarly, measures of neural conduction velocity or cortisol levels in blood involve empirical data. The advantage of such measurements is that there is no guesswork, no estimation or inference. When you see a bystander assist a person (confederate) in distress, you don't have to wonder what happened. You observe it directly and can be sure your record is authentic.

In Chapter 3, I mentioned two types of empirical dependent variables: behavioral and biological. In addition, recall that a decision was made to use each type of measure in our model experiment. Specifically, a behavioral rating scale and heart rate were selected as measures of stress and anxiety.

The OSBD was chosen as a behavioral measure. This scale (the behavioral categories are shown in Figure 5–2) yields a total distress score based on records of observable behaviors such as crying and nail biting. Heart rate is a biological measure that is taken from an EKG similar to the one shown in Figure 5–3.

Including a behavioral and biological measure in our model experiment is essential to fully evaluating the impact of our experimental manipulations. If a treatment intervention has a positive effect on stress reactivity in our model

Cry
Scream
Physical restraint
Verbal resistance
Requests emotional support
Muscular rigidity
Verbal fear
Verbal pain
Flail
Nervous behavior
Information seeking

**FIGURE 5–2** The behavioral categories of the OSBD, one of the instruments to be used in the model experiment we are constructing in this text.

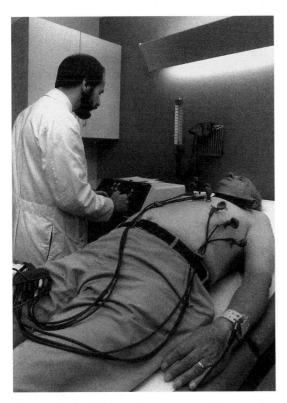

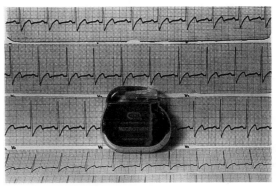

**FIGURE 5–3** An EKG at work and records from an EKG

**self-report inventory**—a measure taken from an individual, based on their own account of how they feel or what they are thinking

study, it will be evident from these measures. Still, we need additional information that we cannot obtain through empirical recording. We need to know more than just what the patient is doing; we need to know how the patient feels. Psychologists have known for many years that the best way to get this information is to simply ask for it. This approach involves self-report measurement.

## Self-Report Measures

A **self-report inventory** is an assessment instrument that measures what people think or feel based on their accounts of their conditions. There are hundreds of self-report inventories ranging in size, complexity, and orientation. Included in the long list of psychological measurements that can be taken with such instruments are self-estimates of feelings of aggression, attitudes toward minorities, perception of physical attractiveness, assertiveness, and even evaluation of the teaching effectiveness of a college professor. Many phenomena at the human level can be indexed via a self-report instrument, and the information yield in such cases is often of great use to the investigator.

There are different types of self-report inventories. One of the more popular inventories is the rating scale. In a rating scale subjects are asked to indicate where they fall along some dimension by choosing a value that corresponds to what they think or feel. An example of a rating scale is the Sports Inventory for Pain (SIP) reproduced in Figure 5–4. This scale was designed to measure how an individual athlete feels about pain and competition. A statement such as, "I owe it to myself and those around me to compete even when my pain is bad," is presented, and the athlete is asked to circle the response that most accurately characterizes how he or she feels about the statement. The response alternatives range from "strongly agree" to "strongly disagree." A numerical code can be used to transform the responses to data values that can be subjected to statistical analyses. For example, a "strongly agree" response might be scored as *1,* an "agree" response might be scored as *2,* and so on. Because R. Likert (1932) was one of the first people to successfully use this self-report methodology, scales of this sort are often referred to as Likert-type scales.

There are a couple of additional points to make about the SIP rating scale shown in Figure 5–4. Notice that the instructions at the top of the scale tell the respondent to select the alternative that ". . . best describes your feelings at this time." Because some traits and attitudes are relatively static and enduring, an individual's position on the scale is not likely to change much. In other cases, however, scale values may shift sharply depending on what the person is feeling. An example is someone's responses to the Beck Depression Inventory

## SPORTS INVENTORY FOR PAIN

Michael C. Meyers, PhD, Anthony Bourgeois, PhD
Arnold LeUnes, EdD

KEY _____

SCORES

RAW

T-SCORE

| | | | | |
|---|---|---|---|---|
| COP | COG | CAT | AVD | BOD |

Below is a list of statements that describe the way athletes often feel about pain and it's influence on competition. Please take your time and read each statement carefully, so that we may find out how you feel toward pain. Then fill in one circle to the right of each statement that best describes your feelings at this time. Please answer honestly. There are no right or wrong answers.

*(Response columns: Strongly Disagree — Disagree — Agree — Strongly Agree, scored 1 2 3 4 5)*

| Statement | Scale |
|---|---|
| ..e pain as a challenge and don't ..t bother me. | COP |
| ..e it to myself and those around ..o compete even when my pain is | COP |
| ..in pain, I tell myself it ..'t hurt. | COG |
| ..injured, I pray for the pain ..top. | CAT |
| ..feel pain during an athletic ..vity, it's probably a sign that ..doing damage to my body. | AVD |
| ..ve little or no trouble with ..scles twitching or jumping. | BOD |
| ..his point, I am more interested ..eturning to athletic competition in trying to stop this pain. | COP |
| ..in pain, I imagine that the ..is outside of my body. | COG |
| ..ain is terrible and I feel ..never going to get better. | CAT |
| ..uld perform as well as ever if ..ain would go away. | AVD |
| ..not worry about being injured. | BOD |
| ..is just a part of competition. | COP |
| ..hurt, I play mental games ..myself to keep my mind off ..pain. | COG |

14. When in pain, I worry all the time about whether it will end. — CAT
15. I have to be careful not to make my pain worse. — AVD
16. I seldom or never have dizzy spells or headaches. — BOD
17. When I am hurt, I just go on as if nothing happened. — COP
18. When in pain, I replay in my mind pleasant athletic experiences from my past. — COG
19. If in pain, I often feel I can't stand it anymore. — CAT
20. The worse thing that could happen to me is to injure/reinjure myself. — AVD
21. I seldom notice minor injuries. — BOD
22. When injured, I tell myself to be tough and carry on despite the pain. — COP
23. When hurt, I do anything to get my mind off the pain. — COG
24. When hurt, I tell myself I can't let the pain stand in the way of what I want to do. — COP
25. No matter how bad pain gets, I know I can handle it. — COP

*(Response columns scored 1 2 3 4 5)*

**FIGURE 5–4** The Sports Inventory for Pain (SIP). (From Meyers, Bourgeois, and LeUnes, 1991.) Copyright 1991 by M. Meyers. Reprinted with permission.

(BDI). You may fill out the self-report one way on one occasion and in quite a different way on some other day, say when you are in a "blue funk," as we all are episodically. Because of the nature of the differences in changing and unchanging feelings and ideas, it is important that the rating scale give explicit instructions about the time period the respondent is supposed to deal with.

Also notice that the instructions on the SIP inform the respondent that there "... are no right or wrong answers." This may not be much of an issue in this case, but it can bias responses in others, such as one in which a personality inventory is administered (see Anastasi, 1988, for a review of these types of self-report scales). As a researcher, you want honest, consistent reactions from your subjects that accurately portray their feelings. If people think they must try to project a positive image (that there are right and wrong answers), then they will generate corrupt records. For this reason the investigator is obliged to remind the respondent of the inherent neutrality of the rating scale.

Along with rating scales, overt behavioral measures can be used as vehicles for self-disclosure. As an example, consider the self-report measure we have selected for use in our model experiment.

In the experiment we are building in this book, the "fear thermometer" shown in Figure 5–5 will be shown to the patient (research participant). As mentioned in Chapter 3, this technique is based on the Self-Report Measure of Fear and Pain developed by Katz et al. in 1982. In order to index the child's estimation of the level of discomfort he or she feels "at this very moment," the child will be asked to place a finger at the point on the thermometer which corresponds to his or her

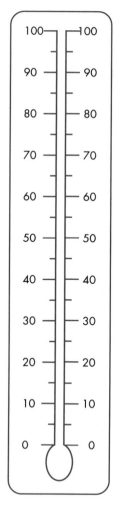

FIGURE 5–5 The "fear thermometer" used in self-reports of stress and anxiety. The children are asked to point to the places that show how much they hurt (how anxious they are), with *0* meaning "no hurt" and *100* meaning "most hurt possible." (From Katz et al., 1982.) Copyright © 1982 by the Children's Hospital of Los Angeles. Reprinted with permission.

level of fear. In this case, an overt physical movement rather than a verbal or written report is used as the self-report measure.

Of course, as I mentioned in Chapter 4, one problem you always face when asking people for personal information is the truthfulness of their comments or responses. When people have preconceived ideas about how they should report, they may present idealized profiles of themselves or someone else. For example, in the case of the fear thermometer test we plan to use in our experiment, a child may be extremely fearful and apprehensive, yet feel compelled to display courage. This is not what the investigator wants. Recall that the ultimate purpose of the project is to determine more precisely which variables contribute to successful therapy in chronically ill children of different ages and to therein improve the children's chances for receiving real benefits. This cannot be accomplished when the child does not give you an accurate self-report. With a dishonest response, you don't know what you have. Even with the appropriate inducements, control statements, cautions, and so on, errors will creep into self-report data. Accordingly, when possible it is a good idea to include other measures to corroborate the self-report profile, as we have done here (behavioral and biological dependent measures will also be recorded).

## WITHIN CHAPTER REVIEW AND STUDY QUESTIONS

### TYPES OF MEASUREMENT

1. Measures that are based on indirect estimates of a change in unobservable phenomena are called:
   a. covert measures
   b. empirical measures
   c. self-report measures
2. Give three examples of empirical measures. What empirical measures are we using in our model experiment?
3. List the two types of self-report inventories mentioned in the text and provide examples of each type that are not identified in the discussion. What are the relative strengths and weaknesses of self-report inventories?

## MEASUREMENT VALIDITY

When considering the type of measurements that are to be taken in an experiment, one must ask the question, "Is this measure going to give me what I want?" As we have seen, many different types of measures are available to the

**validity**—the extent to which a measure actually measures the intended value

**face validity**—the surface-level validity of a measure; the extent to which a measure looks like it measures what it is supposed to measure

investigator, some of which yield sophisticated records and detailed information that can only come from precise instruments. Although obtaining results is critical, the real issue is the appropriateness of those results. Does the measure tell me what I need to know to answer the central questions I have posed? When an experimenter is concerned with the purchasing habits of consumers in the Midwest, for example, it is hardly useful for the experimenter to know the individual's height and weight, political orientation, or favorite color. This information may be of value to someone else, but the data are incidental to the purpose of assessing consumer behavior.

The issue of selecting a measure that is appropriate for the study to be conducted deals with **validity.** Validity refers to the degree to which a measure actually measures what you intend to measure. The validity of a measure not only tells you *what* your scores mean, it tells you *how well* you have done with respect to selecting a variable that provides useful information (Anastasi, 1988).

When a measure is valid, it reports data along only one dimension and prevents the investigator from making erroneous conclusions about the nature of results. Consider what could happen in a study on the effects of age on artistic expression. The researcher may devise a test of artistic skill that strongly depends on the mechanical drawing ability of the subject. In such a case, performance is tied directly to motor coordination, which naturally improves with age, and it may or may not be associated with an underlying artistic talent. If you intend to assess artistic ability, then do so, and don't permit other, intrusive measures to invalidate your results.

As summarized in Figure 5–6, there are different types of validity. I mention four types as they relate to measurement selection and use: face validity, content validity, construct validity, and criterion-related validity.

## Face Validity

**Face validity** refers to the extent to which, on a surface level, a measure appears to measure what it is supposed to measure. That is, when a measure "looks like it makes sense," it has face validity. Although measures of face validity would seem to be easily identified, the concept may be deceptively simple. For example, several years ago I devised an experiment aimed at examining the relation between frustration and aggression (see Nation & Cooney, 1982, for the full report). Using college students as subjects, I induced strong frustrative reactions in the participants by placing them on an extinction schedule on which it was impossible to obtain the rewards they wanted. This involved building an elaborate piece of equipment which permitted the subjects to move dowels through a maze. If the subjects were successful, they would garner tokens they

| Face validity | When a measure seems to measure what you intended it to measure, when the measure looks like it makes sense, it has face validity. Face validity often makes results more believable to an unsophisticated audience. |
| --- | --- |
| Content validity | A measure has good content validity when it reflects all elements of an underlying behavioral distribution. This type of validity is concerned with representing the selected measure. |
| Construct validity | Construct validity addresses the degree to which a measure provides information useful to understanding some fundamental hypothetical idea. |
| Criterion-related validity | This form of validity yields information about how well the scores of one measure correlate with scores from a second measure. This type of validity is extremely important for psychometrics and psychological testing. |

**FIGURE 5–6 Different types of measurement validity**

could later exchange for a highly valued reward. Concurrent with this task, the subjects had to turn off a loud noise that activated every minute. They could turn the noise off with a "nonaggressive button push" or with an "aggressive pad smash." The idea was that when subjects did well on the maze component, they would respond nonaggressively and prefer the button. Conversely, when the maze task was rigged to make the subjects unsuccessful (the extinction condition), it was predicted that the resulting frustration and anger would lead the subjects to behave aggressively and choose the foam rubber pad.

Indeed, this is exactly what happened. During extinction, in tandem with appreciable cursing, equipment kicking, and epithets hurled in the direction of the experimenter (me), the subjects switched from what was apparently a nonaggressive button press to an aggressive pad strike. In terms of face validity, this experiment seemed grounded in bedrock. But how valid was the pad strike measure, really? May it have been that I was actually measuring some dimension of human behavior other than aggression? The answer was clearly yes.

It occurred to me that I might be looking at an extinction-induced shift from preferred responding to nonpreferred responding. That is, the unsuccessful maze performance may have caused people to "try something different." If so, my pad strike was an invalid measure of aggression. I explored this idea by running another experiment (Experiment 4, Nation & Cooney, 1982) which offered a nonpreferred knob turn as an alternative to the button press. The participants did not choose the knob during extinction on the maze problem, however, which confirmed my original suspicion that the pad strike was indeed a valid measure of aggression. As you can see, however, face validity is not always trustworthy.

**validity coefficient**—a statistical expression of the correlation between a measure and some other recordable event

**content validity**—the extent to which a measure covers a broad class of behaviors or characteristics

Technically, it is not possible to determine the degree of face validity. That is, unlike with other more objective measures of validity, with face validity it is not possible to calculate a **validity coefficient.** A validity coefficient expresses the statistical correlation between a measure and some other recordable event (Armstrong, 1995). As a rule, the greater the value of the validity coefficient, the better the measure at yielding meaningful information. However, with face validity there are no values to correlate with some other external criteria because all you do is guess that something "looks right."

Then why even talk about face validity? Why would a research scientist be interested in something so scientifically nonconfirmable? Because that something is a public relations move. After all, the purpose of the research is to inform, and this means you attempt to sell an idea. You can sell an idea better when the measurements seem to make sense in a purely superficial, unscientific way. For example, medical school applicants would likely be puzzled if they were told their admission to medical school was contingent on their performance in a gymnastics competition. In comparison, basing their admission on grades in biology and chemistry courses would be more believable. Face validity is important because it attaches credibility to the research.

## Content Validity

**Content validity** refers to the extent to which a measure covers a broad class of behaviors or characteristics. Rarely do psychologists study a behavioral or mental event that is purely unidimensional. Rather, most psychological phenomena exist as arrays, complex miniature universes of basic physical, emotional, and cognitive elements. As a result, when psychologists choose to examine specific events, they must be careful to adopt measures that sample from each region of the measurement universe and to do so proportionally.

 Think about the measures we have selected for our model experiment. Recall that the objective of our study is to determine the effects age has on the effectiveness of different forms of treatment for chronically ill children. To achieve satisfactory content validity, we need measures that will yield information about the entire domain of stress reactivity. We need to include records of observable and unobservable dimensions of stress. We also need an index of every aspect of the way the child (patient) reacts. Have we accomplished this? Do you think the scores that will become available from the OSBD (see Chapter 3) will have good content validity? How about the other measures we plan to use? How valid are they?

On the whole, we can feel fairly secure that we enjoy good content validity in the experiment we are constructing in this text. We have a sufficient range of dependent measures and they seem to cover most dimensions of stress, including both overt behavioral corollaries and self-perceptions of the participants' (patients') feelings. Although we appear to have the representation that we seek, even with fair samples of what we intend to measure, we must exercise caution not to overgeneralize. That is, we must maintain an awareness that the content of our measures are valid only under the conditions imposed on our experiment. Other experimental conditions may demand a different sample of behaviors and thus dictate the use of altogether different measurements.

## *Construct Validity*

Because so much of psychological research is theoretically driven, individual investigators often finds themselves asking the question, "Do my data tell me anything about the nature of the hypothetical process that formed the rationale for the experiment in the first place?" The aim in such cases is to provide information that will either confirm or refute a particular doctrine. To the extent that a measure maps a specific hypothetical trait, that measure is said to have **construct validity.** Construct validity, then, refers to how well a measure empirically matches an idea. As I mentioned in Chapter 2, the hypothesis is the starting point for psychological research, and most of the time the hypothesis is generated by a particular theoretical formulation. It follows that the experiment must address the specific concepts of the theory. In this regard construct validity is essential.

Historically, the term *construct validity* was first used officially in 1954 when it was introduced in the *Technical Recommendations for Psychological Tests and Diagnostic Techniques.* The following year, Cronbach and Meehl (1955) advanced the concept by formally evaluating it within the framework of test construction. They argued that test results should mean something in terms of psychological theory. When a finding occurs, it should speak to a given theoretical agenda and therein promote further research.

This raises a crucial question in psychological research. Specifically, what is the role of theory in research? Proponents of theory point to the **heuristic** value of theory. The heuristic value of any model refers to the model's ability to stimulate ideas and promote further investigation. The belief is that the organizational framework of theory provides a logical basis for proceeding systematically. In essence, theory prevents us from going in random directions and simply gathering unrelated facts that do not fit into any integrated mold. In contrast, opponents of the heuristic theory (and the notion of construct validity) argue that premature speculation

**construct validity**—the extent to which a measure maps a specific hypothetical trait

**heuristic**—the ability of a model or theory to stimulate additional research

**criterion-related validity**—the degree to which a measure corresponds to performance on some other task or to behavior in another situation

creates a deception that events are ordered in a prescribed manner, which can lead to false assumptions about the true nature of behavioral relations. The position of the latter camp is that as a developing science, we should look for commonalities between and among our data and ultimately build a base on which meaningful statements can be made. So, although construct validity is important for psychological research in most cases, understand that some investigators actively and conscientiously ignore the concept.

Because the model experiment that we are building throughout this text is directly concerned with intervening and treating stress in chronically ill children, we must be concerned about the construct validity of the measures we have chosen for our planned research project. Stress, as it relates to psychological processes, carries substantial emotional baggage and has traditionally been addressed within a theoretical framework. Conventional models describe stress and fear as a central emotional state that cannot be measured directly (Mower, 1960). Alternative accounts view stress and anxiety as more of an amalgam of cognitive and physiological changes (Lazarus, 1983). Whatever the orientation, the concept of stress demands that we deal with it abstractly. Given that stress is central to our model experiment, construct validation is an issue for us.

While the coverage here is necessarily limited, it should be acknowledged that it is possible to statistically document the construct validity of the measures we have selected for our model study. This would involve establishing relationships with other variables known to be directly tied to stress and anxiety, and it would require sophisticated treatment of the data. In any event, construct validity helps us understand the meaning of findings in a larger context, so in this sense it is extremely important.

## Criterion-Related Validity

**Criterion-related validity** refers to how well a measure corresponds to performance on some other task or to behavior in some other situation. As Benjamin et al. (1994) outlined, suppose we are interested in constructing a test that measures the trait "honesty." We could devise questions aimed at measuring people's honest dispositions, then compare their profiles of responses with their behavior in an unsupervised situation in which they are required to handle large amounts of cash. To the extent that scores on the honesty test correlate with actual honest performances, the test can be said to have high criterion-related validity.

Other examples of criterion-related validity are the relation between scores on the Scholastic Aptitude Test (SAT) and grades in college coursework, the relation between intelligence and job performance, and the relation of a person's performance on a flight simulator to that person's success as a professional pilot. In each of these cases, notice that the measure is taken, and then it is compared to a criterion. This is a requirement for determining criterion-related validity.

## WITHIN CHAPTER REVIEW AND STUDY QUESTIONS

### MEASUREMENT VALIDITY

1. When a measure just "looks like it is appropriate" for the experiment, what type of validity is being expressed?
   a. face validity
   b. content validity
   c. construct validity
2. How is content validity determined? Why is it important in psychological research?
3. Define *criterion-related validity* and indicate how the procedures for establishing this form of validity differ from those used to determine concurrent validity.

## MEASUREMENT RELIABILITY

Even when a valid record that measures what you want to measure is taken, there is the additional question of consistency. When a measure is consistent across several different recordings, the measure is said to possess good **reliability.** Unfortunately, reliability in psychological experimentation is often difficult to determine.

Part of the problem with establishing reliability in psychological research stems from the nature of the experimental designs. When hypotheses for studies are formulated and design features are established, dependent variables are selected for the studies. Once a subject completes participation, it is unlikely the investigator will ever choose to take another record from that subject. That is, most studies are one-shot experiments where

**reliability**—the consistency of measurement

**interrater reliability**—the statistical correlation between or among the observations of independent observers who record the same behavioral sequences

one measure is taken and the next question is addressed with minimal regard for what would happen if the same study were conducted a second or third time.

Even if you did choose to rerun an experiment using the same subjects and the same measures, it is unlikely that you would have perfect reliability. Because the conditions of two separate experiments can never be identical, some variation in measurement has to occur. For example, if you administered the State-Trait Anxiety Inventory (STAI) to a clinical patient on successive occasions, it is unlikely you would obtain precisely the same pattern of scores each time. What if an unexpected source of stress were introduced in the patient's life between the first and second recordings? What if the patient's attitude toward taking the test shifts? Events that change anything about the precise character of the experiment intrude and contribute to unreliability.

It does not follow from what I have stated here that psychological experiments are totally inconsistent and irreproducible, however. It just means you are not likely to get *exactly* the same results every time you run a study. You can, however, achieve a degree of consistency where the same fundamental pattern of findings is obtained across experiments. In Chapter 1 I talked about the importance of replication. When an experiment is replicated by another laboratory, and when the overall pattern of results fits the pattern of the initial investigation, the reliability of the measurements is enhanced. True, the experiment will not happen exactly the same way the second time, for reasons mentioned previously, and it would be inappropriate to attempt any statistical operations that would yield reliability coefficients. However, it is possible to show that a given measurement is consistent with a general theme that is expressed throughout the results of many different research projects.

There are some types of reliability in psychological research where it is appropriate to statistically determine reliability coefficients. One such example is **interrater reliability.** This type of reliability is meaningful when multiple observers score the same event. For example, an investigator may be interested in sharing behavior among 3-year-old children who are either with their mothers or in a playroom by themselves. Because one observer who is assigned the task of watching and recording "sharing" may inadvertently bias the results, it is desirable to have two or three observers watching the same events. Once the independent records of the observers are made, it is possible to compute a reliability coefficient. The reliability coefficient essentially tells the extent to which the "raters" agree.

Finally, be aware that reliable data do not always tell the truth. Let me show you a case in point.

# Spotlight on Research: THE UNRELIABILITY OF RELIABLE DATA

**S**everal years ago, I was interested in the effects of a particular chemical agent on the operant response rates of rats responding under a simple variable-ratio (VR) schedule of reinforcement. In this type of schedule, a reward is delivered after differing numbers of lever-press responses are made. For instance, an animal may be rewarded after 8 responses on the lever, then 14, then 3, and so on. There is no consistent pattern of reward delivery, and the result is a very high, stable rate of responding.

I administered the chemical agent to one group of rats and a control substance to a second group. Over a period of weeks, not much happened. The rates of responding for the two groups were essentially the same. I was getting very consistent (reliable) data, and they were telling me the chemical had no demonstrable effects.

Toward the end of the project, I noticed something unusual about the pattern of responses. True, the overall rates of the treatment and control groups were identical, but the allocation of responses over time were very different. The group of rats that had received the chemical treatment responded in bursts, quit for a while, then responded again in another burst. In comparison, the control animals exhibited the typical steady profile of response that characterizes the VR schedule condition. So, even though the groups showed similar overall rates which were reliable across many test sessions, on closer inspection there were some major differences in the manner in which the data were distributed.

As you can see, even good reliability can be misleading. Reliable results may fail to depict the true circumstance. ■

## WITHIN CHAPTER REVIEW AND STUDY QUESTION

### MEASUREMENT RELIABILITY

1. Why is reliability often difficult to determine in psychological research? What can be done to ensure reliable measurement?

## SELECTION OF EQUIPMENT

Up to this point, our discussion of measurement has centered on the various types of measurements that can be recorded in psychological experimentation, whether or not those measurements really measure what you want them to measure. Then there is the issue of consistency. A related concern in most experiments conducted in the 1990s is the selection of appropriate equipment.

Regardless of the area of emphasis, psychology research today usually involves automation. This means that rather than one investigator or a group of investigators manually observing the behavior of subjects, some machine or recording device collects the data. For example, in animal research, the researcher is often interested in the general activity profile of an animal. Someone interested in the different effects of a stimulant (drug) on male and female rats may want to record how many movements the animal makes in a 30-minute time period following drug application. Years ago, you would simply place the rat in a rectangular-shaped box with different quadrants marked off on the flooring, and merely index the number of times the rat crossed into each quadrant. Even with the interrater reliability techniques discussed previously, this effort typically translated into a crude representation of the rat's movement behavior.

In comparison, in the modern laboratories of today, a sophisticated computerized monitoring system such as the Digiscan apparatus shown in Figure 5–7

**FIGURE 5–7** The Digiscan activity monitoring system

provides an integrated account of every horizontal and vertical movement the rat makes. This piece of equipment, which is commercially available frrm Omnitech Electronics, Inc., Columbus, Ohio, updates the rat's position in three-dimensional space every 10 milliseconds. When the rat breaks various photo (light) beams, information is passed to a synthesizer that processes the data and provides a printout of exactly where the rat is and what it is doing. It even tells you when the rat is doing the same thing over and over (this dependent measure is referred to as "behavioral stereotypy"). Ultimately, the Digiscan yields fourteen different dependent measures of animal activity, and the data can be stored automatically as computer files for later statistical analyses. Obviously, this sort of measurement mechanism is far in advance of the simple observational methods that once characterized research in animal behavior.

On a more personal note, I recall an incident early in my career when I faced the task of building an operant laboratory after I was awarded my first academic job. I was only able to purchase four operant chambers (Skinner boxes), and these pieces of testing apparatus were in a small, 6-foot × 6-foot room. Cables from each chamber ran to an adjacent control room where all of the recording, scheduling, and programming equipment was located. There were relays, switches, pulse formers, and mack panels with pins placed to deliver rewards under certain conditions. Cumulative recorders, which actually were graphs drawn by a stylus marking a page as the page turned on a cylinder, informed me what the animals were doing in terms of pressing levers for food reinforcements. With a few whistles, buzzers, and strobe lights added, this recording arena would have looked like something out of a 1943 science fiction movie.

Today, I continue to conduct experiments that involve more than a dozen such operant chambers, and everything I described with respect to data collection and measurement is handled by one inexpensive computer that is only sightly larger than the book you are reading. So, while animal labs today may have lost some of the lustre and quaintness of labs of years gone by, modern recording instruments offer the advantages of efficiency, space saving, and speed.

Measurement automation is also evident in human subject experiments. Even a few years ago, videotaping an exchange in a study of social interaction was viewed as an impressive technological model for measuring social behavior. After the session was filmed, independent evaluators could replay the tape, several times in fact, and document the frequency of a variety of behaviors such as aggressive remarks, acceding to the demands of others in the group, the number of times of conversation initiation, and so on. Today, this technology is obsolete. In today's social psychology laboratories, machinery such as the Interactive Audio-Visual System (Wood Electronics, Inc., Lehigh Valley, Pennsylvania) permits the evaluator to verbally identify what happens as the tape rolls, indicate frequency of responses as they occur, automatically transfer this information to a computer program, and then immediately retrieve the statistical results when the tape is turned off. These and other automated recording instruments have become common in psychological research laboratories using human participants.

What are the real advantages of automating experiments? Obviously, there is the issue of time. It is of great benefit to be able to turn on a piece of equipment, begin your experiment, and then go to the library, to class, or to a meeting and know that your experiment is running while you accomplish other things. There is also the issue of accuracy. Machines are not as likely to err as humans, and they do not judge. To the equipment, the behavior is either there or it is not. The result is that automation provides more consistent and unbiased measurement, and it should be used where possible. Of course, not all dependent measures can be adapted to automation. In fact this is the case for some of the measures we have chosen for our experiment. It is difficult to imagine how the fear thermometer measure that is planned for use in our model experiment could be automated. Nonetheless, where possible, automatic recording should be employed (for a more expansive coverage of techniques of automation, refer to Deni, 1986).

Having said this, I feel obliged to say something about the "imagination" of research as it contrasts with the "automation" of research. Consider the following comments.

## ✳ Thinking About Research

Throughout my career, I have enjoyed working with (and sometimes around) many different colleagues. As with every human domain, research scientists present an impressive array of individualism. No two investigators are alike, and in some cases they define opposite anchors along a common continuum. Conspicuous in this regard are the different attitudes people take about the need for equipment.

I recall one case where a colleague literally stopped doing his research because he lost his external funding and consequently was unable to continue to do the work. Contrast this with the behavior of a second person who had the identical experience. She had been the beneficiary of years of external financial support, but ultimately the money ran out. In the absence of the support she had to shut down her research operation, but she did not quit. She began reading literature in a new area, where research could be conducted with minimal costs. In this case the area was "learned helplessness," which remains a viable model of depression in experimental psychopathology. A key publication by Hiroto and Seligman (1975) provided a methodology whereby a research project could be completed using nothing more than 5-inch × 5-inch wire index cards. Now the woman had a lab and had outfitted it for under $5.00!

The point is, resourcefulness can replace expensive equipment. The famous experimental psychologist Edward L. Thorndike created mazes out of books placed on edge. His resulting research findings shaped learning and conditioning theory for 50 years. As you can see, automation is nice, and it is probably preferred, but it is no substitute for creativity. If you really want to find something out, you can make it happen regardless of your circumstances.    ■

---

## WITHIN CHAPTER REVIEW AND STUDY QUESTION

### SELECTION OF EQUIPMENT

1. What are some of the advantages of automating experiments? Is there ever a situation in which manual recording is preferred over automatic measurement?

---

# DESCRIPTION: MEASURES OF CENTRAL TENDENCY

Thus far in this chapter we have focused on measurement. Given that an investigator has settled on a particular measure that will provide the kind of information he or she holds to be of interest, there is the added issue of how best to represent the data in summary form. Which mechanisms are available to provide a method for monitoring our results, and which will give a general account of what our findings mean?

Often, researchers look to **measures of central tendency** for quick summaries of their findings. *Central tendency* refers to the idea that in any distribution of scores taken on a single measure, it is likely that most scores will cluster in the center of the distribution and that very few scores will fall at the extremes. For example, if we were to measure the intelligence of every first-year college student enrolled at your institution, the majority of students would have similar IQs. However, a few students would have exceptionally high IQs, and a few would score on the low end of the range.

When a scientist actively collects data during an experiment, it often helps to have a single representative measure that indicates how the experiment is proceeding. This information may be useful in terms of adjusting the procedures, determining the need to test more subjects, and so on. The three most common measures of central tendency for these purposes are the mean, the median, and the mode.

**measures of central tendency**—summary values of a distribution of scores; the mean, median, and mode

**mean**—the average score in a distribution

**median**—the middle score in a distribution

## The Mean: The Arithmetic Average

The **mean** is a simple numerical concept that is familiar to each of us. It is an arithmetic average of all the scores taken on a given measure. Every score is added, and the sum is divided by the number of observations in the addition. The computational formula for the mean is:

$$\bar{X} = \frac{\Sigma X}{N}$$

where $\bar{X}$ = mean, $\Sigma$ is the Greek symbol for "the sum of," $X$ is each individual raw score, and $N$ is the number of observations in the addition.

As we will see in Chapter 11, the mean is especially useful because it permits more elaborate inferential statistical operations to be performed. For our present purposes, it is sufficient to note that the mean tells us something general about our findings. For instance, an investigator may run a preliminary experiment to the main experiment (this preliminary experiment is called a "pilot study"). In this case, the researcher is interested in the effects of sleep deprivation on spatial reasoning. Initially, participants in the sleep study are deprived of only 2 hours sleep a night for a week. As shown in Figure 5–8, the mean performance of people in the sleep deprivation condition is not different from that of controls who are not sleep deprived. This tells the experimenter that the degree of sleep deprivation may be insufficient to produce the intended effects. Consequently, the sleep deprivation participants are placed on a regimen where they receive only 4 hours sleep a night for a week. As the mean results profiled in Figure 5–8 indicate, substantial impairment in cognitive functioning (spatial reasoning in this example) is evident under these conditions. The investigator uses mean data in the pilot study to make decisions about which levels of deprivation to use in the real experiment. Here is a case in which a representative measure describes results that can be useful in completing the grand project.

| Moderate sleep deprivation | Percent of correct items |
|---|---|
| Deprived condition | 78.2 |
| Control | 79.4 |
| | |
| Extreme sleep deprivation | |
| Deprived condition | 53.5 |
| Control | 78.9 |

**FIGURE 5–8** Average (mean) score on a pilot study of spatial reasoning under conditions of moderate sleep deprivation (2 hours sleep loss each night for 1 week) and extreme sleep deprivation (4 hours sleep loss each night for 1 week)

## The Median: The Middle Score

Because the mean value can be drastically affected by extreme scores, it sometimes is not the best indicator of the score distribution. Under such conditions, the **median** value is often a better general measure of what the scores mean. The median value is the "middle" score. That is, the median reflects the point in the distribution above which half the scores fall and below which half the scores fall (this actually is another label for the 50th percentile).

Consider the following distribution of scores taken from readings of systolic blood pressure of patients in a hospital setting: 121, 123, 125, 126, and 186. In this group of five patients, one of the patients obviously is an outlier and has an unusually high blood pressure reading. If we were to compute the arithmetic mean of these scores, the value would be 136.2, which would not represent the blood pressure readings of most patients. However, the median or middle score in this distribution is 125, which is a quite accurate indicator of the scores of this particular group.

Therefore, if there is some question about the overall pattern of scores you obtain when collecting data, you may want to use the median as a barometer of how well your measure is working. Of course, it is not a bad idea to take a look at both the mean value and the median value and to use all information when making experimental decisions.

## The Mode: The Most Typical Score

When an experimenter tracks the results of a study while the study is underway, it is sometimes the case that the most frequently occurring score may be of interest. When the researcher wishes to know the most frequent or typical score, the **mode** is the method best suited for representing the data. Because the mode is the most frequently occurring score, extreme values or additional data entries do not necessarily have an effect.

An example of when the mode might be of interest in psychological research is a scientific study of forensic psychology. Forensic psychologists are concerned with such issues as documenting the psychological profiles of criminals or of people who may be at risk of engaging in criminal conduct. Clearly in this circumstance, identifying the most frequent profile could provide law enforcement agencies clues about which types of individuals may be suspects for different types of criminal behavior. Along other lines, it may be of interest for persons running for political office to know which socioeconomic group is most likely to favor a particular political agenda. Here, frequency

**mode**—the most frequent and thus most typical score in a distribution

is more important than any other factor, so it makes sense that modal values would be of great use.

Most distributions yield a unimodal value, which means that only one value occurs frequently. However, in some situations an investigator may find that the distribution presents a bimodal pattern. In a bimodal pattern, two different values in the distribution occur with the same high frequency. This type of pattern might result from an experiment on the various strategies male and female college students use to solve quantitative problems. Males may prefer one approach over all others, females may consistently adopt a quite different approach. The result would be that there would be two modes in the overall distribution, one reflecting the male preference, the other reflecting the female preference.

We see that each measure of central tendency has unique features which make it attractive to an investigator who is attempting to characterize the general pattern of results, either as the experiment proceeds or, as we shall discuss later, when the findings are presented in final form.

## WITHIN CHAPTER REVIEW AND STUDY QUESTIONS

### DESCRIPTION: MEASURES OF CENTRAL TENDENCY

1. If you were asked to present a measure of central tendency that represented the average American's annual salary, which of the following measures would you use?
   a. mean
   b. median
   c. mode
2. What rationale did you use to arrive at your answer to Question 1?

## DESCRIPTION: GRAPHS AND CHARTS

Even when an investigator has gathered information about the reliability and validity of a particular measure and has calculated central tendency values which characterize the general pattern of results, it is sometimes difficult to get an overall feel for the data. You need something quick, something you can glance at and render a decision from that may change the course of a project. This is where charts and graphs are helpful.

Because of the automation that exists in most modern laboratories (see previous discussion), it is not uncommon for a researcher to visually inspect the results of a project daily (or even hourly). As each participant's performance in the experiment is completed, you can automatically update your data set, and most computer programs have graphics capabilities which permit the experimenter to track the findings with considerable scrutiny. There are a number of graphs and charts to pick from, and the selection of the visual representation of the data is often dictated by the nature and demands of the study. Here I mention histograms, frequency polygons (line graphs), and pie charts. Each of these portraits of the data is useful in providing the investigator with summary information that requires nothing more than a sharp eye and a keen sense of what constitutes a "blip" on the record.

## *Histograms*

Before describing the distinguishing features of specific graphs and charts, there are a few comments to make about graphs in general. First, the accepted practice is to plot values of the independent variables on the **abscissa** or horizontal axis (also called x-axis). These variables might include different drug doses, the number of trials an animal is run in a radial arm maze, or different ethnic groups. On the **ordinate,** or vertical axis (also called the y-axis), the various values of the dependent variable are plotted. Therefore, in a study on the effects of early childhood intervention on reading performance, the higher the reading skill, the higher the entry along the vertical axis.

The **histogram** illustrates data graphically using a horizontal and vertical axis. A histogram, or bar graph as it is commonly called, presents a bar for each value of the independent variable. These bars are arranged along the abscissa. The top of each bar corresponds to some value of the dependent variable, such as the frequency of scores, the mean of a sample, or the median point in the distribution. Figure 5–9 shows what a histogram might look like for students enrolled in a research methods class who had just taken an exam.

## *Frequency Polygons and Line Graphs*

When an investigator is concerned with profiling only a few levels of a variable, bar graphs are appropriate because they are simple and easy to read. When several values of a variable are represented in an experiment, however, a **frequency polygon** may be the preferred method for presenting the data. A frequency polygon is created by connecting the

**abscissa**—the horizontal axis on a graph

**ordinate**—the vertical axis on a graph

**histogram**—a bar graph used to summarize data

**frequency polygon**—a bar graph that is converted to a line drawing by connecting lines to the peak of each bar

points that reflect the peak of each bar on a bar graph or some other common measurement. For instance, if we were to convert the bar graph in Figure 5–9 to a frequency polygon, it would appear like the polygon in Figure 5–10. The data sets are the same, but these figures show how the information can be portrayed differently.

Frequency polygons are actually a basic form of a more general method for presenting summary information, which is called a line graph. Line graphs are like frequency polygons in that they connect key measurement points with lines, but line graphs typically involve more complex expressions of multiple variable experiments. For example, Figure 5–11 shows the results of a study conducted in 1981 by psychologist Gordon Bower of Stanford University. Bower's study was designed to assess the effects of different mood states on memory. As you can see, the line graph indicates that people recall events better when they are in the same mood state they were in when they learned the material, regardless of whether or not the mood state was positive or negative. In this case, a line graph communicates the overall findings of the experiment in a way that might be cumbersome if profiled in any other manner. Line graphs are the most popular vehicle for presenting summary findings because modern psychological research usually involves multifactor designs (I discuss these designs in detail in Chapters 8 and 9), and the line graph adapts readily to such designs.

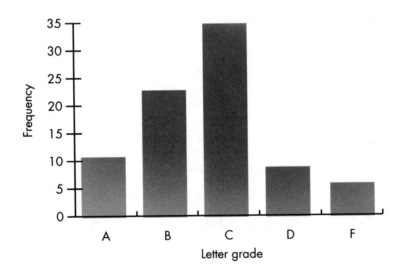

**FIGURE 5–9 Histogram for a hypothetical distribution of scores (letter grades on a test) of students enrolled in a research methods class**

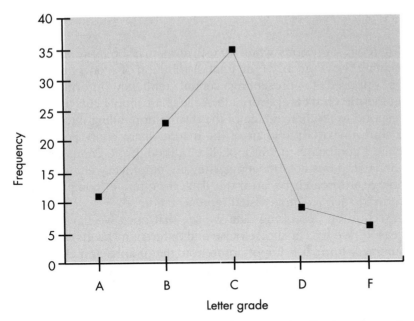

**FIGURE 5–10** Frequency polygon of the score distribution shown in Figure 5-9

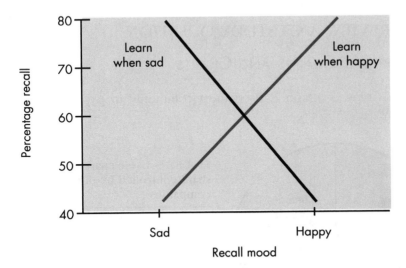

**FIGURE 5–11** Line graph reflecting the percentage recall of material learned in either a happy or a sad mood, as a function of mood at time of recall. (From Bower, 1981.) Copyright © 1981 by the American Psychological Association. Reprinted with permission.

**pie chart**—a graphic portrayal of the percentages of categories of score distributions

## Pie Charts

There are occasions when investigators may be more interested in presenting "how much" of the total distribution of scores falls into each category, as opposed to presenting central tendency information. In these situations, the **pie chart** is appropriate. A pie chart simply cuts a circle into slices that correspond to the percentage of the distribution falling into a category. Figure 5–12 shows what a pie chart of the market share controlled by competing petrochemical companies might look like. Although pie charts are common in organizational and business meetings, they are employed relatively infrequently in psychological research because the data are often so complex that they do not conform to such a simple visual representation.

In this section on describing data we see that once we have selected a particular measure, we have a choice of several different methods of presenting that data in summary form. It is important to note that graphs and charts are used as much by experimenters during the course of the experiment as they are when summarizing the findings in final form. By visually tracking your day-to-day results, you can make informed decisions about how best to adjust your procedures in the future.

## WITHIN CHAPTER REVIEW AND STUDY QUESTION

### DESCRIPTION: GRAPHS AND CHARTS

1. What type of graph is used most commonly in psychological research? Why?

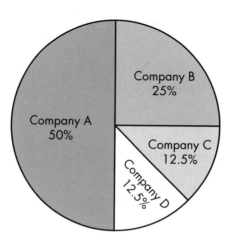

**FIGURE 5–12** Pie chart of the relative market share controlled by different petrochemical companies

## The Model Experiment

In this chapter on measurement and description we have reviewed the various types of measurements that are available, and we have documented the importance of employing measures that are solid measures of what we wish to index (valid measures) and that express some degree of consistency (reliable measures).

We have opted for two empirical measures to be used in the model experiment we are building. One is the OSBD, which has been thoroughly documented with respect to its reliability as an empirical measure of fear and stress (Jay, Elliott, Ozolins, Olson, & Pruitt, 1985). The heart rate measure we have chosen to use obviously has substantial face validity as a marker of stress level, and it has been correlated positively with numerous other measures of stress (refer to Doring, Schneider, & Koenig, 1995). Finally, we also have selected the "fear thermometer" as a self-report measure, which should provide added information about how the participants in our study on the effects of age on the therapeutic effectiveness of cognitive treatment of chronically ill children really feel.

Now that we are more comfortable with the measures we have chosen for our experiment, we are ready to consider additional matters. Of particular significance is how we go about selecting our subjects (participants) and collecting data. These topics are addressed in the next chapter.

# Subject Variables and Data Collection

Once decisions have been made about which dependent measures are to be used in an experiment, it is time to think more seriously about whom to include in the study. Depending on the nature and ultimate purpose of the investigation, a particular kind of subject must be recruited to participate in the project. If you are concerned about the different attitudes Mexican Americans, African Americans, Asians, and Caucasians living in Detroit hold toward police brutality, it makes sense that you would want to include each of these racial categories in your experimental design. More specifically, you would only want people from these respective racial groups who live in the city of Detroit. The attitudes of other subgroups or people from other cities would be of no value for this narrowly defined topic, which is concerned with a specified population.

After the type of subject for the experiment has been identified, there are numerous practical and methodological details to be worked out. First, how do you select subjects? Do you advertise in the paper, make phone calls, enlist friends or relatives? How many subjects do you need, and what guidelines are there for determining how many subjects should be placed in each group? Does the number of groups in your experiment affect the group subject size?

Questions relating to selecting subjects for research participation are not unique to experiments using human participants. When animals are used for experimentation, an equal number of considerations must be addressed. You start by asking questions about which kind of animal is most appropriate for the study. You may want to use mice in your experiment because they are cheaper than rats and, because they also mature more quickly, you can look at the effects of aging more easily. Elsewhere, an investigator may be concerned with the effects of an experimental "smart pill" on concept formation. Because concept formation requires a relatively high level of cognitive integration, it would be a mistake for the investigator to attempt the project using pigeons as subjects. It would make more sense to use chimpanzees or some other infrahuman primate that is capable of performing the task.

These issues, and other factors relating to subject selection, are the focus of this chapter. In addition to these discussions, I comment on a few basic principles to consider when collecting data from your subjects. I begin by addressing an economical question: How can you test everyone when you have limited time and resources?

# POPULATIONS AND SAMPLES

Consider for a moment that you are interested in the attitudes all people older than age 25 and living in Laguna Beach, California, have toward capital punishment. This is a legitimate topic, and it may be useful when contrasted with the capital punishment attitudes of others living in different regions of the nation. The problem is that the Laguna Beach population is somewhere around a half million. Can you expect to ask each person in the city, "Do you favor the use of capital punishment in the United States?" The answer is, no, you cannot obtain responses from everyone in the city. In fact, if you attempted to do so, by the time you finished the attitudes of the people you surveyed early in the project may have shifted sharply. Consequently, your findings would be worthless. What do we do in situations such as this one?

The problem of dealing with large information pools is handled through **sampling.** Sampling refers to a procedure in which you select a subset of a larger number of observations. As we shall see, there are several different sampling methods that can be used, and each has certain features that may make it ideal for a given experimental design. Although sampling techniques may differ, they all have a common, underlying assumption: a sample represents a broader population.

A **population** consists of all relevant cases in the experiment. For instance, in the previous Laguna Beach experiment, the population would be every person living within the city limits of Laguna Beach, California, who is older than 25. This population is finite. If we wanted to work hard enough to determine it, an exact number of people could be provided. In contrast, a **sample** is a subset of the population. The top of Figure 6–1 presents a hypothetical population of events. For our purposes, the events themselves aren't important. What is important, however, is that these events represent all relevant cases. The bottom part of Figure 6–1 represents a sample of the larger population of events. Note that although every event in the sample is also included in the population, the reverse is not true. Not every event in the population is included in the sample.

There are many advantages to using sampling procedures. Chief among them is the fact that samples are manageable. When investigators collect information from samples drawn from broader populations, they compile data sets that can be stored, manipulated, statistically analyzed, and otherwise examined. To put it simply, a task can be completed with a sample. In most cases, a task can't be completed with an entire population.

It is extremely important that a sample reflect all the features of the population. If your sample biases one dimension of the population, then your findings will be invalid because nothing you have to say will match the population you are studying. For example, assume that we are interested in the frequency with which male and female executives make assertive remarks in group situations. Because the present organizational climate is configured such that there are many more male than female executives, it would be a mistake to create a sample that contained equal numbers of males and females. If it did, the sample would not mirror the population and you would risk prejudicing the results. A similar

**sampling**—a procedure in which a subset of subjects is selected from a larger number of observations

**population**—all relevant cases in a data set

**sample**—a subset of a population; each member of the sample is included in the larger population

**FIGURE 6–1** The relation between a sample and the population from which the sample is drawn. Note that only a subset of population values are included in the sample.

Population

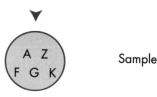

Sample

argument can be made when an animal researcher selects only the healthiest animals from an animal colony for a research project. The animal researcher has not sampled from the colony as a whole; he or she has sampled from the "healthy animal pool" and in effect has redefined the population. Therefore, great caution must be exercised to ensure the sample is representative. In the sections that follow, I discuss some of the procedures traditionally used to ensure representative samples.

## Random Sampling Procedure

In a **random sampling procedure,** population events are selected randomly until a sample of adequate size is created. In this type of procedure, every member of the population has an equal chance of being selected for the sample distribution.

Random sampling techniques require some basic grasp of probability theory (see Hurlburt, 1994, for a more comprehensive discussion of this topic). Probability models are concerned with estimating the likelihood that a particular event will occur. With great mathematical precision, you can predict the frequency with which an event will show up one time, two times, or any number of times. Certain features of the score distribution you are working with, such as the number of scores in the distribution, determine the probability that a given event will occur. For our purposes, it is sufficient to note that probability is a quantitative mechanism which permits us to estimate the chances of obtaining a particular outcome.

Probability and chance are often illustrated through the simple case of a coin flip. Given that you have a truly unbiased coin that is "heads" on one side and "tails" on the other, the probability of getting either a head or a tail on a given toss of the coin is 0.50, or fifty-fifty. Similarly, the chances of drawing a queen of diamonds from a shuffled deck of playing cards is 1 in 52, or approximately 0.02.

It is important to recognize that these probabilities are unchanging as long as the population characteristics remain the same. That is, if 52 cards remain in the deck, the chances of getting the queen of diamonds is the same on the second draw as it was for the first draw. Many people fail to grasp this fundamental principle of probability theory, and something known as the "gambler's fallacy" results. A person playing at a blackjack table, and losing consistently, may stay with the game because, "My luck has to get better, because the averages will work in my favor if I play long enough." This person assumes that his or her previous bad luck somehow will increase the chances of drawing better cards in the future. In truth, each turn at the table is independent and the chances of getting good cards are no more and no less than they would be had the person not played the game previously.

This independence of events principle also holds for random sampling procedures. Each member of the population must be independent. Under such conditions, when the sample is drawn from the population, each element of the population has an equal probability of being selected for the sample distribution. No single member is favored over another, so the sample on the whole should represent the population. This is true, at least, when every event in the population has been identified. When the total population is not identified, exact statements of probability are not possible, and independence cannot be guaranteed. More often than not, this situation exists. Because we rarely know everything about a population, we can never be certain that our random selections have produced sample characteristics we can trust. Still, with a random sampling technique we are safe to say that our sample represents the population pretty closely. The procedure may not be perfect, but often it is the best we can do.

One thing that can be done to improve your chances of obtaining an adequate sample is to randomly select a large number of members from the population. As a rule, the greater the sample size, the greater the similarity between the sample and the population. Of course, time and resources place constraints on this selection process (indeed, this is the rationale for taking a sample in the first place). Therefore, how many subjects do we need? When can we stop randomly assigning subjects to groups and declare a group "full?"

**random sampling procedure**—a procedure in a sample is drawn from a population of values based on some random principle; this prevents systematic biases in the sample

## ✺ Thinking About Research

**U**nfortunately, there are no hard-and-fast rules about how many subjects are needed for each group. Because subject characteristics often dictate how large the sample needs to be, the optimal number of subjects changes with every experiment. For instance, if I am running a study using genetically outbred albino white rats as subjects, I may feel comfortable using 8 to 10 rats per group because the rats do not differ greatly. Human subjects come into the laboratory with appreciably different backgrounds, experiences, and attitudes, so it makes sense to put more human subjects in a group.

Given this, how many human subjects should we use? Cowles (1974) has suggested that about 15 people should suffice when you have several levels of a given independent variable. However, this guideline must be viewed cautiously because, once again, subject and design features may require the use of more subjects per group. If your experiment is concerned with subtle differences, such as the changing brain wave patterns that occur when a person is hypnotized, it follows that you will need a large number of people in your experiment to detect small but reliable changes.

Some other investigation dealing with gross motor activity may not mandate the inclusion of so many subjects.

So what is the answer? How many subjects do we use? The answer is you include as many subjects in each group as you have to in order to provide an adequate test of the hypothesis. This means you do what you have to do to complete the project. As Bowden (1992) noted, researchers have different ideas about issues such as the sensitivity of their findings, the confidence levels they will accept, and a variety of other events that can affect what is known as the power of the statistical test being used to determine group differences (I discuss this idea more fully in Chapter 11, Drawing Inferences About Results). The concept of power need not concern us at the moment. It suffices here to acknowledge that ultimately the researcher makes judgments based on what works. If you can answer your essential questions with only a few subjects in each group, then use only a few. If you require more than a few subjects, then keep the randomization process going.  ■

Regardless of how many subjects you decide to include in your random sample, you must have some vehicle for assigning the subjects to different conditions, and this method must be without bias. One such procedure involves the use of a **random numbers table.** In a random numbers table, like the one in Figure 6–2, a lengthy series of numbers are presented such that the next number in the sequence is not possible to predict. That is, there is no rule or scheme which determines the next value.

Random number tables have been used for decades in psychological research, and there are almost as many ways to use them as there are people who use them. Because there is nothing systematic about the table, you can enter the table at any point, move in any direction, skip as many numbers as you like, and

| | | |
|---|---|---|
| 1864 | 4103 | 1289 |
| 3419 | 2912 | 3535 |
| 2387 | 4300 | 2438 |
| 1134 | 1413 | etc. |
| 2374 | 2976 | etc. |
| 3321 | 2525 | |
| 3358 | 1778 | |
| 1191 | 1312 | |
| 1277 | 3654 | |
| 1155 | 3761 | |
| 3817 | 2334 | |
| 2411 | 1356 | |
| 1123 | 4109 | |
| 1654 | 2387 | |

**FIGURE 6–2** An example of a random numbers table used to assign subjects to treatment conditions randomly

virtually employ the chart in any style you choose. The only requirement is that you make a rule about how to use the chart.

For example, say we are conducting an experiment in which 45 participants must be randomly assigned to three groups. We decide to enter the table shown in Figure 6–2 at the upper left (number *1864*). We further decide that the first two digits of every other number will be used to establish group assignment. Digits *1* to *15* will be assigned to Group 1, digits *16* to *30* will be assigned to Group 2, and digits *31* to *45* will be assigned to Group 3. As subjects enter our laboratory, we methodically move through (down) the list and, based on the subjects' numbers, assign them to one of the three groups. Therefore, if the fourth subject corresponds to *3358* in the list of random numbers (based on the rule of skipping every other value noted earlier), that subject is assigned to Group 3 because the initial two digits of the number (*33*) fall between *31* and *45*. This process is repeated until all groups contain the appropriate number of participants. Because the sequence of numbers used to make the group assignments is random, subject placement in groups is also random. As mentioned previously, this randomization process is imperfect, but it offers a reasonable approximation of a large population.

In practice, investigators often use less sophisticated approaches to achieve random assignment. Some very informal system, such as placing every third person in Group 2 or placing people with last names beginning with letters *A* through *J* in Group 1, may be used. Integral to this assignment procedure is the belief that there is an inherent randomness; people will appear at the laboratory randomly, last names should not systematically bias the experiment, and so on. The essential element is that there is no *a priori* prejudice, nothing that intrudes on the requirement that every

**random numbers table**—a lengthy series of numbers compiled according to some random scheme that can be used to assign subjects to treatment conditions randomly subject have an equal opportunity to gain group membership. With randomization, representation is not ensured, but it is probable.

With regard to subject selection for the model experiment we are building as we proceed through this book, random assignment to treatment conditions provides an orderly and acceptable method for subject assignment. Consider the following procedures for our model study.

Recall the basic design of our model experiment. The study will employ three treatment conditions (cognitive coping strategy, sensory information, and contact control; Note: these particular group labels are defined by specific treatment procedures outlined in later chapters) in two age ranges (4–6, 10–12) equal Ns design (which means each condition will have an equal number [N] of subjects). Our objective in assigning participants to conditions is to ensure that our sample represents the traits and characteristics of the population about which we wish to generalize (see following).

The participants in this study will be 96 English-speaking pediatric patients undergoing treatment for cancer at the University of Texas M. D. Anderson Hospital and Tumor Institute in Houston, Texas. Participants will be selected from all medical services (leukemia, lymphoma, solid tumors, and rare solid tumors) except conditions involving brain tumors. These patients will be omitted because their affliction may prevent them from responding to the demands of the various treatment interventions.

Based on the chosen design, the eligibility criteria will include: (a) is age 4 to 6 or 10 to12, (b) speaks English, (c) is in sufficiently good health to respond to the various points of intervention, and (d) has experience as both an inpatient and outpatient. Because our model experiment focuses on the differential effectiveness of cognitive treatment strategies in alleviating intense stress in younger and older children faced with painful medical treatments, all patients will receive treatment that requires a series of at least four bone marrow aspirations (BMAs) and lumbar punctures (LPs). These criteria will ensure that all subjects meet the minimum requirement of confronting an extremely stress-inducing medical manipulation before psychological intervention.

Forty-eight participants from each age range will be randomly assigned to receive one of the three interventions. Because we are using three different strategies for each age range, 16 subjects (patients) in each age range who meet the criteria will be randomly assigned to receive one of the three treatments (N = 16/group). The random number table in Figure 6–2 will be used to assign participants to the therapeutic treatment conditions. As discussed in this section, this randomization process prevents any systematic differences from appearing between the various conditions and increases the chances that our sample distributions will mirror the populations from which they have been drawn.

Each child's precise age, gender, type and date of diagnosis, maternal educational level, primary provider's occupation, and family income will be obtained from family members and hospital staff. These demographic data will be used to confirm that the sample distributions are equivalent before the treatment interventions are introduced.

## *Stratified Samples*

As useful as random samples are in psychological research, truly random sampling may distort experimental findings in some cases. Consider the following hypothetical study.

An investigator is interested in the relative incidence of obesity in younger and older men and women. The investigator decides to use subjects who fall between ages 25 and 35 for the younger sample and subjects between 65 and 75 for the older sample. The investigator recruits subjects by randomly selecting names from a local phone directory in a large city in the midwestern United States until 50 male and 50 female participants in each age range agree to come to the laboratory and fill out questionnaires, have body fat determinations made, and so on.

On the surface, this approach seems reasonable, and the random selection process appears to prevent any systematic biases from intruding on the experiment. However, the selection procedure is likely to be inappropriate. The probable sampling flaw rests with the changing characteristics of the populations under study. In the United States, the life expectancy for women is greater than that for men. As a result, while the 50/50 split in gender representation may mirror the male/female ratio of people in the 25 to 35 age range, it may not parallel the population of men and women in the 65 to 75 age range. A more accurate estimation of population values could be achieved by creating samples in which the relative percentages of male and female participants corresponded to the different percentages in the younger and older populations.

To match samples and populations subsets with discrepant features, a **stratified sampling procedure** can be used. In a stratified sampling procedure, the investigator identifies how the overall population is configured and then randomly assigns subjects to the subgroups such that the sample values reflect the population subgroup values. For instance, if in the previous example we know that among 25- to 35-year-olds the ratio of women to men is 52:48, then we can assign subjects until we have the same gender representation in our sample. Similarly, if among people in the 65 to 75 year condition we know that the ratio of women to men is

**stratified sampling procedure**—a procedure based on population characteristics in which efforts are made to ensure that the sample mirrors the population and that the sample and the population are parallel

**extraneous variables**—variables that are known to correlate significantly with the dependent variable but that are not included in the design

**matched samples**—samples that are matched along particular dimensions

60:40, then we can stratify our sample and randomly place 60 women and 40 men in this condition. Research indicates that this stratification technique yields more valid results than does the corresponding case in which a simple random sampling procedure is employed (Warwick & Lininger, 1975).

An obvious shortcoming of stratified sampling procedures is that the investigator must have detailed and accurate information about key variables in the population which may affect the project findings. Often this information is unavailable, and it may be impractical to expect to accurately characterize the relevant features of a specific population. Therefore, while the stratified sample is clearly preferred over the random sample in some situations, a blind decision to stratify could substantially compromise the credibility of a study.

## Matched Samples

While randomization protects against biases that may occur when an uncontrolled variable influences the data, and while stratification techniques increase the chances for adequate representation in the sample, there are some cases where even greater equivalency between samples is desired. This is especially true when the different effects an experimenter expects to see on the dependent measure are likely to be small and when one or more **extraneous variables** are known to correlate significantly with the dependent variable. An extraneous variable is a variable that is not being experimentally manipulated or that is not included in the design but which may affect the outcome of the results. Examples of extraneous variables include sex (gender), intelligence, job experience, single parent status, age, fine-motor skills, number of years spent in a formal educational setting, and so forth. Depending on the experiment, ignoring the influence of any one of these variables may result in uninterpretable findings.

In order to control for the intruding effects of extraneous variables, many investigators opt for **matched samples.** When researchers use matched samples, they attempt to create samples that are identical in every way. If this can be accomplished, and if manipulating the independent variable produces differences, you can be reasonably sure that the differences are due to the different values of the independent variable and nothing else. In actuality, of course, it is not possible to equate (match) groups on all subject characteristics. It is possible, however, to match samples closely on those variables which are most likely to affect the data.

There are several different methods by which matching may be accomplished. I will mention three of these methods: equating groups, yoking procedures, and the randomized block design.

**Matching by Equating Groups.** On a surface level, it would seem that the easiest way to establish matched samples would be to randomly assign people, all of whom have common features and characteristics, to different groups. In theory this would be the ideal procedure for matching. In practice, however, it is not possible to select subjects who are exactly alike. Subjects may be similar but not identical with respect to size, intelligence, political orientation, sexual preference, educational background, religiosity, and a host of other psychosocial variables. Because it is the natural order that subjects will differ, to create truly equivalent groups the experimenter must use precision matching or range matching techniques.

In **precision matching,** subjects with identical scores or characteristics are paired, and then each member of the pair is randomly assigned to a condition. Figure 6–3 illustrates how a precision matching procedure works. In this example, the concern is that intelligence (IQ) may be an extraneous variable that will influence the reading skill scores to be used as the dependent variable. Accordingly, subjects are administered an IQ test and equal pairs are formed. Two people score 112, so they are a matched pair, two others score 104 and they are a second matched pair, and so on. Once the pairs have been matched, a random technique is used to assign one person from each pair to Condition A and the other person to Condition B. The result of this process is samples that are identical or equivalent, at least with respect to the variable you are concerned about controlling.

The chief problem associated with precision matching is that it may take an extraordinarily long time, and considerable effort, before you come up with samples of sufficient size. In the previous example, the probability that any two people from such a limited sample will score exactly the same on an IQ test is statistically low. If you collect enough data, people will score the same on a given measure of intelligence, but this task is certain to be labor intensive. Moreover, the situation worsens when you have more than one variable on which to match, which is the usual case.

As an alternative, psychological researchers often equate groups or samples using the **range matching** technique. In range matching, subjects are allowed to fall within discrete yet arbitrary ranges. For instance, use the IQ example that was used to illustrate precision matching. Rather than require pairs to form based on identical IQ scores, however, we will match people whose scores fall within 5 IQ points. Therefore, as

**precision matching**—a technique in which pairs of identical subjects are randomly assigned to one of two treatment conditions

**range matching**—a technique in which pairs created on the basis of falling within a specified narrow range of values are randomly assigned to different treatment conditions

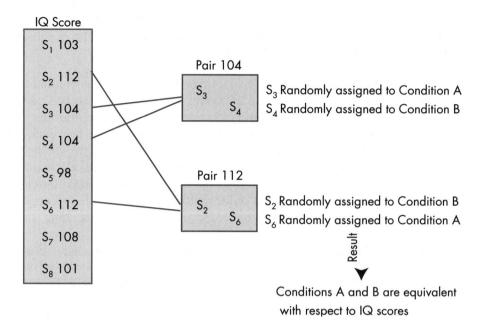

**FIGURE 6–3 An example of precision matching where identical pairs are created and then assigned to one of two treatment conditions. In this case, people with the same IQs are randomly assigned to Conditions A and B, which reflect different experimental manipulations that may affect reading skill scores.**

Figure 6–4 depicts, an individual scoring 111 is placed with a second person scoring 114 to form a matched pair. At this point each member of the pair is randomly assigned to Condition A or Condition B. This process is repeated until a sufficient number of subjects are placed in each condition. Even though the matched samples will not be precisely the same, the range matching procedure allows you to feel secure that you have functionally equivalent samples.

One of the major difficulties with the precision and range matching techniques is that it is often difficult to determine the precise value of a variable. For instance, what if you wanted to match on political conservatism? How could you do it? You might create a questionnaire or some other assessment device, but without the appropriate psychometric documentation you could not be certain what your scores reflect. Another problem with precision and range matching is that in some cases you will have subjects who do not match with anyone. Consequently, these subjects must be discarded from the experiment, and the resulting subject selection bias can affect your ability to generalize (see following section on generalization). Still, the precision and range matching procedures of-

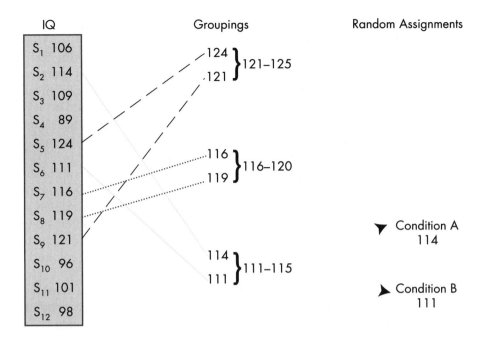

**FIGURE 6–4** An example of range matching where people who fall within the same narrow range of IQ values (create pairs within 5 IQ points) are randomly assigned to treatment Conditions A and B.

---

fer psychological researchers sampling methods that enhance the scientific credibility of their findings.

**Matching with Yoking Procedures.** In psychological research, **yoking** refers to a matching technique that ensures that the same events a subject experiences in one condition are experienced at the same time and in the same sequence by a partner subject in another condition. This procedure, which is used more often with animal research than human research, is ideal for controlling extraneous variation based on temporal (timing) factors or the different effects that may be associated with the pattern by which seemingly identical events are experienced.

There are many good examples of the advantages yoking procedures afford. An experiment conducted by Cook, Mineka, and Trumble (1987) provides one illustration. In this study, which used rats as subjects, one aim was to determine the comparative fear (anxiety) levels produced by controllable and uncontrollable electric shock. Is it worse to receive

**yoking**—a matching procedure in which a master and a partner receive identical treatment manipulations; this procedure controls for sequential and temporal effects that otherwise might influence the data

aversive stimulation you have no control over, or is it worse when the aversive event can be escaped or avoided if you do the correct thing?

To answer this question, Cook et al. presented rats (masters) with 200 signaled avoidance training trials. When the signal (a tone) sounded, an electric shock followed, but the rats could easily avoid or turn off the shock by pressing a lever. Yoked counterpart rats in identical apparatus which contained no levers, and therefore no method for controlling shock, were administered the signal at the same time as the masters. Depending on the master's behavior, the yoked rat received no shock (the master pressed the lever and avoided the shock), or the shock offset of the yoked rat occurred coincidentally with the offset of the shock for the master when the master finally pressed the lever (made the escape) response. Subsequently, both the master and the yoked rats were presented with the signal (tone) and the amount of freezing (the point at which the rat stopped moving) was measured as an index of conditioned fear. As it turned out, the tone predicting uncontrollable shock proved to be more fear evoking (the yoked rats exhibited greater freezing than the masters).

The advantage of the procedure Cook et al. employed is that the master and yoked rats differed only along the dimension of shock controllability. The number of tone and shock presentations, the pattern and duration of shock deliveries, and every other aspect of the experiment was the same for both conditions. Thus, a real match was achieved and only the independent variable (shock controllability) changed.

With human subjects, various forms of yoking can also be useful. For example, Hiroto and Seligman (1975) ran a study on "learned helplessness" in which exposure to a noncontingency (a condition in which your behavior is unrelated to what happens to you) resulted in deficits in later learning exercises. The exposure to the noncontingency in one case was accomplished by having college students look at various geometric configurations containing several different dimensions such as shape, size, and so on, and then receive feedback about their choices of the "correct" dimension, which the experimenter determined arbitrarily. The feedback about being right or wrong was random, and there was no way the learned helplessness subjects could guess correctly. Consistent with the expectations of the experimenters, these subjects performed poorly on later problem-solving tasks (they exhibited helplessness effects).

Now, think about some interpretive issues here. Could it be that just going to the laboratory and sitting in the testing environment for a long period of time produced fatigue, and that this alone caused poor performance among the learned helplessness subjects? It is, in fact, quite possible that a "length of participation factor" could have been responsible for the observed effects. To control for this possibility, Hiroto and Seligman ran a yoked-control group in which the subjects spent the same amount of time in the laboratory as their learned helplessness counterparts, but they did nothing. The yoked subjects had no difficulty with the later problem-solving task, so the time factor obviously was not an issue. This is an example of how yoking procedures help psychologists control for variables that may be intrusive and bias the interpretation of the results.

Although some legitimate complaints about the effectiveness of yoking techniques have been raised (see Church, 1964), on the whole yoking techniques are quite valuable. Similar benefits are reached from the judicious use of randomized block designs.

**Matching with Randomized Block Designs.** In each of the previous examples, the explicit intent was to ensure equivalency by matching subjects based on some specific organismic characteristic, temporal parameter, or other potentially extraneous variable. The purpose of the matching operation was to avoid the contaminating influence a particular uncontrolled variable might have on the results. However, what if the experimenter, in addition to wanting to avoid extraneous variation, wishes to know something about a matching factor? Can matching variables be incorporated into the design of the experiment and analyzed systematically? Yes, matching variables can be evaluated and examined with respect to their influence by using the randomized block design.

The **randomized block design,** which was named by Sir Ronald Fisher, actually originated from scientific studies of various agricultural procedures. Indeed, much of what we know about experimental design as it is currently used in psychological research is based on agriculture research. For Fisher, the term *block* literally referred to a block of land. Separate blocks or plots of land were designated to receive certain treatments. For example, a new, untested soil amendment might be applied to Block A, a second experimental application might be given to Block B, and so on. Within each block, various agricultural products could be carefully monitored and the advantages for crop production appropriately noted.

Psychologists have used the basic experimental framework of the randomized block design to help them control for some extraneous or matching factor. Figure 6–5 is a graphical representation of how a matching factor can be built into the experimental design and thereby controlled. In this instance we are interested in obedience and, as a follow-up to Milgram's classic work on this topic (refer to Chapter 4), we aim to determine if two quite different sets of instructions produce different degrees of obedience. The precise nature of the instructions are incidental to our coverage here, so let's just say they differ, and we will refer to them as Instruction Set A and Instruction Set B, respectively. Let's further assume that we are interested in males only, so gender is not a variable in our experiment.

The decision to use males only introduces a special problem, however. Is it possible that the number of years a person has spent on active duty in military service might correlate with his willingness to respond

**randomized block design—a** procedure in which the matching variable is included in the experimental design as an independent variable

Blocking (matching) variable
Years of military experience

|  | 1–3 | 4–10 | >10 |
|---|---|---|---|
| Instruction set A | $S_1$<br>$S_2$ and so on<br>$S_3$ | $S_1$<br>$S_2$ and so on<br>$S_3$ | $S_1$<br>$S_2$ and so on<br>$S_3$ |
| Instruction set B | $S_1$<br>$S_2$ and so on<br>$S_3$ | $S_1$<br>$S_2$ and so on<br>$S_3$ | $S_1$<br>$S_2$ and so on<br>$S_3$ |

FIGURE 6–5 An example of a randomized block design where the matching factor (the number of years in military service) forms three blocks. Subjects who fall within the three blocks are randomly assigned to Instruction Set A or Instruction Set B in a study of obedience.

to demands (to perform obediently)? It is possible that this variable could operate extraneously on our data if it is uncontrolled. Consistent with our previous discussion, matched pairs of subjects could be created and randomly assigned to Instruction Set A or B. In this case, however, length of military service and its effect on obedience is something we want to know more about, so we create three distinctively different levels (blocks) of the matching variables and incorporate these blocks into the design as an independent variable. Block 1 contains males with 1 to 3 years of military experience, Block 2 includes those with 4 to 10 years of experience, and individuals with greater than 10 years of experience in military service are assigned to Block 3. Now we are in a position to determine if the extraneous variable (the blocking variable) impacts our findings in any systematic way.

One feature of the randomized block design that is easy to overlook as a student or new reader of experimental design is that the integrity of the randomization process is maintained. That is, in our example of blocking based on number of years spent in military service, the pool of subjects composing each block would be large enough to permit the investigator to randomly sample within the block of available subjects. With this random selection process, other systematic sources of bias, such as IQ, aggressiveness, and so forth, should not creep into the results.

Therefore, we can match by building the matching factor (subject variable) into the research design. Later, when we discuss more complex design considerations in Chapters 8 and 9, we will see that the randomized block design adds information about "interaction effects." For now, however, it suffices to note that psychologists have several alternatives to control extraneous variation through matching.

## *Cohort Samples*

Webster's dictionary defines a *cohort* as a band or a group. In psychological research, **cohort samples** are samples that are drawn from a common population and then designated as separate sample conditions based on some distinct trait or evaluation criterion. Cohort samples are common in developmental studies in which specific generations are followed over a period of years (Schaie, 1983). For example, someone interested in studying the onset of schizophrenia may track subjects born in 1970 for 25 years and index both the frequency of occurrence of the disorder and the year in which it was first diagnosed. The sample of people suffering from schizophrenia may then be compared to cohort controls, and a variety of variables distinguishing the two groups can be assessed.

Cohort samples are especially useful when one or several variables may bias an entire population. For example, McMichael et al. (1992) published an update on the effects of environmental lead exposure on the mental and cognitive functioning of children exposed to the metal in early childhood. In this Australian study, known as the "Port Pirie Cohort Study," 831 pregnant women living near a lead smelter were recruited as subjects. The children born to these women have been followed since 1982. Among other things it has been found that girls, especially those around age 4, are more vulnerable to lead toxicity than their male counterparts. This finding was based on comparing children in the study who had elevated blood lead levels with children in the study who had normal lead concentrations in their blood.

This is why it is so important that a cohort sampling procedure was used in this project. People who would choose or be forced to live near a lead smelter site may have children who would perform differently on neuropsychological tests, but not because of the lead contamination issue. That is, socioeconomic status, the social and educational attitudes of parents, and a host of other demographic variables may be responsible for decreased mental functioning in children living in and around Port Pirie, South Australia. To compare them with a sample from another region or area would be a mistake, because you could never be sure if your observed differences were due to elevated lead levels or demographic peculiarities. With a cohort sampling procedure, however, you are assured that your "high lead" sample and

**cohort samples**—samples drawn at the same time from a common population

your "low lead" sample are equal along all dimensions other than the amount of lead in the samples' bodies. All subjects come from a single, common sample sharing overlapping traits. Mothers of the children composing the two different samples should hold common values, attitudes, and so forth. At the least, there is no reason to suspect that some variable which might affect the data would systematically differ for mothers in the "high lead" and "low lead" conditions.

Therefore, the advantage of cohort samples is that they control for built-in problems and therein maximize the utility of the data. However, it should be noted that cohort samples usually involve large numbers of subjects. Of course, under many circumstances collecting a large sample is just not feasible. An alternative sampling procedure must therefore be selected.

# WITHIN CHAPTER REVIEW AND STUDY QUESTIONS

## POPULATIONS AND SAMPLES

1. What role does probability theory play in the formation of random samples? List three different procedures that could be used to generate a random sample.
2. Under what conditions would you want to use a stratified sampling procedure? What is the chief difficulty in using a stratified sampling technique?
3. Under what conditions would you want to include a randomized block design? Can you think of any disadvantages of using such a procedure?
4. A sample of all males born in Mercy Hospital in Oklahoma City in 1984 would be a _____ sample.
    a. random
    b. stratified
    c. cohort

# GENERALIZATION

Our discussion to this point has centered on samples drawn from a large population of values. Because samples are easier to work with than populations, and because it is often impossible to measure every population value, it is appropriate that the bulk of the coverage thus far has focused on sample characteristics. However, the ultimate aim of the psychological investigator is not defining sample values. Rather, it is defining population values. This brings us to the issue of the generalizability between sample and the population.

**Generalization,** as it relates to research methodology, refers to the ability to apply findings from a sample to other settings within a common population. This means that when researchers collect a given data set that is generated by a specific sample, they hope to be able to say something about a broader scientific context. The belief is that if the sample has been selected adequately, is free of bias, and is representative of the population of which it is a subset, then statements about the population can be made confidently. That is, based on a known set of findings we can generalize to an immense, immeasurable pool of events (population) and feel safe that what we are asserting about the larger set of values is valid.

The importance of the concept of generalization to psychological research can be illustrated by a study conducted by Snyder, Wills, and Grady-Fletcher (1991). In this report, 59 couples who were having marital problems were randomly assigned to treatment conditions in which they received either behavioral marital therapy or insight-oriented therapy. It is sufficient to note here that behavioral intervention strategies employ conditioning techniques aimed at increasing positive, caring gestures while decreasing negative or potentially abusive verbal remarks. In contrast, insight-oriented therapy encourages the couple to interact in a mature, accepting environment in which they can resolve hidden or unconscious conflicts. In a 4-year follow-up comparing the long-term effectiveness of the two different treatment approaches, Snyder et al. discovered that 38% of the couples who had received behavioral marital therapy had divorced. These data contrast sharply with the findings from couples who had experienced insight-oriented therapy. Only 3% of these couples had divorced 4 years after marital therapy (see Figure 6–6).

Obviously the Snyder et al. study has profound implications on the selection of treatment styles for couples seeking marital counseling, or at least this is true if the data are generalizable. If the validity of the Snyder et al. findings holds only for the 59 couples who participated in the research project, then it would be reckless and an outright mistake to encourage marital therapists to adopt an insight-oriented approach to treatment. However, if the results from this sample can be generalized to all couples entering therapy, then some clear recommendations can and likely should be made. The issue rests with the ability to generalize from the sample to the population. If the appropriate selection strategy were implemented (and in this case apparently it was), a persuasive and forceful case can be made for choosing insight-oriented marital therapy over behavioral marital therapy.

In studies such as the Snyder et al. (1991) project, concerns over generalization stem more from selection and adequate representation than the appropriateness of the sample. That is, because the Snyder et al.

**generalization**—the ability to make statements about a broader population based on sample findings

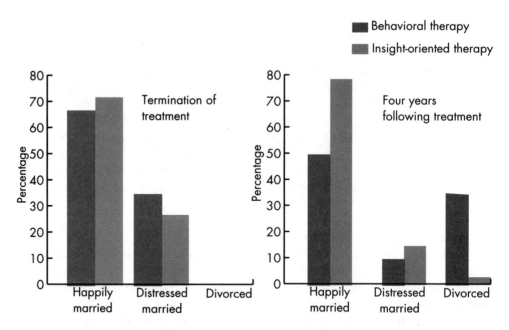

FIGURE 6–6 Data from the Snyder, Wills, and Grady-Fletcher (1991) study showing the percentages of happily married, distressed married, or divorced couples in behavioral and insight-oriented marital therapy conditions at termination and 4-year follow-up. For such data to be meaningful, they must be generalizable to a broader population of couples suffering marital discord. In this case the data are likely to be generalizable. Copyright © 1991 by the American Psychological Association. Reprinted with permission.

investigation was conducted using actual couples experiencing marital discord, you don't have to worry about the credibility of the participants. Certainly, the couples represent a subset of the population to which you hope to generalize, but in most psychological experiments using humans as subjects, the sample may or may not contain members from the broader population. The reason: The majority of psychological experiments using human subjects employ college students.

College students are used in psychological research mostly because of convenience. As I pointed out in Chapter 4, Ethics, forced participation is not permitted, and there are incentives to participate at many institutions, either in the form of material or financial rewards, or as minimal course requirement. As a result, much of what we know about human behavior has come from the performance of college students.

But do college students differ from noncollege students? If there are systematic differences, are we generalizing inappropriately to a population that we really do not know much about? Likely we are. At this juncture, the limited evidence pertaining to the matter is fundamentally at odds. Some studies that have compared college and noncollege subjects have found no differences between the two (Tanford, 1984). Other studies have shown that there are striking differences between the two (Feild & Barnett, 1978). The findings may vary depending on the nature of the experiment. In any event, we should all be aware of the importance of generalizability and the impact it has on the credibility of our data.

## WITHIN CHAPTER REVIEW AND STUDY QUESTION

### GENERALIZATION

1. List sampling events that would compromise an investigator's ability to generalize. In such situations, what can we do with the findings?

## MULTICULTURAL ISSUES

The issue of generalization raises additional concerns about how we conduct psychological research. In addition to questions about the relevancy of data collected predominantly from college students, there is a growing awareness that research findings may be influenced by cultural and ethnic parameters. The study of psychology within the context of cultural diversity is not new—cross-cultural examination of phenomena such as child rearing has been conducted for many years. What is new is that issues related to multiculturalism have emerged as matters of interest throughout the discipline (Bronstein & Quina, 1991).

Richard Majors (1992) addressed the importance of cultural diversity in the communication of emotions in his book *Cool Pose: The Dilemmas of Black Manhood in America*. Majors argues that some black males have adopted certain behavioral styles that are intended to signal very specific feelings or attitudes. A particular posture or look may communicate confidence or discontent, but this emotion may be misunderstood or missed by someone unfamiliar with the black profile. Psychologist Stanley Sue and his colleagues of the University of California, Los Angeles, showed that the success of therapy in mental health clinics is greatly enhanced when clients and therapists are matched according to racial and ethnic backgrounds. The therapists' sensitivity to the traditions and values of the selected cultural groups apparently facilitated discussion and promoted healing.

Given the evidence that culture is a dominant force in behavior, it is not surprising that psychologists have begun to exercise greater caution in interpreting their results. A reliable effect in one cultural population may be of limited significance in another. This is not to suggest that overlap is nonexistent across cultural populations, but it does say something about how far we can or should go with our statements. Perhaps the safest strategy for psychology investigators is to maintain an appreciation for the potential importance of cultural variables as they relate to the outcome of a given study and to incorporate these elements into the overall design of the project when it is feasible to do so.

## WITHIN CHAPTER REVIEW AND STUDY QUESTION

### MULTICULTURAL ISSUES

1. What aspects of Eastern and Western cultures do you think might contribute to differences in a study of the role of older adults in family decision-making processes? What other social behaviors might be differentially determined by cultural factors?

# COUNTERBALANCING AND CARRYOVER EFFECTS

The coverage of procedures relating to subject variables and data collection thus far has centered on sampling techniques, the formation of equivalent samples that are representative of and generalizable to broader populations, and multicultural issues. In addition to the issue of ensuring that subject characteristics and sample features render findings that are scientifically credible, there is the issue of the data collection process. Even with representative samples that are free of the prejudicial effects of uncontrolled sources of variation, if the data collection process is not set up properly, the results may still be uninterpretable.

As a case in point, consider the following experimental protocol. An investigator interested in the effects of three psychoactive drugs (chlorpromazine, ketamine, and scopolamine) on the acquisition and retention of a classically conditioned response, ideally would administer each drug to separate groups of subjects to assess the effects of each chemical on learning phenomena. This is precisely what Scavio, Clift, and Wills (1992) did. They recorded the acquisition and extinction of conditioned eyeblink responses in three groups of rabbits. Each of the three groups received a different chemical treatment (chlorpromazine, ketamine, or scopolamine) after classical conditioning training to see if the learning (conditioning) process was affected by a post-training application of the drug. In this case, ketamine increased conditioning while chlorpromazine and scopolamine retarded performance.

In the best of all possible research worlds, the Scavio et al. (1992) study is the best design to use. But what if you are constrained by resources and can only afford a few animals? What if personnel concerns require that you complete the experiment quicker and with fewer subjects? Can something be done? The obvious answer is to administer all three psychoactive drug treatments to the same animals. This introduces a serious source of bias, however. Although the drugs used in the Scavio et al. (1992) example may operate on different biochemical systems, they may interact, which means one drug may influence the reaction of a second, and so on. By the time you get to the last drug, you may have some profound interpretative problems. Is there any way to run this experiment with fewer animals and yet avoid the problems associated with serial drug administrations? There is a way, and it involves counterbalancing.

## Counterbalancing

**Counterbalancing** is a technique that prevents sequentially dependent effects from intruding on data. In simpler terms, this procedure is used to guarantee that the position of a particular treatment does not systematically affect the experiment results. Let's use the Scavio et al. (1992) example to illustrate how counterbalancing can be used. We can label each of our three chemical treatments as Treatment A, B, and C, respectively. As Figure 6–7 shows, different subjects receive Treatments A to C in different sequences. In this arrangement, Treatment A is in the second position as often as Treatment B or C. This is true for the first and third positions as well. Every chemical appears equally often in each sequential location. The result: Because sequence is not a factor, it cannot systematically affect the results.

Counterbalancing techniques are used a great deal in psychological research because they are economical. Often, you can answer the

**counterbalancing**—a technique used to prevent the biasing effects of sequence in testing; it eliminates test order as a variable

Chlorpromazive = Variable (drug) A
Scopolamine = Variable (drug) B
Ketamine = Variable (drug) C

| Subject number | Sequence of drug administration |
|---|---|
| 1 | A B C |
| 2 | B C A |
| 3 | C A B |
| 4 | A C B |
| 5 | C B A |
| 6 | B A C |

FIGURE 6–7 An illustration of counterbalancing where three drugs are tested using the same animals as subjects

same questions with less expense and effort. It should be understood, however, that in some cases sequence may be a variable of interest to the experimenter. This leads to the next topic.

## Carryover Effects

There are many instances in psychological research where antecedent conditions impact events. Antecedent events are by definition events that "occur before." Depending on the nature of the experiment, antecedent conditions can alter the outcome of experimental manipulations that take place later. When the effects of a treatment condition are influenced by antecedent treatment operations, the phenomenon is referred to as a **carryover effect.**

That a treatment event which occurs first in a sequence may change the behavioral effects produced by the second treatment in the sequence can often be problematic. One example of the complications carryover effects create is the well-known phenomenon of sensitization in behavioral pharmacology research.

In sensitization effects, drug responsiveness increases with each successive administration of the drug. Schenk, Snow, and Horger (1991) reported such an effect in a study that examined the effects of cocaine administration on general motor activity. The psychostimulatory (motor-activating) properties of cocaine have been well demonstrated. In this case, each experience with the drug increased the subject's sensitivity to the activating properties of subsequent cocaine applications. When the independent

**carryover effect**—result when an antecedent treatment condition differentially affects a later test phase

variable is "drug dose," sensitization issues make it difficult to assess the precise effects of different drug doses, even if a counterbalancing design is employed, because you cannot be sure how much of the observed effect is due to experience with the drug.

One way to address the problem of carryover effects like these is to make "order of treatment" an independent variable. That is, analyze treatment sequence and see if it makes a difference. Indeed, there are some cases where the analysis of carryover is critical to understanding the results of an experiment. This was very much the case in a series of experiments I conducted two decades ago on the phenomenon of behavioral contrast.

Positive contrast effects are said to occur when an upward shift in reward magnitude elevates performance in the case where the higher reward amount has been experienced all along. In a study I conducted (Nation, Roop, & Dickinson, 1976), I examined the possibility that a sudden upward shift in reward magnitude would produce a different pattern of results than a gradual upward shift to the same high level of reward. As Figure 6–8 shows, the gradual shift condition produced an even greater positive contrast effect than the abrupt shift condition.

Carryover effects were at the core of our 1976 study. In fact, had we not observed carryover from the preshift (before shifting reward magnitude upward) to the postshift phases of the experiment, contrast effects would not have been observed. In this instance, because we treated preshift phase-postshift phase as an independent variable, the sequence of treatments, rather than being a nuisance, afforded important information.

Therefore, sequential effects in psychological research can be an adversary or a partner to the investigator. It is up to the experimenter and the nature of the topic under investigation to decide which is which.

## WITHIN CHAPTER REVIEW AND STUDY QUESTIONS

### COUNTERBALANCING AND CARRYOVER EFFECTS

1. Under what conditions should counterbalancing be used? Design an experiment involving counterbalancing where human subjects take three forms of an IQ test. What information is lost in such a design?
2. If you were testing for the effects of reinforcement schedules on resistance to extinction, would you want to treat acquisition training and extinction training as an independent variable? Why or why not?

**confounding variable**—an un-controlled variable that systematically biases the results of an experiment

**internal validity**—the degree to which the hypothesis that forms the basis of the experiment is tested free of the biasing influence of the extraneous factor

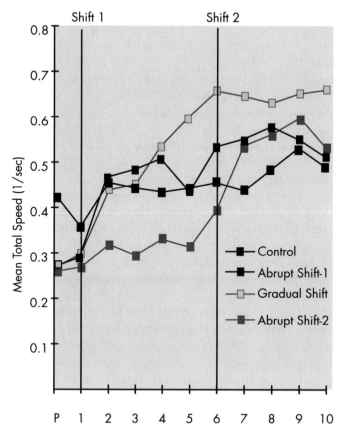

**FIGURE 6–8** This graph demonstrates the importance of carryover effects in that the preshift events (gradual or abrupt increases in reward magnitude) had different effects on a later, postshift phase. (Adapted from Nation, Roop, and Dickinson, 1976.)

# CONFOUNDING

One of the main concerns an investigator has about data collection is that a variable which is not included in the experimental design may be influencing the data. When an uncontrolled variable systematically biases the results of an experiment, it is called a **confounding variable.** There are many potential confounding variables that can corrupt the **internal validity** of an experiment. *Internal validity* means the degree to which the research design provides a fair test of the hypothesis that forms the rationale for conducting the experiment

(Campbell & Stanley, 1963). Effectively, internal validity deals with the issue of whether your results are due to the treatment effect you have opted to manipulate experimentally or to some uncontrolled confounding variable.

Can you think of some obvious confounds that, if left uncontrolled, might prejudice the results of an experiment? What about something as simple as the age of the subject? At the low end of the age range, maturational elements may have a strong effect on performance because cognitive and intellectual processes change rapidly during our formative years. Indeed, this very important variable has been selected as one of the independent variables for the model experiment we are building as we move through this book. In fact, early age differences is the centerpoint for the idea behind the model experiment. But what about age differences in adults? Could they also be a confounding source? They could, because even in the absence of maturational problems, experience that is correlated with age can make a substantial difference with respect to subject performance.

In addition to age, other variables that have the potential to confound the results of a study are the laboratory conditions at the time of testing (e.g., noise or distractions), apparatus malfunctions, and inappropriate representation (i.e., too many males in the sample). In cases where such variables may operate conspicuously as confounding elements in a research project, the threat is nominal. The possibility that such an uncontrolled source of variation may ruin an experiment is so clear that the experimenter knows to control for it. It is when the confounding variable is more subtle that problems arise. This is evident from a controversial report on the causes of homosexuality.

## Spotlight on Research: IS HOMOSEXUALITY BORN OR BRED?

As an Englishman with a Ph.D. in neuro-anatomy, Simon LeVay spent 12 years at Harvard before accepting a position at the Salk Institute in La Jolla, California. As a successful scientist, LeVay became interested in the true causes of homosexuality when his male lover of 21 years died of AIDS. Based on some preliminary findings from other laboratories and an enduring belief that being gay is a biologically determined phenomenon, LeVay launched a scientific investigation into a matter that sparked a fiery debate on the causes of sexual preference.

Using cadavers as subjects, LeVay scanned the brains of 16 heterosexual males and 19 homosexual males. In an astonishing discovery, LeVay found that there was a statistically significant difference in the size of a tiny portion of the hypothalamus that is believed to control sexual activity. This sex-regulating area was much smaller in gay men than in heterosexual men (LeVay, 1991).

Based on these data, LeVay began to promote the idea that gay men may respond to a biological imperative in exercising their sexual preference.

He believed that men are homosexual because of differences in their brain morphology, not because of a peculiar environmental or experiential history (LeVay & Hamer, 1994). Support for LeVay's contention came from studies of identical twins which showed that when one identical twin is gay, the other is almost three times more likely to be gay as compared to men in the same scenario who are fraternal twins (refer to Pillard & Bailey, 1995).

*Prima facie,* these data seem to be compelling and make a strong case for biologically determined sexual orientation. However, closer inspection reveals that all 19 homosexuals in the original study died from AIDS; only 6 of the 16 heterosexuals died from the disease. Do you think there could be a confounding variable here? Could AIDS alter brain morphology? It is possible, but as yet the variable is uncontrolled and therefore confounds the research.

In addition, the twins who were used in the study were reared together. Consequently, the shaping influences that are known to exist in the social environments of identical and fraternal twins might be responsible for the observed effects. The possibility of such a confound prompted Anne Stirling, a developmental biologist at Brown University, to remark, "It's such badly interpreted genetics" *(Newsweek, February 24, 1992, p. 48).*

So, is gayness among males born or bred? If we go on just the reports cited here, it would be a hazardous call one way or the other.    ■

Confounded experiments are often difficult to avoid. It is sometimes difficult to anticipate which organismic or environmental factors will systematically influence your findings. Nonetheless, every effort should be made to control for confounding events.

## WITHIN CHAPTER REVIEW AND STUDY QUESTION

### CONFOUNDING

1. An experiment is designed to determine the relation between IQ and the ability to solve anagrams (puzzles in which letters must be unscrambled to form a word). How many different confounding variables can you think of that might affect performance on this task?

# SELECTING ANIMAL SUBJECTS

Because animal research is such an integral part of psychological experimentation, it is appropriate that I make a few comments about matters relating to the selection and treatment of laboratory animals.

While there are a few psychology laboratories that use infrahuman primates, such as the chimpanzee or the rhesus monkey, as subjects, clearly the bulk of animal researchers use pigeons or albino white rats in their experiments. The latter is more common, and much of what we know about the relation between behavior and environmental events is the result of decades of observing the common laboratory rat.

Different institutions adopt different approaches with respect to maintaining animal colonies. Some facilities prefer the "in house" approach where the breeding colony is on site. This requires carefully controlled breeding operations and close supervision of dam/pup interactions. Other investigators, and I am one of them, prefer to purchase rats from a separate, remote breeding facility where cohorts of animals are shipped directly to investigators at their laboratory sites. Firms like the Holtzman Company in Madison, Wisconsin, offer different strains (e.g., Long Evans, Sprague-Dawley), a narrow range of body weights (you might order animals that arrive at the laboratory weighing between 180 and 200 grams, for instance), or combinations of male and female rats.

Regarding this latter issue, I note that more than 90% of all animal research that is conducted using rats as subjects use males. Given recent findings that female animals respond very differently to the same experimental manipulations that are administered to males (in this case, the study was on patterns of alcohol consumption [Lancaster & Spiegel, 1992]), one is left to ponder the validity of the wealth of information in the area of animal learning, which is based mostly on the performances of the male laboratory rat. How generalizable are the findings to females? What might be the implications for extrapolating to the human condition?

## Concerns over Individual and Genetic Variation

Anyone who has ever conducted a research project using animals knows that while animals are more alike than humans, no two animals are exactly alike. Placed in an operant chamber (a Skinner Box), some animals learn to lever press for a food reward within a matter of minutes. Others, however, can take hours to learn the task, and some will never learn to lever press at all, regardless of your patience or how long you try to train them. Eventually some animals will be discarded from the experiment. What's the problem here? What biases are immediately introduced into the study?

Certainly, you have affected your ability to generalize, because you have a truncated distribution that does not represent the animal population in general. So, what can you do about it? Not much, other than always report your every procedural move, including how many animals were lost to training difficulties, death, and so forth. Let the reader judge the generalizability and credibility of your findings. If all details are not reported in a scientific article, the reader cannot make an informed appraisal of the validity of your findings. Always be meticulous in reporting procedural anomalies where animals are concerned—it can make a big difference.

In addition to individual differences between animals of the same gender, strain, body weight, and so on, there is the issue of behavioral differences that occur due to genetics. This phenomenon is acutely evident in the aforementioned area of alcohol consumption in rats. The ALKO LTD laboratories, the national alcohol research facilities for Finland in Helsinki, have selectively bred alcohol accepting (AA) and alcohol nonaccepting (ANA) strains of rats. Numerous studies have shown that AA rats respond more frequently for alcohol rewards than do ANA rats, and they are more responsive to the drug in general (George, 1987). There are many other instances where genetic lines produce prominent differences in behavioral patterns, including visual discrimination tasks, activity, reactivity to aversive stimulation, and a host of other behavioral end points (see Domjan, 1996, for more coverage on this topic). Therefore, when designing an experiment it is important that the investigator keep in mind that genetic variation is an essential variable that must be considered.

In summary, animal research is not as "tight" as many people might think. There is always the nonresponder, the animal that refuses to cooperate or develops an infection, and on it goes. The selection and use of animals in psychological research must be executed with the same level of scrutiny that is demanded in human subject research.

## WITHIN CHAPTER REVIEW AND STUDY QUESTION

### SELECTING ANIMAL SUBJECTS

1. Why are animals even used in psychological research? Do you believe that we can learn anything about human behavior by studying animals?

## The Model Experiment

Subject selection and the methods by which they are assigned to various experimental treatment conditions are critical to the success of any experimental operation. Of the several procedures available to us, we have decided to use a random sampling technique for assigning subjects (patients) to the six treatment conditions in the model experiment we are building as we move through the chapters of this book. Specifically, 48 patients ages 4 to 6 undergoing medical treatment for cancer will be randomly assigned to one of the three therapeutic intervention conditions we have selected for the project (cognitive coping strategy, sensory information, and contact control; N = 16/group). Similarly, 48 cancer patients ranging from age 10 to 12 years will be randomly assigned to one of the three intervention conditions, creating an equal Ns design.

Each participant is required to meet specified criteria for inclusion in the study, and the functional equivalency of subjects before introducing any experimental manipulations is ensured. Having satisfactorily addressed potential problems relating to subject characteristics, we are now in a position to look at other factors more directly tied to the experiment. In the next chapter, we will discuss experimental control and what actually takes place in the research setting.

## CHAPTER 7

# Experimental Control and the Research Setting

In 1912, W. B. Cannon and his graduate student, A. L. Washburn, set out to determine the true cause of hunger. Because the simplest ideas are those that should be examined first in scientific investigations, Cannon and Washburn decided to test the notion that we eat when our stomachs are empty and we stop eating when our stomachs are full. As a practical evaluation of this straightforward account, Cannon persuaded Washburn to swallow a balloon. When the balloon was inflated, crude seismic recordings of stomach contractions could be made and correlated with subjective estimations of hunger. After several sessions, the data were conclusive—hunger does result from an empty stomach and its attendant pangs and growlings.

Hunger researchers today know that hunger control mechanisms are not centered in the stomach. It now appears that endocrine mechanisms, lipid (fats) stores, and other complex physiological processes determine hunger motivation (Carlson, 1991). In any event, the early experiment Cannon and Washburn conducted is worth mentioning here because it provides several good examples of what *not* to do in psychological research. First, Cannon and Washburn did not isolate the role of the stomach in hunger. To declare the stomach the true determinant of hunger, an experimental manipulation that would show all other events are insufficient to produce hunger would have to be performed. That this is not the case was made evident by subsequent animal and human studies which showed that eating is discontinued after a regular size meal, even when all nerves from the stomach to the central nervous system were cut or blocked. Also, Washburn was both subject and experimenter in this famous early work. Because Washburn suspected the the stomach and hunger were linked before commencing the experiment, do you think he was capable of being unbiased? Do you suspect that Washburn's knowledge of his hunger contractions may have contributed to his subjective appraisal of how hungry he was feeling at any given point in time? These are major flaws in the experimental design, and they could have been controlled.

In this chapter, control issues and what the research setting should be about are our topics. I begin with one of the basic methods for controlling experimental variation: operationalism.

# CONTROL THROUGH OPERATIONALISM

Consider the following experiment conducted by psychologist Stanley Schachter in 1959. Schachter had developed a theoretical model of affiliation (the need to be with others), and his aim was to provide evidence that affiliation needs increase when we are threatened or otherwise placed at risk. Using a laboratory model with college students as subjects, Schachter had women confronted by an extremely intimidating authority figure who was alleged to be a medical researcher. (In actuality, the authority figure was a confederate who worked for the experimenter.) In addition, the women were shown a frightening apparatus they were told would deliver electric shocks of varying intensities. This was also a deception, of course, and no shocks were actually given. Subjects in the "high anxiety" condition were told they would receive extremely intense shocks. Conversely, subjects in the "low anxiety" condition were told they would receive hardly noticeable electric shocks. After these initial, stress-inducing remarks were made, the experimenter would announce that there would be a short delay before shock testing, and he or she would ask the subject to wait their turns to participate. Each subject was given the option of waiting in a room alone or with several other people.

The results of the Schachter experiment are summarized in Figure 7–1. In support of Schachter's model, subjects in the "high anxiety" condition preferred waiting with others twice as often as subjects in the "low anxiety" condition. Other experiments by Schachter and his colleagues would show this ratio to hold only when the subjects were told they could speak with others while in the waiting room. In cases where the subjects were informed they could not speak with anyone, the preference for waiting with others was not nearly so strong.

|  | Permitted to speak with others | Not permitted to speak with others |
|---|---|---|
| High anxiety | Preference for waiting with others was *high* | Preference for waiting with others was *low* |
| Low anxiety | Preference for waiting with others was *low* | Preference for waiting with others was *low* |

FIGURE 7–1 An example of experimenter effects. When subjects were under a condition of high anxiety, they opted to wait with others in a waiting room. This was less likely when they were told they could not speak to anyone (from Schachter, 1959).

**operationalism**—the use of observable events and operations to define various procedures of an experiment

**operational definition**—a special case of operationalism where an independent variable is defined according to the observable events used to produce it

**measured operational definition**—a definition in which operational definitions are used to define a dependent variable

This experiment appears to show that, when people are frightened, what they really need is a sympathetic voice.

The value of the Schachter study for our coverage here is that the experiment's overall design demonstrates the principle of **operationalism.** For psychology researchers, *operationalism* is the practice of defining various procedures of an experiment according to observable operations. Often, in experimental psychology you will see the term **operational definition** which is a special case of operationalism where the independent variable is defined by the observable events used to produce it. For example, Schachter operationally defined the "high anxiety" group by telling us precisely what the subjects experienced by way of instructions, options, and other procedural details. Similarly, we know exactly what Schachter meant when he referred to the "low anxiety" condition. Although there may be some disagreement over whether these manipulations really qualify as "high anxiety" or "low anxiety," there can be no confusion about what was done to the subjects. When experimenters operationalize a variable, they clarify which events occur during an experiment.

The advantage of using operational definitions in psychological research is that they enhance replication. When an investigator provides clear operational descriptions of the variables that were manipulated or changed in the experiment, someone who is interested in reproducing the results of the experiment does not have to attempt to replicate the study with minimal clues. When variables are operationally defined, you know what was done and you can do the same in your laboratory. This increases the chances that you will cut down on the variability that is inherent across experiments conducted in different laboratories, in different locations, and so forth. Operationalism aids science through replication.

Kerlinger (1973) has proposed that in addition to operationally defining independent variables, as was done in the Schachter (1959) experiment, dependent variables can be operationalized. Kerlinger referred to this as composing a **measured operational definition.**

An example of the use of a measured operational definition is available from an alcohol research study conducted by Harford et al. (1992). The purpose of this study was to examine the effects of family history on alcohol abuse in young adults (people between the ages of 14 and 21) in the United States. It is assumed that in order to gain some understanding of the relation between family background and current drinking habits, you must know something about how much alcohol the person actually consumed. Harford et al. coded drinking profiles as follows: average consumption was obtained, using a self-report measure, by dividing the total number of drinks by the total number of days alcohol was consumed in the past month. The resulting codes were 0 = 0; 0.1–1.4 = 1; 1.5–2.4 = 2; 2.5–3.4 = 3; 3.5–4.4 = 4; 4.5–5.4 = 5; and anything greater than 5.5 was scored 6. Therefore, if a person reported a total of 8 drinks during 6 days the person was assigned a score of 1.33 (8 ÷ 6), and this was recoded as a *1*.

With this type of operational description of drinking behavior, the reader has a clear index of the authors' meaning. To simply speak in terms of "excessive drinking" or "moderate drinking" would leave one wondering about the essentials of the report. In this case, however, because the investigators provided a measured operational definition of drinking alcohol, it was easy to discern what happened in the experiment.

## Hypothetical Constructs and Intervening Variables

Almost a half-century ago, MacCorquodale and Meehl (1948) elaborated on the distinction between *hypothetical constructs* and *intervening variables*. A hypothetical construct is defined as some theoretical variable that is attached to some antecedent condition on the one hand and some consequence or behavior on the other. Even though such variables are not directly observable in experimental operations, the investigators conducting the study believe that these variables influence the outcome of performance. In the case of psychological constructs, the experimenter invokes the unseen variable with the belief that there is a physical or tangible counterpart to the construct. Intervening variables are viewed in much the same way as psychological constructs in that they are tied to events that precede (antecedents) and events that follow (the consequences or behavior). However, intervening variables do not necessarily refer to a process that may eventually be defined according to a phenomenon that actually exists.

An example of a variable that may operate as a construct or an intervening variable, depending on the theoretical persuasion of the person using it in research, is learning. No one has actually observed learning take place. We infer a change in the learning process based on detectable changes in behavior. Some learning researchers prefer to think of the variation in learning processes in terms of alterations of real, though as yet unidentifiable physiological processes (constructs), while others are content to interpret learning as an abstraction that carries no additional baggage.

Regardless of whether or not an investigator adopts the position that a variable conforms to the definition of a psychological construct or an intervening variable, from a strictly experimental perspective the circumstance is the same—we cannot directly measure the variable so we must infer its existence in our experimental manipulations. This is where operationalism is of value. Constructs and intervening variables such as "heterosexual responsivity in males" can be operationalized, by physiologic recordings of penile erection, to a set series of stimuli that vary along a continuum of eroticism. Similarly, when we define "high thirst motivation" as 23 hours of water deprivation, we bypass the issue of an underlying theoretical commitment to the essence of a posited hypothetical state.

Regardless of one's philosophical bent, with operational accounts of variables that cannot be observed directly everyone has a firm grasp of what manipulations were performed in the laboratory or field operation.

Before leaving this section on operationalism, it is important to note that several different operational definitions may be used to identify the same construct or variable. Aggression, for example, may be defined in physical terms in one experimental context, such as in the classic experiments by Bandura, Ross, and Ross (1963) where children who had observed models striking dolls similarly acted physically against the dolls when playing with them. Alternatively, aggression can be defined as the number of abusive remarks or exchanges that occur between and among patients participating in group therapy sessions (Merchant, 1990). In either instance, operational accounts of references to aggression permit the reader to follow the events which took place during the experiment and, if so desired, to reproduce the events in a related experiment.

# WITHIN CHAPTER REVIEW AND STUDY QUESTIONS

## CONTROL THROUGH OPERATIONALISM

1. Why are operational definitions important to psychological research? In the example used in this section, "anxiety level" was operationally defined. Consider a study on "altruism" (helping behavior) and its effect on people of different races and ethnic backgrounds. Can you think of some method by which "highly altruistic" people and "mildly altruistic" people could be defined operationally?

2. A theoretical variable that is attached to some antecedent condition on the one hand and some consequence or behavior on the other, and which is believed to have a physiological counterpart, is called a(n):
   a. operational variable
   b. psychological construct
   c. intervening variable

# EXPERIMENTER EFFECTS

In Chapter 6, I acknowledged that subject variables, when left uncontrolled, can corrupt the outcome and interpretation of an experiment. In addition, as we have just discussed, it is essential that operational definitions of variables be used in research if future attempts at replication are to be successful. In all cases, our discussion to this point has centered on controlling events that relate to the manner in which the experiment is constructed and defined. However, there is another, exceedingly important control element that must be considered, and this source of influence falls outside the formal framework of design consideration. It has to do with the person or people who actually conduct the investigation—it has to do with experimenter effects.

**Experimenter effects** are said to occur when the investigator unwittingly or unintentionally contributes to the performance of a participant in the experiment by disclosing what is expected or by treating participants differently. Also, it has become increasingly clear in recent years that the biosocial attributes of the experimenter interact with the attributes of the subjects to affect performance outcomes. That is, depending on the respective characteristics of the experimenter and the subject, you may get totally different results. Let's take a closer look.

## *Biosocial Attributes*

Have you ever thought about how you behave when you are around someone of your gender compared to how you act when you are with someone of the opposite gender? Are your mannerisms consistent, or do you alter your style of interaction based on who you are with? What about your behavior when you are with someone of a different race or ethnic background? Are you reluctant to bring up racially sensitive topics, or do you feel obliged to broach such issues to get them out in the open or to increase your perspective on racial events? Are your responses to older adults different than your responses to younger people, even though the social circumstances may be the same? Does someone's religious convictions alter your responses?

Psychological research tells us that the answer to each of the above questions is "yes." Gender, race and ethnic variables, age, and religious

**experimenter effects**—what result when an investigator unintentionally affects a subject's performance via biosocial attributes or by communicating expected results

**cross-gender comparisons—** combinations where the experimenter and subject are of the same or different sex; various combinations can influence the outcome of an experiment

orientation all affect the way we react to people. Moreover, in the next few sections we shall see that these biosocial attributes can affect the outcome of an experiment.

**Gender of Experimenter and Subject.** There is a very large pool of literature on the differential effects produced by male and female experimenters which dates back to the 1950s. For example, Binder, McConnell, and Sjoholm (1957) had college students learn various lists of words and found that an attractive female experimenter obtained significantly better learning from her subjects than did a male experimenter who was described to the subjects as an "ex-Marine." Even when subjects are children instead of college students, the gender of the experimenter seems to make a difference.

Stevenson and Odom (1963) used two male and two female experimenters in an experiment that required children between the ages of 6 and 11 to pull a lever for a reward when various pictures were shown on a filmstrip. The study was designed such that for the first minute no rewards were given in order that a baseline (normal) index of lever pulling could be determined. Then, when the appropriate responses were made, rewards were delivered. The results from this early experiment indicated that the subjects made over 30% more lever-pulling responses when the experimenter was male than when the experimenter was female. In fact, this was true from the very beginning, even during the baseline period. Surprisingly, this pattern was maintained even when the experimenter left the room in which the participant was performing. Apparently, the simple fact that the instructions for the experiment were given by either a male or a female was sufficient to produce appreciable differences in behavior.

Clearly, the results from these early experiments indicate that the gender of the experimenter can make a difference in the behavior of subjects. But what about the special case where **cross-gender comparisons** are made? Cross-gender comparisons involve combinations where the experimenter/subject are of the same or different gender (male experimenter, male subject; female experimenter, female subject; male experimenter, female subject; female experimenter, male subject).

The degree to which different gender combinations can influence the data is evident from a procedure reported by Rosenthal, Friedman, and Kurland (1965). In an experiment on perception of personal qualities, Rosenthal et al. asked participants to rate the degree of "success" or "failure" reflected in the faces of people in photographs (the same photos were used throughout). The ratings of the faces could range from -10, which corresponded to "extreme failure," to +10, which meant the person looked "extremely successful." Five female and five male experimenters conducted the study on roughly equal numbers of female and male subjects. The results of this famous experiment are shown in Figure 7–2.

The findings revealed that, relative to all other experimenter-subject combinations, female subjects in experiments run by females tended to rate the photographs as less successful looking. Why such profound differences occurred is unclear. It is possible that the subjects' expectations about what a female experimenter wants by way of negative or positive evaluations may make a difference in the response profile, but why would such expectations exist for women and not for men? In any event, one thing is certain. Cross-gender comparisons are important in psychological research using humans as subjects.

More recent illustrations of cross-gender effects in psychological experimentation are available from studies in the area of clinical psychology and therapeutic intervention. Much of this work has been summarized by Beutler, Crago, and Arizmendi (1986). Before reporting the information that has been obtained from investigations in this area, however, I would like you to first ask yourself some questions and then to answer them. Then we can see if your attitudes match those of most people.

Now, assume that you have just terminated a long-term romantic relationship with someone you felt strongly about. The sorrow you have been experiencing for several weeks seems to be increasing in a downward spiral, and you feel that you need to seek counseling because a potentially dangerous depression may emerge. Consider the following:

1. Would you prefer a counselor of the same sex or a different sex?
2. Do you have more confidence in male or female therapists, generally speaking?
3. Would the appearance or dress of the counselor make any difference to you? What about the counselor's preference for maintaining a formal treatment environment, or a more relaxed environment, and would your attitude about environment vary depending on the gender of the therapist?

The evidence that is available indicates that most people have very clear preferences for certain types of therapists and that these preferences can have a dramatic impact on the success of treatment. Clients generally report that they feel

|  |  | Sex of experimenter | |
|  |  | Male | Female |
|---|---|---|---|
| Sex of subject | Male | +0.14 | +0.40 |
|  | Female | +0.31 | -1.13 |

FIGURE 7–2 The mean photo ratings obtained by male and female experimenters from male and female subjects. A negative value indicates the subject rated the photo of the person as a "failure." (From Rosenthal, Friedman, and Kurland, 1965.)

more satisfied at the end of treatment when they are of the same sex as their therapists. Male patients feel more relaxed and seem to be more open when they talk with a male counselor. Female patients say they feel less intimidated and that the therapeutic environment is warmer when the therapist is a woman. In addition, the other variables mentioned previously (e.g., style and dress) are important determinants of therapeutic effectiveness. What does this say about the model experiment we are building in this book? Have we done anything to control for cross-gender effects?

Recall that in our model experiment, we have selected two independent variables: age of chronically ill patients (4 to 6 and 10 to 12) and treatment strategy (cognitive coping strategy, sensory information, and contact control). Implicit in our design is that the gender of subject/gender of experimenter effects discussed in this section of the book are essentially uncontrolled in our model experiment. Practical matters will likely make our experiment include both male and female therapists (experimenters) and both male and female patients (subjects), so cross-gender effects may occur, and yet we are not addressing this very important issue. Why?

The reason has to do with *a priori* expectations. Nothing in the literature in this area suggests that we should include sex of experimenter/sex of subject as additional independent variables. This does not mean that such interactions involving gender do not occur, only they have not been reported. More importantly, once the data are collected, we can arrange our statistical analyses (I address statistical tests in detail in Chapter 11, Drawing Inferences About Results) to determine if gender issues need to be considered. In other words, for our purposes, cross-gender effects, if they exist, can be controlled some other way than through design considerations. This means that we can stay with the two independent variables we have identified for our model experiment and leave other matters until later.

Finally, I note that the sensitivity to gender effects in psychological research has been elevated to a point that gender differences are examined as a matter of routine (cf. Sonnert, 1995). The standard now is to either incorporate gender into the design as a variable (which we have opted not to do) or to statistically analyze for gender effects once the data collection process has been completed (which we have opted to do). The advantage of the latter is that it makes project logistics simpler. Now let's turn to another important biosocial attribute of the experimenter, race.

**Ethnicity.** As ethnic groups in North America define increasingly subpopulations of the broader cultural mosaic, psychologists are attending more to the behavior diversity inherent in a group that holds firmly to selected beliefs, attitudes, and interactive styles. One psychologist who has been instrumental in promoting cultural approaches to the study of psychological phenomena has been James Jones of the University of Delaware (Figure 7–3). Jones's numerous contributions to the literature on behavioral diversity between distinct ethnic populations have contributed greatly to a growing consciousness that questions the validity of past findings. Virtually everything we know about human behavior has been derived from carefully controlled experimental operations based on the performances of white, middle-class Caucasians. As a result, we as a scientific body may have unwittingly presented a distorted, or at least incomplete, picture of human behavior.

The fact that ethnic groups express distinctive behavioral profiles is pertinent to the issue of experimenter effects. More than three decades ago, psychological researchers were examining the interactive effects of race of experimenter and

**FIGURE 7–3** James Jones, a professor of psychology at the University of Delaware, has been influential in making psychologists aware that cultural diversity and ethnic affiliation can be important determinants of response outcome.

race of subject. For example, Summers and Hammonds (1965) conducted a survey research study where all white respondents were asked to complete a questionnaire concerned with racial prejudice. In one condition, the two-person research team (the experimenters) was composed only of whites, whereas in a second condition the team was racially mixed, consisting of one black and one white experimenter. The results showed that when both investigators were white, 52% of the subjects responded according to a pattern that identified them as "highly prejudiced." In contrast, when a black experimenter was part of the research team, the number of respondents falling into this category declined to only 37%. What makes these data even more intriguing is that the responses were made with total anonymity—the subjects were free to say what they pleased, knowing they could never be identified. Nevertheless, the race of the experimenter produced a profound effect on subject performance.

Other early demonstrations of experimenter/subject interactions along ethnic lines were aimed at determining the impact of race on performance on psychological tests. Katz, Robinson, Epps, and Waly (1964) employed a test of hostility using black subjects but experimenters of varied race (i.e., half the time the experimenter was black and half the time the experimenter was white). As an added manipulation, Katz et al. told the black subjects in one condition that the task had nothing to do with intelligence or native reasoning ability. In a second condition, the black subjects were instructed that the task correlated with intelligence. The results from this experiment showed that experimenter race made no difference when the task was presented as neutral. When the task was presented as an indication of intelligence, however, significantly less hostility was registered when the experimenter was white. The authors argued that when the white experimenter was present, there was greater pressure on the subjects to project a "proper" response profile.

More recent evidence underscoring the importance of ethnic considerations in psychological research has expanded to include topics such as aptitude test performance, memory processes, and a litany of other relevant psychological events. The issue of racial congruence between experimenter and subject is certainly evident from experiments that show the performance of black children improves on tests of mental ability when the examiner is also black (refer to Benjamin et al., 1994, for a discussion of these findings). Rita Smith and her colleagues have looked at memory and recall of details from stories in children of different races when the characters in the stories are of the same or different race as the children. The amount of material the children remembered and the specific events they recalled were clearly tied to issues of racial compatibility (Sewell, Chandler, & Smith, 1983).

Considering racial issues from a historical perspective, it is not surprising that all of the examples used here involve comparing blacks and whites in various combinations in their roles as experimenters or participants in studies. The scientific study of the behavioral characteristics of blacks is burgeoning, as witnessed by the proliferation of journals, such as the *Journal of Black Psychology,* and "special topics" books and chapters that focus on interpersonal and intrapersonal behavioral features of the black population. But what about other ethnic and culturally diverse groups? Are experimenter/subject effects equally important for Native Americans, Asians, Cubans, Haitians, and other minority populations? If so, how far along are we really when it comes to understanding the world view of psychology? These issues deserve the vigorous attention of psychological investigators. As minority populations increase, so will our need to include ethnic variables as design features. For someone interested in a career in psychology, the study of ethnic and cultural influences would therefore have to be an attractive option.

**Age.** Many people feel more comfortable with people their own age than they do with people who are older than they. Correspondingly, older people often adjust their social styles when interacting with younger women and men. Perhaps societal expectations or socially prescribed roles dictate that "you act your age," but whatever the determining force it is clear certain behavioral profiles are correlated with specific age ranges. It is also true that the response expectancies associated with age carry over to the experimenter in the laboratory.

Research on this topic demonstrates that the age of the experimenter is particularly important when the nature of the study addresses sensitive issues. As long ago as 1961, Ehrlich and Riesman found that the reaction of women of different ages varied depending on whether or not the experimenter was under or over 40. In this experiment, women from ages 20 to 60 were asked by a younger or older interviewer (experimenter) to comment on the acceptability of an individual engaging in behavior that was forbidden by that individual's parents, when the only reason for doing so was to please the individual's peer group. For younger women, the age of the interviewer really did not make much difference. They responded "unacceptable" with equal frequency in the presence of the younger and older interviewer. In contrast older women responded "unacceptable" 44% more frequently when the interviewer was young than when the interviewer was older. Perhaps the older women felt obligated to maintain a mature profile in the presence of someone from a younger generation and therefore adopted a more conservative stance.

Other early studies on age variables showed that subjects were more likely to respond openly and frankly to questions relating to sexual matters when the interviewer was younger (see Rosenthal, 1976 for a review). This was particularly true when the subjects were 40 or older. More recent investigations on age as it relates to experimenter effects have taken on cross-cultural orientations and reveal that the age variable is significantly more important as a source of influence

**Pygmalion effect**—the tendency for a subject to respond based on what the experimenter expects her or him to do during the course of the experiment

in certain cultures. Therefore, age, like gender and ethnicity, is a biosocial variable you may want to consider when designing an experiment.

**Religiosity.** Not much recent information is available on the effects of the experimenter's religious orientation, but the historical record clearly indicates this variable can be important in specific types of experiments, most notably in the field of survey research (cf. Rosenthal, 1976). For instance, Hyman, Cobb, Feldman, Hart, and Stember (1954) asked Jewish and non-Jewish respondents if they felt the Jewish community had too much influence in business in the United States. They found that the non-Jewish subjects responded "yes" 50% of the time when the interviewer was introduced as non-Jewish, but only 22% of the time when the interviewer was introduced as Jewish. Apparently, the behavior of the subjects changed in an effort not to offend the experimenter. Therefore, at least in very selective circumstances the religious beliefs of the experimenter can alter the results of an experiment.

In addition to the biosocial attributes that have been discussed here, other experimenter effects can be major sources of variation in an experiment. Chief among these are expectancy effects.

## Expectancy: The Pygmalion Effect

Let's say you are interested in studying differences in quantitative expertise among separate ethnic populations. As an experimenter, you believe that African Americans have greater aptitude in mathematics and spatial reasoning than do Caucasians or people of oriental ancestry. Moreover, you express this belief to groups of subjects as they come into the laboratory for testing. Do you think your statement as an experimenter may influence the performance of the participants in the study, or are the subjects likely to demonstrate their relative proficiencies independent of your biased remarks?

There is an extensive body of literature which indicates that what the experimenter expects of the subject indeed alters that subject's performance commensurate with the experimenter's expectations. This tendency to respond differently based on the preconceived expectations of the experimenter is often called the **Pygmalion effect.** This phenomena is named after Pygmalion, a legendary figure who, after several attempts at sculpting the perfect woman, finally succeeded, only to fall desperately in love with his creation (Figure 7–4). When you believe something strongly enough, and subjects are inclined to believe in the authority of the experimenter, you tend to alter your behavior in an effort to conform to an agenda created by an integral, intact belief system, mythical though it may be.

FIGURE 7–4 Pygmalion was a legendary figure who fell in love with the sculpture of a woman he had completed. The term *Pygmalion effect* has come to mean that when subjects believe strongly enough that something is true, it affects their behavior even if the premise under which they operate is false.

The bulk of the work on the Pygmalion effect or the impact of experimenter expectancy on subject performance has come from psychologist Robert Rosenthal. In one experiment conducted with Jacobson that is now considered a classic in the area, Rosenthal was able to show that experimenter expectancies can alter the performance of school children in a classroom setting (refer to Rosenthal, 1976). After a number of assessments, including IQ, were made, students were identified as gifted, and this information was passed to the teachers of these students. In truth, the names that were given to the teachers were selected randomly. There were no significant differences between the so-called gifted students and any of the other students. The teachers were told that because of their exceptionally high scores, the students designated as gifted would likely do very well throughout the year. At the end of the year, all students were retested, and the students identified as gifted registered greater gains.

Perhaps the teachers spent more time with the "gifted" students, or they may have been more encouraging. It is even possible that the instructional styles of teachers changed when they believed they were working with students of unusual ability. Whatever the reason, the same phenomenon occurs with rats as students. When students in an animal laboratory are told they are conducting an experiment with genetically bred "bright" animals and genetically bred "dull" animals, the "bright" animals perform more efficiently on a maze task, even though all animals come from the same genetic stock. The animals are probably handled differently based on predetermined attitudes about their abilities, and it is likely that other encumbrances such as facing the rats the wrong direction in the start box, are inadvertently placed on the rats.

All of this underscores the need to control for experimenter expectancies when conducting psychological research. When expectations are ignored, major misinterpretations of the data can result, as one of the most famous research projects in the history of industrial/organizational psychology demonstrates so vividly.

## Spotlight on Research: THE HAWTHORNE STUDY

In an industrial environment, it is especially important to have some understanding of the various features of the workplace which affect the output of workers. In this regard, management must carefully monitor the social conditions under which work is performed and alter those conditions in an effort to promote productivity. This was precisely the theme of a series of studies carried out between 1924 and 1933 at the Hawthorne, Illinois, plant of Western Electric.

In these classic experiments, workers assembling telephone parts were called into the offices of their supervisors and told that they had been selected to participate in a study on the effects of implementing certain changes in working conditions. The participants were segregated from other workers, and their social and physical environment was changed over a period of several months. Although the workers in the experiment were not explicitly told that their performance would be closely monitored, it was implied by management. Included in the "new policies" were changes in the method of payment so that each worker was paid according to how many pieces he or she fully assembled each day. In addition, rest breaks ranging between 5 and 10 minutes were introduced, and workers were served a light snack in mid-morning and mid-afternoon. The results from these early industrial psychology experiments indicated that the participants did in fact increase their work output significantly above previous levels (Roethlisberger & Dickson, 1939).

The problem with the Western Electric experiments is that the data showed that performance increased systematically, regardless of whether anything was changed. That is, improvements occurred even when no new policies were instituted, which means that increased output was more likely tied to the workers' knowledge that they were in an experiment and not that they were in a specific experimental manipulation. This effect, where subjects in an experiment change their behavior because they realize they are participating in an experiment, is now called "the Hawthorne effect" and can be an intrusive source of influence for an investigator. Something must be done to control for the expectancy effects associated with experimental participation or it becomes impossible to determine the true reason behind the findings from a study.

The Hawthorne effect has been instructive in the sense that it has educated human subject researchers about the unwitting effect an experimenter can have on data. Experimenters must exercise extreme caution because just their presence can create change.    ■

In this section we have seen that experimenter effects and expectancies can have a profound impact on the pattern of results obtained in psychological research. In the next section, I cover some methodological considerations for controlling such unwanted sources of influence.

## WITHIN CHAPTER REVIEW AND STUDY QUESTIONS

### EXPERIMENTER EFFECTS

1. Which one of the following biosocial attributes of the experimenter was not included in our discussion of experimenter effects?
    a. gender
    b. status
    c. age
2. What is meant by the term the *Pygmalion effect?*

# CONTROLLING EXPERIMENTER EFFECTS

The observations made in the last several pages of this chapter make it clear that experimenter bias is a potential source of contamination in an experimental setting. The attributes, mannerisms, and even the most subtle gestures made by an experimenter may unintentionally cue the subject about what is appropriate and what is unexpected in terms of experiment participation. So what can be done to prevent, or at least minimize, the biasing effect of the experimenter? Actually, there are several design features which can help along these lines. I mention a few of the more commonly adopted methods for controlling experimenter effects.

## Multiple Experimenters

For most experiments, the size of the sample population is set before the experiment commences. That is, the research is designed in such a fashion that we know beforehand how many subjects are going to be assigned to Condition A, how many will be assigned to Condition B, and so forth. Given that subject size is fixed, it follows that if the number of experimenters conducting the investigation is increased, each experimenter will interact with fewer subjects.

There are several advantages associated with using multiple experimenters in a research project. First, problems like those described previously, such as those associated with age, ethnicity, gender differences, and so on, are easier to control. If you purposely employ experimenters who define a broad range of attributes, then the chances that a particular experimenter trait may systematically bias the data decrease. Figure 7–5 outlines a hypothetical case where experimenters with different characteristics might be assigned to subjects according to a procedure that ensures balanced representation.

Apart from trait and attributional issues, there is some evidence which indicates that experimenter bias is a learned phenomenon (see Rosenthal, 1976). The position taken here is that the experimenter is involved in a social circumstance with the subject. In this interactive setting, the subject and the experimenter may both become increasingly more sensitive to nonverbal and verbal behaviors during the course of the testing session. For example, an experimenter conducting an experiment on reaction time in a verbal learning task may find that his or her voice inflection when presenting a stimulus word makes a difference in how quickly the subject gives a response word. The key here is that the experimenter is unaware that he or she is picking up this information and therefore unwittingly contributes to the performance of the subject. This bias grows more prominent with successive subjects. The more subjects you test, the greater the likelihood you will learn how to influence the subject unintentionally. Accordingly, it is reasonable to assert that if the experimenter has fewer subjects to run in an experiment, there will be fewer opportunities to learn a biasing style.

| Experimenter | Subject number and condition |
|---|---|
| **Male** Physically attractive | $S_1$ (Condition A) $S_5$ (Condition B) |
| Physically unattractive | $S_3$ (Condition A) $S_7$ (Condition B) |
| **Female** Physically attractive | $S_2$ (Condition A) $S_6$ (Condition B) |
| Physically unattractive | $S_4$ (Condition A) $S_8$ (Condition B) |

**FIGURE 7–5** Using multiple experimenters who possess different traits and judiciously assigning them to subjects from different conditions can reduce systematic experimenter bias.

With multiple experimenters and a fixed sample size, you limit the impact of learned sources of experimenter effects.

In Chapter 6, I mentioned that "generalizability" is an integral part of any research project. Data are not worth much to the scientific community if they have no meaning beyond the sample you have selected for your experiment. Employing several different experimenters can enhance generalizability. Each of the different experimenters brings unique behavioral styles and characteristics to the study. Some may be more confident or at ease in an experimental interview, others may possess a distinctive accent or a distinguished countenance or look. Any one of these experimenter differences could affect the outcome of a study. Incorporating multiple experimenters reduces the chances that any single personal trait may prejudice the findings because different points along a continuum are represented. So many diverse personality elements are present across the total experiment that no one element stands out.

## Selecting and Training Experimenters

Consider yourself as a participant in each of the following two experiments. In one case, you are greeted by a well-groomed, articulate, polite person who introduces you to other subjects who are waiting in a holding area before participating in the experiment. In another case, the person who meets you is slovenly and gruff and has very little to say other than, "Take a seat and wait your turn." How do you think you would react to these two different initial encounters with the experimenter? Would your perception of experimenter competency affect your performance?

Although there are no empirical data on the issue, there would probably be a difference in your response profile in these cases. People tend to respond more favorably to well-educated professionals than to people they see as disinterested lackeys carrying out the demands of an assignment. It follows from this that you would want to select interviewers or primary contact people who are personable and demonstrate professional competency. This often means that the project director must carefully screen prospective experimenters, both for the requisite criteria for experimenter efficiency and for consistency. An experimenter who is focused on one occasion and adrift the next only adds response variation to the project and may make the study more difficult to complete.

In addition to carefully selecting experimenters based on individual characteristics, an essential component of experimenter behavior relates to how much and what type of training the person has been given. Even the most gifted graduate student may be unaware of the importance of instructional consistency, eye contact, maintaining a constant distance from the participant (subject), and other seemingly insignificant details that can alter the subject's behavior. With deliberate instructions and training sessions, experimenters can be schooled on fundamental principles of experimenter decorum and conduct and thereby decrease the chances that experimenter effects will corrupt the data.

Selection and training procedures for experimenters are important to the success of any research project. Even when experimenters are carefully coached about proper technique, however, inadvertent cluing may occur. Think about the following example of experimenter effects.

## ⚛ Thinking About Research

Inexplicably, we have an inherent tendency to find those events that elude scientific description and interpretation most intriguing. Certainly, in the broad realm of psychology, **paranormal phenomena** have been a source of intellectual animation for the general public. Such events have also received serious attention from psychologists, most conspicuously J. B. Rhine (see McVaugh and Mauskopf, 1976, for a review of this research).

One paranormal activity which is often referred to is mental telepathy. Telepathy involves transmitting information from one human mind to another, apart from the normal sensory channels. While most psychologists consider the topic "hokey," it is possible to examine the issue within the framework of scientific analysis. Any attempts to document the legitimacy of the effect have to be carefully controlled, however. I know—I attempted such an experiment years ago, and here is what happened.

One experimenter (an undergraduate male volunteer) was sent to a designated room in a building adjacent the building where I had an office. That experimenter was to concentrate on a geometrical configuration (a triangle) and attempt to transfer his mental image of this object to a subject seated in a room in my building. A second experimenter (also an undergraduate volunteer) was sitting across from the "receiving" subject and recording the "perceptions" of the signal being transmitted from the "sender."

The data from this project were striking. The ability of the "receiver" (subject) to pick up the image was remarkable and proved to be statistically significant. It goes without saying that there was great excitement in the laboratory.

As would be appropriate for any investigator stumbling on such a discovery, greater attention was warranted. As a result, I decided to observe the experimenter who was recording the comments of the "receiver" through a one-way mirror. What was happening, even though it was unintentional, was that when the receiver would make a remark such as, "It's some kind of animal," the experimenter would look down and almost imperceptibly shake his head indicating, "No, that's not right." When the subject, also a male, would move on and say something such as, "It's a pattern of some kind, something shaped, something sharp with angles," the experimenter gave the slightest affirmative nod. Of course, the subject eventually chose "triangle" because he was effectively shaped (trained) to do so. I replaced the experimenter with a more stoic, perhaps less ambitious experimenter, and found that my results washed out. I could get no significant results confirming telepathy. Can you think of anything else I could have done to control for experimenter bias in this study?    ■

This illustration of experimenter bias is not apocryphal. It actually happened. But the problems I faced in this early attempt to investigate the unbelievable could have been avoided. Had I exercised sufficient foresight, I could have more carefully crafted a blind experiment.

**paranormal phenomena**—events that cannot be explained by normal sensory processing; telepathy is one example

## *Single and Double Blind Experiments*

Because of subject expectancies and the issues associated with demand characteristics, as discussed previously, it is unlikely and unadvisable for subjects to know which experimental condition they are in or to have any grasp of what the experimenter expects to happen in a particular condition. When group assign-

**single blind technique**—a psychological research procedure in which group assignment is known to the experimenter but not the subject

**double blind technique**—a psychological research procedure in which group assignment is unknown to both experimenter and subject

ment is unknown to the subject, but it is known the experimenter, the experiment uses what is called a **single blind technique** (see Figure 7–6). As I have mentioned repeatedly, many problems arise when the experimenter has information about which condition the subject has been assigned to, but at least single blind studies avoid subject expectancies.

One method for controlling experimenter as well as subject expectancies, and for correlated confounding influences, is known as the **double blind technique** (see Figure 7–6). In the double blind procedure, group assignment is unknown to both the experimenter and the subject. Because the experimenter has no idea about which condition the subject is really in, the experimenter cannot systematically bias the subject's behavior. For example, suppose an investigation is concerned with the effects of marijuana on assertiveness. If the experimenter knows that a participant is being administered the drug (the single blind case), then the experimenter may inadvertently alter her or his interactive style and therein induce or retard the assertive behavior the subject exhibits. However, it is possible to conduct this experiment such that both the subject and the participant are blind to the presence or absence of marijuana. Individual snack squares, called "brownies," can be provided. Some of the brownies will contain the active drug ingredient and some will not. A second experimenter, who does know the subject's group assignment, but who does not interact with the subject, can supply the "blind" experimenter with brownies that are to be consumed by the participant. Because the "blind" experimenter,

Possesses knowledge of group assignment

| | Single blind | Double blind |
|---|---|---|
| Subject | No | No |
| Experimenter | Yes | No |

**FIGURE 7–6** Single blind and double blind procedures used in psychological research

who interacts with the subject in this double blind situation, cannot predict reliably whether the brownie contains the drug, experimenter bias would not be an issue. At least, it would not be an issue in terms of experimenter expectancies.

It would seem that double blind procedures would be preferred over single blind procedures. However, most psychological experiments conducted over the last 50 years have employed single blind procedures. Why? If the double blind technique offers more control and avoids adding a source of variation, then why isn't it used routinely? The answer usually rests with economics and practical realities. Double blind procedures require more personnel, and they are more difficult to organize and manage. Also, there are simply some cases in which it is impossible to disguise the condition in which the experimenter is operating. The model experiment we are building in the book is one such case.

> In the model experiment we are forging as we move through this book, recall that our design calls for three different intervention strategies (cognitive coping, sensory information, and contact control). Inasmuch as the individual therapists (experimenters) must receive specific training and instruction regarding the procedures to be employed, they obviously cannot be deceived regarding which treatment condition the subject has been assigned to. Indeed, the experimenter defines the treatment condition in our model experiment. Therefore, the use of a double blind strategy is not an option.

We see that although certain methods may be available for controlling experimenter bias, sometimes the ideal control procedure may not be an option. In such instances, exercise as much control as possible and simply be aware that experimenter effects may contribute to your findings.

## WITHIN CHAPTER REVIEW AND STUDY QUESTIONS

### CONTROLLING EXPERIMENTER EFFECTS

1. What advantages are there to using multiple experimenters? Can you think of any problems that may be introduced when multiple experimenters are used in a study?
2. What essential factors are involved in selecting an experimenter?
3. When group membership is unknown to both the subject and the experimenter, this is called a _____.
   a. single blind technique
   b. double blind technique
   c. dual deception procedure

# EXPERIMENTER EFFECTS IN ANIMAL RESEARCH

When psychological researchers think about problems associated with experimenter effects, they typically discuss human studies. Experiments with human subjects presents the greatest challenge with respect to control, and it is in this context that experimenter bias is most likely. However, it should be understood that animal research is not free of experimenter effects.

Consider the following example. Two separate laboratories are conducting identical experiments with albino white rats in commercially made operant chambers (test boxes). The rats are under exactly the same food deprivation regimens, they are operating under the same schedules of reinforcement (say, a fixed-ratio [FR] 4 where every fourth lever press is rewarded [reinforced]), and they receive the same food rewards which are commercially made and come from a common supplier. Nevertheless, one laboratory records response rates that are 30% higher than the other. Why? It seems that the performances should be virtually the same.

On close inspection, we discover that in one laboratory (the one in which the rats respond at a higher rate) the experimenter conducting the simple learning and conditioning study handles each rat for 15 minutes before placing it in the test chamber for a 1-hour testing session. This handling involves taking the rat out of its home cage, holding it, and petting it while it snuggles against a lab coat worn by the experimenter. In the other laboratory, the experimenter never touches the rat before it is removed from the home holding cage and placed in the operant test chamber. As a result of these differences in handling, the levels of the rats' anxiety differ going into the test session. Although it is only moderately stressful for a rat to be taken from its familiar home cage environment and placed in a small enclosure with lights, levers, a grid floor, a pellet trough, and so forth, there may be sufficient stress to affect response rate, particularly early in the session. An experimenter may reduce stress levels with handling and consequently increase the rat's rate of lever pressing. Now we know why the laboratories obtained different patterns of responding.

Other experimenter variables that can affect animal behavior include how much noise the investigator makes, odors from laboratory clothing (imagine the stress evoked in a white rat with a sensitive olfactory system by odors emanating from a lab coat worn by an experimenter who has just sacrificed another group of rats), and the method of treatment, injection, or other manipulation the animals receive before being placed in the test environment. I once observed a graduate student (not one of mine), toss a rat to a second experimenter so that the second experimenter could place the rat in a drug-test chamber. Do you think an experimenter effect was likely produced here? Surely such treatment, in addition to violating ethical standards for conducting animal research (refer to Chapter 4), has a profound impact on the animal's behavior. Even in less obvious cases, the experimenter's treatment of the animal may contribute to the pattern of results, so every effort needs to be made to be consistent and to tell the reader all the details of the testing procedure—including such seemingly insignificant issues as how often the animals were handled each day and when.

Finally, it should be mentioned that the investigator's experience can make a difference in animal performance (Domjan, 1996). For example, someone who is well trained and knows what to look for may detect that an animal is developing an upper respiratory infection, while a less experienced animal researcher may not. Everyone who has ever supervised an animal laboratory knows the value of having the same personnel in the laboratory for several years. There is a certain skill involved in conducting animal research, and there is no substitute for repetition. Just conducting research over and over makes you more knowledgeable and a better researcher.

## WITHIN CHAPTER REVIEW AND STUDY QUESTION

### EXPERIMENTER EFFECTS IN ANIMAL RESEARCH

1. List three things an experimenter could do to alter the outcome of an animal learning study.

## AUTOMATION AND EXPERIMENTER EFFECTS

In the 1930s, behavioral psychologist B. F. Skinner was conducting basic animal learning and conditioning research using conventional mazes, choice tasks, and so forth. By his own admission, Skinner grew weary of repeating the same perfunctory operations. He would place a rat in the start box area of a straight alley maze and then watch as the rat traversed the length of the maze and entered the goal area. At this point, Skinner would take the rat out of the cage and place it in a holding bin for a couple of minutes, then repeat the same procedure. As boredom set in, Skinner began to think of creative alternatives that would permit the animal to record its own data. The result was the invention of the operant chamber (or Skinner Box, as it is commonly called—a term Skinner loathed). In the operant chamber, a lever response by a rat or key peck by a pigeon immediately registers on another piece of equipment. Once the animal responds, it is free to respond again. The experimenter is out of the picture and has no part in recording the data.

**automation**—use of instrumentation in psychological research so that program operations and recordings are carried out automatically by equipment; the experimenter is not in contact with the subject

The engineering technology Skinner employed is an example of **automation** in psychological research. As discussed in Chapter 5, in automation, response profiles are created by electronic and computerized recording and delivery systems which operate independent of the experimenter. The result is that many of the experimenter biases discussed previously are no longer issues. Because the experimenter has no contact with the subject during the data collection period, it is impossible for the investigator to have any impact on responses.

As a control technique, automation is commonly used in human subject research as it is in animal research. Figure 7–7 shows laboratory equipment from

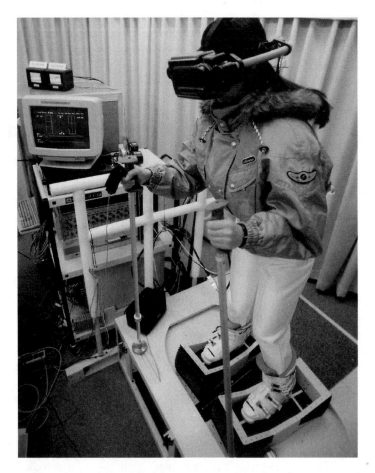

**FIGURE 7–7 A scientific laboratory equipped with automated programming and recording instruments which permit subjects to respond in a "virtual reality" context**

a research setting that focuses on "virtual reality" experiments. In such studies, human participants interact with sophisticated computer simulations of what appear to be real environments. For example, a person being trained as a fighter pilot may perform in an artificial laboratory environment that simulates an actual flight closely. There are those who argue that such training techniques match the effectiveness of training programs using real aircraft, real targets, and so forth. In any event, in the simulation environment behaviors are recorded automatically, information from these behaviors is fed into a computer, the data are analyzed online, and the results are available as soon as participation ends.

## WITHIN CHAPTER REVIEW AND STUDY QUESTION

### AUTOMATION AND EXPERIMENTER EFFECTS

1. How do automated systems assist in controlling experimenter effects in psychological research?

## The Model Experiment

For the model experiment we are building as we move through this book, we have acknowledged that a single blind procedure (instead of a double blind procedure) is our only option. Because the experimenters (treatment specialists) must be trained to provide specific intervention services, it is not possible to take the experimenter completely out of the picture. Nevertheless, we can be vigilant in attending to the impact such experimenter variables as expectancy, gender, race, and so on, may have on the data, and we can attempt to diminish the effects of these variables as much as possible.

Having set the groundwork for our model experiment, it is now time to focus on the structural framework of the experimental design.

# Between-Subjects Designs

**research design—a structural plan used for data collection**

Throughout the coverage thus far, I have made rather general reference to design considerations involving subject selection, participation, control, and so forth. At this juncture, it is appropriate that the discussion move to a more formal description of design characteristics. Commensurate with this move, I shall use the term **research design** to refer to the overall structure or layout of the plans used for collecting data. The aim of this chapter is to demonstrate how the careful definition of groups or conditions can control the menacing influence of variation and therein increase our chances for obtaining valid results. Research design manipulations are important in psychological investigations because, in the absence of an appropriate analytical framework, the wrong information is obtained and the wrong interpretations are rendered.

It is important to note that no design affords the investigator total control. There will always be uncontrolled sources of variation because not every variable that affects a given outcome can be included in the design. Consequently, it is understood that uncontrolled sources of variation are unavoidable in psychological research. Nonetheless, a great deal of useful information can be gained from research designs that adequately control for the major sources of variation or influence in the experimental project. If intelligence and educational background are the principal determinants of performance on problem-solving tasks, for instance, and if these two factors are incorporated into our design as independent variables (see Chapter 3), then we can be reasonably certain that the findings from our study reflect a true picture of the relation between independent and dependent events. The exact values of the dependent measure may be determined by the slight variation of another factor, but omitting that factor from the design outline is not likely to result in a substantial difference in the pattern of the data.

Another feature of research designs that is worth noting is that no single design is necessarily better than another. The suitability of a given design rests with the nature of the questions being asked. It makes no sense to employ a complicated multifactor design when the issue at hand is simply defined by a single environmental or organismic variable. Introducing complex and unnecessary features into a design format is a waste of resources and may complicate interpretative issues by creating a fog which makes it difficult to see the essential result. Correspondingly, it is inappropriate to attempt to answer complicated questions with simplistic designs that will yield bogus results. The rule is, "Match the design to the complexity of the issue, and include only those variables that are required for generating meaningful results."

In the sections that follow, I examine the requirements for what has become known as a between-subjects design (see the next section), and introduce the different types of experimental structures that fall under this general rubric. In later sections of the chapter, issues relating to the selection of the most appropriate between-subjects designs are discussed.

# BETWEEN-SUBJECTS DESIGN REQUIREMENTS: WHAT DOES IT TAKE?

There are many situations in psychological research where it is not practical to use a given participant or subject a second time. In a human subject study on the effects of stress and arousal on completing a complex puzzle within a specified time, for example, you cannot use one person for both "low arousal" and "high arousal" conditions, because that person may have already solved the puzzle and you would therefore corrupt the problem-solving element of the investigation. Similarly, in animal research reusing a subject may be contraindicated, even impossible, because of the type of question being asked. For example, Nehas, Trouve, Demus, and Von Sitbon (1985) conducted a neurochemical study on the effects of a calcium channel blocker (nitrendipine) on the lethality of cocaine. Because the behavioral end point in this experiment was death, the investigators faced a formidable task if they expected to use the same subjects twice. Incidentally, Nehas et al. did show that nitrendipine antagonizes the lethal impact of an overdose amount of cocaine, and this research has helped neuroscientists better understand the nature of the biochemical disturbances that are produced by this commonly abused drug.

When separate subjects must be used for each experimental condition, the design is called a **between-subjects design.** In a between-subjects design, an individual who is in Condition A never participates in Condition B. In effect, in a between-subjects design the subject is locked into only one group designation, and that is the extent of his or her contribution to the experiment. This is in stark contrast to the **within-subjects design** where the same subject may appear in both Condition A and B. I cover within-subjects designs in the next chapter.

As noted, the most basic requirement for a between-subjects design is that subjects are assigned to participate in only one set of conditions. The obvious advantage of this approach is that serial dependencies do not form, and each subject's data express a "clean" profile that is free of the possible contaminating influence of experience, transfer of training, and so forth (Domjan, 1996). A conspicuous disadvantage of between-

**between-subjects design**—a design in which participants are assigned to only one experimental condition and experience only the treatment effects of that condition

**within-subjects design**—a design in which participants are assigned to more than one experimental condition

**control group**—a group in which the value of the independent variable is either neutral or unchanged

**experimental group**—a group in which the value of the independent variable is manipulated or changed

subjects designs is that they are costly. By definition, when you use a between-subjects approach you need more subjects to fill the conditions than you would have had if you had decided to allow the same subject to participate across conditions. More subjects translate into more time for the experimenter and in many instances, such as in animal research, more money. There is also the issue of individual variability. Some argue that using the same subjects across conditions decreases variability, insofar as individual differences are likely to be less than they would be when comparing different subjects (Hurlburt, 1994). Still, between-subjects designs are preferred in many cases (see preceding discussion).

As with all designs, a second criterion for between-subjects designs is that the format and structure be crafted such that you can answer the questions that have formed the rationale for conducting the investigation. A tight experimental design is of no value if the experimental framework fails to yield information that is relevant to the hypothesis (Kerlinger, 1973). Moreover, there are some rhetorical issues. Consider the question, "What is the current population of the Sudan and Egypt?" This question is not answerable because by the time you count the last person who was alive when you started, others will have been born or died. You may estimate the respective populations of the Sudan and Egypt and even use a between-subjects design in the process, but you can never provide a true answer to the question. Therefore, for between-subjects designs to be of value, the design must allow a given, testable idea to be confirmed.

The third requirement a between-subjects design must meet is that it must ensure internal validity. An experiment is said to possess high internal validity to the extent that the observed effects can be determined to be due to the influence of the independent variable(s) and not some uncontrolled source of variation (see Chapter 3). Typically, this requires including at least two groups: a control group and an experimental group.

In a **control group,** the value of the independent variable is either neutral or unchanging. Using randomizing or stratifying procedures like those discussed in Chapter 6, the complexion of the control condition should be made to represent a larger population. Because no manipulation is carried out on subjects in this group, behavioral effects should remain relatively stable over time and across groups (samples). For instance, for someone interested in the effects of marijuana on sleep patterns, it would be useful to know what sleep patterns look like under a nondrug state. This would require that the experimenter compile sleep records of people who were simply sleeping and had not received any treatment. Such a group would qualify as a control condition.

For a between-subjects design, a separate group of subjects must be assigned to the **experimental group.** Unlike their control counterparts, subjects in the experimental group experience a non-neutral value of the independent variable.

The independent variable is manipulated in the experimental group. In the aforementioned study of marijuana intoxication and sleep patterns, for instance, subjects in the experimental condition would be exposed to the psychoactive effects of the drug and would subsequently sleep. Differences in the records (e.g., EEGs, EKGs, pulse rate, and breathing patterns) between the control group and the experimental group ostensibly would be due to the manipulation of the independent variable (amount of marijuana) in the experimental group.

It is essential that the character of the control group and the experimental group be identical in every respect except one—the value of the independent variable. Age, socioeconomic status, gender representation, and any other factor that might influence the data must be equally represented in both conditions. If the integrity of this "sameness" is maintained, and the independent variable is changed carefully across conditions, then the internal validity of the experiment is virtually ensured.

A fourth requirement for between-subjects designs relates to **external validity.** External validity refers to the extent to which the results from an experiment can be applied to members of a broader population. Essentially, external validation addresses questions tied to generalizability, as discussed in Chapter 6. You have selected subjects from a larger pool of subjects and assigned them to control or experimental conditions. Given that the selection and assignment procedures were unbiased, what do the differences mean for rest of the population? Can you say anything about the characteristics of the population members who were not included in the experiment? Although we can never accurately delineate the exact boundaries, limits, or relevance of experimental findings, it is fair to say that on the whole increased generalizability means increased external validity.

## WITHIN CHAPTER REVIEW AND STUDY QUESTIONS

### BETWEEN-SUBJECTS DESIGN REQUIREMENTS: WHAT DOES IT TAKE?

1. What criteria are used to evaluate between-subjects designs? Which of these criteria is/are peculiar to between-subjects designs?
2. Define external validity and indicate why it is important for between-subjects designs.

**external validity**—the extent to which the results of an experiment can be applied to a broader population

# ONE-FACTOR TWO-GROUP DESIGNS

The most elementary type of between-subjects designs is the **one-factor two-group design.** For this design, because the term *factor* is used to connote the number of independent variables included in the study, only one variable is manipulated. One-factor two-group designs typically take the form of one control group and one experimental group, as discussed earlier. However, this design does not require the value of the independent variable to be neutral or unchanged in one condition. This means it is possible to experimentally manipulate the value of the independent variable in both conditions and still maintain the integrity of the one-factor two-group design.

For example, an investigator interested in the effects of alcohol on human aggression may conduct a study where people consume 1 ounce of ethanol or 5 ounces of ethanol. The interest in the experiment lies with quantitative variation in the independent variable (i.e., the amount of the drug) (see the section later in this chapter on One-Factor Multiple-Group Designs). Therefore, even in the absence of a true control group (in which there is no change along the dimension of the independent variable) a one-factor two-group design may yield information.

Of course, with simple designs that do not contain a group where the value of the independent variable is neutral, it is not possible to make statements about the degree to which the introduction of the independent variable produced change. This is apparent in the alcohol research illustration provided previously. Because you have no way of indexing what the 1-ounce manipulation did with respect to boosting or attenuating aggressive behavior among humans, you have no idea about the overall shape of the ethanol/aggression function or where your groups fall along that function. Let's say there are no differences between the patterns of aggression exhibited by people in the 1-ounce and 5-ounce conditions. Does this mean alcohol has no effect on human behavior? Not at all, because 1 ounce of the drug may suffice to produce maximum change in the dependent variable. Adding more alcohol will produce no discernable effects, so group differences would not be expected in our example. With a true control the information is of increased value because it more fully and systematically characterizes the relation between two values along the continuum of the independent variable.

Because of issues like these, many psychological researchers have chosen to launch preliminary experiments with the more traditional no manipulation (control group)-manipulation (experimental group) format. This is also an economical way to determine if the independent variable and the dependent measure are linked. If they are, you can design more elaborate programs. Still, you should understand that sometimes even the most basic projects must employ one-factor two-group designs that do not contain a conventional control group. In this regard, assume that I wish to examine the relation between intelligence and big toe length. Because it is impossible, despite what some may view as contradictory examples, to possess "zero" intelligence, it follows that you must go with two "nonzero" conditions, such as low intelligence and high intelligence. Here, a one-factor two-group design that has no control group is the most appropriate design and one that will yield valuable results (assuming you are interested in the question being asked).

We can further subdivide one-factor two-group designs. In Chapter 6, I covered four sampling or data collection techniques: random sampling, stratifying, matching, and cohort sampling. Each of these procedures can be used when faced with one-factor two-group design considerations.

## Simple Randomized Design

As discussed in Chapter 6, in a random sampling procedure each member of a population is randomly assigned to an experimental condition. This general rationale is used in forming groups based on a **simple randomized design.** In the simple randomized design, subjects are randomly assigned to one of two groups. Figure 8–1 uses the control group-experimental group dichotomy to illustrate how random assignment procedures are used in one-factor two-group designs. The first step is to select an overall sample from a population of possible participants. Subsequently, some randomization vehicle, such as a random numbers table, is used to assign members of the overall sample to one of two conditions (i.e., the control group or the experimental group). This randomization process continues until the overall sample has been exhausted or until a predetermined group number (N) has been reached. At this point, differential treatment experiences are introduced, which in this case means that the value of the independent variable is changed in the experimental group but remains unchanged in the control condition. Given adequate internal validity, differences observed in dependent measure values reflect the influence of the treatment manipulation.

In the animal behavior sector, the simple randomized design is very popular among neuroscientists because the simple two-group design allows the distinctive impact of selective drugs, lesions, or other environmental interventions to be assessed. For instance, albino white rats were randomly assigned to receive injections of physiological saline (fluid that has no detectable biochemical effects) or a drug known as Ro15-4513 before receiving an acute exposure to alcohol (cf. Kolata,

> **one-factor two-group design—** design in which two groups differ on one independent variable
>
> **simple randomized design—a** type of one-factor two-group design (see previous entry) in which subjects are assigned randomly to each of the two groups

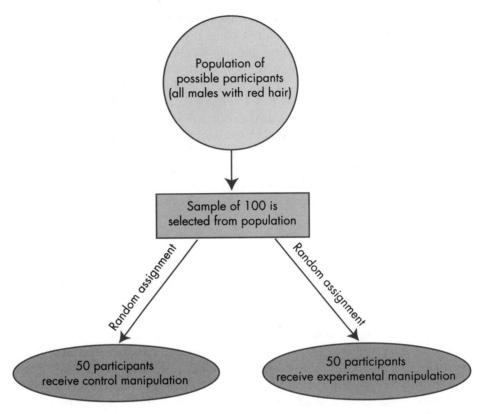

**FIGURE 8–1 An example of the formation of groups in a simple randomized design**

1986). Animals in the control (saline) condition passed out within a few minutes, but animals given the Ro15-4513 (the experimental group) were unaffected—they continued to walk around and explore as if nothing had happened. Because the random assignment process virtually ensured that the two groups were equal, we can feel reasonably secure that the group differences were due to the various drug manipulations. Similarly, in the classic human study on conformity by Soloman Asch (1956), the comparison of two randomly formed groups on a single factor was sufficient to make an important point. On a perceptual-judgment task, subjects were asked to pick a line that matched a "standard line" shown to them before testing. When subjects were alone during the test (the control condition), they made very few errors. However, when confederates of the experimenter were present and purposely made incorrect choices (the experimental condition), the subjects went along with the incorrect opinions. This basic randomized format portrays the elegance of the one-factor two-group design: you can keep it simple and answer some very important questions.

## *Stratified Design*

As discussed in Chapter 6, it is not uncommon in psychological research to engage an issue where truly random assignment may bias the result. Previously, the relation between age and gender was used to illustrate such a case. Specifically, because of differential life expectancies for men and women, it would be inappropriate to represent males and females proportionately in younger and older samples. To accurately represent population values, more women than men would need to be assigned to the older condition. This could be accomplished by **stratifying** subjects and judiciously creating conditions that mirror the elderly population statistics. For example, if the population has 60% women, then the sample should have 60% women.

Regarding one-factor two-group designs, a stratified sampling procedure might take the form of the subject assignment procedures outlined in Figure 8–2. Let's say we are interested in the relative effectiveness of cognitive-behavioral therapy and psychoanalytic therapy. Further, based on the work of Sue and Zane (1987), we know that different ethnic

**stratifying**—the act of assigning subjects to groups according to their rank along some continuum

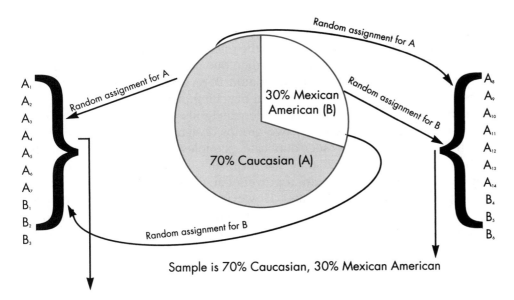

Sample is 70% Caucasian, 30% Mexican American

**FIGURE 8–2** Method for assigning subjects to groups in a stratified design. Note that the sample features mirror those of the population.

**matched-pairs design**—a type of one-factor two-group design in which subjects are matched on some variable and then assigned to one of two groups

**cohort design**—a type of one-factor two-group design in which group designations are made according to differences between subjects selected from a common pool

groups respond differently to specific types of intervention programs. Inasmuch as we want to avoid having greater minority representation in one condition than the other, the first step is to determine how the population is configured (see Figure 8–2). Where *A* corresponds to Caucasian and *B* corresponds to Mexican American, it is estimated that the population about which we hope to generalize is made up of approximately 70% whites and 30% Mexican Americans. Accordingly, subjects are randomly assigned to each treatment condition until the percentage requirements of that condition are met. At this point, no further assignments of people with that particular ethnic background are made. The result is that when the assignments are complete, the configurations of the samples will be identical to the broader population in terms of ethnic diversity (see Figure 8–2), thereby controlling for a potential confounding element.

Of course, stratified designs assume that you know something about the population parameters of the larger data matrix. Even when that information is not available, it may be possible to control for subject characteristics that may encroach on your experiment. This can be accomplished with the matched-pairs design.

## Matched-Pairs Designs

In a **matched-pairs design,** at least for the one-factor two-group case, two subjects are matched on some variable and then one member from each pair is randomly assigned to Condition A or Condition B. As discussed in Chapter 6, this can be accomplished either by precision matching or range matching. Because the previous discussion in Chapter 6 adequately illustrates how matched pairs would be assigned in a one-factor two-groups design (refer to Figures 6–3 and 6–4), there is no need to present duplicate examples here. Just understand that matched-pairs designs forfeit some statistical sensitivity (Myers, 1991) and may compromise some of the strength or power of an inferential test (see Chapter 11, Drawing Inferences About Results). However, the gains likely will outweigh the losses. What you give up in statistical sensitivity will be compensated by increased experimental control and minimization of unwanted sources of variation.

## Cohort Designs

In Chapter 6, a *cohort* was identified as a group sharing a common distinctive trait. A **cohort design** as relates to one-factor two-group designs, then, involves the formation of two groups from an initial subject pool, where group designations are determined by differences along some dimension. Figure 8–3 shows how such a design might unfold. Because cohort samples were discussed in great detail earlier, extensive coverage of this topic is not warranted here. It suffices to say that the most elementary use of the cohort sampling approach to conducting research is evident in the one-factor two-group situation.

## WITHIN CHAPTER REVIEW AND STUDY QUESTIONS

### ONE-FACTOR TWO-GROUP DESIGNS

1. In the _____ group, the value of the independent variables is neutral or unchanging.
   a. experimental
   b. control
   c. manipulation
2. Under what conditions would a stratified one-factor two-group design be preferred over a simple randomized design? What limitations are imposed in the stratified design?

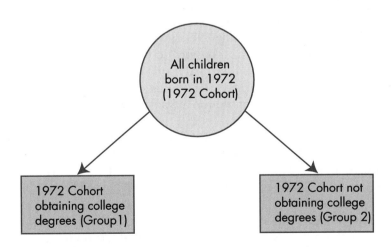

FIGURE 8–3 A cohort design that involves only two groups

# ONE-FACTOR MULTIPLE-GROUP DESIGNS

In the early days of psychological research, the one-factor two-group design was commonly employed. Given the infant status of the discipline and the basic nature of early inquiry, using the simplest approach available was clearly indicated. In today's experimental setting, however, the questions being asked are more complex and the demand for thorough analyses is far more advanced than it once was. Accordingly, it is somewhat rare today to see a simple one-factor two-group design. Contemporary experimental designs are more likely to include several experimental groups and, in some cases, several control groups.

A **one-factor multiple-group design** is a research plan wherein a single measure (the dependent variable) is recorded for more than two levels of one independent variable. One of the typical conditions (levels) is a control group where the value of the independent variable remains neutral—it is unchanged. The remaining groups are defined by their respective levels of change introduced along the dimension of the independent variable. These changes can be qualitative or quantitative. In the former case, there is no discrete separation between groups. Rather, the conditions differ categorically, which means the groups are of different types and possess distinctive characters and that it is not possible to specify how much they differ. Conversely, in experimental situations that incorporate quantitative differences along some dimension, it is appropriate to address the extent of group separation and to indicate the amount of difference in the value of the independent variable.

An experiment by Bandura et al. (1988) can be used to illustrate a one-factor multiple-group design where qualitative differences exist among groups. The idea underlying this study was that cognitive control can be a powerful strategy for dealing with pain, stress, or other health-related situations. Based on preliminary information, Bandura et al. speculated that coaching people to think about things that would direct their attention away from the source of discomfort might alleviate suffering.

To assist the subjects in this regard, Bandura et al. introduced a cognitive control strategy that was designed to divert people's attention away from the pain associated with an aversive stimulus, specifically, plunging hands into ice water. As Figure 8–4 shows, subjects in this condition increased their ability to withstand painful stimulation by almost 60% relative to their baseline pain tolerance. In comparison, subjects in a placebo group who were simply told they were being given something that would help them deal with pain and a control group who received no experimental manipulation failed to exhibit increased tolerance. Therefore, this experiment shows that cognitive control is extremely effective in altering pain tolerance. More important for us, this research provides an example of a one-factor multiple-group design.

When one examines the groups, it is obvious that the groups differ in kind but not amount. To be sure, the cognitive intervention group experienced events neither the placebo group nor the control groups experienced, and the placebo condition was treated differently than the true control condition (even taking an inactive substance is perceived as an experimental manipulation). These differences withstanding, it is still not possible to say how much the groups differed. The group designations are nominal (recall the discussion of scales of measurement in Chapter 5), and although they are separated by procedures, it makes no sense to specify group differences along some continuum.

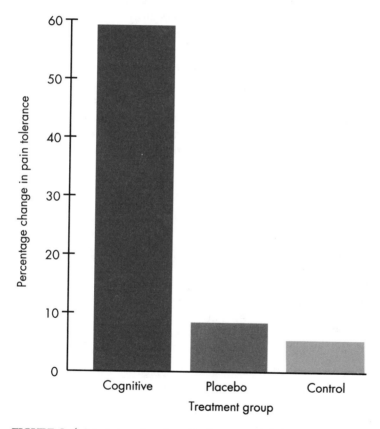

FIGURE 8–4 An example of a one-factor multiple-group design in which qualitative differences in the independent variable are used to designate groups. (From Bandura et al., 1988.) Copyright © 1988 by the American Psychological Association. Reprinted with permission.

**one-factor multiple-group design**—a design that includes more than two levels of one independent variable

With respect to one-factor multiple-group designs in which the experimental manipulation is performed on a quantitative variable, it is appropriate to specify group differences along some dimension. One of the oldest experiments in the history of psychology can be used to illustrate this popular research model. In 1885 Hermann Ebbinghaus conducted the first systematic study of long-term memory in human subjects. In this classic experiment, Ebbinghaus used himself and anyone else he could find as subjects. Each subject was presented with a list of nonsense syllables such as *KLH, YTW, OJS,* and so on. As Figure 8–5 shows, the subjects were then asked to immediately relearn the syllables from the list or to relearn the syllables immediately and after 9 hours of rest, 24 hours of rest, or 2 days of rest. The results from the Ebbinghaus project showed that retention diminished over several hours. Specifically, the time to relearn the list to a particular criterion (savings) was reduced appreciably by 9 hours, and retention continued to fall off even more over the next couple of days.

To account for this phenomenon, Ebbinghaus postulated the formation of a memory trace which erodes with time. What is important to us is that the design of this archival memory experiment employed multiple values of the independent variable "time since original learning," and that these values are separated by amount. That is, it is possible to say how much difference exists between a 9-hour retention group and a 24-hour retention group. Therefore, unlike the qualitative case in which group membership is defined by distinctively different

FIGURE 8–5 An example of the use of quantitative variation in the formation of groups. (From Ebbinghaus, 1885.) For each group designation, a memory test was administered after differing amounts of time since learning.

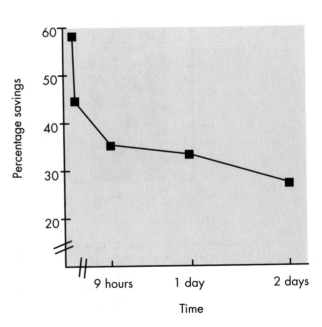

categories, in the quantitative design we may specify the degree of variation along the continuum of the independent variable.

Because the character of quantitative designs permits groups to be arranged by order and increasing values of the independent variable, it is appropriate to plot the data on a line graph such as the one in Figure 8–5. It is possible to just glance at such a graph and determine if trends exist. Of course, this is not possible with a qualitative design where groups are placed along the horizontal axis arbitrarily. In qualitative experiments, bar graphs are more commonly used.

## WITHIN CHAPTER REVIEW AND STUDY QUESTION

### ONE-FACTOR MULTIPLE-GROUP DESIGNS

1. Differentiate between qualitative and quantitative one-factor multiple-group designs. Give examples of each and show how the graphic representations of the results would differ.

# MULTIFACTOR DESIGNS

Psychological phenomena are often complex and determined by the joint effects of several different variables. It follows that in many, if not most, instances, experimental designs consider the impact of multiple independent variables that are manipulated simultaneously. Of course, it is possible to conduct a series of one-factor (one independent variable) experiments and eventually gain some understanding of the effects of these factors on the dependent variable, but this would be costly in terms of time and number of subjects. Perhaps even more important is that there would be no way to distinguish the effects that are due to the combined exposure of two or more variables. That is, the joint effects of Variable A and Variable B on a given subject may produce a response pattern that is very different from that which would be produced by isolated manipulations of these variables. Because of the complex nature of psychological research and the need to assess cotreatment effects, multifactor designs are commonly employed by investigators in the 1990s.

In a **multifactor design,** two or more independent variables are studied simultaneously. Within each independent variable the investigator

**multifactor design**—a design that incorporates more than one independent variable

**factorial design**—a design in which each level of one factor is combined with each level of other factors

may opt to include only two levels, or he or she may manipulate multiple levels. In either case, because we are discussing different examples of between-subjects designs in this chapter, it should be understood that individual subjects who appear in one condition (e.g., a given level of independent Variable A combined with a given level of independent Variable B) do not appear in a second. Unlike the within-subjects version of multifactor designs discussed in the next chapter, in the designs here participants perform only once under a specified set of conditions.

## The Factorial Design

The most common of the between-subjects multifactor designs is known as the **factorial design.** In a factorial design, each level of one factor (independent variable) is combined with each level of the other factors (independent variables). The symmetry of the factorial design is evident in a study by Smith (1986). This experiment (Experiment 3 in the report) was concerned with the effects of environmental context on recognition memory. Smith's research centered on the idea that the context in which learning originally takes place may provide an important source of retrieval cues and thus become an integral part of the memory matrix. It follows that if people learned material in a certain context and recalled that material in the same context, they would perform at a higher level than in a test situation where the memory task was presented in a context different from the one in which they had originally learned.

As Figure 8–6 shows, Smith used a factorial model to examine the role of context in memory by combining the independent variables *learning environment* (a barren cubicle or a large classroom with windows, a blackboard, and 25 desks) and test context (same context [SC] or different context [DC]). Four groups comprised of separate subjects were created by this arrangement: cubicle-SC subjects learned 50 word pairs in the small cubicle and were administered a recognition test in the same cubicle; classroom-SC subjects learned the 50 word pairs in the large classroom and were given the memory test in the same classroom; cubicle-DC subjects learned the word pairs in the cubicle but received the memory test in the classroom; and classroom-DC subjects learned the word pairs in the classroom but received the memory test in the cubicle.

In a factorial design that involves two independent variables, it is customary in psychological research to refer to the combination of two values along each independent variable as a *cell*. For example, assume that $A_1$, $A_2$, and $A_3$ correspond to the three levels of the first independent variable and that $B_1$, $B_2$, and $B_3$ refer to the three levels of the second independent variable. Subjects participating in the first level of Treatment A and the third level of Treatment B would therefore fall in Cell $A_1B_3$. Similarly, subjects falling in the cell of the second level of the first variable and the first level of the second variable would be in Cell $A_2B_1$. The advantage of cell configurations in experimental design is that they permit us to think in terms of collapsing across one factor within a given level of the other factor. By collapsing, I mean that all the data within a given factor is combined to create a single data set. This concept relates to what is known as a main effect in a between-subjects multifactor design.

## Main Effects

A **main effect** refers to the impact of one independent variable in an experimental framework that manipulates multiple factors. In an experimental situation that involves three levels of Treatment A and three levels of Treatment B, for instance, we may be interested in the differential effects of the three levels of B apart from the influence of A. In this case, by combining or collapsing across $A_1$, $A_2$, and $A_3$ at each level of B we are able to assess the action of $B_1$, $B_2$, and $B_3$ independent of A. That is, because all levels of A are represented in each level of B, systematic differences due to the respective levels of A are not a concern. Later in this book I discuss the availability of statistical tests that make it possible to determine if the resulting differences in $B_1$, $B_2$, and $B_3$ reflect real or chance differences (see Chapter 11, Drawing Inferences About Results). If the differences are real, then we can say that a significant main effect for B has been obtained.

The role of main effects in psychological research can be illustrated by inspecting the pattern of results produced in the study by Smith (1986) (refer to Figure 8–6). Recall that this experiment was concerned with the effects of learning

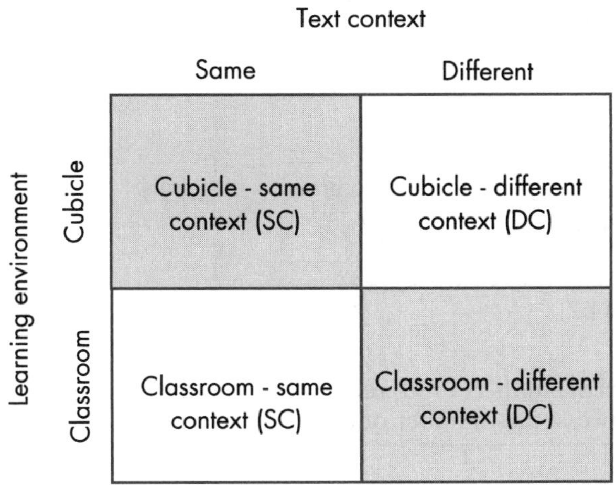

Text context

|  | Same | Different |
|---|---|---|
| **Cubicle** | Cubicle - same context (SC) | Cubicle - different context (DC) |
| **Classroom** | Classroom - same context (SC) | Classroom - different context (DC) |

Learning environment

**FIGURE 8–6 The factorial model Smith used, 1986**

**main effect**—the impact of one independent variable in a factorial design

context on recognition memory. Human subjects learned word pairs in a small cubicle or a large classroom and then were asked to recall the words in SC or DC. The results of Smith's experiment are profiled in Figure 8–7.

If we designate *learning environment* as Treatment A (with two levels, a cubicle or a classroom) and *test context* as Treatment B (also with two levels, same or different), we can say that Cell $A_1B_1$ corresponds to the condition where subjects learned in the cubicle and received the memory test in the same cubicle, Cell $A_1B_2$ corresponds to the condition where subjects learned in the cubicle but were tested in the large classroom, and so on. Now, let's say that we are interested in determining whether SC or DC produced a difference in word recognition independent of where the original learning took place. In other words, we have expressed curiosity about a main effect for B. By pooling or combining the data from $A_1B_1$ and $A_2B_1$, and then separately combining the results at $A_1B_2$ and $A_2B_2$, we can create the new data sets $B_1$ and $B_2$. It is now possible to compare performances where the material was learned and remembered in SC or DC, regardless of specific context features.

It is apparent from the mean (average) number of recognition errors shown in each cell of Figure 8–7 that the performance of subjects under the SC condition was better (fewer errors were made) than under the DC condition. That is, the average of $B_1$ (SC) would be 4.67 errors and the average of $B_2$ (DC) would

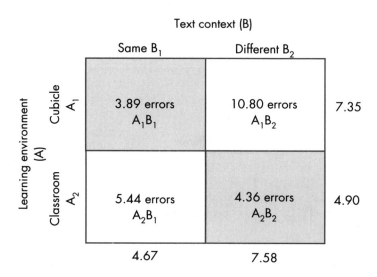

**FIGURE 8–7 The results of Smith's (1986) recognition memory study. The data are expressed as number of errors.**

be 7.58 errors in this study given equal Ns (subjects/cell). In addition, because statistical analyses revealed that these differences were not likely due to chance, we can assert that people remember events better if at testing they are in the same place they were when they originally acquired the information. You might want to remember this the next time you start preparing for an exam!

Smith interpreted his data within a theoretical framework tied to the concept of retrieval. He believed that the richer the memory matrix, the more cues that are available for retrieval. Ostensibly, because the environmental stimuli that defined a setting became integral to the memory matrix, when the subject was in the same environment during testing more retrieval cues were present. Also note that had we been interested in the main effect for Treatment A, it would have been just as simple to compare recognition performances in the cubicle and the classroom independent of whether subjects tested in each of these rooms had learned the words in SC or DC. By collapsing across the two levels of B at $A_1$ and $A_2$ and combining the data sets from the respective cells, it would be possible to determine if context was influential in altering recognition memory. However, unlike the issue of same-different comparisons that are linked to a large pool of literature on retrieval phenomena, there is minimal theoretical cause for assessing the role of room size and features on memory functioning. Therefore, although the information on the main effect for Treatment A is readily available, it would receive scant attention from the investigator.

Let's return to the main effect for Treatment B that Smith observed in his study. If we scrutinize the results of this experiment, it becomes apparent that our main effect is created largely as a result of the discrepancy that exists for SC and DC subjects who originally learned the 50 word pairs in the small cubicle. Specifically, when subjects learned in the cubicle and received the recognition test in the same cubicle, only 3.89 errors were made on the average. In comparison, subjects who learned in the cubicle but were tested in the large classroom made 10.80 errors. This pattern is appreciably different from the one exhibited by subjects who originally learned the material in the classroom. In both testing settings (cubicle and classroom), approximately 4 or 5 errors were made. Therefore, it would seem that the main effect for B we discussed earlier may not tell the whole story. Indeed, it may misrepresent what occurred in the Smith study.

## Simple Interaction Effects

This leads us to a discussion of **interaction effects** in psychological research that employs a between-subjects multifactor design. Interaction effects are said to occur when the effect of one independent

**interaction effects**—when the effects of one independent variable change across the different levels of a second independent variable

variable produces a different pattern of results when separate values of that independent variable combine with different values of a second independent variable (Gravetter & Wallnau, 1995). The simplest expression of interaction effects in a between-subjects multifactor design is the case involving only two independent variables, each with two levels. Given that Treatment A and Treatment B define relevant experimental manipulations, it is possible that at level $A_1$ the influence of $B_1$ (Cell $A_1B_1$) is very different from the influence of $B_2$ at $A_1$ (Cell $A_1B_2$), and that this pattern of separation is very different from the impact of $B_1$ and $B_2$ at level $A_2$ (Cells $A_2B_1$ and $A_2B_2$, respectively). Similarly, at a given level of B, say $B_1$, the effects of $A_1$ and $A_2$ may differ compared to the other level of B ($B_2$).

Returning to the Smith study, we see an example of simple interaction effects. Figure 8–8 profiles the numerical data in Figure 8–7. Conventionally, Treatment

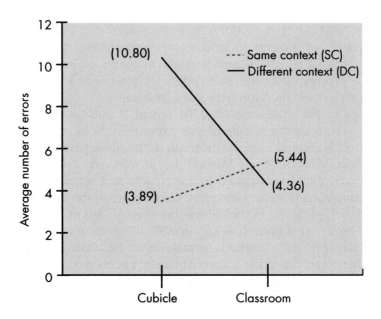

FIGURE 8–8 A graphic representation of the findings from the Smith (1986) study regarding the effects of context on memory. Note the interaction between the original learning environment and the SC or DC status of the test environment, as well as the significant main effect for Variable B (SC or DC).

Variable A is plotted along the horizontal axis and Treatment Variable B is denoted by different symbols in the legend. At $A_1$ (learned in the small cubicle) substantial separation is apparent between conditions where participants performed under SC or DC conditions ($B_1$ and $B_2$, respectively). In contrast, at level $A_2$ (learned in the large classroom), it did not make much difference whether subjects were tested in SC or DC. This pattern reflects a significant interaction.

One subtle, and admittedly imprecise, rule that exists for interactions is evident from Figure 8–8. Notice how the lines converge. That is, although the lines that define $B_1$ and $B_2$ are far apart at $A_1$, they meet and cross over at $A_2$. This convergence pattern offers the investigator a clue that an interaction effect may exist. Of course, it is not possible to assess the significance of this interaction without analyzing the data with the appropriate statistical tests (see Chapter 11, Drawing Inferences About Results). Even when separated lines would appear to converge, should you continue the lines beyond the points plotted from the data, a significant interaction effect will likely be observed.

Therefore, as indicated, the Smith results illustrate the case where you have a significant main effect for B and a significant interaction effect. Now consider what a significant main effect for Treatment Variable A and a significant interaction effect might look like. Figure 8–9 represents hypothetical data where collapsing across levels of B, $A_1$ and $A_2$ clearly differ. This means that if you combined the performances of all subjects who received Treatment $B_1$ or $B_2$, performance at $A_1$ would still be noticeably lower than performance at $A_2$. Even with this apparent main effect, on closer inspection it is evident that the various

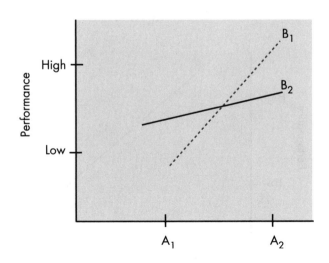

**FIGURE 8–9 An illustration of a significant main effect for Variable A and a significant interaction**

levels of B have different effects as we move across the two levels of A. Specifically, at $A_1$, the cell that incorporates $B_1$ is below that defined by $A_1B_2$. This pattern reverses at $A_2$, and once again the lines of the graph converge and cross over. In this example, no main effect for B exists because when the performances of all subjects in $A_1$ and $A_2$ are compared, the points $B_1$ and $B_2$ occupy fall squarely on top of one another.

It is further possible for an investigator to find a dramatic interaction effect in the absence of any main effect differences. This situation is shown in Figure 8–10. Consistent with the rule of convergence mentioned earlier, one sees again that the lines in the graph created by the changing values of A and B cross. Unlike in the previous illustration of interaction effects, however, when we collapse across the two levels of B, $A_1$ and $A_2$ are the same. Similarly, collapsing across the two levels of A results in values of $B_1$ and $B_2$ that occupy virtually the same place on the graph. Nonetheless, a whopping interaction between Variables A and B occurs. At $A_1$, participants receiving $B_1$ are far below participants receiving $B_2$, and this pattern reverses at $A_2$ (subjects in $A_2B_1$ perform at much higher levels than subjects in $A_2B_2$). In more concrete terms, this pattern might occur in a study of males and females (Variable A) trained on one of two social skills programs (Variable B). For males, one training program may produce much better social skills development, while females might have an advantage in the other training program. Overall, males may not be different from females, and the effectiveness of the two training programs may be essentially equivalent. Still, prominent and meaningful differences would be evident in this study from the significant interaction effect.

**FIGURE 8–10 An illustration of experimental findings where no main effects were found but a significant interaction is apparent**

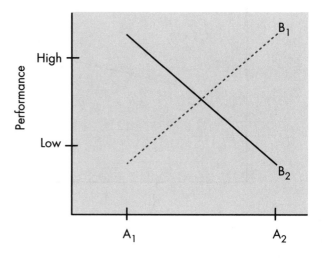

Finally, it should be understood that even in the simplest case of the between-subjects multifactor design, it is possible for a researcher to witness a pattern of findings that reveals significant main effects for both Variables A and B, as well as a significant interaction effect. Figure 8–11 shows how the results from such an experiment might appear in graphic form. Collapsing across $A_1$ and $A_2$ obviously renders values that indicate a main effect for Variable B, and the same can be said for Variable A when the scores of $B_1$ and $B_1$ are combined. Moreover, the separation that is apparent between $B_1$ and $B_2$ at level $A_1$ is augmented at level $A_2$. Therefore, it is clear in this illustration that an interaction effect occurs.

This feature relates to a previous comment made above. Recall that I remarked how in some cases involving interaction effects lines converge and cross over, while in other cases you might have to extend the lines beyond the points associated with the data to achieve the crossover effect. Figure 8–11 is a case in point. If you were to continue the slopes in this graph, the lines would eventually cross.

Given that it is possible to obtain a significant main effect or main effects and a significant interaction as well, how do we make decisions about the relative importance of each finding? Interpreting such results requires that we follow certain rules and that we ask questions in a prescribed sequence.

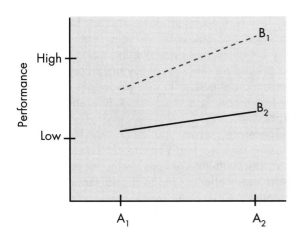

FIGURE 8–11 An illustration of experimental findings where both main effects (A and B) are significant and the interaction effect is significant as well

## Spotlight on Research: NOW THAT I'VE CAUGHT IT, WHAT DO I DO WITH IT?

**W**hen I was a kid, I had a dog that suffered from a number of behavioral afflictions, not the least of which was its inappropriate torment of wild bunnies. For reasons that were unclear to me, and surely were unclear to my dog, he would chase any rabbit we happened to disturb during our daily walks in the dappled meadows of Oklahoma. The chase always ended the same way: the dog caught the rabbit and, because he was motivated only by catching his prey, he did not know what to do next. I was no help in this regard. I was as puzzled by my dog's behavior as he was.

My experience has been that psychological investigators sometimes find themselves in a predicament similar to that of my dog. They collect data systematically, but then seem uncertain about what to do next. In factorial studies, this dilemma may be especially troublesome because you may have so much information you may not be sure where to begin. What piece of the experiment do you interpret first?

The answer is that you always interpret the interaction effects before examining the main effect differences (Howell, 1995). This is true for a couple of reasons. First, it is possible that your main effect differences may be a byproduct of the interaction effect and therefore be essentially meaningless. Take the hypothetical example of male and female college students (Variable A)

who perform on tests of reading skill under conditions of sleep deprivation or being rested (Variable B). Although males and females do not differ when rested, females exhibit substantially greater reading performance than males under sleep deprivation conditions. In fact, the differences between sleep-deprived males and females is so vast that overall performances by gender show females to be superior to males in reading skill. Obviously, such a finding is misleading. It would be more appropriate to address the data in terms of the interaction effects. Therefore, it makes sense that you interpret the interaction before making statements about main effects.

A second reason for looking at interactions first is that even in cases where a legitimate main effect occurs, scores may vary across the other factor. That is, the pattern of results may be such that the impact of one variable on a second variable may be greater at one level than at another (see the preceding discussion). By first interpreting the interaction effects, a more reasonable account of the true meaning of main effect differences can be expressed.

Therefore, when you catch something when chasing an idea and you are not sure what to do next, start with interactions and work your way toward main effects. You will find that your interpretations make more sense.  ■

## *Higher-Order Interaction Effects*

Throughout this text, I have remarked on the complex nature of psychological phenomena and the care the investigator must exercise when designing an experiment. Often this means that three, four, or even five independent variables must be included in the design structure. Similar to the simple interaction effects discussed previously for the multifactor between-subjects design where only two independent variables are present, it is possible that each variable in a more complex experiment may interact with every other variable in that experiment. Such interactions are commonly referred to as **higher-order interaction effects,** and if you are not careful your design can yield statistically significant differences that are virtually impossible to decipher.

Consider a hypothetical experiment that incorporates Treatment Variables A, B, C, and D. This is called a four-way design because four independent variables are being studied. Several two-way interactions may be obtained here, such as the A × B interaction, the A × C interaction, the B × C interaction, and so forth. The key in all cases is that only the influence of two independent variables are being compared. In contrast, in a three-way interaction cell comparisons are made according to the impact of three factors. A significant A × B × C interaction permits $A_1B_1C_1$ to be compared to $A_1B_1C_2$, for instance. However, this same interaction also permits comparisons between $A_1B_1C_1$ and $A_2B_1C_1$. In both comparisons, the effects of all three treatment variables on the performances of subjects in a particular condition (a cell) are evaluated relative to separate combinations of different levels of the same three variables. You can imagine how difficult it is to unravel the meaning of the differences in such interactions. Further imagine the challenge inherent in interpreting a four-way interaction where all possible combinations of Variables A,B,C, and D must be assessed (see Figure 8–12). Clearly, practical concerns limit how far we can extend multifactor between-subjects designs. It serves no useful purpose to design an experiment, however elegant, if at the end of the data collection phase you are overwhelmed with information that leaves you wondering what you have done.

With a better conceptual understanding of the features of multifactor between-subjects designs, it is appropriate to return to the model experiment we are developing as we move through the chapters of this book. In each of the previous seven chapters elements of the model project have unfolded. It was determined that the experiment, which is intended to demonstrate the relative efficacy of a cognitively based treatment strategy in younger and older chronically ill populations, would incorporate two independent variables: type of treatment (cognitive coping strategy, sensory information, and contact control) and age range (4 to 6 years old and 10 to 12 years old).

Therefore, we see that our design is a simple, two-way, multifactor between-subjects design. That is, subjects (chronically ill cancer patients) of a given age range who receive one of the three types of therapy experience no

**higher-order interaction effects**—interaction effects associated with comparing data from cells defined by three or more independent variables

FIGURE 8–12 The higher-order interactions that can be produced in a four-way design involving Treatment Variables A, B, C, and D

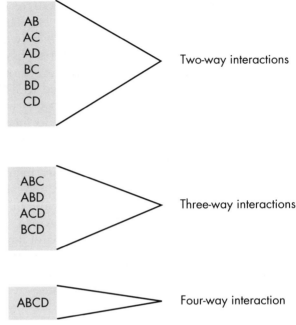

further experimental manipulations. The between-subjects character of our model experiment means that the size of our sample will have to be large (recall from Chapter 6 that because 16 subjects from each of the two age ranges will be assigned to each of the three treatment conditions, a total of 96 patients will be required for this study).

However, including two variables in the overall experimental framework permits us to examine two-way interaction effects and therein more deliberately determine the role of age in the success of cognitive intervention. Indeed, if the interaction tests were not set up and made possible by design, we would compromise our ability to make statements about the issues that formed the rationale for the experiment. Remember from Chapters 2 and 3 that the prediction for our model experiment is that the cognitive coping strategy manipulation will be more effective for 10- to 12-year-olds than for 4- to 6-year-olds. Should we decide to conduct separate experiments on each age range using the indicated therapeutic interventions, it would not be possible to make direct comparisons across experiments. That is, no statistical analysis permits a determination of relative differences between groups when the groups are part of different research projects conducted at different times, under different conditions, and in potentially diverse medical climates. However, if the groups are evaluated within a common experimental framework, and an "age range x type of treatment" interaction becomes evident, it would be appropriate statistically to compare Cells $A_1B_1$ (4- to 6-year-olds, cognitive coping strategy) and $A_2B_1$ (10- to 12-year-olds, cognitive coping strategy). If age (A) differences appear here that are not apparent at other levels of B (other treatments), then we may feel reasonably confident that our suspicion about the limited utility of cognitive strategies for young children is sound.

Therefore, the two-way model we have selected allows us to answer the central question that is the driving force behind the project. Thoughtful, considered design issues are as critical to creative research as good ideas. Many beautifully conceived notions have been wrecked by ugly design decisions.

In addition to concerns over how many independent variables an experimenter should include in a study, it should be noted that there is also the question of how many dependent measures are desirable for a given project. This issue relates to multivariate experimental designs.

## ⚛ Thinking About Research

Beginning students are often misled by the attempts of professors and textbooks to keep the coverage of research methodology as simple as possible. Obviously, it makes sense that the instructive process is better served if the material can be presented in a straightforward manner where the inessentials have been cut back, leaving only the crux of scientific information. Sometimes in our ambition to keep the material simple, however, we promote deception. In our efforts to make an area more understandable, we inadvertently omit key topics or concepts.

In the 1990s, one aspect of psychological research that is often misrepresented concerns selecting dependent variables. Typically, coverage of this topic leads students to believe that one dependent measure is used, even when the experi-

mental framework is defined by multiple independent variables. For example, in a study of stress reactivity, the format presented to the uninitiated student of psychological research may include scores on an anxiety questionnaire. In addition, this format is offered as the only available, or best, index of distress. This type of procedure, in which only one dependent measure is employed, is called a **univariate design.**

In actuality, it is becoming commonplace to use several dependent measures, a procedure which is known as a **multivariate design.** With stress

**univariate design**—a design where only one dependent variable is recorded

**multivariate design**—a design where two or more dependent variables are recorded

reactivity, for instance, you might want to include a behavioral measure, a self-report measure, and a physiological measure.

> This is precisely what we did in the model experiment we are constructing in this text (i.e., the OSBD, a self-report of pain measure [the fear thermometer], and heart-rate were chosen for our model experiment—refer to Chapter 3).

The advantage of the multivariate approach is that in addition to increasing the chances for ob-taining a significant result, it also permits you to define the limits of your effects. That is, it is some-times as important to know what events are not af-fected by your experimental manipulation as it is to identify the events that *are* influenced by your treatment effects.

Therefore, as you think about which indepen-dent variables to include in your study, also consider which dependent measures are appro-priate. Thinking ahead is basic to attaining goals in all areas, including scientific research.    ■

## WITHIN CHAPTER REVIEW AND STUDY QUESTIONS

### MULTIFACTOR DESIGNS

1. Describe the relative disadvantages and advantages of factorial designs. Provide an example of a factorial design that is concerned with the effects of socioeconomic status and age on memory.
2. Define each of the following terms:
   a. main effects
   b. simple interaction effects
   c. higher-order interaction effects

## SELECTING THE BEST BETWEEN-SUBJECTS DESIGN

In this chapter, several different types of between-subjects designs have been covered. It was acknowledged that the most elementary form of the between-subjects procedure involves only two groups. Typically this means that the value of the independent variable is changed for the experimental group and un-changed or neutral for the control group. It was further noted that in many instances several values of one independent variable must be examined across separate groups in a multiple-group design. Finally, designs that incorporate multiple independent variables were discussed.

With the demonstrated utility of between-subjects designs and an array of designs to choose from, it follows that psychological researchers are placed frequently in the position of selecting a plan from an overall package. How do they choose? What criteria do researchers employ when deciding on design considerations? Are there rules to follow when selecting the best possible between-subjects procedure for our experiment?

It is appropriate when attempting to answer these questions to look more closely at why we selected the design we did for the model experiment that we are building in this book. Why did we decide to use a 2 x 3 factorial design? Should we have gone with some other strategy?

The initial point that must be addressed is that we chose a between-subjects design. Regarding the independent variable of age range (Variable A), there is obviously no alternative but to use a between-subjects procedure. You cannot at once fall into both the 4- to 6-year-old age range and the 10- to 12-year-old category. But what about the "type of treatment intervention" variable (Variable B)? Why use separate subjects in all three therapeutic strategies? Most notably, a between-subjects approach is preferred because it is possible, even likely, that any one of the treatments selected for our model experiment may result in improvement (i.e., diminished stress and anxiety among individual patients). Accordingly, to accurately determine the relative efficacy of the different treatment interventions, experimentally naive (untreated) patients are required. This can only be accomplished using a between-subjects design.

Earlier, in the section on interaction effects, I commented on the need to be able to assess interaction effects in our model experiment. In the absence of a factorial design, it would not be possible to gauge directly the relative efficacy of a cognitive treatment for younger and older children. Therefore, a multifactor design was mandated by the hypothesis under investigation.

Finally, why did we choose only two age ranges and three different types of treatment? As mentioned previously, a good experiment is designed economically and includes the fewest levels of each variable that are necessary to answer the question at hand. The literature tells us that we have sufficient separation between age groups to establish appreciable differences in levels of cognitive functioning, and three types of treatment intervention suffice to determine the specificity of the effects of age on therapeutic success. Indeed, the number of subjects in this applied study is large already (96), so extending the number of levels could produce additional logistics problems that would make it difficult to complete the project. Therefore, logical as well as practical concerns were important when we selected the design for our model experiment.

It should be apparent from these remarks that the answer to the question about whether there are rules for selecting the best between-subjects design is "no." There is no recipe or cookbook account of design considerations to follow. In the final analysis, the investigators must make decisions that are dictated by the nature of the questions they are asking. It is not the easiest part of experimental psychology, but it surely is one of the most critical.

## WITHIN CHAPTER REVIEW AND STUDY QUESTION

### SELECTING THE BEST BETWEEN-SUBJECTS DESIGN

1. What were the chief factors we considered in selecting a 2 × 3 between-subjects design for our model experiment?

### The Model Experiment

Throughout this chapter, the value of between-subjects designs has been discussed. Although assigning subjects to separate experimental conditions carries expensive baggage in some ways, it can be quite cost effective in others. When experience in one treatment setting affects performance in a second, a between-subjects design provides an option that ensures you will not have flawed results, and thereby find yourself returning to "square one."

We have selected the between-subjects design format for our model experiment because the nature of our experiment is such that participation in one treatment condition may result in improvements that would render performance in a second condition meaningless. That is, in a 2 [age range (4 to 6 years and 10 to 12 years)] × 3 [types of treatment (cognitive coping strategy, sensory information, and contact control)] design that aims to look at the therapeutic effectiveness of different interventions on stress reactivity in chronically ill patients, it makes sense that if experience with one condition successfully alleviates anxiety, it is nonsensical to attempt to measure impact of a second intervention. Simply stated, you cannot alter something that doesn't exist. As a result, different subjects must be used in separate conditions in our model experiment.

Of course, between-subjects designs are not the answer in all cases of experimental psychology. Alternative design frameworks may be more suitable when other types of questions are being asked. In the next chapter, a few of these alternatives are discussed.

## CHAPTER 9

# Within-Subjects, Mixed, and Single-Subject Designs

**within-subjects design**—an experimental framework within which repeated observations are made on the same subjects; often called repeated measures designs

Throughout the previous chapter we discussed the merits of the between-subjects model where participants only experience one treatment manipulation. With no further elaboration, it is sufficiently noted that such designs are integral to a successful experimental outcome, at least in selected cases. It is also true, however, that in some instances assigning subjects to different experimental conditions is wasteful and inefficient. Moreover, it is outright inappropriate to use between-subjects designs in some research environments.

In this chapter, I cover several alternatives to using the conventional between-subjects design in psychological research. Included in this chapter are discussions of (a) the role of within-subjects designs, (b) instances where both between and within features are incorporated into the model (the mixed design), and (c) single-subject designs. As you will see, there are certain circumstances in which each of these specialty design formats is best suited to answering the questions under investigation. First, let's look at the within-subjects model that has become popular in the psychology of learning and conditioning, personality, memory, and other research areas where repeated recordings are likely to be made.

# WITHIN-SUBJECTS DESIGNS

On several occasions earlier in this book I referred to the need to provide adequate experimental control. Otherwise, you will find yourself in a defenseless, untenable position from which you will be unable to argue compellingly about issues. Control, as we have observed, can be accomplished by judiciously manipulating different values of the independent variable(s) and randomly assigning subjects to separate control and experimental conditions. However, control can also be achieved using the subject's performance as a basis for judging the strength of experimental effects. In this type of design, which is known as a **within-subjects design,** each subject serves as his or her own control. Within-subjects designs present an experimental framework wherein the same participants receive different treatments or experience different levels of a given independent variable. More often than not this means that each subject is tested repeatedly across all experimental conditions. Because participation is recurrent, and the same dependent measure often employed, within-subjects designs are sometimes referred to as repeated-measures designs. Figure 9–1 portrays the most elementary within-subjects design where each subject participates in both Treatment 1 and Treatment 2.

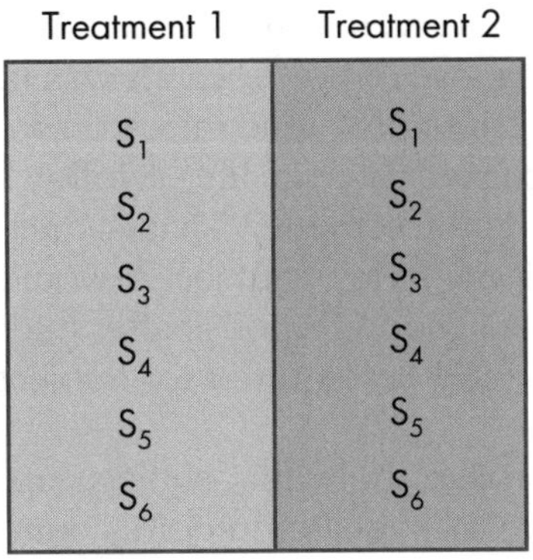

| Treatment 1 | Treatment 2 |
|:---:|:---:|
| $S_1$ | $S_1$ |
| $S_2$ | $S_2$ |
| $S_3$ | $S_3$ |
| $S_4$ | $S_4$ |
| $S_5$ | $S_5$ |
| $S_6$ | $S_6$ |

**FIGURE 9-1** A simple within-subjects design where the same subjects participate under the conditions of two successively presented treatments

The within-subjects model is attractive for a variety of reasons. A few of these reasons are discussed in the sections that follow, and some of the unique characteristics and problems associated with reusing the same subjects across treatments are highlighted.

## *Advantages of Within-Subjects Designs*

As indicated, on occasion a within-subjects approach is preferred over all others. Let's look at some examples.

**Sometimes Nothing Else Works.** Consider the following social psychology research project conducted by Metalsky, Abramson, Seligman, Semmel, and Peterson (1982). In this study, which focused on the importance of attributional styles and life events on depressive mood reactions, college students were tracked over an entire semester. Metalsky et al. were particularly interested in the reactions of certain types of students to low grades reported at mid-term. The investigators determined that people who exhibited a tendency to attribute setbacks and failure to internal ("It was my fault"), stable ("I'll never get any better"), and global ("I'm not good at anything") factors were more likely to respond to low mid-term grades by becoming depressed than were people who tended to attribute failure to external ("The exams were unfair"), unstable ("I'll do better next time"), and specific ("This is just one situation") factors. Metalsky et al. believed that different types of attributional styles confer protection against, or foster the formation of, depressive episodes triggered by negative life events.

Taking a closer look at the Metalsky et al. study we see that given the nature of the phenomena under investigation, it would have been inappropriate to employ a between-subjects design. Think about the constraints that would have been imposed in this study had the research team opted for a between-subjects analysis. This would have meant that attributional-style information would have had to be collected for Subject A, and then the investigators would have had to

**subject variation**—the differences that exist between subjects in the same group or condition

observe Subject B's reaction to low grades received at mid-term. Obviously, this makes no sense. Because the purpose of the research was to assess the effects of a given individual's attributional tendencies on reactions to negative life circumstances occurring later in life, it follows that the same subjects must be used at both points in the semester. That is, measurements would have to be made and the attributional style of Subject A would need to be determined and used to predict Subject A's mood response after mid-term grades were posted. The same information would be required for Subject B, and so forth.

In research projects such as the Metalsky et al. project, the within-subjects approach is mandated. When the rationale underlying the research requires comparisons of related events in the same individual, within-subjects applications are required. It is of no value to measure a dependent variable that is tied to common factors if you consider only one factor and ignore the second. Only when you know an individual's performance on the first event does that individual's performance on the second event take on meaning.

Within-subjects designs also are necessary when only one independent measure is used and sequentially dependent effects are an issue. You may be interested in the effects of practice on learning and performance in rats responding in a straight-alley maze, for instance. Latency to traverse the length of the alley is recorded on Trial 1, then again on Trial 2, and so on until maximal or asymptotic performance levels are reached, or the experiment is terminated. Trial-to-trial behavior changes are critical in such research settings because they are believed to represent parallel changes in associative and cognitive learning processes. Although it might be possible to compare the performance of Rat 1 on Trial 15 with the performance of Rat 2 on Trial 16, it makes no sense to do so. The difference between the two scores could be a function of training conditions, the rats' different statuses, or a host of other factors. In contrast, the difference between Rat 1's latencies on Trial 15 and Trial 16 would provide an index of true change—a change based on one rat's experiences in the same learning context.

Therefore, we see that occasionally there is no alternative to using the same subjects more than once in an experiment. In fact, in many cases it is appropriate to use the same subjects in all conditions. In addition to meeting the practical demands of research questions, within-subjects designs offer additional advantages, such as controlling for variation.

**Reducing Variation.** As I have noted previously, subject differences, or **subject variation** as it is often called, limits the sensitivity of an experimental manipulation. This issue is discussed in much greater detail in Chapter 11 when the statistical concept of error variance is described more fully. At this juncture, it is sufficient to say that we understand that when some subjects in a given condition respond in one way and other subjects in the same condition respond in another, the investigator is not likely to be able to report that a difference is meaningful, regardless of its magnitude. It follows that design considerations that are aimed at reducing subject variation are favored over those that are less effective in controlling subject differences.

Because the same subjects are used in Condition A and Condition B in a within-subjects design, this model is ideally suited to control for subject variation. The within-subjects design, which may be considered a totally matched design (see the discussion on matching in Chapters 6 and 8), ensures that subject characteristics across groups are similar if not identical. Because the same subjects are used across conditions, the only subject differences that should occur are minor changes in mood, fatigue levels, motivational status, or other variables that are subject to moment-to-moment fluctuation. Oscillations along these lines are not likely to make much of a difference one way or the other, so they can be treated as constants. The important thing is that certain subject variables, such as intelligence, gender, attributional style, educational level, and spatial reasoning ability, remain the same. These factors may have a profound effect on the dependent measure, but they tend to be stable across a variety of situations. For example, a person's attitude about domestic violence in Scotland or the United States is not likely to shift, at least not any time soon. Consequently, when the same subject is used again in an experimental condition, there is a match on this factor and the experimenter does not have to worry about its contributing to subject variation.

**The Economical Approach.** In addition to reducing subject variation, within-subjects designs offer the advantage of decreasing the required number of subjects. This feature is depicted in Figure 9–2. In a hypothetical study of the effects of number of years of formal education on performance of verbal and quantitative tasks, it is possible to employ a between-subjects model. As the top panel of Figure 9-2 shows, different groups of people with 1 to 12 years of formal education (high school or lower), 13 to 16 years of formal education (college educated), and greater than 16 years of a formal education can be assigned to take either the verbal ability test or the quantitative ability test. If we decide that we want 15 people in each of the 6 conditions created by this $3 \times 2$ design, then we require a total of 90 subjects.

In contrast, look at what is needed in the within-subjects design outlined in the bottom panel of Figure 9–2. Because the same people who have 1 to 12 years of formal education perform on both the verbal and the quantitative tasks, the number of people in this group can be decreased by one half. Similarly, the number of participants in the other groups may be cut. The result is that only 45 total subjects would be required to accomplish the same result produced by the between-subjects arrangement.

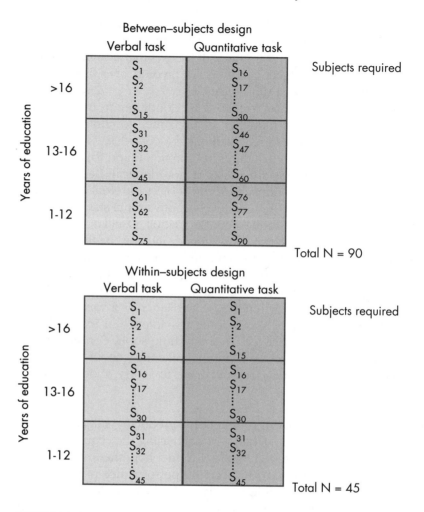

**FIGURE 9–2 The sample sizes (N) necessary to complete a hypothetical study on the relation between number of years of formal education and performance on verbal and quantitative tasks. The between-subjects design is shown in the top panel; the within-subjects design in the bottom panel.**

In some instances, savings like those shown in Figure 9-2 may not be of a great deal of interest. In cases where an almost unlimited supply of participants is available, it may actually be more desirable to employ the between-subjects approach, for reasons that I address shortly in this chapter. But what about when it is difficult to obtain even one subject, let alone many?

Take the case of an investigator who is interested in examining the effects of Rasmussen's encephalitis on motor dexterity, for example. The researcher will find it difficult to recruit a large number of individuals who suffer from this degenerative neurological disease because it is rare. The logistics of going from hospital setting to hospital setting will also be problematic, and other practical matters, such as the subject's need for constant medical attention, changing health status, and so on, will pose obstacles to conducting the research. Accordingly, it would make sense for the researcher to make maximum use of a subject once one is found and feels well enough to participate. In such circumstances, a within-subjects design is desirable because a great deal of information can be obtained from one subject.

The within-subjects approach is also valuable when collecting data from a given participant is expensive. I use a firsthand account to illustrate this advantage.

## Spotlight on Research: WHERE DOES THE MONEY GO?

For several years my laboratory has focused its research efforts on the effects of chronic exposure to metal pollutants (lead or cadmium) on psychoactive agents such as alcohol (Nation et al., 1991; Nation et al., 1993) and cocaine (Grover et al., 1993; Nation & Burkey, 1994; Nation, Livermore, & Bratton, 1995). The pattern has been one of decreased responsiveness to acute administrations of the drug, combined with increased self-administration of the drug. Our assumption has been that the increased voluntary administration of either alcohol or cocaine reflects a compensatory effect where more of the drug is needed to gain the same effect that would normally be produced.

Because all our work prior to 1993 had been conducted using rats, there was a real need to examine the relation between metal toxicity and drug use in humans. The opportunity to examine cocaine use/abuse patterns in human subjects was made available to me in the summer of 1993 when Dr. Donald Meck of the Applied Psychology Center in Warner-Robbins, Georgia, agreed to collaborate with me on a joint project. Dr. Meck's facility treated numerous people abusing cocaine, and the hospital setting provided a convenient place to draw blood samples and conduct metal screens. Still, there was a problem—cost. Each analysis of blood lead residues or blood cadmium residues would cost $183.00. Because numerous subjects would be needed in a project that aimed to establish a relation between metal contamination, cocaine use, and cognitive disturbance, the overall expenses were a concern.

As a result, we decided to use the same subjects on several different cognitive tasks. Using this within-subjects model we could minimize our expenses and still obtain the necessary information. For each $183.00 investment we were able to correlate lead or cadmium burdens with scores on a variety of psychological measures. There would have been no way for us to afford separate assays on each individual had we used a between-subjects design. Therefore, by using the same subjects again and again we were able to keep the budget within a manageable range and go forward with the research. The project is still proceeding, and although we don't have answers yet, with the cost-saving features of the within-subjects design we believe we will have something to say soon. ∎

**power**—the ability to detect real differences between conditions

**transfer effects**—result when experiences alter the manner, intensity, or direction of a behavior recorded in a subsequent experiment phase

Therefore, within-subjects designs provide an economical method for gathering data. In addition, they may offer increased sensitivity.

**Power.** Earlier I mentioned that subject variation limits an investigator's ability to detect significant differences, and that this issue is discussed more thoroughly in Chapter 11. As we shall see in Chapter 11, the **power** of a design is compromised by excessive subject variation. A powerful design effectively detects real differences between conditions, even when the absolute value of the differences is small.

For now, it suffices to acknowledge that because within-subjects designs restrict the degree of subject variation, they improve the power of the experiment. This means that within-subjects designs provide a more sensitive test of the effects of the independent variables and a better chance for demonstrating separation between or among groups. As an added benefit, the increased power associated with within-subjects designs may permit fewer subjects to be used. That is, you may not need as many participants in an experiment to achieve the same level of sensitivity. As noted in the preceding sections, fewer numbers can translate into real savings in time and money.

## Disadvantages of Within-Subjects Designs

Because so much space has been devoted to the strengths of within-subjects designs, you may be inclined to think that such designs are superior in all circumstances. Why would you even want to consider a between-subjects approach? What possible reasons could there be for not using an economical design that decreases subject variation and increases sensitivity?

Actually, there are several disadvantages to using a within-subjects procedure. In fact, there are instances in which it would be a mistake to do so. Included in this list of problems are transfer effects.

**Issues Involving Transfer.** Because experience is central to developing behavior and mental function, it should come as no surprise that antecedent conditions relate directly or incidentally to performance measures and may therefore bias those measures. When experiences alter the manner, intensity, or direction of a behavior measured at a later time, **transfer effects** are said to occur. In some cases transfer effects may be the focus of the experiment, but in others they confound the results or create problems for the investigator. The special cases of habituation, sensitization, contrast, and transfer of training (acquisition) can be used to illustrate the diverse effects associated with transfer.

**Habituation. Habituation** refers to a very general process that occurs in all organisms. It takes the form of reduced reactivity to a stimulus following repeated exposure to that stimulus (Petri, 1981). Habituation may be so complete that the behavior is lost. This is the effect you seek in some instances, such as training a horse to accept a saddle. Initially, the horse may react violently to the saddle by bucking and kicking. With further experience, however, the horse exhibits less displeasure and eventually shows little or no reaction to saddling. Transfer effects are evidenced in this example by the horse's reducing its violent responses because of prior saddling events.

Habituation in a laboratory setting can be illustrated by the classic experiments carried out by Sokolov (1960). Sokolov observed the behavior of animals under conditions where a tone was introduced according to a schedule. When the tone was introduced in a predictable, constant manner, the animals became disinterested and stopped orienting to the noise. Conversely, when the same tones were presented in an irregular order, the animals exhibited an arousal response. Clearly, this phenomenon was not due to receptor fatigue or adaptation because the animals' responsivity increased with irregular presentations, but decreased with regular presentations, even though the overall level of stimulation was the same for both conditions (Groves & Thompson, 1970).

Examples such as these highlight more positive aspects of habituation effects where the outcome is anticipated. Sometimes, however, the transfer is not intended and may limit an investigation or compromise the clinical utility of an intervention. For example, an experimenter attempting to induce stress by having participants watch an especially gory accident film may find that the participants' stress levels rise quickly and then fall off. Because the subjects may grow used to the shock, it doesn't bother them as much. Or, as Dyck et al. (1986) observed, repeated administration of a drug that stimulates the immune system (POLY:IC) is associated with diminished effectiveness of medical treatment (drug tolerance). In these types of settings, habituation or transfer effects are not desired and corrupt the procedures. Unless other manipulations can be introduced to handle these difficulties, the within-subjects methodology is contraindicated.

**Sensitization.** Prior stimulation does not always result in decreased responsiveness, as it does in habituation. Sometimes experience with a particular stimulus or event can augment an organism's reaction to the same stimulus when it is presented later. This phenomenon is referred to as **sensitization.**

There are many practical and laboratory examples of sensitization effects, and for the most part they involve aversive situations. For example, a child who has suffered through an extended illness and has been forced to endure repeated, painful injections may exhibit an increasing fear of needles. Or, in the midst of a violent thunderstorm, successive

**habituation**—a reduction in response that occurs due to repeated presentations of a stimulus; it is not due to receptor fatigue

**sensitization**—an enhanced reaction to a stimulus that has been presented several times previously

**contrast effect**—results when the value of a reward or punishment is determined by comparisons with other hedonic events

claps of thunder may evoke increasingly greater emotions among people with storm phobias. In animal research, it is well known that reinstating an intense electric shock can produce a stronger reaction the second time (Domjan, 1996). With sensitization, it is as if the sensory system is primed by prior experience and is maximally charged and prepared to activate the appropriate behavioral systems.

Regarding within-subjects designs and sensitization effects, caution must be exercised to control for the contaminating influence of early experiences. In a study of the effects of cold on attentional processes, if the same subject participates under conditions of moderately cold and extremely cold, you cannot be sure if the greater attentional disruption associated with the more extreme environment is due to the absolute cold condition or a sensitization effect. Accordingly, a within-subjects design would be inappropriate here.

**Contrast Effects.** In Chapter 6, I mentioned a contrast experiment I conducted several years ago (Nation et al., 1976). In this experiment, rats that had been receiving small rewards began to receive large rewards. Following the shift to the larger reward condition, these animals performed at a higher level than animals that had always received the larger reward. This phenomenon illustrates what is called a **contrast effect.** In contrast effects, the value of a behavioral outcome (reward, punishment) is determined by comparisons with other hedonic events.

When an investigator is not interested explicitly in contrast comparisons, this system of evaluating incentives via comparison can be problematic. For instance, should a psychotherapy researcher be interested in establishing the efficacy of a particular intervention or treatment strategy, contrast effects can be particularly misleading. A treatment that may normally produce only nominal gains may have profoundly positive effects when viewed in the context of an aborted treatment procedure or a procedure that is especially unpleasant for the client. In such a situation the investigator may be led to make false claims about the value of the therapy—it may be proclaimed effective when in truth it only works when it follows a disastrous treatment attempt.

Obviously, what is needed is a clean analysis of the therapy program of interest, and you may not be able to get this using the same client across different therapeutic conditions. Because of possible contrast effects, a within-subjects design that uses Therapy A and Therapy B for the same client and then looks to see which is more effective might prejudice your findings. If contrast is a concern, a between-subjects model or some other design may be more suitable.

**Transfer of Training (Acquisition).** In basic psychological research, there are two dimensions to behavior change. There is the impact of the experimental manipulation on the incidence of change and there is the effect of the manipulation on the maintenance of change. In the former case you are concerned about initiating the behavior (response acquisition), while in the latter you are concerned about keeping the behavior going. Depending on the questions that are being addressed in the project, an investigator may focus on the effects of the independent variable on one dimension or both.

Consider the role of excitatory amino acids (EAA) in the initiation (incidence of change) and expression (maintenance of change) of behavioral sensitization to cocaine. Behavioral sensitization to cocaine is said to occur when repeated administration of the drug produces a progressive increase in the locomotor activating properties of the drug. It has been shown that using a drug to block EAA activity in a particular brain region (the ventral tegmental area) selectively interferes with the initiation (acquisition) but not the expression (maintenance) of cocaine sensitization (Kalivas, 1995). Thus, here is a case where a given drug manipulation produces very different effects depending on whether the incidence of change (acquisition) or maintenance of change is the effect of interest.

Issues relating to response acquisition versus response maintenance involve a special case of transfer of training. **Transfer of training** refers to a general process where what is learned under one set of conditions facilitates learning and performance in another (Leahey & Harris, 1993). When responding on Trial N promotes responding on Trial N+1, transfer of training occurs. Regarding acquisition and maintenance, limited transfer places us in an acquisition phase; with extended transfer we deal more with response maintenance. Therefore, where we are in our behavioral analysis is dictated by how much transfer has occurred.

Normally, within-subjects transfer is crucial to the task—in its absence no improvement would be possible. But in specific situations, however, transfer of training effects may restrict analysis and work against a researcher.

Problems associated with transfer of training can be illustrated using the model experiment we are developing in this book. In the previous chapter, I noted that one of the reasons for opting for a between-subjects design for our model experiment is that any one of our three interventions (cognitive coping strategy, sensory information, and contact control) may produce improvement. That is, patients may show decreased fear and anxiety following exposure to a single, particular therapy procedure, so we would be hard pressed to demonstrate change on a second treatment. How can you decrease anxiety that does not exist?

This issue relates to transfer of training effects that underlie the acquisition versus maintenance distinction discussed previously. Insofar as we may consider the response being learned in our model experiment a "coping response" which diminishes the level of subjects' anxiety, it follows that when a treatment is newly introduced, response acquisition is the behavioral dimension of concern. That is, if there have been no prior attempts at intervention, we must rely

**transfer of training**—situation when what is learned under one set of conditions affects performance under another set of conditions

**order effects**—result when location in a test sequence influences performance

**one-factor two-treatment within-subjects design**—a design in which there are only two levels of one independent variable and all subjects participate in both conditions

on our present treatment manipulation for change and record improvement (the acquisition of coping responses) accordingly. Conversely, if a prior treatment intervention has generated improvement (the incidence of coping is high), then a second intervention must deal with response maintenance. Because our model study is concerned with the relative effectiveness of the three treatment interventions in younger and older chronically ill children, we must concentrate on response acquisition rather than response maintenance. Therefore, we must ultimately favor a between-subjects format because we cannot risk the transfer of training effects that may arise from a within-subjects design where the same patients would be treated more than once.

Any time an experiment, such as our model experiment, aims to measure the incidence of behavior change (acquisition), transfer of training must be limited. To the extent that a within-subjects design permits extensive transfer, it undermines the integrity of the experiment.

**Issues Involving Order.** The preceding remarks on transfer are concerned with that special situation where there is a carryover effect from Event A to Event B in a prescribed sequence. Transfer, then, deals principally with the impact of a specific experimental antecedent on subsequent phases of the study. A related concern is the mutual effects two or more treatment manipulations may have on each other, regardless of their order of occurrence in the experiment. When this circumstance arises, **order effects** are said to exist.

To illustrate one instance where order effects may be an issue, refer back to Figure 9–2. Recall that a three hypothetical levels of formal education (1 to 12 years, 13 to 16 years, greater than 16 years) × 2 tasks (verbal, quantitative) design was suggested, with tasks serving as the within-factor. A possible problem associated with this design is that performance on one task may facilitate, or impair, performance on the other. Perhaps perceived success on math problems would dispose a person to try harder on verbal material that was presented later, or maybe having the opportunity to perform on a reading task may influence concentration on quantitative problems that are attempted later. The truth is that we have no way of knowing about such potentiation effects, nor can we gauge interference from one task to the other should it occur.

There are several ways to control for order effects. One method involves counterbalancing and the other has to do with treating order as an independent variable. Both of these topics were discussed in detail in Chapter 6. Here I merely reiterate that in within-subjects designs, order of treatment can have a major effect on the data and should be controlled accordingly.

## *Types of Within-Subjects Designs*

In Chapter 8, I outlined several of the various subtypes of between-subjects designs. Within-subjects designs are similarly broken down into different subclassifications. The types of within-subjects models I comment on in this chapter are summarized in Table 9–1. Because this topic was given extensive coverage in the between-subjects designs discussion, I comment only briefly on the within-subjects counterparts, which are similar in many respects to the previously discussed models.

**One-Factor Two-Treatment Designs.** The most elementary form of the within-subjects design is the **one-factor two-treatment within-subjects design.** In this simple model there are only two levels of one independent variable, and all subjects participate in both treatment conditions. As discussed earlier, because transfer or order effects may influence the results, the investigator may want to counterbalance the level of independent variable experienced first. In any event, mean (average) performance in one treatment is compared with mean performance in the other, with the mean values in both cases defined by the same subjects.

Examples of the basic one-factor two-treatment design are provided by clinical follow-up studies that monitor success rate. In these sorts of experiments, behavior is measured for a group of participants once during therapy and again at some point after therapy has been discontinued. If you consider an intervention strategy such as brief group therapy (cf. Evans & Connis, 1995) and record the change in psychological status of patients at the end of treatment and 1 year

| | |
|---|---|
| One-factor two-treatment within-subjects design | A design in which there are only two levels of one independent variable and all subjects participate in both conditions |
| One-factor multiple-treatment within-subjects design | A design in which all subjects perform under all levels of one independent variable |
| Multifactor within-subjects design | A design in which all subjects perform under each level of two or more independent variables |

TABLE 9–1  Types of within-subjects designs

**one-factor multiple-treatment within-subjects design**—a design in which all subjects perform under all levels of one independent variable

later, essentially you have a one-factor (time after therapeutic intervention) two-treatment (end of therapy, 1 year after therapy terminates) within-subjects design. The same subjects are involved at both levels of the independent variable.

A word of caution is appropriate here regarding the statistical approach to be used in this type of research design. Because you have only two treatment conditions, a t-test is the recommended parametric analysis tool (I discuss t-tests in Chapter 11). However, the scores under each treatment are likely to be correlated even when transfer and order effects are controlled as much as possible. Thus, a t-test for dependent data would be the appropriate test statistic.

**One-Factor Multiple-Treatment Designs.** In psychological research, it is not uncommon to gather information on the same subject on more than two occasions. When subjects participate under three or more levels of one independent variable, the design is referred to as a **one-factor multiple-treatment within-subjects design.** Therefore, a given subject might perform under the conditions of Treatment A, then Treatment B, and finally Treatment C. In this situation, note the systematic progression across treatments. Serial dependencies will develop as the subject moves from one treatment to the next, but this may be an interesting aspect for the investigators.

For example, someone interested in practice effects may be interested in monitoring the relative amounts of increase in performance early and late in training. Because acquisition functions are typically negatively accelerated (the degree of improvement decreases as training trials increase), one would expect that the change in performance from Trial 4 to Trial 5 would be greater for a given subject than would the change from Trial 21 to Trial 22. Here, the independent variable (trials) is a cumulative factor and observations based on serial position are integral to the experiment. In such situations it is essential that all subjects experience each level of the independent variable in the same sequence.

Figure 9–3 presents the results from a one-factor multiple-treatment within-subjects study where the sequence of observation (treatment) was important to the outcome of the study. Employing what is known as the "preference technique" in developmental research, Fantz and Nevis (1967) exploited infants' tendencies to examine one stimulus more often and longer than another. To achieve this, a bull's-eye pattern and an arrangement of straight lines were placed in a mechanism above the infant's crib, and the infant's time spent looking at each stimulus was recorded. As Figure 9–3 shows, very young infants exhibited no

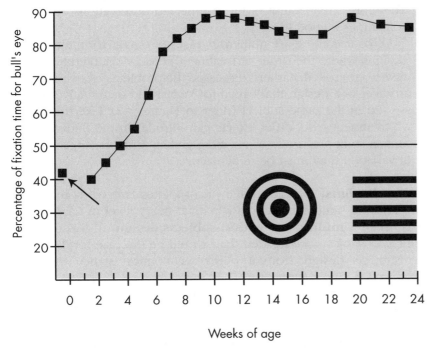

**FIGURE 9–3** Looking preferences for infants between 2 and 24 weeks for a bull's-eye pattern and an arrangement of straight lines. By about 8 weeks the infants show a strong preference for the bull's-eye. This illustrates a design in which the same subjects are observed repeatedly under different levels of one independent variable (a one-factor multiple-treatment within-subjects design). [Adapted from Fantz & Nevis, 1967, and Hopkins, 1974.) Copyright © 1974 by St. Mary's College of Maryland. Reprinted with permission.

preference for pattern. However, by the time the infants were a couple of months old, they began showing a clear preference for the bull's-eye pattern.

These data have been attributed to a maturational process which leads young children to prefer curved lines over straight ones—because curvilinear patterns are more intriguing for some reason, they are looked at more frequently and for longer periods of time (Hopkins, Kagen, Brachfeld, Hans, & Linn, 1976). In any event, in the within-subjects investigation Fantz and Nevis conducted, the sequence of different levels of the independent variable (weeks of age) was fundamental to the success of the project and could not have been altered.

**multifactor within-subjects de-sign**—a design in which all subjects perform under each level of two or more independent variables

Therefore, a consistent order of repeated observations or treatments is sometimes a good thing.

Of course, there are numerous cases of one-factor multiple-treatment designs where the order of treatment must be counterbalanced or otherwise controlled. Earlier I discussed the problems associated with transfer or carryover in a design that called for verbal and quantitative performance to be assessed in the same subject (refer to Figure 9–2). Like this simple one-factor two-treatment case, order effects can intrude on the findings of designs which contain multiple levels of an independent variable. Consequently, as a source of variation they must be minimized.

**Multifactor Designs.** When a design incorporates two or more independent variables and the same subjects participate at every level of each variable, the design is called a **multifactor within-subjects design.** In this design format, because fewer subjects are needed than would be the case for the comparable between-subjects design, from a purely economical stance the multifactor within-subjects design is attractive.

Consider the advantages of this experimental model in studies concerned with special populations. You are a researcher interested in characterizing the unique abilities of female left handers and thus are faced with the challenge of locating a sufficient number of women who are left-hand dominant. Left handedness, which is rare enough, is especially rare in women (see Benjamin et al., 1994). It follows that when you finally locate a restrictive subpopulation of left-handed females, you want to make the most of it and collect as much information from each subject as possible. This is where the multifactor within-subjects design affords some assistance.

In a design framework that calls for an evaluation of psychomotor dexterity using the left hand or right hand under timed or untimed conditions, a subject could participate in all treatments (this is depicted in Figure 9–4). As mentioned before, insofar as performance under one treatment transfers benefits or impairs performance on another, order effects would need to be controlled by counterbalancing or some other design feature. In any event, you can see how a multifactor within-subjects design lessens the burden of an investigator confronted with sampling from a limited population.

In animal behavior research, similar sensitivity to maximizing the use of one subject may be evident, if not because of the rarity of the population then because of expense. A rhesus monkey, for example, may cost as much as $2,000. Not surprisingly, psychological researchers using these monkeys employ totally repeated multifactor designs to keep numbers and costs down.

As noted for within-subjects design in general, multifactor within-subjects designs also have the advantage of checking individual variation. In research areas like those concerned with indexing perceptual accuracy under different experi-

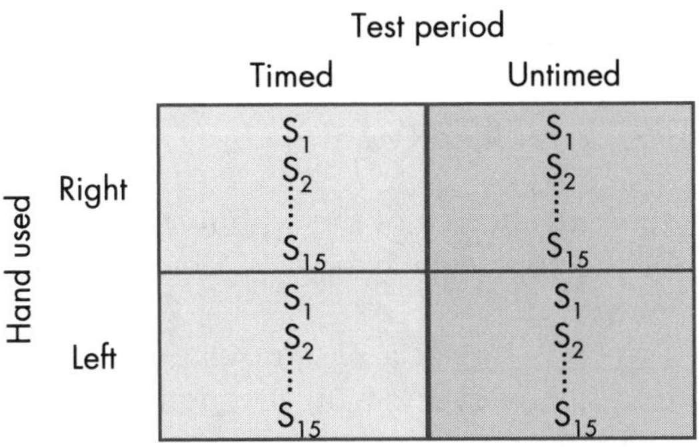

Test period

| | Timed | Untimed |
|---|---|---|
| Right | $S_1$ $S_2$ ⋮ $S_{15}$ | $S_1$ $S_2$ ⋮ $S_{15}$ |
| Left | $S_1$ $S_2$ ⋮ $S_{15}$ | $S_1$ $S_2$ ⋮ $S_{15}$ |

Hand used

FIGURE 9–4 An example of a multifactor within-subjects design. Note that the same subjects participate in all four conditions of this research project which interacts two levels of the hand (left, right) and testing period (timed, untimed). Because order effects would need to be controlled, the sequence of tests would need to be counterbalanced.

mental conditions, individual differences in perceptual judgment can be a major source of experimental error and make it difficult to obtain significant results (Goldstein, 1988). When the same subjects are used in all experimental treatments, individual variation becomes less of an issue because basic perceptual functions are relatively more consistent from one test session to the next. This permits the experimenter to gauge more precisely the impact of a specific manipulation on a value of the independent variable.

As seems to be true for all research designs, there is a down side to using the multifactor within-subjects design. The principal difficulty is associated with the excessive time commitment and attendant fatigue and boredom that go with long-term participation. It is one thing to ask that subjects remain attentive for a couple of test sessions and it is something else again to ask them to remain alert for six tests. Yet this is what each subject must do in a simple $2 \times 3$ multifactor within-subjects design. If this design were expanded just one level on the first factor (a $3 \times 3$ design) the number of treatment combinations jumps to nine. Of course, adding a third independent variable would be out of the question because the design would likely exceed the practical limitations of the participants. Therefore, even though there are decided advantages to using multifactor within-subjects designs, the questions of interest must be addressed deliberately and in small steps. More ambitious projects probably will need to use between-subjects models or some combination of between- and within-subjects designs, which is the topic of our next section.

## WITHIN CHAPTER REVIEW AND STUDY QUESTIONS

### WITHIN-SUBJECTS DESIGNS

1. What are four advantages of the within-subjects designs mentioned in this chapter? Of the four, which do you consider to be most important and why?
2. The _____ of a design relates to the design's ability to detect the differences, however small, that reflect real separation between or among conditions.
   a. variation
   b. power
   c. significance
3. What are the chief disadvantages of using within-subjects designs?
4. List the four special cases of carryover used to illustrate transfer effects.
5. What type of within-subjects design involves same subject participation at each level of two or more independent variables?
   a. one-factor two-treatment designs
   b. one-factor multiple-treatment designs
   c. multifactor designs

# MIXED DESIGNS

In this chapter and the one preceding, much of the discussion of between-subjects and within-subjects designs has been devoted to the positive features of these models. Given that each type of design framework offers a unique experimental advantage, it is not surprising that research psychologists employ more elaborate designs that incorporate elements of both types of models. Indeed, the most popular design in experimental psychology is likely the **mixed design,** which combines between-subjects and within-subjects factors.

When a design includes both a "between" factor and a "within" factor, it is sometimes referred to as a "split-plot design." The split-plot design, which is really a mixed design subtype, takes its name from agricultural research. For example, in order to accurately access the crop enhancement properties of a new agricultural product, say Cornpone XL, a field would first be subdivided into separate and distinct plots of equal size, soil characteristics, fertility, and so forth. Differing concentrations of Cornpone XL would then be designated for each plot and each plot would be subdivided further to form "mini-plots." The mini-plots would also receive different manipulations on another variable, say the amount of water added to the soil. The result would be an array of plots receiving varying levels of the Cornpone XL amendment (the "between" factor) and all water treatments (the "within" factor). By creating plots and splitting them into smaller units we would be able to determine the enhancement effects of different concentrations of Cornpone XL under a particular watering condition or across all watering conditions. This relates to the aforementioned differences in main effects and interaction effects (see the discussion in Chapter 8).

Translating the split-plot design from farming to psychological research is straightforward. Plots correspond to a group of subjects that performs under only one level of Variable A. The mini-plots correspond to the individual members who compose the respective groups and perform under every level of Variable B. For a 2 × 3 mixed design, then, a subject participating under $A_1$ conditions would never participate under $A_2$, but he or she would perform at all three levels of B.

To illustrate the mixed design in psychological research, assume that we are interested in differences in the maladaptive attitudes of clinically depressed and normal people at two different points in time. This question actually interested Hamilton and Abramson (1983), who measured the number of negative attitudes of people in the throes of acute depressive episodes, and then again following the people's recoveries. In this quasi-experimental design (refer to Chapter 10), because time of testing had to be controlled, it was essential to test normal, nondepressed control subjects when their counterparts were suffering bouts of depression. As Figure 9–5 reveals, Hamilton and Abramson were able to show that although the depressed population exhibited more maladaptive attitudes during depressive episodes, upon recovery their thinking did not differ significantly from those of normals, whose attitudes remained relatively consistent.

In the Hamilton and Abramson example, the participants' psychological status served as the between-subjects variable. Because it is illogical to assume that a person can be depressed and nondepressed at once, participants were mutually excluded from the other category. Conversely, because monitoring the attitudinal changes that accompany improvement requires that the same subjects be tested during and after the depressive episode, this factor by definition must be a within-variable. In this study, the mixed nature of the design was axiomatic—it could not be otherwise.

Mixed designs are often much more complex than the Hamilton and Abramson experiment, which illustrates combinations of "between" and "within" variables in the simplest form (a one-between, one-within format with only two levels of each variable). Some mixed models have six or more variables with assorted combinations of "between" and "within" factors. As a rule, the ratio of "within" factors to "between" factors in more elaborate designs favors more between-subjects variables because of the

**mixed design**—a design that includes at least one "within" factor and one "between" factor

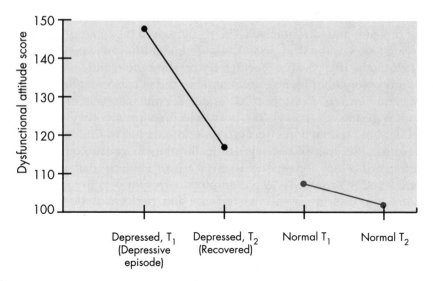

FIGURE 9–5 An example of a mixed design. Depressed and nonde-pressed people (the "between" factor) were assessed in terms of mal-adaptive attitudes when the depressed people were experiencing depressive episodes and again when they recovered (the "within" fac-tor). (Adapted from Hamilton and Abramson, 1983.) Copyright © 1983 by the American Psychological Association. Reprinted with permission.

reasons noted earlier. If you attempt to use the same subject in too many test sit-uations, transfer effects and fatigue may intrude on your findings. Still, because the advantage associated with the judicious use of resources remains in within-subjects analysis, experimenters incorporate variables into models whenever feasible. For the mixed model, repeated observations on the same subject restrict individual variation and sample sizes.

Although a detailed, sophisticated treatment of quantitative and statistical op-erations in psychological research falls outside the instructional boundaries of this book, a caveat concerning proper analysis of mixed models is duly regis-tered here. One of the concerns with mixed designs is practical and relates to the identification of appropriate error terms. As I discuss in greater depth in Chapter 11, drawing inferences about the significance of differences between and among treatment conditions requires some estimate of variation. In non-technical terms this means we must have some method for determining chance differences. Suffice it to say experimental psychologists and statisticians have provided an impressive arsenal of mathematical tools for the task. The problem with mixed designs is that one estimate of variation must be used for the "between" comparisons of treatment differences, while another must be used for the "within" comparisons. As you deal with more complicated multifactor models and the intricate interactions that surface in them, the situation becomes even more challenging. Although computations are possible with these more elaborate projects, caution must be exercised when forming the appropriate statistical tests. While computer packages take care of this task in simpler cases, many of the "canned" analytical systems will not accommodate more sophisticated models. Therefore, the investigator must make the appropriate statistical decisions and adopt the correct procedures. Otherwise, the interpretations will be flawed.

A second concern over the use of mixed models has been raised by theoretical statisticians. The statistical tests that are used in more complex studies, such as the analysis of variance (ANOVA), require that certain assumptions be met (cf. Howell, 1995). One of these assumptions is independence of subject errors (variation), and there has been no shortage of statisticians who have pointed out mixed designs that include "within" components violate this assumption. There are ways to limit the problems associated with this inherent violation, but the problems remain and must be acknowledged. Therefore, as has been true for the other designs discussed thus far, investigators must weigh the merits and perils of employing a mixed model and select an experimental framework that best suits their projects.

## WITHIN CHAPTER REVIEW AND STUDY QUESTIONS

### MIXED DESIGNS

1. List two advantages and two disadvantages of mixed designs. Examine your list and select the most important consideration, then explain why you made your selection.
2. What is the origin of the term "split-plot design"?

# SINGLE-SUBJECT DESIGNS

Several references have been made in this book about the importance of inferential statistics and the ability of psychologists to determine whether a particular finding is truly significant or simply due to chance variation (Chapter 11). Such statistical concepts have grown out of probability theory which has its

**single-subject design**—a design in which the behavior of one subject is recorded following different experimental manipulations

**baseline**—the steady state of responding that occurs before new experimental conditions are introduced

roots in England, most conspicuously in the work of scientist and mathematician Sir Francis Galton (1822–1911). Galton noted that people differ to some extent along virtually every dimension of behavior, and that therefore variation in performance is expected. Probability estimates and inferential statistics, then, may be used to discern if such variation is built in or due to some experimental manipulation.

Curiously, Galton's recognition of individual variation has been the impetus for promoting group comparisons. In some ways, this has obscured the importance of reliable differences between and among members of a population. Some experimental psychologists have argued that group data tell us very little about human behavior. They contend human behavior must be studied on a person-to-person basis (Bergin & Strupp, 1970). Predictive validity is compromised for the individual case when estimates are predicated on what the average (mean) person in the group looks like.

The appreciation for the importance of the individual has resulted in the development of the **single-subject design.** This design, championed by the followers of behaviorist B. F. Skinner (1974), tracks and records the details of one organism's performance over time or across treatment manipulations. The experimental single-subject design should not be confused with the *case study* approach (see Chapter 10), however, which describes an individual who operates under one or more set of conditions. In the case study, the researcher documents the behavior and activity of one subject as events unfold. In contrast, in a single-subject design, an independent variable is experimentally manipulated and observations are made on the effects such changes have on a previously identified dependent measure.

In its most elementary form, a single-subject design consists of pretreatment recordings and posttreatment recordings. This means that the experimenter measures an individual's responses before introducing an experimental manipulation (a period Skinnerians refer to as **baseline**), then applies a given treatment and records the differences in response patterns. In psychotherapy, this type of design is illustrated by the introduction of a specific intervention strategy. When a psychologist or psychiatrist records the frequency of auditory hallucinations in a schizophrenic patient before and after the administration of the drug Haldol, a basic single-subject design is employed. In such cases, an assessment of the influence of a given level of the independent variable (the drug dose) is possible because the treatment involves a planned introduction.

The problem with the simple single-subject design is that you can never really be sure that behavioral changes are a consequence of the treatment. That is, the observed pattern of change may reflect naturally occurring shifts in responding as much as anything else. For the Haldol example we just used, for instance, improvement that is defined in terms of reduced hallucinations may have occurred anyway, even if the drug had not been administered. Even if you have an extended period of baseline recording, you can never be sure about what caused the change in your subject. Clearly, something more elaborate and compelling is required if single-subject research is to provide useful information. In the sections that follow we see that such alternatives are readily available.

## *Reversal Designs*

One of the more popular methods for determining the efficacy of single-subject models is the **reversal design.** Reversal designs are commonly employed in behavior therapy and involve the systematic introduction and withdrawal of the therapeutic intervention (Spiegler & Guevremont, 1993). At minimum, reversal designs involve an initial baseline recording phase, the introduction of some treatment regimen, and the reinstatement of the baseline conditions in a third phase. This type of reversal design is called an **A-B-A design,** where *A* refers to the nontreatment period and *B* the period of treatment.

**The A-B-A Design.** The purpose of A-B-A designs that involve one subject is to assess the value of the treatment intervention. If the treatment (B) truly determines change, then with the reversal and reinstatement of the conditions that occurred before (when A is reinstated) responding should return to baseline levels. Borrowing from Martin and Pear (1988), Figure 9–6 shows how the results of an A-B-A single-subject design might look.

In this case, the subject's name was Billie. As a second-grade student, Billie was disruptive and resisted attempts to complete the assigned number of math problems. Billie's teacher, Ms. Johnson, reasoned that rewarding Billie for working math problems with extra time in his physical education might improve his academic performance and decrease his disruptive behavior. Ms. Johnson first recorded the number of math problems Billie completed during a 1-week period (baseline). Subsequently, for a comparable time period, 1 extra minute was added to Billie's physical education class when he completed a math problem (treatment). Finally, the special incentive conditions were dropped and Billie was observed for 1 week under normal conditions (reversal and reinstatement).

From Figure 9–6 it is clear that the manipulation was successful because when the treatment was taken away, behavior returned to baseline levels. The only difference between baseline and the treatment period was the incentive of extra time in physical education class, so this must have produced the desired effect.

**reversal design**—a design which involves the systematic introduction and withdrawal of some treatment

**A-B-A design**—a type of reversal design in which baseline records are maintained, then a new treatment is introduced, behavioral measurements are made, and the original baseline conditions are reinstated and behavioral changes are noted accordingly

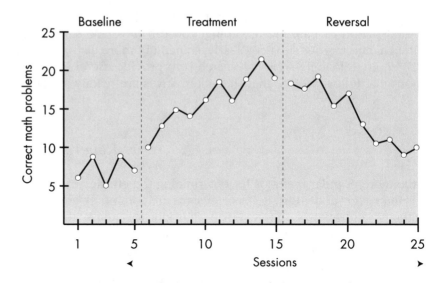

**FIGURE 9–6** Hypothetical example of an A-B-A design. In this example, Billie, a student, is rewarded for completing math problems with extra time in his physical education class (treatment). Subsequently, the treatment is withdrawn and Billie's behavior drops off (reversal). (Adapted from Martin and Pear, *Behavior Modification: What It Is and How to Do It*, 1992, 4e.) Reprinted by permission of Prentice Hall, Inc., Upper Saddle River, NJ.

It should be understood that although a return to baseline response levels following reversal in an A-B-A design affirms the validity of treatment, failure to observe a return to baseline responding in no way ensures a devaluation of treatment utility. That is, if A is reinstated following a change in behavior observed during B and the behavior pattern remains as it was during B, this does not mean necessarily that the treatment was ineffective. Rather, it means that you cannot be sure that the treatment is responsible for the observed results.

For instance, for the case involving Billie, the incentive system installed during B may have been responsible for Billie's improved performance. However, recognition from Ms. Johnson, peers, parents, or other uncontrolled natural reinforcers may have taken over and sustained a change that originally resulted from the introduction of the experimental treatment. Therefore, although A-B-A designs can be used to establish treatment efficacy, they cannot be used to challenge treatment efficacy.

**The A-B-A-B Design.** In practice, a therapist who has been successful in demonstrating the effectiveness of treatment using a reversal strategy is not going to abandon a client during the return to baseline period. If you have reason to believe that the incentive system used with Billie really worked, it makes sense that you would want to use it again. Accordingly, single-subject research often employs an **A-B-A-B design,** where the treatment is introduced, reversed to baseline, and then reintroduced to provide the subject (client) with the benefits of therapy. Figure 9–7 profiles the data from a hypothetical A-B-A-B study of Billie's behavior.

Reversal designs are not problem free, however. Spiegler and Guevremont (1993) have noted the three following issues associated with using single-subject reversal designs in psychotherapy:

> **A-B-A-B design**—a design in which a treatment is introduced, withdrawn, then introduced again; a type of reversal design where the subject is guaranteed to receive treatment benefits

1. Only certain types of behaviors change rapidly enough to permit the use of reversal designs. If the target (selected) behavior becomes ingrained and relatively permanent in the client's repertoire, changes toward baseline are unlikely during reversal. If you are successful at training assertiveness skills, these behaviors may enhance self-esteem and become self-sustaining. Consequently, reversal manipulations are probably not going to show positive results.
2. What works with one patient may not work with others. Some clients may respond favorably to treatment while others may not. In the absence of the

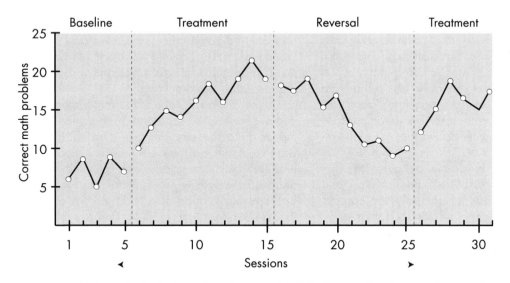

**FIGURE 9–7** Hypothetical data showing an A-B-A-B design for the student Billie. (Adapted from Martin and Pear, *Behavior Modification: What It Is and How to Do It*, 1992., 4e.) Reprinted by permission of Prentice Hall, Inc., Upper Saddle River, NJ.

ability to generalize, predictive validity is compromised and selecting an appropriate therapy becomes ad hoc.

3. There are ethical concerns over ever withdrawing a successful treatment. What if the treatment will not work a second time? If positive change is produced, shouldn't you leave the client alone?

With these practical problems there are concerns about reversal designs from a purely experimental perspective. Baseline performance may be troublesome, for example.

## ✸ Thinking About Research

The advantage of baseline assessments is that they permit comparisons when two or more conditions differ from the beginning. In effect, a subject or group is compared against its earlier performance. What happens, however, when individual baselines are unstable? Under what conditions do baselines fail to return to preexisting levels and what does this mean for the experimenter?

It was noted previously that natural reinforcers or other intrusive events can sustain changes that are produced by experimental manipulations. Often, there is not much to be done about this, and the subject will not return to baseline. Occasionally, however, the problem of an unrecoverable baseline rests with some inadvertent act of the researcher.

For example, in a classic behavior therapy study conducted by Hart, Allen, Buell, Harris, and Wolf (1964), a 4-year-old named Allen continually cried at the preschool he attended. Hart et al. recognized that the staff rewarded Allen for crying. Each time Allen cried, he was attended to quickly. As a result, the investigators decided to place Allen's crying behavior on extinction and ignore it. Predictably, during extinction there was a decrease from the baseline crying rate, so it appeared the intervention procedure had worked. When the reinforcement (baseline) conditions were reintroduced (the staff began attending to Allen's crying), however, operant crying did not return to its higher baseline levels. On closer inspection, Hart et al. determined that the staff were giving Allen ". . . comfort and attention whenever he merely looked like crying" (p. 324). When true reinforcement procedures were employed and only full-scale cries were rewarded, the previous high rate of crying behavior returned. The A-B-A manipulation was successful in documenting the value of extinction (B).

Unlike this case, where the experimental procedures corrupted a return to baseline performance in a reversal design, in many instances baselines shift on their own. In my research on lead/ethanol interactions, one rat exhibited pronounced changes in reactivity to exactly the same baseline application of a radiant heat source to its tail (Burkey et al., 1994). Perhaps changing animal body temperature or some other factor contributed to this fluctuating pattern, but the end result was unstable baselines. What do you do in a case like this? Are meaningful comparisons possible? What are your alternatives when you face single-subject research?

The answers are not simple. Shifting baselines create interpretive problems for psychologists because it is difficult to know why baseline performance does not return. In cases where baselines change, it may be better to turn away from reversal procedures and use the multiple-baseline approach, which is discussed in the following.

■

## Multiple-Baseline Designs

When baseline vagaries and changes are a concern, the **multiple-baseline design** is an attractive alternative methodology. In a multiple-baseline design, there is a successive shifting to a new treatment following the achievement of steady-state responding after the previous shift (Ollendick, 1995). This means that if Treatment B were introduced following performance under Treatment A, we would continue recording until behavior during B was consistent, reliable, and steady. At this point, Treatment C would be introduced and we would once again continue recording until a steady state was achieved in C. Then we would introduce Treatment D, and so on. Each treatment in the serial presentation serves both as an experimental manipulation and a baseline for the ensuing phase.

Unlike in the reversal designs discussed previously, comparisons with the initial baseline data are not always important in a multiple-baseline design. Rather, the evaluation of performance relative to the most recent antecedent events is critical. In other words, ancient history is less important than what just happened. The advantage of the multiple-baseline approach is that as long as behavior is consistent, treatment effects can be indexed and interpreted free of comparisons that span several phases.

There are several different types of multiple-baseline procedures. I mention only two here: multiple-baselines across behaviors and across situations.

**Multiple-Baselines Across Behaviors.** In a multiple-baseline across behaviors design, several different behaviors are monitored in the same individual. The treatment manipulation is performed on one behavior and changes in that behavior are noted. Because the treatment manipulation has not been performed on other behaviors, those measurements should remain largely unchanged. When changes in the initial behavior are evident and relatively stable, the treatment manipulation is performed on the second variable, and so on until all target behaviors have been examined.

Figure 9–8 illustrates hypothetical data using the multiple-baseline across behaviors procedure. This example is based on the aforementioned case of Billie who was used to illustrate a reversal design (refer to Figure 9–6). This time, the reward of adding time to Billie's physical

**multiple-baseline design**—a design that involves successively shifting to new treatments once a new baseline is established

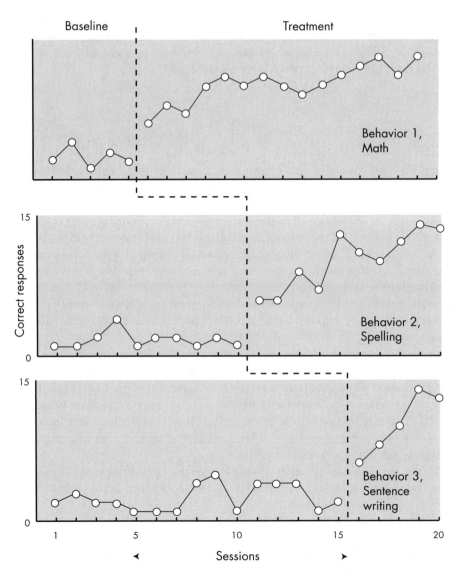

**FIGURE 9–8** Hypothetical response profiles for Billie using a multiple-baseline across behaviors design. Note that when the treatment is introduced for one behavior, the remaining behaviors are stable until the treatment is applied to those behaviors. (Adapted from Martin and Pear, *Behavior Modification: What It Is and How to Do It*, 1992, 4e.) Reprinted by permission of Prentice Hall, Inc., Upper Saddle River, NJ.

education class is used first with math, then with spelling, and finally with sentence writing. For each behavior, once the treatment is introduced it continues for the rest of the investigation. Because behavior change is not apparent in a given behavior until the treatment application is made for that specific response class, we can be relatively confident that the treatment controls the changing pattern of responding.

For demonstrations of multiple-baseline across behaviors to be convincing, the behaviors must be independent. If changes in one behavior generalize to another behavior, both will be altered by treatment and the results will be undecipherable. When other behaviors change with the target behavior, you effectively have an A-B reversal design and you cannot be certain which behavior produced the change, for reasons noted previously.

**Multiple-Baselines Across Situations.** When a treatment is effective in one situation, it is often desirable to know whether it works in other situations. In addition, from an experimental point of view it may be important to determine if the changes observed in new stimulus settings are due to generalization or to the contingencies of the intervention.

In a multiple-baseline across situations design, a treatment is introduced in one situation, then another, and so on. For example, Corte, Wolf, and Locke (1971) showed that self-abusive face hitting in an institutionalized child could be suppressed by electrically shocking the self-abusive behaviors in a "small room" setting. This manipulation, however, had no effect in a "general ward" setting. When the same punishment contingencies were later introduced in the general ward environment, a decrease in self-abusive behavior was observed for this situation as well. As Martin and Pear (1988) noted, by offsetting the introduction of the treatment across situations, Corte et al. were able to establish that improvement was tied specifically to the treatment manipulation.

Therefore, we see that a number of options regarding data collection from one subject are available. Decisions concerning which procedure to select must be made carefully, of course, and the investigator must be flexible and adjust based on the issues at hand.

## WITHIN CHAPTER REVIEW AND STUDY QUESTIONS

### SINGLE-SUBJECT DESIGNS

1. What advantage does the A-B-A-B design have over the A-B-A design?
2. Define each of the following:
   a. multiple-baseline across behaviors
   b. multiple-baseline across situations

**The Model Experiment**

In this chapter, we have seen that repeatedly observing the same subject increases power by reducing individual variation and is more economical in most cases. However, within-subjects designs are not indicated for some situations where transfer effects are an issue. This is precisely the problem with the model experiment we are building in this book. Because any one of the three therapeutic interventions we have selected (cognitive coping strategy, sensory information, and contact control) may effectively alleviate fear in the face of medical treatment for both younger (4 to 6 years old) and older (10 to 12 years old) children, it might prove difficult to index the therapeutic effectiveness of a second intervention administered to the same patients.

Because our model experiment requires that we measure the effectiveness of different therapies in ameliorating anxiety in chronically ill children of two age groups, a between-subjects design is necessary. A history of treatment, or differing treatments, would compromise our ability to assess the relative merits of a given therapy regimen. Therefore, although within-subjects designs are preferred in many situations, with some projects the experimental procedures must involve different subjects. We will continue discussing research options in the next chapter where quasi-experimental designs are covered.

# Alternative Research Designs

**observational method**—the process of indexing an event as it occurs in a natural or laboratory setting

Thus far, the discussion has focused on experimental manipulations as they are performed under well-controlled laboratory conditions. Because so much psychological research employs such methodologies, it is appropriate that experimental approaches be allocated the bulk of space in this book. Still, alternatives to experimental analysis are available, and in many instances these alternatives are better suited to answer the basic questions at hand than are true experiments. In this chapter, I discuss five alternatives to experimental designs: the observational method, the survey method, the case study, the correlational method, and the special issue of quasi-experimental designs.

# THE OBSERVATIONAL METHOD

For all types of psychological research, data collection involves a vigil. As we have seen with the experimental method, in laboratory settings this vigil takes the form of watching changes in the dependent variable that are causally tied to changes in the value of manipulated treatments (independent variables). The "watch" in this case consists of monitoring EEGs, computer printouts, counters, clocks, decisions, the number of nonsense syllables recalled, the number of hostile exchanges, the number of altruistic gestures, and assorted overt measures of experimental influence. In many cases, our observations are based on representations of behavior rather than behavior per se.

The **observational method** as it is traditionally used in psychological research offers a means of directly indexing behavior. In the observational model, the investigator keeps a detailed log of when and where a specific event occurs. This event may take the form of a narrowly defined behavior, such as biting, or it may be more inclusive and refer to a class of behaviors, such as aggressive displays. In either case, records concerning the frequency and duration of spontaneous responses are kept. There is no attempt to elicit a reaction from the participant. Rather, behaviors are noted as they occur and are documented as part of an aggregate profile established over time by the subject.

Consider a researcher who is interested in the developmental onset of "sharing behavior." Constructing an experimental framework within which 2-year-old children are induced to share with playmates is difficult in itself. Even if the investigator is successful, the data may be biased. Is the investigator looking at genuine social behavior, or are the children responding to expectancies created by the experimenter? When you arrange opportunities for sharing, what does this tell you about the likelihood of sharing in more typical situations? In truth, you cannot be certain about legitimate patterns of social interaction among children of any age group unless you observe them under normal conditions. To answer the question about the age at which sharing is truly initiated, the investigator would need to carefully monitor the spontaneous behavior of children as they interact with their peers in a playroom, an outside environment, or some other realistic social setting.

An obvious challenge observational methods present relates to quantifying behaviors that may occur infrequently over a long time span. In the case of assessing the developmental onset of sharing, for example, the researcher may have to wait a considerable time between incidents of sharing. Are there ways to more judiciously use the time committed to the project? Can something be done to reduce the workload to manageable levels?

One strategy researchers employ to use their time in observational studies more efficiently is called **interval recording.** In this procedure, a specific observation period is designated before recordings begin. With the aid of a prerecorded tape, a timer, or some other mechanism, a signal tells the researcher when the interval begins. During this interval, a specific behavior or category of behaviors is recorded. Records of responding typically index only the presence or absence of the behavior up to a maximum of once per interval. Although the length of the interval is dictated by the nature and base frequency of the behavior being studied, as a rule the investigator attempts to record using short duration intervals. This approach provides a more complete picture of behavior and increases efficiency in recording (Badia & Runyun, 1982).

To illustrate the use of interval recording in observational research, assume that the behavioral measure of interest is the frequency of hostile remarks made during group therapy sessions. For a 1-hour session, it has been predetermined that measurements will be taken in successive 5-minute intervals for each of six patients. Therefore, every 5 minutes a beeper sounds and the observer notes the first hostile comment for each of the six patients participating in the session. If no hostile remarks are made, a *0* is recorded; if several such comments are made, a *1* is recorded (recall that in interval recording only the presence or absence of a response is noted, regardless of how frequently it may occur in the interval). Because the observer is only concerned with registering whether a hostile remark was made during the 5-minute period, monitoring all six patients at once should not prove too difficult.

On many occasions, the length of the recording session will be so long that interval recording will be rendered impractical. For example, if you are concerned about monitoring attentiveness in gifted and normal IQ children during a normal school day, it is unrealistic to expect to record this behavior throughout the day. An alternative would be to use a procedure called **time sampling** in which the presence or absence of the behavior is recorded during brief intervals that are separated by

**interval recording**—the act of recording a specific behavior or category of behavior during an interval that is signalled by some external mechanism

**time sampling**—a process in which the presence or absence of a behavior is recorded during brief intervals that are separated by periods of time uniform periods of time. For example, an observer could score attentiveness (i.e., attending to the teacher, attending to work at a desk) as occurring or not occurring during a 1-minute time interval beginning at the top of every hour. Using this approach, one observer could follow several children throughout the day. Figure 10–1 shows what a record of such a study might look like.

Interval recording and time sampling techniques are limited in that they only provide frequency information. If you wanted to know something about the duration or strength of the response, additional measures would be necessary. Commonly, psychological researchers combine recording strategies, such as not-

|  | Gifted | | Normal | |
|---|---|---|---|---|
|  | Attending to teacher | Attending to work at desk | Attending to teacher | Attending to work at desk |
| 9:00AM | 16 | 18 | 11 | 13 |
| 10:00 | 17 | 17 | 13 | 14 |
| 11:00 | 9 | 14 | 10 | 11 |
| 12:00PM | 14 | 11 | 11 | 10 |
| 1:00 | 11 | 12 | 9 | 8 |
| 2:00 | 12 | 16 | 9 | 12 |
| 3:00 | 9 | 11 | 7 | 6 |

FIGURE 10–1 A record of time sampling the presence or absence of behavior for gifted and normal IQ students over a normal school day

ing the duration of responding using a time sampling technique (Powell, Martindale, & Kulp, 1975). Keep in mind that there are no rigid guidelines for formulating a recording strategy; customize and employ the techniques that will render the most useful information.

## *Concerns in Observational Research*

Although there are clear advantages associated with using the observational method, there are also unique opportunities for error. Because observational methods involve humans, mistakes in interpretation and recording are always possible. Sometimes the source of error rests with the observer, but often the problems stem from inadequate design considerations.

One of the major sources of error and inaccuracy in observational research is in defining the response (Hawkins & Dotson, 1975). When an observer is given vague or misleading instructions about what to record, it makes sense that the observer will make mistakes in recording. If an observer is given only general directions to record "aggressive behavior," she or he must arbitrarily determine what constitutes an aggressive response. One person may interpret a rude remark as aggressive, while another would not. Consequently, there would be inconsistencies in the record log, which would contribute to erroneous reporting. Although such difficulties are not likely to be eliminated, they can be minimized if the person training the observers provides detailed instructions about what to record and what to ignore. This can be accomplished by telling the observer to record "only behaviors where one person physically touches another" or "only the frequency of degrading remarks." Because everyone would then clearly understand what to look for in such situations, more consistent recording would be possible.

Another problem that must be addressed in observational research is designing a suitable data sheet. If the structure of the sheet on which the entries will be made is poorly thought out, observers will find it difficult to keep up during the recording session. In addition, if the data sheet fails to provide an appropriate framework for record keeping, observers may jumble entries that will lead to confusion later when others try to decipher the notes and codes. Most of these issues can be resolved by taking the time before the research begins to craft a straightforward, logical plan for recording (Conrad & Maul, 1981).

Of course, in observational studies that include more than one observer, and this is usually the case, there are always problems of **interobserver reliability**. Interobserver reliability refers to the extent of agreement between or among two or more people who are observing

**interobserver reliability**—in observational studies, the extent of agreement between or among two or more people observing a common event

**unobtrusive recordings—obser-vations made by a concealed investi-gator who does not interfere with the research setting**

the same event. Because personal biases, fatigue, boredom, emotional status, and a host of other individual differences may intrude on a rater's observations, differences in the record log are inevitable. However, certain actions can be taken to ensure consistent recording and thereby increase interobserver reliability. First, training sessions for observers can be carefully conducted and the overall level of competence elevated. This will not guarantee attentiveness, but it will provide some assurance that a common degree of sophistication exists among the observers. Also, explicit instructions about factors that contribute to inaccuracy and unreliability can be provided. If an observer knows beforehand that every incidence of the target behavior must be reported, a more accurate account of responding will likely result, and interobserver reliability will improve.

## Naturalistic Observation

In Chapter 1, naturalistic approaches to research were contrasted with laboratory investigations. In this section of the book, I describe how research using naturalistic observation is actually carried out. A few of the difficulties associated with this type of research are also mentioned.

**Gathering Information.** Recall from Chapter 1 that naturalistic observation is defined as "a research method that permits the investigator to collect information in a naturally occurring environment." The aim of this type of data collection procedure is to observe behavior as it unfolds naturally in a habitat, workplace, or routine environment. Naturalistic observations can take the form of peeking around bushes in the wild or watching the behavior of pedestrians at a busy intersection in midtown Manhattan. Even the interactive styles of executives in the boardroom may be studied by naturalistic observation. The only requirement in all of these illustrations is that events flow normally and are free of artificial influences and arbitrary changes in the environment.

Regardless of the natural environment, it is essential to this kind of research that all observations be unobtrusive. **Unobtrusive recordings** are observations made by a concealed investigator who remains undetected in the environment and does not interfere with the natural processes being studied (Webb, Campbell, Schwartz, & Sechrest, 1966). In animal behavior studies, concealment may take the form of a blind or remote location where the observer remains outside the perceptual field of the animal but has the ability to track the animal. Using binoculars or telephoto recording equipment, the observer is able to document the animal's movements in the environment and yet not become part of the environment. The animals are permitted to behave in ways they normally would. In addition, because the animals are unaware of the observer, the genuineness of their behaviors is ensured.

Technically, there is one way unobtrusive recordings can be made in a natural environment when the researcher is detectable. This occurs when researchers become such a familiar element of the environment that the animals effectively ignore them, or at least do not view them as intrusive. The work of primatologist Jane Goodall mentioned in Chapter 1 is one such example. Goodall has been in the natural environment of the primates she studies in Africa for so many years that, if anything, her absence would present a more unnatural context than would her presence. The animals are accustomed to Goodall's being around, jotting down notes on a pad, and so on. Consequently, she is able to unobtrusively enter records of the animals' behavior patterns even though she is conspicuous in their habitat (see Miller, 1995, for a recent summary of Goodall's fascinating life among humans' closest relatives). Similarly, when a fourth-grade teacher in a public school system maintains records of the amount of time children spend with the caged iguana in the corner of the room, he or she makes unobtrusive observations. The teacher is supposed to be in the classroom, so his or her presence does not stimulate unnatural or artificial behaviors.

One problem that often occurs in naturalistic observation, however, is that the researcher may want to become part of the environment and contribute in ways that will corrupt the recording scheme. For example, when a marine biologist monitors the activity of a blue whale for 6 months only to discover that the animal inexplicably attempts to beach itself, she or he may feel obliged to intervene. In such situations, a judgment must be made: Is it more important to save the animal or to study the animal? Intervening means contaminating the research because the events being observed would no longer be truly natural. Separating personal and professional ambition is never easy, but it is essential to obtaining accurate natural records.

A second concern when gathering data from naturalistic environments relates to the methods used for making the recordings. You can imagine the disruption caused by the click of a camera in the wild or the presence of an audiotape recorder in the kitchen of a dysfunctional family. The hardware used to store data changes the circumstances of the recording session. In some cases, less intrusive alternatives may be available, or the data can be collected remotely. In other cases, however, there may be no way to conceal the mechanism of recording. In these cases, about all you can do is acknowledge the potential source of bias and accept that your observations may not be truly natural.

Therefore, as a first step in naturalistic observation, do everything you can to keep the observer out of the research environment. This may require elaborate concealments, careful selection and deployment of recording devices, and extensive training on how to remain inconspicuous in animated settings. Once you have accomplished this task, you are ready to move to the next step in naturalistic observation: making sense of your findings.

**Interpreting Naturalistic Observations.** The process of observing behavior in a natural habitat requires that you attend to those behaviors identified *a priori* as relevant to your task. This means concerning yourself with the frequency or incidence of a behavior rather than its absence. Such an approach obscures the importance of nonparticipation, however, and can lead to misleading interpretations. For example, an educational psychologist who is interested in cooperative behavior among kindergartners may keep detailed records of the children who choose to interact with one another. But what about the children who choose to play or work alone? Obviously, the tally of cooperative behaviors for the independent children will be *0,* because there is no interaction. The real story here is the children's lack of participation, not their lack of cooperative responding.

It is useful in such cases to develop a recording methodology that allows for reports on nonparticipants. The researcher may find that the positive findings from a study apply only to a minority population. Note that this restriction in no way lessens the importance of the findings for that population, it just limits what you can say.

Another issue for naturalistic studies that relates to interpretive matters is the completeness of the behavioral profile. Even in cases where all members of the group being observed are active, information will be missed. In a research environment where behaviors occur naturally at a high frequency, it is impossible to register every occurrence of a target response. When you are examining the frequency of "rough-and-tumble play" in elementary school children, for instance (Nurss, 1989), you will find that it happens so often you cannot keep track of it. You can turn to interval recording techniques or some of the other methods discussed earlier, but the result will be only a sample of what the children did during the observation period. Consequently, inferences about the actual behavioral picture must be made, and this needs to be recognized by the researcher and the reader of the report.

With naturalistic observation, as with all recording procedures, an awareness of the strengths and limitations of the research model must be maintained. Obviously, decisions to use a particular approach are based on the approach's perceived advantages, but it is no less crucial to address the approach's boundaries of interpretation. Caution is the key to advancement in scientific research. When it is exercised appropriately, everyone benefits.

## WITHIN CHAPTER REVIEW AND STUDY QUESTION

### THE OBSERVATIONAL METHOD

1. Discuss some of the strengths and weaknesses of the observational method. Do you think such methods are preferred to the experimental methods discussed earlier? Why or why not?

# THE SURVEY METHOD

In **the survey method,** the researcher questions subjects regarding their attitudes, beliefs, and opinions on some position. The survey method shares a characteristic with the observational approach discussed in the previous section, which is that no experimental manipulations are performed. That is, in neither method is there an attempt to alter the environment to see what would happen. Rather, the investigator's aim is to describe events as they presently stand.

One discernable difference between the survey method and the observational method is that in the survey strategy there is no attempt at concealment. Unobtrusive recording is out of the question, of course, because the presence of the investigator is required to distribute and administer the survey. Even in cases involving mail or telephone surveys, it is not possible to keep the researcher concealed, because the participants know that they are responding to a questionnaire that someone else will evaluate. Although this alone may bias response patterns on the questionnaire, on the whole survey data are extremely useful. As a result, the technique has been popular among psychology researchers for decades.

Survey research has several functions, one of which is to predict responses. This is seen most conspicuously in the results published by national pollsters who attempt to predict such things as voter behavior, job opportunities over the next 5 years, the number of people who enter college in the fall of 2000, and a myriad of other futures. The Gallup Poll is perhaps the best known of professional polls, at least in politics.

Figure 10–2 shows the vote predicted for the 1992 U.S. presidential elections for the week March 31, 1992, to April 1, 1992, as well as trends before that period (Gallup, 1993). Notice that the attempt was to predict how responders would behave. Because such survey data can be used to chart strategies, identify target areas, and so forth, they are extremely valuable to people like political candidates who must be concerned

**the survey method**—a procedure in which subjects are asked about their attitudes, beliefs, and opinions

*Asked of registered voters: Suppose the 1992 presidential election were being held today. If George Bush were the Republican candidate and Bill Clinton were the Democratic candidate, whom would you vote for? [Those who were undecided were asked: As of today, do you lean more to Bush, the Republican, or to Clinton, the Democrat?]*

Bush . . . . . . . . . . . . . . . . . . . . . . . . . . . . . . . . . . . . .54%
Clinton . . . . . . . . . . . . . . . . . . . . . . . . . . . . . . . . . .34
Undecided; other . . . . . . . . . . . . . . . . . . . . . . . . . . . .12

SELECTED NATIONAL TREND

|  | Bush | Clinton | Undecided; other |
|---|---|---|---|
| 1992 | | | |
| March 20–22 | 52% | 43% | 5% |
| March 11–12 | 50 | 44 | 6 |
| February 19–20 | 53 | 43 | 4 |
| February 6–9 | 53 | 38 | 9 |

**FIGURE 10–2** Gallup Survey, April 1992. Predicted vote of the 1992 U.S. presidential elections. (From Gallup, 1993.) Copyright © 1993 by Scholarly Resources Inc. Reported by permission of Scholarly Resources Inc.

with how people are going to behave. Of course, the predictive utility of survey results is short lived, as Figure 10–2 also shows (Bush lost to Clinton in 1992). Therefore, updates are necessary to forecast accurately.

In addition to predicting responses, survey results are used to characterize attitudes or behaviors. Depending on the topic, questions may be designed to yield attitudinal information that is peculiar to a time and circumstance, or they may target more enduring opinions that reflect a person's position over time. Often, questionnaire data are compared to previous reports made along the same lines, and the results are combined to establish trends in attitudes or behavior.

For example, Figure 10–3 presents the results of a November 1992 Gallup poll on gambling activity. Because similar information is available from surveys that were administered as long ago as 1938, national trends in gambling participation can be determined selectively by comparing the current data with choice previous results. A quick visual inspection of the patterns of responding in Figure 10–3 reveals that certain changes in behavior have occurred over the years. For example, the percentage of respondents who purchased a state lottery ticket rose sharply from 1982 to 1992. This sort of information can be useful to those

## December 16 ■ Gambling: Participation
Interviewing Date: 11/20-22/92   Survey #GO 322034

*Please tell me whether or not you have done any of the following in the past twelve months:*

| Played bingo for money? | | | 1982 | 9 |
|---|---|---|---|---|
| | | Yes | 1950 | 4 |
| National | | 9% | 1938 | 10 |

| | Yes |
|---|---|
| SELECTED NATIONAL TREND | Yes |
| 1989 | 13% |
| 1982 | 9 |
| 1950 | 12 |

| **Bought a state lottery ticket?** | Yes |
|---|---|
| National | 56% |
| SELECTED NATIONAL TREND | Yes |
| 1989 | 54% |
| 1982 | 18 |

| Visited a casino? | Yes |
|---|---|
| National | 21% |
| SELECTED NATIONAL TREND | Yes |
| 1989 | 20% |
| 1984 | 18 |
| 1982 | 12 |

*Bet on a professional sports event such as base-ball, basketball, or football?*

| | Yes |
|---|---|
| National | 12% |
| SELECTED NATIONAL TREND | Yes |
| 1989 | 22% |
| 1984 | 17 |
| 1982 | 15 |

| Bet on a horse race? | Yes |
|---|---|
| National | 12% |
| SELECTED NATIONAL TREND | Yes |
| 1989 | 14% |
| 1984 | 11 |

**FIGURE 10-3.** Gallup Survey, December 1992. National trends in gambling participation. (From Gallup, 1993.) Copyright © 1993 by Scholarly Resources Inc. Reprinted by permission of Scholarly Resources Inc.

in the gambling industry, and it may also be useful to state officials who must anticipate revenue gains from such endeavors.

Although survey results may stand alone in some psychological research studies, most investigators use survey data with other behavioral measures. This can take the form of self-report information that is used as one of several dependent measures.

Recall from Chapter 5 that a self-report technique will be used as a dependent measure in the model experiment we are building as we move through this book. The fear thermometer, which is a self-report technique, will be used with two other measures (the OSBD and a heart rate measure) to assess fear levels in younger

(4- to 6-year-old) and older (10- to 12-year-old) children receiving one of our three treatment interventions (cognitive coping strategy, sensory information, and contact control). Although the fear thermometer is not a conventional survey, it still qualifies as a questionnaire because participants are asked to report how they feel.

In addition to serving as dependent measures, survey findings may be used to establish levels of an independent variable. This is illustrated by the study conducted by Hamilton (1974), which was designed to evaluate the effects of need achievement on task selection.

Based on models set forth by psychologists David McClelland and John Atkinson (see Atkinson & Birch, 1978; McClelland, 1985), it was proposed that people who had a strong desire to be successful (high need achievement) and a low fear of failure would select moderately difficult tasks. These tasks would ensure a high probability of success, which would bring these people satisfaction. In contrast, it was predicted that people with a low need achievement and a high fear of failure would select either very difficult tasks that would cause minimal shame and embarrassment should they fail or very easy tasks that would virtually guarantee failure could be avoided.

Accordingly, a need achievement questionnaire was administered first to establish two distinctive groups: high need achievement and low need achievement. Subsequently, all subjects were allowed to select from tasks varying from "easy" to "very difficult." The findings confirmed Hamilton's predictions. More important for us, this study shows how a survey can be used to establish different levels of an independent variable.

## Developing Surveys

A great deal of time and planning should be given to developing a survey before it is administered. Because a flawed survey ensures failed survey research, it is essential to work out the details of the assessment tool before commencing data collection. There are three issues in the development of a good survey: the kinds of items that should be included, the construction of these items, and the physical features of the survey.

**Selecting Survey Items.** The decision to use one type of item in the questionnaire is determined partly by the nature of the study. If an investigator is interested in an individual's perception of the importance of close family relationships to the maintenance of cultural and ethnic identity, for instance, it may be important to incorporate unstructured items into the survey. An **unstructured item** refers to a question that is intentionally ambiguous. This type of item does not restrict the range of alternatives. Rather, the respondent is free to respond as he or she sees fit. An example of an unstructured item is:

> How does the role of the father differ in the African American community relative to the Mexican American community?

To such an item, the respondent may briefly remark about cultural diversity, or he or she may expand on the perceived sociocultural impact of the dissolution of the nuclear family in the United States. The advantage of the unstructured format is that trends and behavior patterns that were unexpected when the survey was constructed may emerge. With the broader behavioral picture created by the unstructured approach, new directions in research may be identified.

Perhaps the greatest difficulty with unstructured items is that it is often difficult to score their responses. Because the questions are open ended and their answers are diverse, it may be difficult to classify the reactions of the respondents. Coding schemes may assist in this regard, but coding means losing information and compromising the value of the unstructured format. Also, the investigator cannot be certain that the respondent understands the question being asked. Because uncertainty is integral to this kind of item, the respondent may answer with responses that are tangential and unrelated to the survey.

When a survey researcher wants to limit the range of possible responses, **structured items** are preferred. With structured items, the respondent is forced to select only one of several answers provided by the investigator. An example of a structured survey that is familiar to many college students is the "teaching evaluation form" that is administered at the end of a course. Typically, the student must agree or disagree with statements made about the course. Although the format of such opinion surveys varies across institutions and even across faculty members, in most cases the evaluator must select from a relatively narrow range of response alternatives. Figure 10–4 is the teaching evaluation survey I use for my classes.

Included in the list of structured surveys are rating scales like the Likert scale discussed in Chapter 5. On the rating scale, the respondent must mark a point along some continuum that is anchored by two extremes. In one version of this approach, called a **continuous rating scale,** the respondent is free to mark anywhere along a line that corresponds to a distribution of uninterrupted values. In contrast, the **discontinuous rating scale** requires the respondent to select one of

**unstructured item**—a survey question that is purposely ambiguous and presents an unrestricted range of alternatives

**structured items**—survey questions to which the respondent is forced to select only one answer

**continuous rating scale**—a scale on which the respondent is free to select any point along some continuum

**discontinuous rating scale**—a scale on which the respondent must select from one of several discrete values

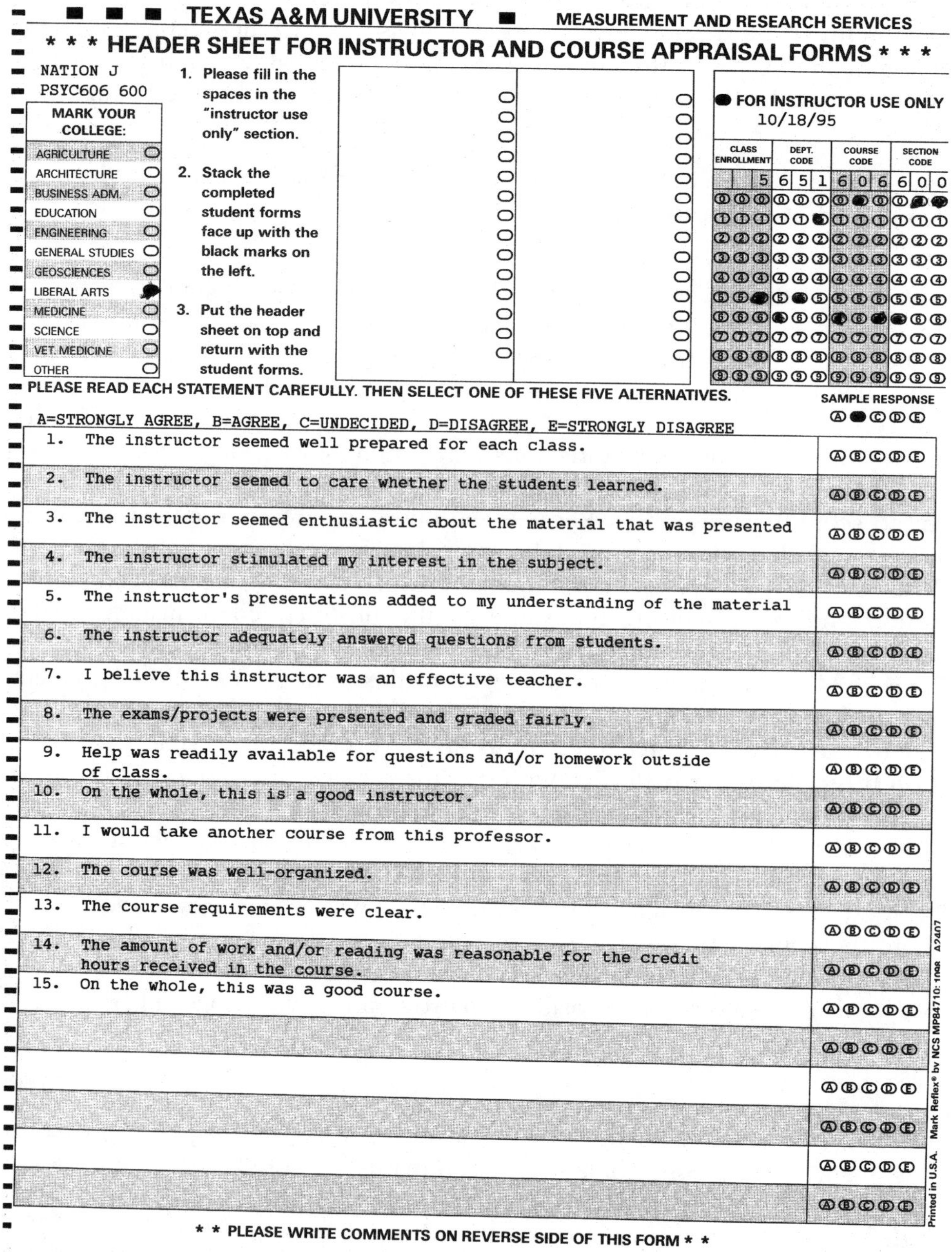

TEXAS A&M UNIVERSITY MEASUREMENT AND RESEARCH SERVICES

* * * HEADER SHEET FOR INSTRUCTOR AND COURSE APPRAISAL FORMS * * *

NATION J
PSYC606 600

MARK YOUR COLLEGE:
AGRICULTURE
ARCHITECTURE
BUSINESS ADM.
EDUCATION
ENGINEERING
GENERAL STUDIES
GEOSCIENCES
LIBERAL ARTS
MEDICINE
SCIENCE
VET. MEDICINE
OTHER

1. Please fill in the spaces in the "instructor use only" section.
2. Stack the completed student forms face up with the black marks on the left.
3. Put the header sheet on top and return with the student forms.

FOR INSTRUCTOR USE ONLY
10/18/95

| CLASS ENROLLMENT | DEPT. CODE | COURSE CODE | SECTION CODE |
|---|---|---|---|
| 5 | 651 | 606 | 600 |

PLEASE READ EACH STATEMENT CAREFULLY. THEN SELECT ONE OF THESE FIVE ALTERNATIVES.

SAMPLE RESPONSE

A=STRONGLY AGREE, B=AGREE, C=UNDECIDED, D=DISAGREE, E=STRONGLY DISAGREE

1. The instructor seemed well prepared for each class.
2. The instructor seemed to care whether the students learned.
3. The instructor seemed enthusiastic about the material that was presented
4. The instructor stimulated my interest in the subject.
5. The instructor's presentations added to my understanding of the material
6. The instructor adequately answered questions from students.
7. I believe this instructor was an effective teacher.
8. The exams/projects were presented and graded fairly.
9. Help was readily available for questions and/or homework outside of class.
10. On the whole, this is a good instructor.
11. I would take another course from this professor.
12. The course was well-organized.
13. The course requirements were clear.
14. The amount of work and/or reading was reasonable for the credit hours received in the course.
15. On the whole, this was a good course.

Printed in U.S.A. Mark Reflex® by NCS MP84710:1098 A2407

* * PLEASE WRITE COMMENTS ON REVERSE SIDE OF THIS FORM * *

**FIGURE 10–4** An example of a structured survey involving teaching evaluation

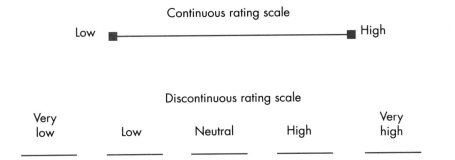

FIGURE 10–5 Continuous and discontinuous rating scales for evaluating the perceived importance of a college education

several discrete values designated by the researcher. Figure 10–5 shows what continuous and discontinuous rating scales might look like for a survey on the perceived importance of a college education.

Once the decision is made about what type of item to include in the survey, the next issue is how best to construct the item. As the next section notes, this is where the survey researcher must be especially careful and thoughtful.

**Constructing Survey Items.** As any writer will tell you, ideas flow freely, but effectively communicating those ideas is a struggle. This is the case for survey construction, where the composition of items determines the quality of responding and ultimately the utility of the results.

**Length of Items.** Although there are no hard-and-fast rules about how best to write an item, a general recommendation can be made: Keep the item short and simple. When a question is too long or complex, the respondent may have difficulty following the intent of the item. This is especially true if the respondent population is poorly educated. Consider the following item:

> Because economic exigency has forced more than 70% of women in contemporary American society to enter the work force, an increasing number of children labeled "latch key children" are left unattended once they are dismissed from school. Given the present social milieu, do you view this emergent policy as problematic?

Even if the respondent can handle the vocabulary, he or she may be confused about what precisely is being asked. Does this mean problematic for society or for the family? What age children are we talking about? What "milieu" is the investigator talking about? In comparison, a more concise item will yield a more definite response. For example, we might ask:

Should children under age 9 be left alone after school?

The respondent should have no trouble deciphering this question. In addition, the yes-or-no answer scheme makes scoring and interpretation simpler.

Of course, the length of the survey itself is a concern. Even with shorter, focused questions, a survey can run too long. Fatigue and boredom lead to inappropriate responses and corrupt the survey process. If possible, construct the survey so that the average respondent can complete it in just a few minutes.

**Cultural and Ethnic Issues.** When constructing items for a survey, cultural and ethnic diversity matters must be considered. A questionnaire on pain that is administered to a tribal "celebrant" in parts of East India has to be very different from one that is administered to college students on the Nebraska Wesleyan campus in Lincoln, Nebraska. Native members of certain East India tribes have a much different tolerance for pain than most Americans (Melzack & Wall, 1988). Therefore, the kind of references they make to painful experiences are specific to their environment. It makes sense to fashion the survey instrument to address the unique values of the East Indian people by amending the survey's language, style, and format.

Sensitivity to minority concerns is also a must for successful survey research. As noted in Chapter 6, Stanley Sue is a psychologist who has contributed substantially to the literature on the delivery of mental health services to ethnic-minority populations. Among Sue's findings is that Native American and African American survey respondents are less likely to respond openly when the questionnaire is administered by whites (cf. Sue & Zane, 1987). Sue and his colleague, Zane, recommend that the possible respondents interact with ". . . persons who share the unique perspective, value system, and beliefs of the group . . ." (p. 38).

**Physical Features of the Survey.** Several writers have commented on the need to incorporate certain physical features into a written survey (Bordens & Abbott, 1988; Dillman, 1978). The questionnaire must be neatly formatted with a clear typeface, and it must have lettering that is sufficiently large to avoid reading difficulties. From the instructions on, the survey must be visually appealing, easy to follow, and logically organized. Figure 10–6 summarizes several key points to consider when making a survey "look right."

1. Organize the items logically.
2. Choose a clear and legible typeface.
3. Use a print size that is large enough to be read easily.
4. Make the entire package visually appealing and the instructions easy to follow.
5. Keep the survey as brief as possible.

**FIGURE 10–6** Points to consider when designing a survey

## WITHIN CHAPTER REVIEW AND STUDY QUESTIONS

### THE SURVEY METHOD

1. In survey research, a(n) _____ item is purposely ambiguous.
   a. structured
   b. unstructured
   c. objective
2. What three issues regarding the development of a good survey were discussed? How are they interrelated?

## THE CASE STUDY

Administering and scoring surveys is an important element of psychological research because a large amount of information can be compiled for many different people in a relatively short time. On occasion, however, it is more useful to collect a great deal of information on one individual over a longer time. This is when the case study is appropriate.

For our purposes, a **case study** is defined as a thorough analysis of one person's behavior or mental activity. The case study may focus on one act or trait, or it may document a wide range of behaviors. Regardless of scope, the case study is intended to provide in-depth information on the details of the case and therein yield data that would normally be obscured or missed in a more global assay.

**case study**—a thorough analysis of one person's behavior or mental activity

A classic report of brain injury can be used to illustrate the value of the case study approach. On September 13, 1848, a 25-year-old railroad construction foreman named Phineas P. Gage had a tragic accident. An explosion hurled a 3-cm wide, 109-cm long tamping iron through Gage's brain (see drawing below). Not only did Gage survive, but with the aid of his men, he was able to walk to a nearby physician's office!

Under the care of his physician, John Harlow, Gage recovered fully, at least physically. However, his behavior changed dramatically. Before his accident, Gage had been an intelligent and socially appropriate man whom everyone liked. After the accident Gage developed a predilection for profanity and a disdain for social convention. As the months and years passed, it became apparent to Harlow that Gage had lost "the equilibrium or balance, so to speak, between

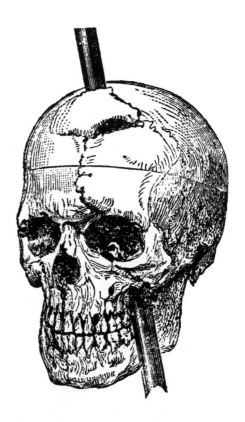

Case studies such as the Phineas Gage case further our understanding of specific phenomena by providing detailed information on one individual over a relatively long time.

his intellectual faculty and animal propensities" (Harlow, 1868). In the words of his friends, "Gage was no longer Gage."

Had the Gage case been presented as a part of a greater study involving numerous patients who had suffered severe head injuries, much of the detailed information about the case would have been obscured in summary format. As it stands, however, the careful records Harlow maintained, combined with a reexamination of the precise location of Gage's lesion (Damasio, Grabowski, Frank, Galaburda, & Damasio, 1994), provide clues about the involvement of the prefrontal cortex in rational decision making and the processing of emotion. In the words of Damasio et al., "The mysteries of frontal lobe function are slowly being solved, and it is only fair to establish, on a more substantial footing, the roles that Gage and Harlow played in the solution" (p. 1105).

Of course, case studies like these are limited in their generalizability, and their full dynamics can never really be known. However, case studies add significantly to the scientific literature and, when combined with more conventional experimental analyses, yield special products.

## WITHIN CHAPTER REVIEW AND STUDY QUESTION

### THE CASE STUDY

1. Under what conditions do you think case study information would be most useful?

## THE CORRELATIONAL METHOD

Surely the richness of psychology attracts many to the field. The variety of subject areas and the great number of topics within each area provide investigators with an enormous range of phenomena that merit inspection. On occasion, these phenomena may involve events over which the investigator has minimal control. The effects of prolonged inclement weather on mood, the impact of early religious experience on moral development, and the importance of parental support to academic achievement are all issues that interest psychologists, but in none of these cases is it possible for the researcher to experimentally manipulate the variables of concern. Still, there are investigative approaches that permit the relation between and among such factors to be analyzed. One of the most popular is the correlational method.

**Correlation** refers to the degree to which two or more events vary together. When two or more events change in the same direction, they are said to be positively correlated. For example, there is a positive correlation between age and height because as you age, your body height increases. Conversely, when two or more events change in opposite directions, they are said to be negatively correlated. An example of negative correlation is the relation between interest rates and lending activity. When interest rates successively increase, loan applications are likely to decline. Both positively and negatively correlated events are instructive for psychology researchers because they allow us to predict certain events and establish links that would otherwise go unreported.

The value of the correlational approach in research is evident from an adoption study of human obesity. Albert Stunkard et al. at the University of Pennsylvania reported findings in 1986 which showed that the body fatness of 540 adults who had been adopted immediately after birth was more positively correlated with the body fatness of the adults' biological rather than adoptive parents. That is, whether obese, average weight, or thin, adult adoptees were more likely to have the body builds of their biological parents than the builds of the parents who actually reared them. These data argue that genetics influence obesity and that the role of the family environment is minimal in many cases. By restricting the target populations for treatment to people who are most likely to benefit from psychotherapy, psychologists have now improved their chances of controlling certain types of eating disorders.

As useful as correlational methods are in situations where the variables cannot be experimentally manipulated, they do have limitations. First, correlation does not imply causation. It tells us nothing about cause-effect relations. Two events may vary together, but one does not necessarily cause the other. For example, no one is likely to assert that an increase in height promotes musical expression, even though the two have a strong positive correlation. It is true that as we grow older and our body sizes increase, we become more proficient using musical instruments. Obviously, however, other factors are at issue in this correlation.

Related to problems associated with causality, correlational data may reflect trends that are actually produced by another variable. This issue, which is typically referred to as the *third variable problem* in correlational research, stems from the fact that two events may vary together because they are both caused by a third event. For instance, there is a high positive correlation between drug abuse and crime. Although it is reasonable to assume that criminal behavior may be influenced by psychoactive drugs, it can be safely asserted that both activities derive prominently from flawed socialization experiences, inadequate support networks, inappropriate modeling, and a host of other idiosyncratic determinants of human conduct. Viewed within this context, the fact that two variables are correlated (drug abuse and crime) is incidental to the causal relation between both variables and a common social variable (personal background). In this case, it would make more sense to study the causal connections and their respective mechanisms of influence than to examine the correlation between two events that just happen to vary together and in the same direction.

Despite certain weaknesses, it should be understood that the correlational approach to conducting psychological research has decided benefits. When experimental manipulation is not possible, correlational techniques can be used to describe and predict behavioral events. Indeed, for certain projects correlational methods are preferred over all others.

## WITHIN CHAPTER REVIEW AND STUDY QUESTION

### THE CORRELATIONAL METHOD

1. Think of a research setting where a correlational analysis would be appropriate. What would be the ultimate value of your findings?

## QUASI-EXPERIMENTAL DESIGNS

Within the confines of a laboratory, carefully executed experimental control can be expected. The researcher manipulates only those variables that are of interest and holds constant or randomizes other factors so as to prevent systematic influence. Conducting research outside the laboratory may require greater compromise, however. In many instances it is impossible to exercise effective control over extraneous variables that may influence your results. When experimental control is compromised by practical considerations, the investigator may want to turn to a **quasi-experimental design,** which is a design that attempts to reduce the number of explanations of an effect. I mention two such designs: the nonequivalent control group design and the time series design.

**quasi-experimental design**—a design that reduces the number of rival hypotheses but compromises control

## *Nonequivalent Control Group Designs*

Psychologist Dwayne Simpson heads the Behavioral Research Program (BRP), which is housed on the campus of Texas Christian University in Fort Worth, Texas. A chief objective of the BRP is to evaluate and document the effectiveness of various drug intervention programs that have been introduced throughout the United States over the last two decades. Often, the behavioral patterns of patients must be tracked for years after treatment is terminated. The ultimate task for Simpson and the BRP, then, is to determine the efficacy of the experimental treatment in producing lasting recovery from drug addiction (Simpson, 1980). The following hypothetical investigation illustrates the kind of research decisions that people conducting program evaluation research must routinely make.

In an ideal research world, program evaluation researchers like Simpson and his colleagues would randomly assign people with a history of heroin abuse to an experimental treatment condition involving the introduction of an experimental drug we will call Amylen or to a control condition involving placebo administration. By monitoring patient progress for members of each group over the next 18 months, it might be possible to determine the true impact of the experimental drug. However, because ethical issues constrain the investigator, some form of treatment must be offered to all people in the study who are addicted to heroin. This does not mean all patients must continue treatment, only that convention prevents the investigator from doing nothing for these patients for 18 months.

As an alternative to random assignment and traditional experimental control, the investigator may permit experimental and control groups to form along different lines. Specifically, assume that 50 people addicted to heroin are offered Amylen for an 18-month experimental period. Each week for 1 month, each patient is required to report to the drug rehabilitation center where the medication is dispensed. During each visit extensive neuropsychological data and self-report information on the frequency and incidence of heroin use are collected. Corroborating evidence is obtained from friends, relatives, police records, and other sources.

At the end of the 1-month preliminary evaluation period, it is determined that 15 patients "definitely would like to continue with the program," and that 15 others "do not want to participate further in the experimental program." The responses from the remaining 20 patients categorized them as "uncertain." At this time, it is further determined that the amount of drug use for those wishing to continue treatment is somewhat less than that of the "dropout" group. Is it possible to assess the treatment effectiveness of Amylen using these subjects?

It is possible to make statements about the effects of Amylen intervention using the design outlined in Figure 10–7. This design is called a **nonequivalent control group design** because the two groups differed from the very beginning. In addition to reported heroin use, what factors do you think might contribute to differences between a group of 15 addicts who agree to continue treatment and a comparable group of addicts who decline treatment? Is motivation an issue? Is length of addiction, and its attendant perceptions of hopelessness, an uncontrolled source of variation? What about age, access to heroin and other psychoactive drugs, social support networks, health status, or a host of other determinants? Are there likely to be differences on these variables between those who want to continue and those who don't, and isn't it likely that such differences will bias the results?

> **nonequivalent control group design**—procedure in which two unequal groups receive treatment and are compared based on change or difference scores

For a quasi-experimental design of the sort shown in Figure 10–7 to be of any value, the researcher must look at change or difference scores. A difference score is calculated by subtracting a postmanipulation value from a premanipulation value. For example, for the nonequivalent control group design in Figure 10–7, the difference score would be calculated as the difference between the incidence of heroin use before the introduction of the 18-month treatment with Amylen and the incidence of heroin use after treatment was terminated. If a participant in the study decreased heroin use from four times a week to once a week, the change or difference score would be −3. Similarly, if drug use increased from once a week to three times a week, the difference score would be +2. Figure 10–8 shows what the results from a study like the one in Figure 10–7 might look like.

The obvious advantage of using difference scores with this type of design is that the groups are compared according to a common metric. Even though group differences may exist before treatment, comparisons are still possible because we measure change from individual baselines. This is not to say that the

|  | Pretreatment Measure | Treatment | Posttreatment Measure |
|---|---|---|---|
| Group 1 | $X_1$ | Yes | $X_2$ |
| Group 2 | $X_1$ | No | $X_2$ |

**FIGURE 10–7** The general framework of the nonequivalent control group design. In this hypothetical case, Group 1 refers to a group of people with a history of heroin abuse who have opted for continued treatment with the experimental drug Amylen. Group 2 is defined as similar heroin users who have declined treatment. $X_1$ and $X_2$ represent the same dependent measure recorded before and after treatment.

|  | Pretreatment | Posttreatment | Difference score |
|---|---|---|---|
| Continue with program | 3.6 | 0.8 | -2.8 |
| Dropout | 4.1 | 3.9 | -0.2 |

Mean heroin use per week

FIGURE 10–8 The results of a hypothetical study on the treatment of heroin addiction using a nonequivalent control group design

change is due to the treatment manipulation, of course, because group separation in difference scores could occur for a variety of reasons, including those that distinguished the groups at the outset.

As mentioned, the nature of quasi-experimental designs is such that cause/effect statements can never be made forcefully. You simply attempt to limit the number of competing alternative explanations and provide a plausible account of the results. To assist in this process, some investigators may attempt to match subjects in the two nonequivalent groups (see the discussion of matching procedures in Chapters 6 and 8). For instance, in our hypothetical study of heroin addicts we might want to match a subset of patients on factors such as age, length of addiction, and incidence of drug use during the premanipulation phase. However, problems with this approach are that you further reduce sample size, regression toward the overall group mean (average) is likely (Loft, 1989), and conditions may remain different on other uncontrolled variables.

Given this, what good are nonequivalent control group designs? First, they tell us something about the feasibility of a connection between events. The results obtained from this type of design are instructive insofar as they provide a more informed guess about the relation between some experimental manipulation and behavior change. Also, there are numerous circumstances in which clear cause/effect determinations are incidental. Our hypothetical experiment on treating heroin addiction falls into this category. If Amylen decreases heroin use among only a select subpopulation of clients who want to use it, who cares why it works? What produces the effect is relatively unimportant. What does matter is that there is a treatment that offers hope to an identified group of dependent clients.

## *Time Series Designs*

The field of sport psychology is a rapidly growing specialty area within psychology, and the demand for demonstrations of techniques that decrease anxiety, enhance motivation, and improve performance is escalating (cf. LeUnes & Nation, 1996). Although the psychology of sport and sport behavior encompasses many subareas, the area of performance enhancement among elite athletes has attracted the most attention. I have worked and published scientific reports in this area (e.g., LeUnes & Nation, 1982; Nation & LeUnes, 1983), and I have had a chance to monitor the development of procedures that seem to offer genuine benefits for competitive athletics. One such line of research deals with imagery and performance. As the next section shows, however, the early research on this topic suffered from a few methodological weaknesses.

 ## Thinking About Research

**R**ichard Suinn of Colorado State University is a practicing sport psychologist and one of the pioneer experimental investigators in this popular field. Because of Suinn's proximity to ski slopes and the availability of elite competitors, he expressed an early interest in the performance enhancement of downhill racers (Suinn, 1972).

One technique that Suinn and his colleagues introduced in an effort to improve ski performances is now referred to as **mental practice,** or imagery training. As it relates to downhill racing, mental practice involves visualizing movements along the ski course. Before participating, the skier imagines himself or herself at the starting gate, anxiously awaiting the signal to go. The skier then imagines every turn on the course, every mogul, and points of ice or rough snow as he or she mentally races the course and accelerates at the finish line.

Preliminary attempts to demonstrate the validity of mental practice on race performance were encouraging. World-class downhillers initially skied the course as they normally would, and their times to the finish line were recorded. Subsequently, each downhiller engaged in mental practice, rehearsing his or her previous run and visualizing how to improve the

**mental practice**—imaginal rehearsal technique that is used as an intervention to enhance performance

next attempt. The results were striking: records of the postintervention trial (following mental practice) indicated a reliable decrease in the time it took the skiers to finish (see Suinn, 1983). The technique of mental practice seemed to have worked, but had it really?

Do you see a problem with this type of methodology? Were there other factors that may have influenced racing performance on the second trial and thereby bias the recordings? There are, and Suinn and his colleagues were quick to point them out and to caution against accepting the merits of mental practice as a training procedure for skiers. First, "warm-up effects" are an issue. Because only one run was completed before the effects of the imagery manipulation were tested, the improved times of the participants in their second

runs may have simply reflected normal increases in performance. Especially for athletic competition, completing a few practice attempts before competing in the actual event usually enhances performance. Also, one must be concerned about random fluctuations from one trial to the next. Is it possible that a skier's performance varied so much from run to run that the observed differences were due to normal differences in finish times?

Suinn and other sport psychologists have addressed these issues with more sophisticated designs that have yielded results favoring the use of mental practice in athletic competition (Suinn, 1983). One design format that has proven to be especially worthwhile in this type of research is the "time series design" discussed in the following section.                    ■

The interpretive problems of single-group designs that measure behavior before and after a treatment manipulation have caused researchers to consider other experimental methods. On occasion, a special case of the A-B-A within-subjects design that was discussed in Chapter 9 is employed. Recall that this design format requires that the treatment (B) be introduced following baseline recording (A), and that the conditions of baseline then be reintroduced (A). However, it may be impractical in some cases to think in terms of reintroducing baseline conditions. In such situations time series designs may be appropriate.

Technically, a **time series design** is a quasi-experimental design that measures the performances of one group of subjects in a pretest/posttest format. Although conventional control groups are not used in such designs, a degree of experimental control can be achieved by meshing several control strategies that restrict the number of alternative interpretations of the data (Diggle, 1990).

**Interrupted Time Series Designs.** One design that can be used to increase confidence that the observed findings are due to the treatment effect is the **interrupted time series design.** This design involves taking multiple recordings both before and after a treatment is introduced. Figure 10–9 presents the general framework for interrupted time series designs. Several measurements $(X_1–X_4)$ were taken before the introduction of the treatment condition, and several additional measurements $(X_5–X_8)$ are taken after the introduction of the treatment. Notice that the same dependent measure is recorded for the same subjects throughout the observation period.

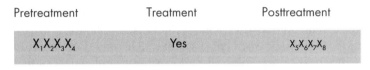

| Pretreatment | Treatment | Posttreatment |
|:---:|:---:|:---:|
| $X_1 X_2 X_3 X_4$ | Yes | $X_5 X_6 X_7 X_8$ |

**FIGURE 10–9 An interrupted time series design**

To illustrate interrupted time series designs, let's return to the mental practice topic we just discussed in the Thinking About Research section. Recall that mental practice employs imagery and other cognitive strategies to improve athletic performance. Using several basketball players as subjects, Kendall, Hrycaiko, Martin, and Kendall (1990) investigated the effects of imagery rehearsal and a self-talk package on a specific defensive basketball skill executed during competition. Figure 10–10 profiles the players' pattern of percent correct performances as a function of each opportunity across a number of games. A visual

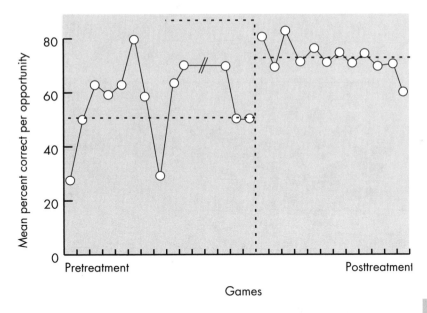

**FIGURE 10–10** The mean (average) percent correct of defensive performances per opportunity before and after a group of basketball players received treatment involving imagery rehearsal and self-talk (across games). (Modified from Kendall et al., 1990.) Reprinted by permission from G. Kendall, D. Hrycaiko, G. L. Martin, and T. Kendall, 1990, "The Effect of an Imagery, Rehearsal, Relaxation, and Self-talk Package on Basketball Game Performance," *Journal of Sport and Exercise Psychology,* Vol. 12 (2): 162.

**time series design**—a quasi-experimental design that measures the performance of one group of subjects in a pretest/posttest format

**interrupted time series design**—a design that involves taking multiple recordings both before and after a treatment is introduced

inspection of the average performances (dashed lines) before and after treatment reveals that defensive efficiency increased following the mental practice manipulation. On closer inspection we see that only 3 of the data points in the pretreatment phase are as high as the posttreatment data points. Using this interrupted time series approach, arguments supporting a genuine treatment effect can be made more confidently because a series of recordings was taken before and after the experimental manipulation. The large number of data points provides no real proof, but it does diminish the possibility of a chance finding.

One distinct advantage of the interrupted time series design is that if there is a particular pattern that could mislead an investigator, it is likely to be detected. For instance, the top panel of Figure 10–11 portrays a hypothetical pattern of re-

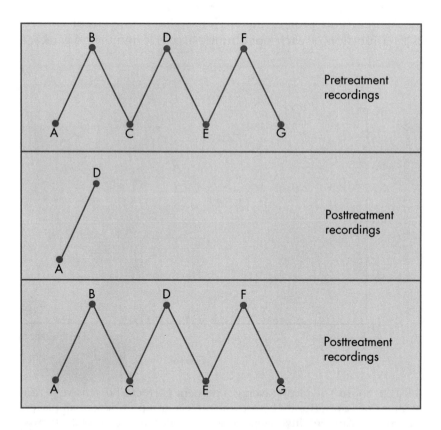

**FIGURE 10–11** (Top) A hypothetical pattern of behavior; (Middle) The pattern that is reported if only two posttreatment measures (A and D) are taken; (Bottom) The pattern that is reported with the full range of posttreatment recordings (A to G)

sults that consistently occurs for a particular measurement. It is clear that for whatever reasons, this measure fluctuates uniformly, first increasing, then decreasing, then increasing again. As the middle panel of Figure 10-11 shows, if a researcher took only two measurements, say at Point A for pretreatment and Point D for posttreatment, the results would be erroneously interpreted as a significant treatment effect. In actuality, no treatment effects were produced, which would have been evident had the full range of recordings (A to G) been obtained (bottom panel). In other words, had an extensive interrupted time series design been used, it would have been clear that the posttreatment pattern continued the previously established pretreatment pattern.

Sampling only a few data points along a constantly shifting but abiding pattern has produced more than one scientific phantom in the history of psychology. On some occasions, the incomplete measurements and flawed initial interpretations set in motion a prejudiced agenda that would survive for years.

## Spotlight on Research: WHATEVER HAPPENED TO THE KAMIN EFFECT?

In animal learning and memory research, the issue of retaining aversively motivated behavior was unexplored until 1957 when Leon Kamin made a surprising discovery. Kamin trained adult rats to avoid electric shocks delivered to a grid floor by teaching them to jump hurdles within a fixed time span. After the rats reached a set criterion, different groups of rats were returned to their home cages for differing retention intervals before retraining on the original avoidance task.

Curiously, Kamin found that although avoidance performance during retraining was excellent when retraining was carried out either immediately or 24 hours after the original training, the rats were unable to perform when the retention interval was roughly 1–3 hours after original training (see Figure 10–12). This U-shaped retention function became known as the Kamin effect and was replicated by several different investigators (cf. Klein, 1991).

Early theoretical accounts of the Kamin effect included such models as "the incubation of fear hypothesis," which proposed that the downward slope of the retention function was due to a linear pattern of forgetting and that the upward slope was due to gradually increasing fear levels that promoted avoidance responding. Within this context, fear incubated over time and by the 24-hour mark had accrued to heights that offset dropoffs in normal retention of a learned event (Kamin, 1957).

Years later, other investigators would discover that the retention function associated with avoidance training is much more complex (e.g., Holloway, 1978). Rather than conforming to the U-shape Kamin described, it seems that the pattern of retention is actually one in which high retention levels rebound about every 6 hours. Rats, as it turns out, exhibit biological rhythms that come full cycle about every 6 hours. Because the internal cues associated with a particular physiological state operate as retrieval cues and thereby promote the retention of learned material, it follows that rats should remember more when the retraining test is administered at 6-hour spacings (on cycle) as compared to 3-hour spacings (off cycle). Looking again at Kamin's original findings, we see that the U-shaped function was created by recordings taken out of phase when retention would be expected to be low (3 hours) and again when the biological rhythms and interoceptive cues were congruent with the state of the animal during original learning (24 hours).

Basically, the more complete interrupted time series model employed by Holloway (1978) and others revealed a more accurate picture of avoidance phenomena. Once again, the more measurements that are taken before treatment (the rest interval in the home cage in this case), the greater the chances of accurately characterizing the nature of the relation between the treatment variable and behavioral changes.                     ▪

In this section, we have seen that the interrupted time series approach offers many advantages over the simpler single-group, pretest/posttest paradigm. However, because every member of a population is exposed to the same conditions in this quasi-experimental design, you cannot be certain that pretreatment activities are not partly responsible for posttreatment results (Campbell & Stanley, 1963). When such pretreatment experiences are a concern for the in-

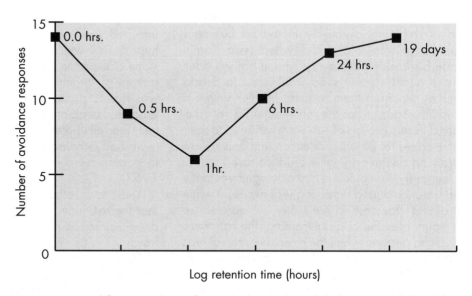

**FIGURE 10–12** The retention of aversively motivated behavior as defined by Kamin (1957)

vestigator, she or he may want to extend the interrupted time series design and include a comparable group that does not receive the treatment manipulation. This leads us to the multiple time series design.

**Multiple Time Series Design.** As with all time series approaches, the **multiple time series design** involves taking a series of measures before and after the introduction of some treatment manipulation. This experimental model, however, includes the use of a comparable group that functions as a more conventional control group. As Figure 10–13 shows, multiple recordings are made in the control condition pre- and posttreatment, in a manner exactly like that for the treatment condition. However, for the control group, during the period of the experimental treatment manipulation subjects either do nothing or engage in some neutral activity.

Had a quasi-control group of basketball athletes from a nearby school been included in the Kendall et al. (1990) study that was used to illustrate interrupted time series designs, a multiple time series design would have resulted. The control group in this case would not receive treatment involving imagery rehearsal and self-talk, and its game performances would be contrasted against those of the treatment group. Figure 10–14 shows how the data from such a project might look should a positive effect be produced in only the treatment group.

Even if the data in Figure 10–14 were real, understand that you would still be limited in interpreting them. Although treatment and control players are from similar schools, are of the same age, have the same athletic ability, and so on, it is still possible that some uncontrolled source of variation produced the group

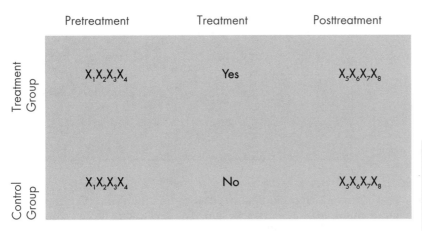

|  | Pretreatment | Treatment | Posttreatment |
|---|---|---|---|
| Treatment Group | $X_1X_2X_3X_4$ | Yes | $X_5X_6X_7X_8$ |
| Control Group | $X_1X_2X_3X_4$ | No | $X_5X_6X_7X_8$ |

**FIGURE 10–13** The general framework of the multiple time series design

**multiple time series design**—a design in which multiple recordings are made for one group before and after a treatment is introduced and are then compared to the same number of multiple recordings of a quasi-control group that does not experience the experimental manipulation

differences posttreatment. What if the control group experienced a mid-season coaching change or a team member died in an auto accident during the treatment period? Do you think such life experiences could have been the true determinants of the results? Perhaps they could—we just don't know. With quasi-experimental designs we must always be aware that a common variable outside the researcher's control may have impacted pretreatment and posttreatment performance. Nevertheless, with such designs you may still be able to

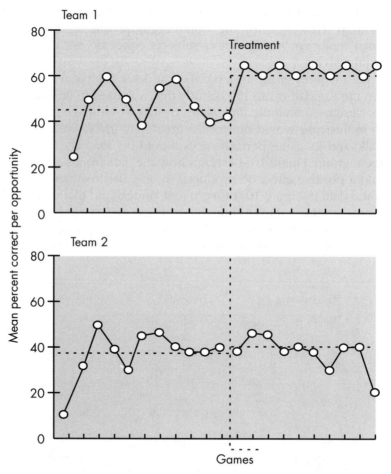

**FIGURE 10–14** Hypothetical profiles of treatment intervention using a multiple time series design. The treatment group (top) is composed of basketball players at a given school, while the control group (bottom) is composed of similar athletes from a neighboring school. Mean (average) percent correct defensive performances per opportunity are shown across basketball games for each group.

make restrictive remarks about the likelihood that a particular treatment effect exists. You do what you can do and try to limit as many alternative explanations as possible.

## WITHIN CHAPTER REVIEW AND STUDY QUESTIONS

### QUASI-EXPERIMENTAL DESIGNS

1. Under what conditions would you use a nonequivalent control group design? When selecting a dependent variable for such a design, why would you want to consider using a change or difference score?
2. What advantage(s) does an interrupted time series design have over a single-group pretest/posttest format?
3. When multiple measurements are taken for one group of subjects before and after one treatment manipulation is introduced, this design is referred to as _____.

## The Model Experiment

In this chapter, we have discussed several alternatives to the conventional experimental approach to conducting psychological research. Although carefully monitored laboratory experiments are essential to the scientific process, advancing our understanding of the world of which we are a part clearly may be accomplished by other means.

Even when rigorous experimental procedures are followed, components of the design alternatives discussed in this chapter may be incorporated into the overall research scheme. For example, in the model experiment that we continue to build as we progress from chapter to chapter in this book, it is clear that we are able to benefit from self-report procedures. As was made clear in this chapter in the section on survey method, self-report data are especially valuable when they are used with other behavioral measures. Regarding our model experiment, we have decided to include a fear thermometer, which is a self-report procedure that yields information about a patient's perception of his or her level of apprehension and anxiety. This measure is to be used with two other measures: the OSBD and a heart rate (HR) measure to evaluate the levels of fear registered by younger (4- to 6-year-old) and older (10- to 12-year-old) children receiving one of three treatment interventions (cognitive coping strategy, sensory information, and contact control).

As a result, we see that the experimental psychologist's arsenal must include design alternatives. The ultimate goal is to match research procedures to the demands of the hypothesis under investigation. Use whatever is available if a more complete understanding of the issue at hand will result.

# Drawing Inferences About Results

**probability theory**—a theory that is concerned with estimating the number of times a particular event will occur given the total number of events

The year was 1796, and the manifold talents of Maskelyne had turned to the heavens. Maskelyne, the astronomer royal at the Greenwich Observatory, was fascinated by planetary motion and the reconfiguration of the stars which suggested an underlying intelligence and order in the universe. At the time, the Greenwich Observatory represented the most sophisticated astronomy laboratory in the world, and the telescopes used there were among the most powerful.

To assist Maskelyne in his efforts to track the movements of various planets and celestial objects, he employed several assistants, one of whom, named Kinnebrook, was given the responsibility of regularly entering readings into a log regarding the precise location of an object and how far it had moved since the last recording. Based on comparisons with his own records of movement, Maskelyne observed that his assistant was repeatedly making errors and, after proclaiming him "an incompetent," he dismissed him (Boring, 1950).

Years later, after closely inspecting the same records, another astronomer named Bessel noticed that the assistant's entries were off a constant eight-tenths of a second from those of Maskelyne. Perhaps what was really at issue was not competency, but an inherent "personal difference." Could it be that some biologically determined difference in perceptual processing might account for the discrepant readings? Could such differences exist between and among all members of the population?

This early recognition of the differences between people contributed substantially to the development of the concept of probability. To the extent that differences occur naturally along some dimension, it makes sense that measures taken along that dimension would reflect the character of the underlying distribution of scores. If we know something about the distribution, we can anticipate what kind of differences should occur based on the essential principles of probability theory.

**Probability theory** is concerned with estimating the number of times a particular event will occur given the total number of events (Tuckwell, 1995). Questions concerning probability address how likely something is or how frequently we can expect something to happen. For example, how probable is it that you will find an African elephant running free in the streets of downtown Appleton, Wisconsin? Certainly this event is less likely than seeing the animal at the San Diego Zoo, so we can feel fairly confident about this statement of relative probability. But what about cases where subtler probability discriminations must be made? What about the differences in scientific recording that were evident for Maskelyne and his assistant? Did these differences truly reflect a systematic separation predicated on some biological substrate, or were they a result of chance? Science needed some mechanism by which such questions could be answered, and the solution was ultimately provided in the form of inferential statistics.

**Inferential statistics** is one method psychological researchers and other scientists use to establish the validity and reliability of their findings. It is a method that allows researchers to make statements about populations based on sample data. As was true for Maskelyne and Bessel over 150 years ago, psychologists today need to know whether the differences in their data are due to chance or causal events. Is the treatment effect genuine, and what is the probability of finding the same result in a repeated experiment?

Regarding the model experiment we are building in the pages of this book, if the results are in a direction that favors our hypothesis, how can we be certain that the age/intervention strategy interaction is robust? That is, if cognitive therapy is more effective with older children (10- to 12-year-olds) than with younger children (4- to 6-year-olds) will this pattern hold for future comparisons? What is the probability that we are making an erroneous conclusion?

In this chapter, we will see that the concept of probability assists us greatly in making decisions about the true meaning of our findings. I begin with a discussion of sampling distributions and their role in the process of drawing inferences about results.

# SAMPLING DISTRIBUTIONS

In Chapter 6, the differences between samples and populations were discussed. Recall that a population includes all members of some specified group, while a sample is a subset of the population. For instance, an investigator interested in characterizing the purchasing habits of all consumers living in Greensboro, North Carolina, (the population) may select a group of 250 people at random (the sample) and closely monitor the people's spending behavior over a set time period. The advantage of a sample is that it is manageable in terms of the time and costs required to study it.

The disadvantage of working with samples is that you can never be certain that the sample truly represents the population. In populations where individual values vary greatly, it is possible to select a sample that does not represent the population. For example, Figure 11–1 presents

**inferential statistics**—a methodology that permits researchers to make statements about populations based on sample information

| | | | |
|---|---|---|---|
| 54 | 61 | 66 | **28** |
| 41 | 58 | 50 | 53 |
| **22** | 43 | 40 | 42 |
| 36 | 44 | **31** | **38** |
| 51 | **23** | 48 | 26 |
| **24** | **26** | 56 | 54 |
| 39 | 56 | 46 | 47 |
| 44 | 49 | **29** | 48 |

**BOLD** = Selected for sample
Population mean = 42.9
Sample Mean = 27.6

FIGURE 11–1 The ages of all 32 employees of Bachman Chemical Company and the mean age of a random sample of 8 employees randomly selected from this population

the mean age of a random sample of eight factory workers employed by Bachman Chemical Company (a hypothetical case). You can see that the sample mean in this instance is a poor estimate of the population mean, which is based on the ages of all 32 employees.

How can we improve our estimations of population characteristics based on sample values? The answer rests with repeated sampling of a given population. If we take a large number of samples from the same population, the probability is that most of those samples will possess values that approximate the corresponding parameters of the population. For instance, for the population of scores in Figure 11–1, if we were to randomly draw 10 samples of 8 employees (N = 8), we would likely find one or two cases where the sample means were off the mark. The remaining means, however, would be pretty close to the mean of the population (see Figure 11–2).

Consider the result of such repeated sampling operations. You would have numerous sample mean values, each an estimate of the population mean but varying one from the other. Because the sample means are based on a common measure (employee age), it is possible to arrange the different mean values in a frequency distribution (see Chapter 5). Statisticians call a frequency distribution of sample means the **sampling distribution of the mean.** Figure 11–3 shows what the empirical sampling distribution of the mean would look like for the 10 means in Figure 11–2.

| | | | |
|---|---|---|---|
| 54 | 61 | 66 | **28** |
| 41 | 58 | 50 | 53 |
| **22** | 43 | 40 | 42 |
| 36 | 44 | **31** | **38** |
| 51 | **23** | 48 | 26 |
| **24** | **26** | 56 | 54 |
| **39** | 56 | 46 | 47 |
| 44 | 49 | **29** | 48 |

Sample mean = 27.6

| | | | |
|---|---|---|---|
| 54 | 61 | 66 | **28** |
| 41 | 58 | **50** | 53 |
| 22 | 43 | 40 | **42** |
| 36 | 44 | **31** | 38 |
| 51 | 23 | 48 | **26** |
| **24** | 26 | 56 | 54 |
| **39** | 56 | 46 | 47 |
| 44 | **49** | 29 | 48 |

Sample mean = 36.1

| | | | |
|---|---|---|---|
| 54 | 61 | 66 | 28 |
| 41 | 58 | 50 | 53 |
| 22 | 43 | **40** | **42** |
| 36 | 44 | **31** | 38 |
| 51 | **23** | 48 | 26 |
| 24 | 26 | 56 | 54 |
| **39** | 56 | 46 | **47** |
| **44** | **49** | 29 | 48 |

Sample mean = 39.3

| | | | |
|---|---|---|---|
| 54 | 61 | 66 | **28** |
| **41** | 58 | 50 | 53 |
| 22 | **43** | **40** | 42 |
| 36 | 44 | **31** | 38 |
| **51** | 23 | 48 | **26** |
| 24 | 26 | 56 | 54 |
| 39 | **56** | 46 | 47 |
| 44 | 49 | 29 | 48 |

Sample mean = 39.5

| | | | |
|---|---|---|---|
| 54 | **61** | 66 | 28 |
| 41 | 58 | 50 | 53 |
| **22** | 43 | **40** | **42** |
| **36** | 44 | **31** | **38** |
| 51 | 23 | 48 | 26 |
| 24 | **26** | 56 | 54 |
| **39** | 56 | 46 | 47 |
| 44 | 49 | 29 | 48 |

Sample mean = 41.8

| | | | |
|---|---|---|---|
| 54 | 61 | 66 | 28 |
| 41 | **58** | 50 | 53 |
| 22 | 43 | **40** | **42** |
| 36 | 44 | 31 | **38** |
| **51** | 23 | 48 | 26 |
| 24 | **26** | 56 | 54 |
| **39** | 56 | **46** | 47 |
| 44 | 49 | 29 | 48 |

Sample mean = 42.5

| | | | |
|---|---|---|---|
| 54 | 61 | 66 | 28 |
| **41** | 58 | 50 | 53 |
| 22 | **43** | 40 | 42 |
| 36 | **44** | 31 | **38** |
| 51 | 23 | 48 | 26 |
| 24 | 26 | 56 | 54 |
| 39 | 56 | **46** | **47** |
| **44** | 49 | 29 | 48 |

Sample mean = 42.8

| | | | |
|---|---|---|---|
| 54 | 61 | 66 | 28 |
| 41 | 58 | 50 | 53 |
| 22 | 43 | **40** | **42** |
| 36 | **44** | 31 | 38 |
| **51** | 23 | **48** | 26 |
| 24 | 26 | 56 | 54 |
| **39** | 56 | 46 | **47** |
| 44 | 49 | 29 | **48** |

Sample mean = 44.8

| | | | |
|---|---|---|---|
| **54** | 61 | **66** | 28 |
| 41 | 58 | 50 | 53 |
| 22 | **43** | 40 | **42** |
| 36 | 44 | 31 | 38 |
| 51 | 23 | 48 | 26 |
| 24 | 26 | 56 | **54** |
| 39 | 56 | 46 | 47 |
| **44** | **49** | **29** | 48 |

Sample mean = 47.6

| | | | |
|---|---|---|---|
| **54** | **61** | 66 | 28 |
| 41 | 58 | **50** | 53 |
| 22 | **43** | 40 | 42 |
| 36 | 44 | 31 | 38 |
| **51** | 23 | 48 | 26 |
| 24 | 26 | 56 | 54 |
| **39** | 56 | **46** | 47 |
| 44 | 49 | 29 | **48** |

Sample mean = 49.0

**BOLD** = Selected for sample

**FIGURE 11–2** The means of each of 10 samples of 8 employees randomly selected from the population of 32 employees of Bachman Chemical Company (see Figure 11-1)

## Features of the Sampling Distribution of the Mean

The sampling distribution of the mean has well-defined features. First, the mean of the sampling distribution equals the mean of the population from which the samples are drawn, at least theoretically given that you can obtain every possible sample of a given size from an identified population of values. It follows that if you want to be really secure in making statements about the agreement between the sampling distribution of the mean and the parent population, you must obtain a large number of samples (Spatz, 1993). The greater the number of sample means the more likely it is that the distribution of sample means will resemble the population distribution.

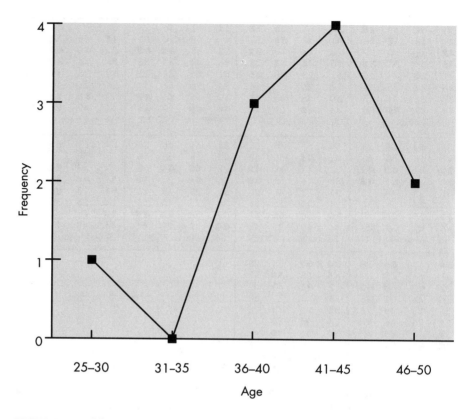

**FIGURE 11–3** The sampling distribution of means calculated in Figure 11-2. Each point on the horizontal axis refers to an age range rather than a specific age value.

Another feature of the sampling distribution of the mean is that each of the equal-size samples must be drawn randomly from the same population. In this vein, every member of the population must have an equal chance of being selected each time a sample is formed. This means that when a particular population value is selected for one sample, that value is replaced in the population and has the same probability of appearing in a second sample. Because the selection process is random, the probability of one population value appearing in successive samples is very low with large populations. However, it is essential that such an event *could* happen.

In addition to these features of the sampling distribution of the mean, there is the issue of the form the sampling distribution assumes with a large number of samples. This leads us to one of the most important principles in inferential statistics: the central limit theorem.

# Spotlight on Research: THE NORMAL CURVE AND THE CENTRAL LIMIT THEOREM

**F**or many years, psychologists have used theoretical distributions. Unlike the other distributions that have been discussed up to this juncture, theoretical distributions are based on mathematical formulas and logic rather than on empirical values. In actuality, the theoretical curves that are generated by these formulas represent best estimates of real-world distributions. Because theoretical distributions are only estimates of real events, they can never be truly accurate. However, they do provide a "best guess" of how the actual events would be distributed.

The theoretical distribution that has proven to be most useful for psychological research is the **normal distribution.** The label "normal" was applied to this distribution by early statisticians who noted that frequency distributions obtained from a variety of different fields and different data sets tended to match this theoretical curve (Patel, 1982). In describing the normal distribution shown in Figure 11–4, statisticians were able to document a number of distinctive features. First, the mean, median, and mode fall at precisely the same point on the curve. In addition, the normal curve that defines the normal distribution is bilaterally symmetrical, meaning that one half is a mirror image of the other.

On closer inspection of Figure 11–4, we see that the y-axis (the vertical axis) of the distribution is omitted. Its presence is assumed, however, and higher points along this axis correspond to greater frequencies of values. The values themselves are represented along the x-axis (the horizontal axis) and are expressed in standard deviation units (see the following). [Note: SD refers to the standard deviation of a sample and the Greek symbol $\sigma$ refers to the standard devia-

tion of a population. For our purposes, SD will be used for either the sample or population standard deviation.]

One of the most useful features of the normal curve is that the area under the curve between any two SD points is fixed. That is, the percentage of the total population that falls between the frequencies of two scores is always the same. For example, from Figure 11–4 it is evident that 34.13% of the total population will fall between the mean of the distribution ($\mu$) and +1 SD units. This is true whether we are dealing with age scores, height, weight, IQ, athleticism, or any other event that can be measured. If the data are normally distributed and we know the SD values that correspond to any two values, we can estimate the percentage of the population that will fall within this range.

There are numerous other advantages associated with the normal curve. It can be used to determine what proportion of population scores fall at or above a particular value, and it can be used to find the score that cuts off a specified proportion of the population. Given these and other uses, it follows that empirical distributions which approximate the normal distribution are especially instructive with respect to probability issues. Because the area under the normal curve is also a probability statement about the events in that area, it is possible to say how many times out of 100 we should obtain a particular score. With respect to the sampling distribution of the mean, for instance, insofar as the sampling distribution is normal, the probabil-

> **normal distribution**—a symmetrical theoretical distribution in which fixed percentages of the distribution fall at precise points on the normal curve

**Central Limit Theorem**—regardless of original form, the sampling distribution of the mean takes on the character of the normal distribution as sample size increases

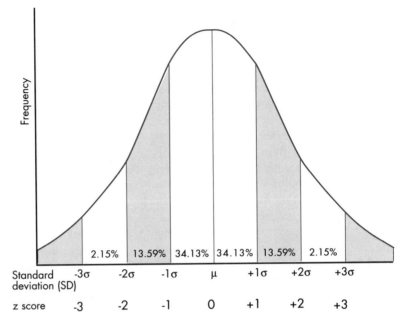

FIGURE 11–4 The normal curve characterizes a theoretical distribution (the normal distribution) with mean = 0 and SD = 1 ($\mu$ = 0 and $\sigma$ = 1).

ity of getting a particular sample mean from a specified population could be expressed.

Fortunately, mathematical statisticians have proven the **Central Limit Theorem,** which states:

> For any population of scores, regardless of form, the sampling distribution of the mean will approach a normal distribution as N (sample size) gets larger. Furthermore, this normal distribution will have a mean equal to $\mu$ and a standard deviation equal to SD/$\sqrt{N}$.

The Central Limit Theorem permits us to make statements of probability about means from a sampling distribution of means even when the population of scores from which the samples were drawn is not itself normal. Now that we know the samples are normally distributed, we can use the sample means to estimate the population mean. More important, we can say how probable it is that a given sample mean comes from a specific population. ▪

# *Variability and Sampling Error*

Variability is inherent in almost every distribution psychologists deal with in a research environment. For example, when an investigator records the amount of time it takes for 20 different individuals to complete a block design on some intelligence test, the probability of any two scores being the same is remote. Similarly, people express different levels of mood disturbance, groups exhibit differing amounts of cooperativeness, rats will traverse a maze at different speeds, and so forth. **Variability,** one of the most important concepts in experimental psychology, refers to the fluctuation of scores about some typical value.

To illustrate the importance of knowing about variability, Spatz and Johnston (1976) presented the following story.

> Two brothers took advantage of a warm Christmas Day in Miami and went water skiing. On average, each brother finished his turn only 5 feet from the shoreline, a position at which he could step off the ski and into only 1 foot of cold water. This average figure did not accurately reflect the excitement of the day, however.
>
> What actually happened was that one brother was so determined to avoid the cold water that he overshot the beach and went 35 feet up the rocky shore. On seeing this spectacle, the other brother overcompensated and stopped 45 feet from the shore and was forced to swim in. Therefore, although the average distance from the shore for the two brothers was perfect, their individual distances were way off mark. (pp. 61–62)

This story shows how essential it is to know something about the variability of scores in a distribution. Some distributions may have scores that are spread widely, while others may be tightly bunched even though they have the same mean. In order to truly understand the significance of a given score, we must know something about the variability of the distribution from which the score was taken.

When applying statistics in psychological research, experimenters are concerned with two measures of variability: the variance and the SD. Although variance must be calculated first, the SD is more important to statistical decision making.

**The Variance.** Figure 11–5 presents a hypothetical distribution of weekly family income for households on one block in Comanche, Oklahoma. Using the simple formula for calculating the arithmetic mean $\Sigma X/N$, where $X$ refers to the individual raw score values and $N$ is the number of observations in the distribution, we see that the mean of this distribution is

**variability**—the fluctuation in scores about the mean

| Household | Weekly family income/week | Deviation score (x) | $x^2$ |
|-----------|---------------------------|---------------------|-------|
| The Smiths | $2300 | $505 | 255,025 |
| The Waltons | 1950 | 155 | 24,025 |
| The Thompsons | 1811 | 16 | 256 |
| The Robertsons | 1754 | -41 | 1681 |
| The Hunters | 1710 | -85 | 7225 |
| The Duvalls | 1245 | -550 | 302,500 |

$$\text{Mean} = \Sigma X/N = \frac{10770}{6} = 1795 \qquad \Sigma x = 0 \qquad \Sigma x^2 = 590712$$

$$\text{Variance} = \Sigma x^2/N = \frac{590712}{6} = 98452$$

$$\text{SD} = \sqrt{\text{Variance}} = 313.77$$

**FIGURE 11–5** Hypothetical distribution of weekly family income for households on one block in Comanche, Oklahoma

$1,795/week. To gain some grasp of the variability of scores about the mean, we calculate the variance. The **variance** is defined as the average of the squared deviations about the mean. Understanding the logic and calculations used to determine the variance requires that we address the notion of deviation scores.

As Figure 11–5 shows, a deviation score $(x)$ is derived by subtracting a raw score from the mean of the distribution. Of course, if all scores in the distribution were the same, $x$ would always be 0. In a heterogenous distribution such as the one in Figure 11–5, however, $x$ takes on nonzero values (plus or minus), the sum of which is 0. Because the sum of the deviation scores always equals 0, we must square each deviation score to preserve its meaning (fourth column). By averaging these squared values we arrive at an index of the variability in the distribution—we calculate the statistic known as the variance.

It is possible to have two distributions that have the same mean but that differ dramatically in terms of dispersion of scores about the mean. It should be apparent from the sample in Figure 11–5 that the farther the scores from the mean, the greater the individual deviation scores $(x)$ and consequently the greater the calculated variance. The variance statistic, then, communicates, in numerical terms, information about the spread in the distribution.

The problem with using the variance to indicate variability is that variance is not technically reported on the same dimension as are the mean and raw scores used in its calculation. Take a closer look at the variance reported in Figure 11–5. You see that it is not expressed in dollars, but as an average of "squared dollars." Practically speaking, squared dollars make no sense, so we must do something to get our index of variability back on the same scale of measurement as the raw scores comprising the original distribution. This leads us to the SD.

**The Standard Deviation.** The **standard deviation** (SD) is the square root of the variance. As we can see from Figure 11–5, when we take the square root of the variance, we render a value that is on the same scale as the values of the original distribution. In this case, our SD value is expressed in terms of "dollars," which makes considerably greater sense than "squared dollars." Therefore, the SD affords an index of variability that is more meaningful than the variance.

It should be noted that another reason for obtaining the SD for a given distribution is that the SD is an essential component of many additional statistical calculations. Because the purpose of this text is not to detail such advanced statistical manipulations, it suffices here that you understand that such operations are necessary in inferential statistics and that without them psychologists would be constrained when trying to uncover the meaning of their data. Therefore, the SD statistic is an important element of the overall research enterprise.

Let's briefly return to the normal distribution that was introduced in the Spotlight on Research section earlier in this chapter. Recall from that discussion that one of the most critical features of the normal curve is that if we know something about where an individual score falls on the normal curve, we can say something about how probable that score is. That is, if we can define the area under the curve we can estimate the number of times out of 100 that we would expect to obtain a particular score. With the aid of z scores, we can enter the normal distribution and make more deliberate statements about the meaning of individual scores in the distribution.

**Z Scores.** A **z score** is calculated according to the following formula:

$$z = \frac{raw\ score - mean}{SD}$$

By definition, z scores indicate, in SD units, how far raw scores deviate from the mean. One of the chief uses of z scores is to enter the normal distribution. Because the normal distribution has μ (the population mean) equal to 0 and an SD equal to 1 (see Figure 11–4), the SD values of the normal distribution correspond to z scores of the same value.

> **variance**—the arithmetic average of the squared deviations about the mean
>
> **standard deviation (SD)**—the square root of the variance
>
> **z score**—a value that indicates, in SD units, how much a given raw score in the distribution differs from the mean

Because it is possible to calculate the mean and SD for any distribution of scores, it is possible to define the corresponding point on the normal distribution for any given value as long as the scores from the distribution that were used to calculate the z score are also normally distributed.

Figure 11–6 shows how z scores might be useful in making statements about a particular IQ score on the Wechsler Adult Intelligence Scale. Because the mean on this test is always 100 and the SD is 15, it follows that based on the z score formula presented earlier that an IQ of 115 corresponds to a z score value of +1 $\left( \dfrac{115-100}{15} = \dfrac{15}{15} = +1 \right)$. From the normal distribution in Figure 11–4, we know that approximately 84% of the population falls below this point. More important for inferential statistics and decision making, we can say that the chances of obtaining an IQ score greater than 115 is only 16 out of 100 (roughly 16% of the population falls above a z score value of +1).

Now that we have some elementary understanding of variability, SD, and z scores, we are in a position to address the importance of these issues for sam-

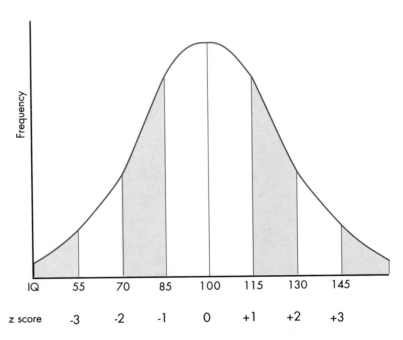

**FIGURE 11–6** A normal distribution of IQ scores (mean = 100, SD = 15) and their corresponding z score equivalents. Refer to Figure 11-4 for the percentages of the distribution falling between specific z score values.

pling distributions. The topic of primary interest along these lines is sampling error.

**Sampling Error.** Recall from our previous discussion of the sampling distribution of the mean and the Central Limit Theorem that the distribution of sample means will have a mean equal to the population mean. However, should we draw only one sample from the population, it is likely that the mean of this sample ($\bar{X}$) will differ from the population mean ($\mu$). It can be further assumed that when samples are repeatedly selected from the population there will be variable sample mean values. Some samples will be close estimates of the population mean, while others will be considerably off the mark. The difference between a sample mean and a population mean is defined as **sampling error.**

As noted in previous sections, the SD is perhaps the most useful method for expressing the degree of variability in a distribution, and the situation is no different when we deal with the sampling distribution of the mean. The standard deviation of a sampling distribution is referred to as the standard error, and when we talk about the sampling distribution of the mean, the SD is called the **standard error of the mean ($SD_{\bar{x}}$).** The standard error of the mean is calculated as:

$$SD_{\bar{x}} = \frac{SD}{\sqrt{N}}$$

Therefore, if we know the SD of the population from which the sample means have been drawn, we can derive the $SD_{\bar{x}}$ by dividing the SD of the population by the square root of the sample size $N$ (the number of observations that went into forming each sample mean).

*Why is it valuable to know* that the sampling distribution of the mean has a mean equal to the population mean ($\mu$) and a SD equal to $SD_{\bar{x}}$? One of the chief reasons relates to the aforementioned Central Limit Theorem. Remember that the Central Limit Theorem states that with large sample sizes the sampling distribution of the mean approximates a normal distribution, regardless of the form of the original population of scores. This places us in an extremely advantageous position with respect to using z scores. Recall that when z scores are derived from a normal distribution, as they would be with the sampling distribution of the mean, we can use the normal curve to tell us the probability of obtaining a particular z score value. Given this information, it is possible to make probability statements about how likely it is that a particular sample mean came from a specified population. Simply take the sample mean value, subtract it from the mean of the distribution of sample means ($\mu$) and divide it by the standard error of the mean ($SD_{\bar{x}}$) to obtain the z score equivalent of the sample mean value. Apply the

**sampling error**—an error that occurs when the sample mean differs from the population mean

**standard error of the mean ($SD_{\bar{x}}$)**—the standard deviation of the sampling distribution of the mean

resulting z score value to the normal curve and you can see how probable it is that you would obtain the sample mean value given the population mean.

To illustrate how we may answer questions about populations based on what we see in sample means, assume that we are concerned with making statements about the representativeness of a sample mean that was obtained from a randomly selected group of collegiate women volleyball players. Each of 36 participants have completed the Profile of Mood States (POMS), which provides an index of overall mood disturbance. Other sources have indicated that the population of women volleyball players has a mean ($\mu$) on this self-report questionnaire equal to 100 and a SD equal to 12. As Figure 11–7 shows, because the mean of our sample of 36 players is 104, the z score equivalent is +2. We arrived at this figure by subtracting our sample mean (104) from the mean of the sampling distribution and dividing this result by the standard error ($12/\sqrt{36}$, or 2). Entering the normal distribution (Figure 11–4), we see that the probability of obtaining a random sample with a mean value of 104 from this population is approximately 2.5 in 100. (Only about 2.5% of the population falls above a z score value of +2.) Needless to say, this raises concerns about the representativeness of the sample.

Using the sampling distribution of the mean in this way helps psychology researchers make decisions about treatment effects (I discuss this in greater detail later in the sections on Statistical Inference and Decision Making in this chapter). If we know whether a treatment mean is likely to have been drawn from a specific population, we are able to speak more persuasively about the significance of our findings.

Sample mean = 104
Population SD = 12
Population mean = 100

$$z = \frac{x - \bar{x}}{SD}$$

$$z = \frac{\bar{x} - \mu}{SD_{\bar{x}}} \quad \text{for sampling distribution of the mean}$$

$$z = \frac{104 - 100}{12/\sqrt{36}}$$

$$z = \frac{4}{2}$$

$$z = +2$$

FIGURE 11–7 The z score value of the mean of a sample of 36 volleyball players who completed the POMS. (The population mean for the scale is 100; the SD is 12.)

## *Other Sampling Distributions*

Before we discuss how the sampling distribution of the mean helps psychologists make decisions about treatment effects, it should be mentioned that other types of sampling distributions exist. In fact, every statistic has a sampling distribution with its own SD and mean, which are referred to as the standard error and **expected value,** respectively. For example, the median statistic or middle score that was discussed in Chapter 5 has a sampling distribution with a standard error of the median and an expected value of the median.

One distribution that is of concern here is the **sampling distribution of a proportion.** The proportion is simply the frequency of an event divided by the potential frequency of that event (Guilford & Fruchter, 1973). Examples of proportions are the proportion of the population under age 25, the proportion of federal judges who are women, the proportion of registered voters who actually cast ballots, and the proportion of high school seniors who attend college. In all these cases the number of times an event occurred is compared to the number of times that event could have occurred.

Like sampling means from a population, a proportion obtained from one sample may or may not provide a good estimate of the proportion of the parent population. In order to determine the accuracy of a sample proportion, we need to know something about the sampling distribution of a proportion. Specifically, the standard error of the proportion ($SD_p$) is calculated as:

$$SD_p = \frac{(p_s)(q)}{N}$$

where   $SD_p$ = standard error of a proportion
  $p_s$ = sample proportion
  $q$  = $1-p_s$
  $N$  = sample size

As *N* becomes larger, the sampling distribution of a proportion becomes more normal. Once again, the z score statistic can be used to help determine whether a sample proportion differs from a population proportion. Simply subtract the sample proportion from the proportion of the parent population and divide the result by the standard error of a proportion. This figure is the z score equivalent of the sample proportion. Enter the normal distribution (Figure 11-4) and you will be able to determine whether the sample proportion represents the population proportion.

For example, a situation may arise where a politician wants to know if her constituents hold the same attitudes about trimming the defense

**expected value**—a value like the mean that is the most representative score from a distribution

**sampling distribution of a proportion**—a sampling distribution that is created by repeatedly drawing proportions from a common population of proportions

budget as the rest of the nation. Assume that the proportion of people nationally who favor cutting defense spending is .61. In the politician's conservative district however, only 47 of the 100 people sampled indicated that they support reducing federal defense spending. Is this enough of a difference to warrant concern? Figure 11–8 provides evidence that the politician should take notice of local attitudes.

So we see that other sampling distributions may be useful in research. However, the sampling distribution of the mean is of primary utility in psychological research. As we shall see in the next section, comparisons of sample mean values permit experimenters to say when an independent variable has an effect and when it doesn't.

$$SD_p = \sqrt{\frac{(P_s)(q)}{N}} = \sqrt{\frac{(47)(.53)}{100}} = \sqrt{.0025} = .05$$

Using the z score formula:

$$z = \frac{P_s - P_k}{SD_p}$$

where $P_s$ = Obtained sample proportion

$P_k$ = Known population proportion

SD = Standard error of the proportion

z is calculated:

$$z = \frac{.47 - .61}{.05} = -2.8$$

The probability of this z statistic, and thus the sample proportion on which it is based, is less than 1 in 100. Therefore, the sample value likely comes from a different parent population (i.e., local attitudes differ from national attitudes).

FIGURE 11–8 Calculation of a z score based on a sample proportion of people favoring cutting defense spending

1. Samples of 20 are drawn 1,000 times from a common population and the mean of each sample is calculated. If the means are plotted, what is the resulting distribution called? Without knowing anything about the form of the underlying population, can anything be said about the character of the newly created distribution?
2. What is meant by the term "sampling error"?

# STATISTICAL INFERENCE AND DECISION MAKING

In any experiment, the researcher must make decisions about treatment effects. Comparing groups receiving different levels of an independent variable always reveals some differences because no two groups are ever exactly alike. The real issue is how much the conditions differ. Has the experimental manipulation produced a pattern of scores that would not be expected under control conditions? Do the groups represent a common underlying population or do they represent different populations?

Although it can never be determined with certainty that a treatment manipulation has produced a real effect, we can use **statistical inference** to tell us how probable it is that a treatment effect occurred. Statistical inference involves making statements about populations based on sample characteristics.

The simplest application of inferential statistics involves comparing one control group and one treatment group. The data from each of these groups can be considered a sample from a larger population data set. In addition, the mean of each sample can be viewed as an estimate of a population mean. As Figure 11–9 illustrates, the control sample ($\bar{X}_C$) and the treatment sample ($\bar{X}_T$) may come from the same population. Therefore, their respective means are estimates of one parent value. In such a case, any differences between the sample data sets can be attributed to sampling error. When sampling error accounts for the only difference between a control group and a treatment group, the treatment effect is said to be nonsignificant.

Now let's assume that the control sample and the treatment sample have been drawn from population data sets with very different means (see Figure 11–10). Each sample mean value and each sample SD are estimates of separate, nonoverlapping distributions (i.e., scores in one

**statistical inference**—a decision about population characteristics that is based on sample data

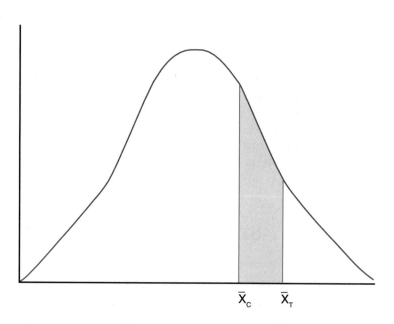

$\overline{X}_c$ = Control sample mean

$\overline{X}_T$ = Treatment sample mean

**FIGURE 11–9** A control sample mean and a treatment sample mean drawn from the same population

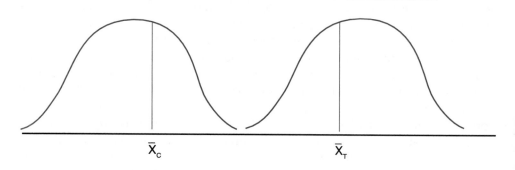

$\overline{X}_c$ = Control sample mean

$\overline{X}_T$ = Treatment sample mean

**FIGURE 11–10** A control sample mean and a treatment sample mean drawn from different populations

distribution do not appear in the other distribution). When the mean of a treatment sample and the mean of a control sample estimate different population characteristics, the treatment effect is said to be significant.

Implicit in a statement of statistical significance is the belief that the treatment manipulation caused the scores to be different. Specifically, the population of scores on which the treatment sample mean is based has been displaced by the independent variable. Take a conditioned punishment study in animal learning as an example. One group of rats lever presses for food reward (control sample). The lever responses of a second group produce both food and an electric foot shock (treatment sample). Because the shock applications in the second group shift the population of lever responses downward (the frequency is reduced), the mean of the treatment sample will be lower than the mean of the control sample. Similarly, when reading scores for a group of fourth-graders who are given special instruction improve significantly, it's because the instructional procedures caused the entire population of reading scores to increase. Because the treatment and control samples are alike in every respect except for the value of the independent variable, the displacement in population characteristics must be due to the effects of the treatment.

In most psychology experiments, comparisons are more elaborate than simply assessing the difference between one control sample and one treatment sample. Certainly this is true for our model experiment, which has been the consistent focus of this book. Once again, our model experiment involves a 2 age range (4- to 6-year-olds, 10- to12-year-olds) × 3 types of treatment (cognitive coping strategy, sensory information, and contact control) factorial design. Comparisons of treatment effectiveness will be made at both age ranges, with particular interest given to the relative benefits of cognitive therapy for older as opposed to younger children.

Note that we are dealing with six independent samples in our 2 × 3 model experiment. For each of the six conditions that is created by interacting age and treatment, a sample mean value will be determined for each of three dependent measures (the OSBD, a self-report of pain, and heart rate [HR]). At issue is whether these sample means will be estimates of the same or different populations. If it is determined that the sample means have been drawn from a common population, then age and type of therapy will be declared nonsignificant. Conversely, if it becomes clear that the independent sample means represent distinctively different parent populations, a significant effect of the independent variable manipulation would be inferred.

Therefore, depending on the design, one or several comparisons of sample means may take place. Whatever the number of comparisons, the objective is the same: to estimate population characteristics based on sample data and to determine if the treatment had a genuine effect on the distribution of scores.

## What's Error and What's Not?

The discussion thus far has assumed a dichotomous decision-making scheme. Instances of drawing samples from one common population or nonoverlapping populations are graphically portrayed in Figures 11–9 and 11–10. In actuality, research psychologists rarely work with such convenient distributions. The bulk of distributions, whether they are based on animal or human subject data, are tied to laboratory or field research, or are theoretical or empirical, will overlap.

Overlapping distributions raise an exceedingly important question, especially when we deal with sampling distributions of means. When a sample mean value is obtained, is it possible to use that value to estimate two different population means? The answer is "yes." Of course, depending on where the sample mean falls in the respective distributions, it may be a good or a poor estimate of the population mean. Figure 11–11 illustrates how one sample mean closely estimates one population mean while misrepresenting a second. Note that sampling error is involved in both instances; it's just greater in one case.

We see from Figure 11–11 that our chances of getting the indicated sample mean value are pretty good if we consider only the population on the left. In contrast, we would obtain this same sample mean value very infrequently should we consider only the population on the right. Based on an awareness of the precise probability that a mean value could come from a given control or from a treatment population, we are able to make decisions concerning treatment effects.

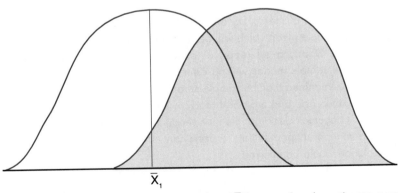

$\overline{X}_1$

**FIGURE 11–11** One sample mean value ($\overline{X}_1$) may closely estimate one population while misrepresenting a second.

If we extend the logic of this case, which involves one sample mean, to a case that involves two sample means, we can express the probability that the means estimate the same or different population means. Regarding treatment effects, it is possible to make statements about how probable it is that a treatment sample mean and a control sample mean came from a common parent population. If it is highly unlikely that the treatment mean was drawn from the population that produced the control mean, then we can infer that the treatment displaced the scores relative to the control condition, thereby creating a separate population of values (i.e., a significant treatment effect has been observed).

**Return to the Null Hypothesis.** In Chapter 2, the importance of stating the **null hypothesis** was addressed. Because it is not possible to prove that a relation between two or more variables exists, we must approach our topic from a different perspective. That is, we must state that there is no relation between or among variables and set up a test that permits us to reject this assertion (the null hypothesis).

For example, suppose that our experiment deals with the effects of social facilitation on motor performance. Our formal hypothesis, or **alternative hypothesis** as it often called, states that performance on a pegboard task will improve as we increase the number of onlookers watching the subject perform. The idea is that the larger the group of onlookers, the greater the subject's arousal and the greater the subject's motivation to do well on this task, which measures manual dexterity (Zajonc, 1965).

When testing is completed, it is clear that the experimental conditions that employed greater numbers of onlookers produced increased performance of the subject on the pegboard task. As we discussed in Chapter 2, however, we can never say with certainty that the enhanced performance was caused by the increased arousal associated with larger groups of onlookers. What we can say, however, is that the manipulation of the independent variable produced a pattern of results that is not likely to be due to chance variation—we reject the null hypothesis. In showing that the null hypothesis is false, we indirectly offer support that the alternative hypothesis is true.

Rejecting the null hypothesis and the argument that the independent variable has an effect on the dependent variable is directly linked to sampling distributions and statistical inference. When we set up the null hypothesis, in effect we say that the means of all treatment groups come from a common population. The differences between the mean value of an untreated sample and the mean values of treatment groups that received different manipulations of the independent variable are due to sampling error. The degree of sampling error can be determined with the standard error of the mean, as was discussed in the previous section on sampling distributions. This rationale only extends so far, however, and then we must

**null hypothesis**—a statement that two groups are not different

**alternative hypothesis**—a statement that the treatment effect produces a significant change in the value of the dependent variable

question whether the mean differences reflect sampling error or whether the means were drawn from separate populations.

Based on probability statements about sampling error, we may be able to argue in favor of a treatment effect. If the observed mean differences between untreated (control) and treated samples are sufficiently great that it is highly improbable that these differences could occur due to sampling error, then something must have produced a different population of scores in the treatment group. Insofar as sources of variation other than those associated with the independent variable have been controlled, there is reason to believe that the treatment manipulation is responsible for displacing scores and creating a new population of values. By rejecting the null hypothesis, we are saying that the untreated and treated sample means have not been drawn from the same population and that it is highly likely that the different populations are a result of the treatment application. The key phrase here is "highly likely." Again, nothing is ever absolute in inferential statistics.

## Statistical Significance

By this time, you may be reeling from all the uncertainty. When are the means from different populations and when are they not? At what point is sampling error no longer a viable reason for the observed differences between sample means? Are there guidelines that can help judge sampling error and treatment effects?

Fortunately, theoretical statisticians and researchers have agreed on a few basic rules that help us maneuver this guesswork. When comparing samples from a common parent population, it makes sense that small mean group differences will be more likely than large mean group differences. Indeed, were we to draw an infinitely large number of samples two at a time from one population, we would see that the sampling distribution of mean difference scores would take the form of the distribution in Figure 11–12. If we assume that the mean of this distribution is 0 and that as we move away from the mean we begin dealing with greater and greater sample mean differences, it becomes clear that the estimated frequency of an extreme difference is virtually nil. Moreover, it is apparent that 99% of all sample comparisons would likely include chance sample mean differences that would be greater than 95% of all sample comparisons. It follows that if you want to allow for cases of sampling error that produce really large differences between sample mean values, you need to include most of the total sampling distribution of mean difference scores.

As noted earlier, at some point we must consider that the observed sample mean difference came from another distribution. In other words, rather than as-

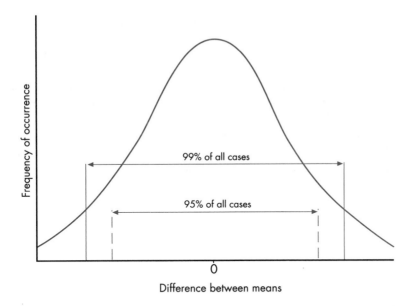

**FIGURE 11–12 Sampling distribution of mean difference scores**

suming that chance variation accounts for the sample mean difference we see, we must consider that the difference was created because samples were drawn from different populations (a treatment effect has occurred). At what point do chance interpretations give way to treatment effects? For experimental psychology, convention holds that if the observed mean difference value would occur in a given sampling distribution of mean difference scores fewer than 5 times in 100, then the means are probably drawn from different populations and sampling error (chance) is not the issue. This criterion is typically referred to as the **significance level.** It is a statement of probability that an observed mean difference is due strictly to chance.

When a comparison of mean differences yields a statistic such as a *t*-test (see following) which tells us that the difference between treatment groups would occur fewer than 5 times in 100 based on chance alone, that comparison is said to reach an acceptable level for statistical significance. If an investigator wants to be very cautious and even more certain that chance is not an issue, a significance level of .01 may be used instead of .05. This means that you would obtain a mean difference of this magnitude simply because of chance only 1 time in 100. Whether you adopt a .05 or a .01 criterion, it should be understood that the investigator sets the criterion before the

**significance level**—a statement of probability that an observed mean difference is due to chance

**Type I error**—the act of stating that a treatment effect exists when it does not

**Type II error**—the act of accepting the null hypothesis when it is false (when a treatment effect exists)

experiment is conducted. Once the significance level is set, it is not to be changed.

Implicit in what I have said here is the notion that inaccurate statements may be made. When I say that a mean difference is statistically significant at the .05 level, I am not saying that sampling error could not account for the difference between means; I am just saying that it is unlikely. Similarly, when a sample mean difference fails to reach an acceptable level for statistical significance, this does not rule out the possibility that the means were drawn from different populations (the treatment does have an effect). Although such sampling outcomes are not probable, they are possible. These matters relate to Type I and Type II errors.

## *Type I and Type II Errors*

Intuitively, it would seem that errors in decision making could be avoided by invoking extremely conservative criteria. If you want to be absolutely certain that a treatment manipulation really produces an effect when you say that it does, why not set the significance level to 1 in 1,000? If you find that your means are significantly different, you are virtually assured that chance played no role in the separation between means. It is not this simple, however. When you adopt such stringent significance criteria, you are more likely to make mistakes of a different sort.

Figure 11–13 profiles the four possible outcomes in statistical decision making. Cell 1 shows the situation where the null hypothesis ($H_o$) reflects the true state of affairs and you correctly fail to reject it. In this instance you accurately indicate that the treatment (independent variable) had no effect on the value of the dependent variable. However, it is possible that based on the selected samples you reject the null hypothesis even though it is true (Cell 2). This is known as a **Type I error**. You mistakenly state that the treatment produced an effect when the only reason for the separation between means was sampling error. Typically, the probability of a Type I error is expressed as alpha ($\partial$).

Now consider Cells 3 and 4 in Figure 11–13. If the null hypothesis is indeed false and you correctly reject it, you have appropriately identified a legitimate treatment effect. However, if a true treatment effect exists and, based on your sample data you fail to reject the null hypothesis, then you have committed a **Type II error.** By committing a Type II error you have effectively overlooked a meaningful relation between the independent and dependent variables. The probability of making a Type II error is expressed as beta ($\beta$).

The true situation

| The decision made based on sample data | | H₀ True | H₀ False |
|---|---|---|---|
| | Retain H₀ | 1. Correct decision | 3. Type II error |
| | Reject H₀ | 2. Type I error | 4. Correct decision |

**FIGURE 11–13** Type I and Type II errors

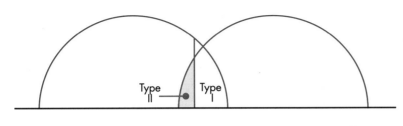

Alpha at .05

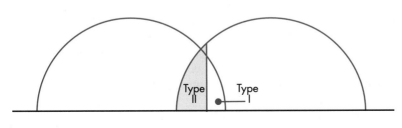

Alpha at .01

**FIGURE 11–14** The effects of shifting the alpha level on Type I and Type II errors

Although it is possible in some cases to manipulate the values of alpha and beta independently, mostly the relation between the two is an inverse one—as alpha goes up, beta goes down, and vice versa. As Figure 11–14 shows, when alpha (the significance level) is set at .01 instead of at .05 for hypothethical nontreatment and treatment populations, the chances of making a Type II error increase. By choosing a lower alpha level you may increase your confidence that if a significant mean difference appears it is legitimate, but you also increase your chances of overlooking a real effect. The reverse is true going the other way. When you adopt an alpha of .05 instead of .01, you minimize Type II errors but elevate the risk of stating that there is a treatment effect when there is none.

Given this, what is to be done? Is there a rule or conventional policy on when to set the significance level higher or lower? Unfortunately, no. Ultimately the investigator must consider the consequences of making one type of error or the other and adjust accordingly.

## Thinking About Research

Assume that you must test the abilities of various chemical compounds to retard AIDS symptoms for the NIH. You are commissioned to conduct the study blind, with no knowledge of the history of the test compound.

In selecting the significance level you weigh the relative risks associated with Type I and Type II errors. If you opt for a smaller alpha level, there is security in knowing that the drug produced real benefits, but there is also a greater chance of missing an opportunity for identifying a desperately needed medical intervention. Alternatively, what happens if you relax the significance level? The chances of passing up on a breakthrough are reduced, but the chances of misleading the medical community with respect to recommending a treatment for AIDS goes up. On further reflection, you realize a Type II error may halt research. If a compound that actually offers some benefits for AIDS victims is shown falsely to have no effect, the compound may not receive further consideration and a rare opportunity will be lost. This, of course, would be a tragedy. You determine, however, that a Type I error would be worse. To present a bogus drug to an AIDS sufferer would mean causing unspeakable torment and perhaps delaying additional efforts to find a legitimate therapy. Therefore, you decide to set a very stringent alpha level and live with overlooking a true effect, ultimately relying on continuing research efforts until a suitable treatment is identified.

This is one case where there is a clear rationale for setting a particular significance level. Under other conditions the choices may not be so straightforward, but usually careful deliberation will lead an investigator to favor taking a chance on a particular type of error. Can you think of other situations where Type I errors would be more tolerable than Type II errors? What about the reverse situation?    ■

## WITHIN CHAPTER REVIEW AND STUDY QUESTIONS

### STATISTICAL INFERENCE AND DECISION MAKING

1. _____ involves making statements about populations based on sample characteristics.
2. How does sampling error relate to statistical decision making?
3. What is the difference between a Type I error and a Type II error? How are the two interrelated?

# POWER AND EFFECT SIZE

In recent years, decision making has begun to focus more on events that contribute to being correct rather than being wrong. For example, instead of speaking in terms of Type II errors, statisticians have concentrated on power (Rosenthal, 1994). **Power** is defined as the probability of correctly rejecting the null hypothesis (Cell 4 in Figure 11–13). Power is calculated as 1 - beta (probability of a Type II error). Therefore, if beta is .25, power has a probability of .75 (1 - .25). This means that if the null hypothesis is false, 75 times out of 100 the results from our experiment will lead to a correct rejection of the null.

Although it is not discussed in detail here, recognize that it is possible to increase the power of a test, (e.g., by increasing sample size), without altering the alpha level (the probability of a Type I error). Then why don't we always make a test as powerful as we can so that we virtually ensure we will not overlook a real treatment effect? The answer rests with effect size.

**Effect size** refers to the difference between the population mean as specified by the alternative hypothesis and the population mean as specified by the null hypothesis. Effect size, then, defines how much the distribution resulting from our treatment and the distribution as characterized under the null hypothesis (where no treatment effect exists) are separated. The problem, as it relates to power, is that a test can be made so powerful that even minuscule, meaningless effect sizes will be detected as significant. For example, say we are interested in the impact of an educational program on student scores on the Medical College Admissions Test (MCAT). Theoretically, it would be possible to test so many subjects that even a 1-point difference between the treated condition and a control condition would yield a significant effect. That is, the power of the test could be

**power**—the probability of correctly rejecting the null hypothesis

**effect size**—the difference between the population mean as specified by the alternative hypothesis and the population mean as specified by the null hypothesis increased to a level where a legitimate, but practically unimportant, effect would be detected.

Therefore, while it is nice to avoid Type II errors, real-world issues and the influence of power on those issues must be considered. Probably the safest thing to do is to report the effect size with information about statistical significance and let the reader decide if the reported differences actually mean anything (Hurlburt, 1994).

## WITHIN CHAPTER REVIEW AND STUDY QUESTION

### POWER AND EFFECT SIZE

1. What is the danger of designing an experiment that is too powerful?

## CHOOSING THE APPROPRIATE STATISTICAL TEST

Throughout this chapter, I have addressed issues relating to sampling distributions, error, and decision making. One theme has been that variation must be considered when determining treatment effects. Any two treatment groups or samples will differ, even when the independent variable has no effect, just as subject scores within the same group will differ. The task of the experimental psychologist, then, is to assess how many of the differences (variation) are due to chance and how many are due to the treatment manipulation. But precisely how is this assessed? What tests are available to evaluate the strength of a treatment effect that takes chance variation into account?

Actually, many statistical tests yield this exact information. I mention only the t-test and analysis of variance (ANOVA) here. See Howell (1995) for more extensive and sophisticated coverage of these and other statistical procedures.

### The t-test

The most elementary experimental comparison involves two samples. This may take the form of comparing a conventional control condition and an experimental condition (see Chapter 8), or two groups that have received differing levels of the independent variable. When two groups from a between-subjects design are compared, the **independent samples t-test** provides a numerical index of the relation between groups.

The t-test formula is:

$$ t = \frac{\overline{x}_1 - \overline{x}_2}{\sqrt{\frac{\left(\sum X_1^2 - \frac{(\sum X_1)^2}{N_1}\right) + \left(\sum X_2^2 - \frac{(\sum X_2)^2}{N_2}\right)\left(\frac{1}{N_1} + \frac{1}{N_2}\right)}{(N_1 + N_2 - 2)}}} $$

where
$X_1$ = individual subject scores in Group 1
$X_2$ = individual subject scores in Group 2
$\overline{X}_1$ = mean of Group 1,
$\overline{X}_2$ = mean of Group 2
$N$ = the respective number of subjects in Groups 1 and 2

For our purposes here, it suffices to note that this formula represents a ratio of the difference between two sample means **(between-groups variability)** and the average variation among subjects in each group **(within-group variability)**. In effect, the mean separation between groups is evaluated and adjusted for the pattern of scores individual subjects exhibit. As the ratio increases, either because of greater mean differences or smaller within-group variation, the greater the probability of a treatment effect. Therefore, the larger the t statistic, the less likely that the observed differences result from chance.

Figure 11–15 illustrates how the t statistic for the grade point averages (GPAs) of two groups of second-year college students is computed (a hypothetical case). One group has undergone training on "How to Study in College" (the experimental group), while the other has not (the control group). We see that a t value of 3.00 is calculated.

But what does a calculated t value of 3.00 mean? What do we do now? As with any test statistic, t has a distribution with an expected value and SD (see previous discussion in this chapter). Because t is an index of true mean differences when no treatment effect is suggested, the expected value of t is 0. Conversely, as t increases, it falls further out on the distribution and offers a statement of probability that the means are from different populations (a treatment effect exists). Because

**independent samples t-test**—a test which yields a numerical value that indicates whether or not two means differ significantly

**between groups variability**—difference between groups

**within-group variability**—difference in scores of subjects within the same group

| Group I (has undergone training) | Group II (no training) |
|---|---|
| GPA | GPA |
| 3.41 | 2.54 |
| 3.16 | 3.10 |
| 2.98 | 2.10 |
| 2.95 | 2.40 |
| 3.26 | 2.80 |
| $\sum X_1 = 15.76$ | $\sum X_2 = 12.94$ |
| $\sum X_1^2 = 49.80$ | $\sum X_2^2 = 34.07$ |
| $N = 5$ | $N = 5$ |
| $\overline{X} = 3.15$ | $\overline{X} = 2.58$ |

$$t = \frac{3.15 - 2.58}{\sqrt{\dfrac{49.80 - \dfrac{(15.76)^2}{5} + 34.07 - \dfrac{(12.44)^2}{5}}{5 + 5 - 2}\left(\dfrac{1}{5} + \dfrac{1}{5}\right)}}$$

$$t = \frac{.59}{.19}$$

$$t = 3.00$$

FIGURE 11–15 The calculation of the t statistic based on the GPA for two groups of college students, one of which had taken a "How to Study in College" course and one of which had not

statisticians have provided a detailed description of the character of the t distribution, we can determine precisely where on the distribution our calculated t falls. Moreover, the associated probability statements based on the value of t permit us to comment on the likelihood that our mean differences have occurred simply as a result of chance.

This brings us back to "significance levels." When the significance level for t is set at .05, we must obtain a calculated value of t that could occur by chance only 5 times in 100. Without getting too involved in the theory, accept for now that for samples of a given size we know what critical value of t on the t distribution corresponds to the .05 significance level. Accordingly, if our calculated value of t exceeds this critical t value, it is safe to say that our observed mean differences are such that fewer than 5 times in 100 would we obtain such mean separation due to chance variation. Therefore, the null hypothesis of no differences between the two groups is rejected.

Returning to the data set in Figure 11–15, we recall that our calculated t statistic is 3.00. Based on the sample size and the related degrees of freedom ($[N_1 + N_2]$ - 2), it is possible to enter a lengthy table (not presented in this book but reproduced in Hurlburt, 1994) and find the value of t that corresponds to the .05 significance level for this comparison. This table value is 2.306, and our calculated value for t exceeds it. Therefore, we reject the null hypothesis and conclude that the "How to Study in College" sessions affected GPA.

As mentioned earlier, in most instances experimental psychologists in the 1990s deal with more elaborate designs involving more than two groups. Certainly that is the case for the model experiment we are building in this book. Let's turn to a statistical test that is used when multiple experimental groups are involved in the design.

## *Analysis of Variance*

When three or more levels of the independent variable are of interest to the investigator, the **analysis of variance (ANOVA)** test is appropriate. The ANOVA is based on the same logic of the t-test, but the ANOVA is applied to more complex designs. As with the t-test, the total variation in the experiment is partitioned into between-groups variability and within-groups variability. Essentially, the F-ratio statistic that is formed by the ANOVA test is determined by the size of the treatment effect plus error relative to error alone (see Figure 11–16). Conceptually, the ANOVA test looks at multiple group differences that occur independent of chance variation.

From this it follows that when there is no treatment effect (i.e., treatment + error = error), the F-ratio is 1. As with the t-test, the F-ratio is distributed with known probabilities for each value of the statistic. When the value of *F* exceeds the table value associated with a particular significance level, say .05, we say that a treatment effect has been produced. That is, one of the three or more groups differs from the others such that it cannot be reduced to simple chance factors.

The most elementary type of ANOVA is the **one-way analysis of variance (ANOVA).** In the one-way ANOVA, multiple groups are compared on only one independent variable. For example, suppose we are interested in the effects of differing levels of incentive on the performance of 10-year-olds in a probability learning situation. We would compare high, medium, and low incentive conditions and determine the ratio of between-groups variability to within-groups variability (the precise mathematical manipulations and formulas need not be presented here; refer to Gravetter and Wallnau, 1995, for further information). We would then compare the resulting value of *F* to the appropriate table value, which

**analysis of variance (ANOVA)**—a test for assessing significant differences between three or more groups

**one-way analysis of variance (ANOVA)**—statistical test in which groups are compared on only one independent variable

**two-way analysis of variance (ANOVA)**—statistical test for examining group differences when two or more independent variables are included in the experimental design

would be determined by the number of groups and the total number of observations in the experiment. If the observed value was greater than the table value, then incentive would have produced a true effect.

When the effects of two independent variables are examined in the same experiment, a **two-way analysis of variance (ANOVA)** test is used. With this test, the ratio of between-groups variability and within-group variability is again established, but this time for each independent variable. The result is that separate F-ratios must be determined for each variable, compared to their respective table values, and the statistical significance of each determined accordingly. In addition, the F-ratio for the interaction of the two independent variables must be calculated (see the discussion of interaction effects in Chapter 8). Although technically speaking each of the F-ratio measures are interdependent, it is possible for one to reach an acceptable level for statistical significance and not the others, or for all or none to be significant.

It should be understood that when two or more independent variables are compared in the same experiment, the ANOVA is the appropriate statistical test even when only two levels of the independent variable exist for each case. For instance, should you want to examine the effects of a low and high dose of alcohol (Independent Variable 1) on the reading performance of females and males (Independent Variable 2), a two-way ANOVA is the recommended statistical test. Among other things, this procedure permits you to test for interaction effects that otherwise would go unreported.

$$\text{F-ratio} = \frac{\text{between-groups variance}}{\text{within-group variance}}$$

where

$$\frac{\text{between-groups variance}}{\text{within-group variance}} = \frac{\text{treatment effect} + \text{error}}{\text{error}}$$

When there is no treatment effect the ratio is 1.

$$\frac{0 + \text{error}}{\text{error}} = 1$$

As the treatment effect increases, the F-ratio gets larger, assuming error remains the same.

**FIGURE 11–16 The conceptual basis of the F-ratio**

Returning to the model experiment we have been building throughout this book, recall that our research agenda calls for a 2 × 3 between-subjects design. Younger (4- to 6-year-olds) and older (10- to 12-year-olds) chronically ill children will receive one of three treatment interventions (cognitive control strategy, sensory information, or contact control). Consistent with what has been stated here, it is appropriate that we employ a two-way ANOVA test. The results of this statistical approach will yield separate F-ratios for age, treatment type, and the interaction of age and treatment type. In all cases, it will be possible to declare whether there is a treatment effect that has been produced which reflects more than mere chance variability.

## *Other Statistical Procedures*

Although comments here have been restricted to between-subjects comparisons (subjects participate in only one group), recognize that appropriate statistical tests are available for other designs. Special versions of the t-test and the ANOVA test are available for within-subject designs where subjects participate in more than one condition. Because the data across groups are correlated in these experiments, special adjustment in the calculation of t and F must be made, but the basic rationale remains. You still compare obtained statistics with table values to determine the significance of treatment.

Also, depending on certain features of the collected data set, *nonparametric* statistics may be indicated. The *parametric* tests discussed in this chapter assume certain features, such as a normal distribution of scores and equal variances across groups. When the data are nonnormal or otherwise violate the assumptions of the t-test, the ANOVA, or some other parametric procedure, alternative nonparametric tests are recommended. For a complete discussion of nonparametric procedures and details on how and when to apply them, refer to Maritz (1995).

## WITHIN CHAPTER REVIEW AND STUDY QUESTION

### CHOOSING THE APPROPRIATE STATISTICAL TEST

1. Under what conditions would you use ANOVA instead of the independent sample t-test?

# The Model Experiment

The process of statistical inference is immensely important to experimental psychology. Because we rarely have access to the data from all members of a population, we must deal with sample values and estimate population characteristics. This involves error and introduces a source of variability that must be considered. By employing statistical tests that control for sampling error, the researcher assumes a more secure decision-making posture.

Because the model experiment we are building as we move through the chapters of this book incorporates two independent variables (age and treatment type), a two-way ANOVA test will be used to assess the differential benefits of cognitive intervention and other therapies on anxiety levels of younger and older chronically ill children undergoing medical treatments. This analysis will have to be performed on the three dependent variables selected for this model project (scores from the OSBD, a self-report measure of fear and pain [the fear thermometer], and heart rate [HR]). The inferences we draw based on these tests will ultimately provide answers to the questions we asked earlier in the book.

We have come a great distance in our coverage of the basic methodology in psychological research. Now it is time to put it all together.

# The Scientific Report

Looking back on what has been covered in this book, we see that we have formulated a research idea, considered our options on how to approach it, and defined the appropriate methodology for analyzing the data. Although the experiment that has been our model throughout the text actually has never been completed, we have examined the essential elements of the hypothetical project in such detail that conducting the research would be relatively simple. Indeed, at this stage executing the experiment would be akin to following a recipe—we would just move from step to step systematically to have the final product.

Well, almost. Certainly you would not meticulously follow the Waldorf Astoria recipe for Red Velvet Cake, creating a delectable dessert (trust me on this, I've done it), and then refuse to serve it to family or guest. Neither does it make sense for a scientist to elegantly design an experiment and carefully collect the data only to leave the results in a file drawer. The ultimate objective of the experiment is to communicate, and the vehicle for communication within the scientific community is *the scientific report.*

This chapter is devoted to writing the research paper that will become the mechanism of communicating the findings from our model experiment. True, we did not really collect the data for our model experiment, but then again inasmuch as it is imagined and not real, we can do whatever we want. And so, it's done. We have finished collecting the imaginary data on the effects of age on the effectiveness of cognitively oriented therapeutic interventions with chronically ill children.

# FEATURES OF SCIENTIFIC WRITING

Writing of any sort can be scary. When I began writing my first book, *Psychology,* in 1983, I took pen in hand and literally wrote the chapters. There was something wonderfully nostalgic and honorable about this style, but there were also times when an empty page prevailed, mocking me as a writer. Beads of blood would form on my forehead as I cudgeled my brain, searching for any kind of thought—not necessarily a good one, any kind would have done! Writing is a learnable skill, however, and you can learn to be effective at it. More specifically, you can be a good scientific writer, and several successful article writers have offered tips for improving your writing skills (e.g., Sternberg, 1992). Here I suggest a few of my own.

## *Keep It Short*

Successful writers, and successful scientists, are targets for seduction. They can become so enamored of their talents that they feel morally obligated to share every thought with the uninformed world. The result is often a long-winded production that could have been better presented in a more concise format.

When drafting a scientific manuscript, follow the basic guideline of presenting the information as briefly as possible. Of course, you would be remiss if you sacrificed completeness for brevity, but don't add gratuitous words and paragraphs that bloat an article and render it more difficult to read and understand. Fellow scientists, practitioners, and anyone else interested in reading the report will be working under time constraints, so don't force them to sift through insignificant rants or opinions that amuse the author more than anything else.

Crafting a scientific report is one task where it is appropriate to be economical in the use of language. Report the necessary facts, and leave lengthy compositions to other literary forums.

## *Keep It Simple*

Webster's dictionary defines a *belletrist* as "a writer of literature that is an end in itself and not practical or purely informative." The belletristic style is flowery, provocative, often stimulating cascades of creative ideas and desultory thoughts. It is also inappropriate for scientific reporting.

Some writers seem to embrace the maxim, "Obscurity is *prima facie* evidence for profundity." Of course, it is an error in syllogistic reasoning to determine that (a) most good articles are difficult to understand, (b) the article I have written is difficult to understand, so (c) therefore my article must be good. The aim of writing is not to challenge people. Rather, it is to get a message across. Therefore, don't purposely weight a scientific manuscript with words and phrases that leave the reader wondering what was said. Select *used,* not *utilized,* and *cause,* not *engender.* If you keep it simple, your reader will be grateful.

## *Broad to Narrow*

When you set out to write a scientific report, use the "funnel approach" similar to that outlined for hypothesis development in Chapter 2. Begin with broad statements and general remarks about the topic area and progress to increasingly narrower descriptions of the task at hand. This approach permits the uninitiated reader to gain some background in the topic area, and it permits the writer to lay out the logical flow of ideas that has led to the formal hypothesis. Of course, depending on the complexity of the subject matter, introductory remarks may run only a couple of paragraphs or they may require several pages. Regardless, inform your reader of general issues and then proceed to more specific concerns.

## Wrap It Up

Don't make the mistake of taking the readers to the end of the manuscript only to have them say, "Is that all there is?" Summarize the significance of your findings and highlight the points that interface with the literature in the area. When an article ends abruptly and leaves the reader to draw the conclusions, the essence of the research can get lost. No one has spent as much time with the project as you have, and no one is in as good a position as you are to identify the major findings. Therefore, take the time to complete the job.

Although there are many acceptable ways to summarize your findings, my preference is to do so in the first paragraph of the discussion section (see following), not at the end of the paper. This permits the reader to gain some perspective about the overall results before moving to the micro-analyses and mini-evaluations of the findings. It also gives rapid readers a "nutshell version" of the report and may signal them where to look for certain details.

# The APA Style

Separate from the issues of manuscript length and style of expression is the article format. By format I mean the appearance and presentation of the report's content. Because different scientific disciplines have adopted unique publication formats, and because diversity is inherent in psychological research, psychologists must write manuscripts in many different formats. The most common, and the one we will use, is that established by the American Psychological Association (APA).

The APA provides psychology researchers with detailed guidelines on how to present a written report in the fourth edition of its *Publication Manual* (1994). The 7-page seminal version of the manual, which was published as a document in the APA journal *Psychological Bulletin* in 1929, has since been expanded to a separate volume of over 300 pages. Included in the manual are instructions on appropriate style (e.g., clarity and smoothness of expression), proper citations, and order and preparation of tables and figures. These and the numerous other rules and recommendations the manual sets forth answer virtually any question a scientific writer may have about manuscript preparation. You are encouraged to read it and refer to it as needed.

Because APA currently publishes 37 different journals in dramatically different areas, a standard format is necessary. Imagine the difficulty of trying to read articles that are on a similar topic but are published in different formats. For example, a clinical psychologist interested in the molecular dynamics of human depression would likely find the results of an article in the non-APA journal *Science* at the beginning of the report, while she would find the summary from a similar study in the APA journal *Experimental and Clinical Psychopharmacology* at the end. The common format of all APA journals eliminates the need to search for information and makes the reader's job easier.

# THE FINAL REPORT

In the following pages, I present the major features and sections of the final research report using the model experiment we have built. As we write our report, I comment on the essential aspects of particular sections and, when appropriate, remark what not to do. Although the sections are presented serially and are interrupted by commentary, keep the overall picture of the manuscript in mind. As the manuscript unfolds and the picture sharpens, you will see all of what we have discussed in this book come together. The final report is the synthesis of scientific thought and ambition.

## *The Title Page*

The initial page of the manuscript is the title page and it introduces the reader first to the topic, and then to the authors. First, let's look at the title which opens the article. Do not underestimate the importance of creating a descriptive title. The title must communicate the topic of the report fully, but concisely. Because of the increased specialization in psychological research, this is not always as easy as you might think. How do you capture the topic, the relation between the independent and dependent variables, the type of subjects, and all other essential elements of the project in 10–12 words? Some writers resort to using semicolons, and I suppose this technique is preferred over omitting key information. Whatever your solution, whenever possible, keep the title brief.

Also on the title page are the names and institutional affiliations of the authors, which are typically centered immediately below the title. Although for a brief period APA publications stopped including the authors' affiliations, in 1994 the policy was reintroduced. As a rule, each author's given name is presented first, followed by the middle initial and full last name. The first author who is listed, called the lead author, has usually contributed the most to the study. Author involvement decreases as you move through the list of names.

Finally, the title page has a page header at the top right and a running head at the top of the article. The page header, which continues across pages, consists of one or two words from the title and includes the page number. The running head is an abbreviated title of no more than 50 characters. The purpose of the running head is to identify the article.

Because we have been partners in developing the model project in this book, it is appropriate that the title page appears as follows:

```
                                              Psychotherapy    1

PSYCHOTHERAPY AND AGE DIFFERENCES


                  The Effectiveness of Psychotherapy
                    for Chronically Ill Children
                         as a Function of Age
          Jack R. Nation              You A. Student
        Texas A&M University      Your College or University
```

## *The Abstract*

The second page of the research report carries the abstract. The abstract provides the reader with a complete summary of the report. For experimental and empirical articles, abstracts should be between 100 and 120 words long. The abstracts of articles that present no new data, such as review papers or theoretical essays, should be somewhat shorter (75 to 100 words long). The word *Abstract* should be centered at the top of the page and the text presented in blocked format (no paragraph indention). The abstract should be completely self-contained, and it should include a statement on why the research was conducted, a description of the methodology, a summary of the overall findings and concluding remarks. Also, it should mention the type of subjects that were used (e.g., animal-human, male-female, or child-adult), the recording instruments or apparatus, and the implications of the results.

This probably sounds like a tall order, and it should. How can you cram so much information into 120 words? You can usually find a way, but it often takes several rewrites. Don't become discouraged when at first draft you realize that you have generated a 300-word summary! Unnecessary material can be pruned, and you can eventually reduce the abstract to an acceptable length.

Keep in mind that the abstract you write for the research report will likely be the first thing other researchers see. For many, it will be the only thing they see. With the numerous computer searches that are now available (see Chapter 2), other investigators and interested individuals can access a broad number of abstracts from a broad number of publications. If you write a poor abstract and omit key information, your findings may go unnoticed because others will see no need to retrieve your full published article.

Understand that it is sometimes better to write the abstract after you have written the rest of the manuscript. For instructional purposes, I present the abstract of our model experiment now. Of course, in so doing I disclose the findings from our imaginary data set. But that's O.K. Like the novel reader, you can find out what you discovered before you read the entire research report!

Psychotherapy    2

Abstract

This study examined the relationship between age and the effectiveness of a cognitively oriented therapeutic intervention in pediatric oncology patients.  Forty-eight patients from ages 4 to 6 and 48 patients from ages 10 to 12, received treatment with a (a) cognitive coping, (b) sensory information, or (c) contact control treatment before receiving medical treatment. Behavioral observations, self-reports, and heart rate recordings were taken immediately before treatment and compared to baseline records. On the heart rate measure, the cognitive coping intervention was effective only in alleviating the older children's anxiety. Conversely, the sensory information treatment reduced only the younger children's fear. The contact control had no ameliorative effects. These data suggest that further investigations of the effect developmental parameters have on various therapeutic strategies are needed.

## Introduction

The introduction is the opening text of the manuscript, before which the title is repeated. The introduction, which unlike the abstract is not labeled "Introduction," begins with general remarks about the literature in the broad area that defines the topic of the research report. In the opening paragraph, it is a good idea to address issues relating to particular problems without discussing what you intend to do to solve those problems. Anticipated solutions and a formal statement of the hypothesis or hypotheses to be tested are stated later. Your task at this stage is not to educate but to document. Specify the area of focus and tempt the reader by underscoring the importance of the topic.

Once you have instructed the reader on the nature of the report in very general terms, the educational phase commences. Although most of your readership will possess some knowledge of the topic area, some readers will be new to the field and therefore will need some remediation. Even readers who are more familiar with the research area may not be aware of recent developments that are pertinent to your research concerns. Therefore, review previous theoretical and empirical articles that have a direct bearing on the narrow research idea that forms the basis for the research you are reporting.

The review of the literature should flow from broad to narrow, as discussed earlier. Using the funnel format, first cite those papers that relate to the research problem in an overall sense, then move to sources that are relevant to the hypothesis that was tested. For instance, for the model experiment we are reporting here, rather than immediately jump into the issue of whether cognitively based therapies for young chronically ill children are appropriate, first document that the respective cognitive apparatus of younger and older children differs in general. Before you can make assertions about the age-related constraints of cognitively oriented interventions, you must first establish that younger and older age children approach the cognitive world from different perspectives. Examine the importance of age in other arenas, such as nontherapy situations where developmental cognitive functioning has been shown to impact performance outcomes.

After referencing material that deals with age-related changes in human cognition in the nontherapeutic environment, shift the discussion to articles concerned with the interaction of cognitive ability and therapeutic effectiveness. Obviously, information on the differential effectiveness of cognitively based therapies for younger and older chronically ill children is not available, or we wouldn't have needed to conduct our study. What is available, however, are reports on developmental cognition and coping with stress (see following). Because such reports validate the importance of pursuing more explicit clinical experiments, they should be woven into the introductory narrative. Again, we move from broad to narrow.

The length of the introduction depends to a certain degree on the richness of the literature in the research area. Some topic areas are either poorly investigated or appeal to only a few. Therefore, the corresponding literature reviews would be brief. Other topics are supported by a very large pool of literature, in which case you would have to identify the essential reports. Whatever the case, economy is the key. Reference only *needed* articles. If you can make your case with fewer articles, do so.

After you have introduced the relevant literature, identified inconsistencies or missing parts of the puzzle, and clarified what is and is not known, it is time to unambiguously state the purpose of your study. Leave no doubt why you conducted the research or what you had hoped to find. In our study, we expected a cognitively oriented therapeutic intervention to be less effective in alleviating the stress of 4- to 6-year-old chronically ill children than the stress of their 10- to 12-year-old counterparts. This hypothesis was predicated on literature that questioned the ability of younger children to invoke elaborate cognitive schemas, and it should be so stated, forcefully and without hesitation. Tell the scientific community why your article deserves to be read.

The introduction for our model experiment follows.

The Effectiveness of Psychotherapy for Chronically Ill Children

as a Function of Age

The developmental aspects of human cognition have long been recognized as important determinants of performance in laboratory settings. It has been demonstrated, for instance, that younger children (5- or 6-year-olds) perform better on extradimensional discrimination tasks than on intradimensional discrimination tasks, while the opposite is true for older children (11- or 12-year-olds) (see Baddeley, 1993; Kendler & Kendler, 1967). One reason rests with the respective cognitive capacities of younger versus older children (Reese & Lipsitt, 1970). Because older children are able to invoke problem-solving strategies and to use abstract decision rules, concepts such as "opposite," which facilitate performance in an intradimensional situation, are immediately available. Conversely, younger children must rely more on their conditioning histories, so they would be expected to perform better on an extradimensional task (refer to Reese & Lipsitt, 1970, for a detailed discussion of this line of reasoning).

Recently, the notion that developmental differences in the cognitive apparatus may affect clinical phenomena has received attention (Gerralda, Kim, & Klein, 1994; Sargent & Liebman, 1985; Weekes, 1995). As a result, it is now clear that learned helplessness that results in the laboratory, which many believe to parallel clinical depression (Abramson, Seligman, & Teasdale,

1978), is more likely to occur in older rather than younger children. Parsons and Ruble (1977) showed that experiences with success and failure has more impact on 11-year-olds than on 3-year olds. That is, the older children's past performances were more likely to affect their future behavior, either positively or negatively. Rholes, Blackwell, Jordan, and Walters (1980) were able to demonstrate that younger children are less susceptible than are older children to helplessness due to age-related differences in casual attributions. Apparently, when younger children deal with failure, their diminished cognitive levels act as a buffer against the negative attributional styles that would emerge with a more elaborate mental network.

As further evidence of the importance of developmental parameters to clinical issues, several papers point to the fact that age differences are responsible for substantially different approaches in dealing with stress. Specifically, Brown, O'Keeffe, Sanders, and Baker (1986) assessed children's ability to cope with a dental injection and found that in the 8 to 18 age range the variety and total number of cognitive coping strategies increased as age increased. Similarly, Curry and Russ (1985) reported coping methods as a function of increasing age. It seems that as the overall cognitive and intellectual ability increases, the reliance on cognitive responses to cope with stressors increases as well. Even in instances of severe medical problems involving chronic, life-threatening illness, coping strategies shift in a more cognitive direction as a child matures. Along

these lines, Worchel, Copeland, and Barker (1987) observed that chronically ill pediatric oncology patients in adolescence were more likely to use spontaneous cognitive interventions to help them cope with such painful procedures as spinal taps and bone marrow tests.

Findings like these and numerous others in this expanding pool of literature raise serious questions about the efficacy of certain types of therapeutic interventions which currently are being recommended for children facing stressful life situations. To date, virtually everything that has been attempted in the area of the interaction between age and coping strategies focuses on indexing the coping techniques children invoke under chronic or acute stress conditions. Perhaps an even more important issue rests with the general suitability of therapeutic interventions that are so solidly tied to events we now suspect are more appropriate for one age group rather than another. Insofar as commonly recommended treatment approaches like the coping program Peterson and Shigetomi (1981) advanced depend on the patient's cognitive sophistication, and given the aforementioned data revealing the disinclination (indeed, the inability) of younger children to use cognitive coping strategies, it follows that such techniques may be comparatively ineffective with this age range. In simple terms, it is likely to do very little good to invite a child to deploy elaborate mental images to combat stress when that child possesses marginal imaging skills.

Accordingly, this study was designed principally to show that a cognitively oriented strategy that is patterned after that by Peterson and Shigetomi (1981) would more effectively alleviate stress in 10- to 12-year-old children diagnosed with cancer than in 4- to 6-year-old children with the same illness. By demonstrating the age-related limitations of a cognitively oriented therapeutic regimen, the need to examine the scope of other treatment procedures would be enhanced.

An additional, adjunctive concern of this study was the role information played during the coping period. Information is known to produce beneficial results in dealing with stressful situations (Miller, Sherman, Combs, & Kruus, 1992), but it appears more true for younger children than for older children (Curry & Russ, 1985). For some reason, younger children seek more information about the source of their stress than do older children. Therefore, we predicted that a technique like sensory information (see Siegel & Peterson, 1980) would be more effective with 4- to 6-year-olds than for 10- to 12-year-olds. The expected interaction between age and therapeutic style would underscore the need to incorporate developmental parameters into studies of treatment efficacy.

## *Method*

The method section follows the introduction. This section of the article provides a detailed account of how the research was conducted. If the method section is presented properly, any individual should be able to replicate the experiment based the information provided. Also, the reader should be able to judge the suitability of the participant (subject) selection procedures, the experimental design, and other aspects of the research protocol.

The method section is typically divided into three subsections: Participants, Materials or Apparatus, and Procedure. As a rule, a detailed description of the participants opens the method section.

**Participants.**   The participant subsection for our model experiment is illustrated below. In this subsection, the essential characteristics of the sample are described. With human participants, this includes specifics on gender, age, and other variables that are relevant to the study. For our model experiment, for instance, certain eligibility criteria had to be met. If you are going to conduct a study on the effects of a particular type of intervention on coping with the stress associated with medical treatment, it makes sense that you would need to use patients who are already identified as needing attention. In addition, because our experiment is concerned with younger and older chronically ill children, the

---

Psychotherapy    6

Accordingly, this study was designed principally to show that a cognitively oriented strategy that is patterned after that by Peterson and Shigetomi (1981) would more effectively alleviate stress in 10- to 12-year-old children diagnosed with cancer than in 4- to 6-year-old children with the same illness. By demonstrating the age-related limitations of a cognitively oriented therapeutic regimen, the need to examine the scope of other treatment procedures would be enhanced.

An additional, adjunctive concern of this study was the role information played during the coping period. Information is known to produce beneficial results in dealing with stressful situations (Miller, Sherman, Combs, & Kruus, 1992), but it appears more true for younger children than for older children (Curry & Russ, 1985). For some reason, younger children seek more information about the source of their stress than do older children. Therefore, we predicted that a technique like sensory information (see Siegel & Peterson, 1980) would be more effective with 4- to 6-year-olds than for 10- to 12-year-olds. The expected interaction between age and therapeutic style would underscore the need to incorporate developmental parameters into studies of treatment efficacy.

Method

Participants

The participants in this study were 96 English-speaking pediatric patients (48 male and 48 female) who were undergoing

---

Psychotherapy    7

cancer treatment at the University of Texas M.D. Anderson Hospital and Tumor Institute in Houston, Texas. Of the 48 male participants, 29 were Caucasian, 15 were Mexican-American, and 4 were African-American. Of the 48 females who participated in the experiment, 31 were Caucasian, 12 were Mexican-American, and 5 were African-American. Half of the male and female participants were from each of the two age ranges included in the experiment (4- to 6-year-olds and 10- to 12-year-olds).

Participants were selected randomly from all medical services (i.e., leukemia, lymphoma, solid tumors, rare solid tumors) except brain tumors. Eligibility criteria included (a) age 4 to 6 or age 10 to 12, (b) English speaking, (c) in sufficiently good health to respond to the various points of intervention (see following), and (d) experienced as both an inpatient and outpatient. All patients were receiving treatment that required a series of at least four bone marrow aspirations (BMAs) and lumbar punctures (LPs).

sample is further restricted and this must be pointed out. Finally, the participant selection procedures should be identified.

If animals are used as subjects, their sex, genus, species, and supplier should be specified. Also, the age of the animals at the time of arrival at the laboratory, their initial body weights, and overall health status should be mentioned.

**Materials.** This subsection, which is often called the apparatus subsection in experiments where specialized equipment is used, describes the "in-house" materials or instruments or the commercially manufactured equipment that was used in the study. For commercially made products, the manufacturer's name and location and model number should be reported. A published scale or questionnaire must be referenced so that others may locate it if need be. In the case of a newly created measurement instrument, it may be necessary to reproduce the instrument or to at least let the readers know how they can obtain a copy of it. Finally, if the experiment involves stimuli that are part of an experimental manipulation, these stimuli must be identified. Again, because the purpose of the method section is to facilitate replication, each of the unique features of the research project must be specified.

The primary materials in our model experiment were concerned with indexing stress levels. This brief subsection appears as follows:

---

Psychotherapy    7

cancer treatment at the University of Texas M.D. Anderson
Hospital and Tumor Institute in Houston, Texas. Of the 48 male
participants, 29 were Caucasian, 15 were Mexican-American, and 4
were African-American. Of the 48 females who participated in the
experiment, 31 were Caucasian, 12 were Mexican-American, and 5
were African-American. Half of the male and female participants
were from each of the two age ranges included in the experiment
(4- to 6-year-olds and 10- to 12-year-olds).

    Participants were selected randomly from all medical
services (i.e., leukemia, lymphoma, solid tumors, rare solid
tumors) except brain tumors. Eligibility criteria included (a)
age 4 to 6 or age 10 to 12, (b) English speaking, (c) in
sufficiently good health to respond to the various points of
intervention (see following), and (d) experienced as both an
inpatient and outpatient. All patients were receiving treatment
that required a series of at least four bone marrow aspirations
(BMAs) and lumbar punctures (LPs).

<u>Materials</u>

    A behavioral rating scale and a self-report scale were used
in this experiment. The behavioral rating scale was the
observational Scale of Behavioral Distress (OSBD) (reproduced in
Smith, Ackerson, & Blotcky, 1989); the self-report scale was the
"fear thermometer," which is easily constructed in house (see
Katz, Kellerman, & Seigel, 1982). In addition, heart rate was
measured using an electrocardiograph (EKG) [model 69-2204]

**Procedure.** In the procedure subsection of the method section, every aspect of the conduct of the experiment is described. It is important to tell the reader about the activities of the experimenter and the participants. Each step in the study should be described in series, beginning with a statement on design features and an account of how individual participants were assigned to conditions. In describing the various experimental manipulations that define the independent variable(s), it may be necessary to reproduce instructions, list items in a questionnaire, specify stimulus elements presented to the participants, or detail other methodological events. Of course, exercise some common sense about what to include; it is obviously not necessary to tell the reader that it was a pleasant day outside or that FaberCastel #2 lead pencils were used to write the subjects' names when they arrived at the laboratory. The guideline is to describe the experimental procedure in sufficient detail that the reader understands how the research was executed and, if so desired, could replicate the experiment. Therefore, be thorough in reporting the procedure subsection, but omit what is unnecessary.

Finally, I recommend closing the procedure subsection with a formal description of the dependent variables used in the study. This caps the method section by telling the reader what the endpoints of the experiment were, and it underscores what was actually measured. Before entering into the next section, which is largely quantitative, it is nice to remind the reader what the numbers (data) stand for.

Given our model experiment, we must provide information in the procedure subsection about our three types of therapeutic interventions (cognitive coping strategy, sensory information, and contact control). This tells the reader what was done to the children, and how we went about it. Whether the reader agrees with the quality of the intervention process or not, there can be no uncertainty about what happened. After all, the point of our research was to establish the differential effects of the independent variable on the dependent variable(s), not to market the treatment concept. Accordingly, our procedure subsection appears on the following pages.

Psychotherapy    8

manufactured by Carolina Biological Supply Company (Burlington, NC).

Procedure

Demographic data. Each child's age, gender, type and date of diagnosis, maternal educational level, primary provider's occupation, and family income were obtained from family members and hospital staff.

Design and assignment to treatments. This study employed a 2 age range (4 to 6, 10 to 12) x 3 treatment conditions (cognitive coping strategy, sensory information, and contact control) equal Ns design. Eight male and eight female participants from each age range were randomly assigned to receive one of the three interventions. (Note: Because of ethical considerations, after the research was completed all participants were offered the most beneficial program as defined by the results of this study, but these results are not presented here.) The same physicians and nursing staff were present throughout the study.

Experimenters. The experimenters (therapists) included graduate students and postdoctoral students who had received extensive training in psychotherapeutic intervention. All personnel had a minimum of 100 practica (therapy) hours of supervised experience with children.

Each experimenter involved in the treatment phase of the proposed project was supervised by a licensed clinical psychologist, certified by the State Board of Examiners of

Psychotherapy    9

Psychologists as a health service provider in the State of Texas. During the data collection phase of the experiment, it was the responsibility of each experimenter to monitor the psychological welfare of the participant (patient) and determine whether or not the participant was at risk.

Medical treatment (stressor). The study was explained to both patient and parent, and the parent signed an informed consent form. All data collectors were blind to the interventions used in the study, and data were collected in the same manner across four scheduled medical procedures. The first two procedures were used to gather baseline data, and the respective interventions were performed before the last two procedures. Parents accompanied children during the procedures in all cases.

After the child was placed in a treatment room and examined by a physician, a research assistant entered the room, attached a heart rate monitor, and had the child complete a self-report (see following) regarding his or her fear or expected pain. Subsequently, behavioral observations were recorded and heart rate was measured. At this point, the intervention was introduced. When the nurse actually brought the medical procedure instruments into the room, behavioral records and heart rate recordings were again taken, for 2 minutes. The data collected for the 2-minute period immediately before the four BMA or LP medical procedures (two baseline and two post-intervention) were used for the analyses.

Psychotherapy    10

Interventions. Depending on treatment assignment, one of the three following intervention strategies was used.

In the cognitive coping condition (see Peterson & Shigetomi, 1981), a research assistant pointed out to the children how good the children felt when they were safely in their homes and that sometimes, when children are hospitalized, they wish to feel those same feelings. The research assistant had already taught these children three techniques to achieve such feelings: (1) cue-controlled, deep-muscle relaxation; (2) mental imagery; and (3) comforting self-talk.

Participants were trained in deep-muscle relaxation by stretching and tensing their muscles, then relaxing completely. After the children had practiced this technique several times, the cue word calm and slow deep-breathing exercises were introduced. The participants practiced each of the components until each was able to demonstrate that relaxation could be achieved quickly using these cognitive-behavioral techniques.

The imaginal distraction technique was then introduced. Participants were asked to imagine a scene that made them quite happy. Scenes such as playing outdoors, lying at the beach, or walking in the mountains were common. The children were encouraged to make the scene as vivid and as positive as possible.

Finally, participants receiving the cognitive coping intervention were given two comforting self-talk phrases: "I will

Psychotherapy    11

be better in a little while," and "Everything is going to be all right." The children were encouraged to say these phrases out loud and to then repeat them silently to themselves.

As a result, the participants who were assigned to the cognitive coping strategy intervention were adept at these tasks before actually being asked to use the intervention during the last two of the four scheduled medical procedures.

In the sensory information intervention, participants were told that one way of learning to cope with the medical procedures was to know exactly what to expect, including what they might think and feel (see Siegel & Peterson, 1980; Smith, Ackerson, & Blotcky, 1989). When the last two of the four medical treatments were conducted, it was explained that the nurse was going to provide this type of detailed information, telling them step by step what she was going to do. An example of what the nurse told the participants is, "I am about to put the numbing medicine in the place I just washed. I'll count to three and then put it in so that you won't feel the needle. You may feel a pinprick as I put the numbing medicine in and, sometimes the medicine stings as it starts to work. OK, one, two, three."

In the contact control condition, a research assistant simply read the children a chapter from Winnie the Pooh or The Never Ending Story. While there was an attempt to keep the intervention times uniform across the cognitive coping strategy, the sensory information approach, and the contact control condition, the inherently shorter time associated with the sensory information intervention could not be avoided.

<u>Dependent Measures.</u> As mentioned earlier in the Materials subsection, a behavioral rating scale, a self-report measure, and an EKG were available for this study. Accordingly, the dependent measures used to index the patients' levels of apprehension before treatment, and thereby determine the relative effectiveness of each intervention with the different age groups, were:

1. Observational Scale of Behavioral Distress (OSBD). This scale (refer to Smith, Ackerson, & Blotcky, 1989) required that two trained observers record behaviors in 11 categories (e.g., crying, nervous behavior, and verbal resistance) in 15-second intervals for 2 minutes to obtain a total distress score. The scale has good reliability and validity and has been described in detail (Jay, Elliot, Ozolins, Olson, & Pruitt, 1985).

2. Self-Report Measure of Fear and Pain. Three visual analog thermometers were used to assess the children's perceptions of fear and expectancies of pain. With this procedure the participant simply points to a location on the thermometer that best describes how he or she feels (0 = no fear; 100 = as afraid as much as possible). This instrument has also been shown to be reliable in studies similar to the one reported here

(Katz, Kellerman, & Siegel, 1982).

3. Heart Rate. Heart Rate (HR) was monitored using the EKG device discussed previously. Chest electrodes were attached to the participants. The HR value was averaged over five beats and appeared as digital beats per minute.

Following the data collection phase, all participants were debriefed and, as indicated earlier, each was given the option of using the intervention technique that produced the most favorable results.

## *Results*

The results section of the report follows the method section. Its purpose is to tell the reader what you found in the experiment. This requires that you provide statistical confirmation of observed effects. When you say that a particular condition or independent variable produced an effect, for example, you must present the supporting information from the appropriate statistical tests. As discussed in Chapter 11, this means you must present the significance values, test value, and degrees of freedom for inferential statistics tests such as the ANOVA and t-test. This does not mean that every possible comparison or test must be presented, of course. To the contrary, you should be as economical as possible and select only tests that are critical to the essence of the research. Don't clutter your report with details from nonsignificant test outcomes or with comparisons that are of no consequence.

When deciding whether to report main effects or interactions (see Chapter 8), avoid redundancy and misleading statistical information. For example, it is possible that the strength of a given interaction effect may be so great that a significant main effect may be produced, primarily by one level of the independent variable. Because the main effect may be incidental in such cases and may add no new or useful information, only the interaction test must be reported.

As a rule, individual data points are not outlined in the results section. Only when you conduct a single-subject experiment or when the pattern of individual scores within a group is of interest (as it is with behavioral pharmacology studies where individual differences in responsiveness to drugs is always an issue) do you present individual scores. The more common approach is to present general group information (e.g., means or medians) in a figure or a table. This summary information allows the reader to see group differences more clearly and to gain some feel for the overall pattern of the results.

Although writing styles vary, my preference is to begin the results section with a story about the findings from the experiment. Rather than immediately present statistical and quantitative information in the form of numbers, use words to tell the reader what you found in the study. You can document your story with numerical details after the reader receives the "take-home message."

Finally, be descriptive in the results section and avoid interpreting what the findings mean. Deciphering the results comes later. For now it suffices to indicate which manipulations were significant.

With these considerations in mind, the results section for our model experiment appears as follows:

---

Psychotherapy     13

(Katz, Kellerman, & Siegel, 1982).

3.  Heart Rate. Heart Rate (HR) was monitored using the EKG device discussed previously. Chest electrodes were attached to the participants. The HR value was averaged over five beats and appeared as digital beats per minute.

Following the data collection phase, all participants were debriefed and, as indicated earlier, each was given the option of using the intervention technique that produced the most favorable results.

### Results

The results of this study showed that the cognitive coping strategy diminished the anxiety associated with medical treatment only in the older participants (10- to 12-year-olds). The levels of the 4- to 6-year-old children did not differ from baseline when this intervention strategy was used. A quite different pattern of results was evident when the sensory information approach was used, however. With this intervention, fear and apprehension concerning scheduled medical treatments was reduced more in the younger age range than in the older age range. The contact control procedure did not alter fear reactions. Finally, regardless of the intervention used, only the heart rate measure showed any evidence that fear and anxiety levels were affected in this study.

Because neither the observational scale data nor the self-

---

Psychotherapy     14

report data showed significant differences due to type of intervention or age of the participant, only the statistical findings on the heart rate measure are presented in this report. The physiological measure of heart beats per minute was totaled over each of the 2 minute recording periods for both the 4- to 6-year-old range and the 10- to 12-year-old range, and behavior (heart rate) during the final two post intervention periods is presented as percent of baseline in Figure 1. A 2 age ranges x 3 interventions ANOVA test showed that the cognitive coping strategy significantly reduced heart rate relative to the other two forms of treatment among the older children, and that the sensory information regimen resulted in significantly greater declines over the remaining two interventions in the younger children (F(2,90) = 4.13, p < .05).

Additional analysis of the heart rate measure showed that there were no overall differences between the two age groups (F(1,90) = 1.48, p < .05). This means that when you compare the two age ranges over all three types of intervention, there is no real difference. Of course, what differs is that one type of intervention worked better with one age range and another type worked better with the other. From the overall pattern of the findings reported here, it seems clear that a given intervention is not uniformly effective for younger and older children.

## *Discussion*

The final section of the main text of the scientific report is the discussion section. The principal purpose of the discussion section is to interpret and give meaning to the obtained results. The discussion should begin with a summary paragraph that tells the reader the overall story. Included in this summary paragraph are remarks about whether the research hypothesis was supported or rejected.

Following the opening summary paragraph, the discussion moves to specific findings and attempts to integrate those findings into the available literature. Any inconsistencies should be indicated. When the findings confirm a previous result or support a particular rationale, it is appropriate to highlight these aspects of the data. Also, the implications of your data for future research may be addressed here.

More than is true for the other sections of the final report, the discussion section permits more license with respect to promoting a personal bias or opinion. Be careful, however. Earlier in this chapter I mentioned the importance of "keeping it simple." Although the scientific community has some tolerance for creative expression, the final report is not intended to be a forum for literary luminance. When simpler phrases work, use them. If you can make your point briefly, do so. The premier requirement of the discussion section is to provide the reader with a scholarly judgment of what your experimental search uncovered. A good and complete discussion accomplishes this task without appealing to gratuitous verbiage.

Finally, when appropriate, finish the discussion section with a few statements about conclusions that can be drawn from your study. This provides the reader with one or two bits of information and increases the likelihood that your major findings will be remembered.

The discussion section for our model experiment appears as follows:

Psychotherapy        14

report data showed significant differences due to type of
intervention or age of the participant, only the statistical
findings on the heart rate measure are presented in this report.
The physiological measure of heart beats per minute was totaled
over each of the 2 minute recording periods for both the 4- to 6-
year-old range and the 10- to 12-year-old range, and behavior
(heart rate) during the final two past intervention periods is
presented as percent of baseline in Figure 1. A 2 age ranges x 3
interventions ANOVA test showed that the cognitive coping
strategy significantly reduced heart rate relative to the other
two forms of treatment among the older children, and that the
sensory information regimen resulted in significantly greater
declines over the remaining two interventions in the younger
children ($F(2,90) = 4.13$, ($p < .05$).

Additional analysis of the heart rate measure showed that
there were no overall differences between the two age groups
($F(1,90) = 1.48$, ($p < .05$). This means that when you compare the
two age ranges over all three types of intervention, there is no
real difference. Of course, what differs is that one type of
intervention worked better with one age range and another type
worked better with the other. From the overall pattern of the
findings reported here, it seems clear that a given intervention
is not uniformly effective for younger and older children.

Discussion

The findings from this study generally agree with the

Psychotherapy        15

rationale that formed the basis for the research. Specifically,
it was shown that an intervention technique based on cognitive
principles (the cognitive coping strategy suggested by Peterson &
Shigetomi, 1981) was more effective in reducing fear of medical
treatment when it was used with older children (10- to 12-year-
olds). Conversely, younger children (4- to 6-year-olds) benefitted
more than older children from a treatment that relied on
information concerning the sensory events that were about to take
place during medical treatment.

The finding which showed that the older participants were
more responsive to the cognitive therapy regimen than were the
younger participants is consistent with a large pool of
literature which shows that developmental stage determines a
person's behavioral orientation in a problem-solving situation.
Discrimination learning (Baddeley, 1993; Kendler & Kendler, 1967)
and reactions to failure and reward (Rholes, Blackwell, Jordan, &
Walters, 1980) are psychological phenomena that depend heavily on
a person's cognitive capacity. It seems that this cognitive
capability is linked to age, with older children demonstrating
greater cognitive capability than younger children. In this
context, it is understandable that a therapeutic approach based
on verbal cues, imagery, and comforting self-commentary might be
appropriate for children ages 10 to 12 but would be
contraindicated for children ages 4 to 6.

Similarly, the greater effects observed with the sensory
information strategy in the younger children may be explained in

Psychotherapy        16

terms of cognitive development. As noted previously, the older a
child becomes, the more reliant he or she is likely to be on
cognitive coping strategies (e.g., Brown, O'Keeffe, Sanders, &
Baker, 1986; Worchel, Copeland, & Barker, 1987). In fact, older
children seem to prefer spontaneous cognitive methods for dealing
with stress, and this may obscure more rudimentary attempts at
fear reduction. In contrast, in the absence of a more elaborate
mental framework, younger children may rely exclusively on simple
descriptive approaches, such as being told what is happening
next. Along these lines, the greater effectiveness of the sensory
information intervention in the younger children is interpreted
as a special case involving distraction: The greater cognitive
tendencies of older children interfere with simple information
benefits. Because younger children are not distracted by such
mental processes, they experience the fear-reducing effects of
knowing just how bad the pain of medical treatment is likely to
be.

Regardless of theoretical issues, the findings from this
study permit one very important conclusion. A given intervention
is not likely to be the most effective treatment across all age
ranges. Greater attention should be given to the impact of
developmental parameters on the efficacy of various therapeutic
techniques.

## *References*

Following the main body of the text is the reference section. All articles, books, and other publications that are mentioned in the text of the final report must be listed in the reference section. References serve two primary purposes: they acknowledge other individuals for their contributions and they guide the reader to more elaborate coverage of a particular theory or empirical issues.

The aforementioned APA *Publication Manual* provides detailed instructions on the accepted reference format for articles published in APA journals. These guidelines specify everything from the order of references in the list to the proper citation for obscure unpublished materials. It would be inappropriate here to attempt a complete review of all aspects of referencing. Understand, however, that very clear rules exist concerning how to form a reference list, and they should be followed.

The reference list for our model experiment, which begins on a new page after the discussion section ends, appears as follows:

Psychotherapy    17

References

Abramson, L. Y., Seligman, M. E. P., & Teasdale, J. D. (1978). Learned helplessness in humans: Critique and reformulation. Journal of Abnormal Psychology, 87, 49-74.

Baddeley, A. (1993). Human memory: Theory and practice. Boston: Allyn and Bacon.

Brown, J., O'Keefe, J., Sanders, S. F., & Baker, B. (1986). Developmental changes in children's cognition to stressful and painful situations. Journal of Pediatric Psychology, 11, 343-357.

Curry, S. L., & Russ, S. W. (1985). Identifying coping strategies in children. Journal of Clinical Child Psychology, 14, 61-69.

Gerralda, M. E., Kim, S., & Klein, S. (1994). Psychiatric adjustment in children with chronic physical illness. British Journal of Hospital Medicine, 52, 230-234.

Jay, S. M., Elliott, C. H., Ozolins, M., Olson, R. A., & Pruitt, S. D. (1985). Behavioral management of children's distress during painful medical treatment. Behavioral Research and Therapy, 23, 513-520.

Katz, E. R., Kellerman, J., & Siegel, S. E. (1982, March). Self-report and observational measurement of acute pain, fear, and behavioral distress in children with leukemia. Paper presented at the meeting of the Society of Behavioral Medicine, Chicago, IL.

Kendler, T. S., & Kendler, H. H. (1967). Experimental

Psychotherapy    18

analysis of inferential behavior in children. In L. P. Lipsitt & C. C. Spiker (Eds.), Advances in child development and behavior. New York: Academic Press.

Miller, M. M., Sherman, H., Combs, C., & Kruus, L. (1992). Patterns of children's coping with medical and dental stressors: Nature, implications, and future directions. In L. Siegel, G. Walker, J. Wallander, & A. La Greca (Eds.), Advances in pediatric psychology: Stress and coping in child health. New York: Guilford Press.

Parsons, J. E., & Ruble, D. N. (1977). The development of achievement-related expectancies. Child Development, 48, 1075-1079.

Peterson, L., & Shigetomi, C. (1981). The use of coping techniques to minimize anxiety in hospitalized children. Behavior Therapy, 12, 1-14.

Reese, H. W., & Lipsitt, L. P. (1970). Experimental child psychology. New York: Academic Press.

Rholes, W. S., Blackwell, J., Jordan, C., & Walters, C. (1980). A developmental study of learned helplessness. Developmental Psychology, 16, 616-624.

Sargent, J., & Liebman, R. (1985). Childhood chronic illness: Issues for psychotherapists. Community Mental Health Journal, 21, 294-311.

Siegel, L. J., & Peterson, L. (1980). Stress reduction in young dental patients through coping skills and sensory

Psychotherapy    19

information. Journal of Consulting and Clinical Psychology, 48, 785-787.

Smith, K. E., Ackerson, J. D., & Blotcky, A. D. (1989). Reducing distress during invasive medical procedures: Relating behavioral interventions to preferred coping styles in pediatric cancer patients. Journal of Pediatric Psychology, 14, 405-419.

Weekes, D. P. (1995). Adolescents growing up chronically ill: A life-span development view. Family & Community Health, 17, 22-34.

Worchel, F. F., Copeland, D. R., & Barker, D. G. (1987). Control-related coping strategies in pediatric oncology patients. Journal of Pediatric Psychology, 12, 25-38.

## *Author Note*

Following the reference section on a separate page is information about the author(s) and the conduct of the study. This includes the authors' names and institutional affiliations and an address where requests for reprints can be sent. Also, acknowledgments and expressions of gratitude may be presented in the author note section. If the research was conducted for a specific purpose, such as completing the requirements of a master's thesis, it should be indicated. In addition, if an agency provided financial support, information concerning the agency, such as the award number, should be presented.

The author note section for our model experiment appears as follows:

```
                                    Psychotherapy     20

                        Author Note
        The original idea for this experiment came from Patricia L.
Nation, Department of Educational Psychology, Texas A&M
University, College Station, TX  77843.
        Jack R. Nation is currently with an academic institution
that offers a course this text supports.
        Requests for reprints should be sent to Jack R. Nation,
Department of Psychology, Texas A&M University, College Station,
TX 77843.
```

## *Tables and Figures*

If tables and/or figures are included in the manuscript, they are presented at the very end of the article on separate pages. Tables appear, on numbered pages, in the order in which they appear in the body of the manuscript. Figures are un-numbered and follow a separately numbered figure caption page.

There were no tables for our model experiment, but we did have one figure. The caption page and figure for our model experiment appear as follows:

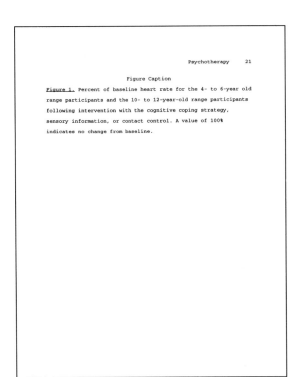

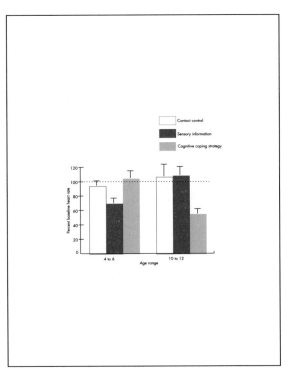

Now, after 12 chapters of detailing how to design and complete a psycholog-ical experiment, we have our final product: a scientific manuscript (see Appen-dix for final version). Now, how do we relay the information? How do we let the broader scientific community know what we have achieved? This important step in the communication process is covered next.

# The Publication Process

In this chapter, I cover the sequence of events that is involved in publishing a paper in a scientific journal. In the previous chapter, we completed the final version of a manuscript based on our model experiment, which dealt with the effects of age on the effectiveness of psychotherapy, and it is this manuscript we hope to submit for editorial consideration. As you will see, there is much to consider.

# SELECTING THE APPROPRIATE JOURNAL

The initial decision in publishing a report involves selecting the appropriate publication outlet. This is not as simple at it might seem, for there are several factors that must be considered. First, which journal is likely to reach the audience that will find the information most useful? It stands to reason that if you have written a report on Pavlovian conditioning following cerebellar lesions in rats, you would not send your article to *Human Memory and Cognition* for review. But where would you send it? There are several options—an impressive array of high-quality animal learning and conditioning journals is available. As a rule, choose a journal that has a history of publishing similar types of papers. Other scientists who are interested in the topic are likely to see your article because they know to expect papers on conditioning or the effects of lesions on behavior, and so forth.

In addition to the "appropriate audience" selection criterion, consider the purpose of the journal. Some journals, such as *Psychological Bulletin,* publish integrative articles that are designed to bring literature together. They do not intend to present new data. Therefore, such a journal would be disinclined to consider manuscripts, like ours, that are based on novel experimental findings. Similarly, journals like the *Journal of Abnormal Psychology* are not likely to be interested in theoretical papers that may be thought provoking but provide no new data. Therefore, consider the objectives of the journal before submitting a paper for evaluation.

You may also want to think about the journal's rejection rate. As with all academic journals, psychology journals vary in their standards. Some journals, like *Science,* are extremely difficult to publish in. Over 90% of the 5,000 papers submitted annually to *Science* are rejected, not because the research is of poor quality but rather because "Darwin happened to submit a paper that week," or "Sir Isaac Newton decided to reformulate *Principia* in a forthcoming issue." The point is that some top-of-the-line journals have only enough space for the very best papers. Therefore, if you have a solid report, but one that is not earth shattering, you may want to select a specialty journal.

Regarding the manuscript we based on the model experiment in this text, after carefully considering our options, assume that we select the *Journal of Consulting and Clinical Psychology (JCCP)* as a possible publication outlet. This journal, which is published under the authority of the APA, specializes in treatment effects. It makes sense, then, that other scientists interested in the relative effectiveness of different forms of psychotherapy would see our report here. *JCCP* principally publishes new experimental findings. Even though *JCCP* has a pretty high rejection rate (71%), it is appropriate that we give *JCCP* the first shot at publishing a "true breakthrough" because we have an outstanding paper.

# THE APA PUBLICATION PROCESS

Because we have selected an APA journal for our initial submission, it is appropriate that we track the publication sequence according the APA publication process outlined in the *Publication Manual of the American Psychological Association* (see Figure 13–1). We begin with the journal editor.

## *Author Submits Manuscript to Editor*

Most journals publish their editorial policies and "Instructions to Authors" sections in each volume. Typically, this information is at the very beginning of the volume, at the end of the volume, or both. Included in this information are the number of copies of the report that are required for submission and the name and address of the editor overseeing the manuscript during the review process.

For our submission, we look through the most recent copy of the *Journal of Consulting and Clinical Psychology* and find that the editor is Professor Larry E. Beutler. Manuscripts are to be submitted in quadruplicate (four copies) to Professor Beutler at Graduate School of Education, University of California-Santa Barbara, Santa Barbara, California 93106-9490.

In addition to the four copies of the manuscript, a cover letter should be sent to the editor explaining the nature of the research. Because the *Journal of Consulting and Clinical Psychology* is an APA publication, concurrent submissions to other journals are not permitted. Indicate in the cover letter that your manuscript is not under review by another publication. In addition, include your telephone number, FAX number, e-mail address, and address for correspondence.

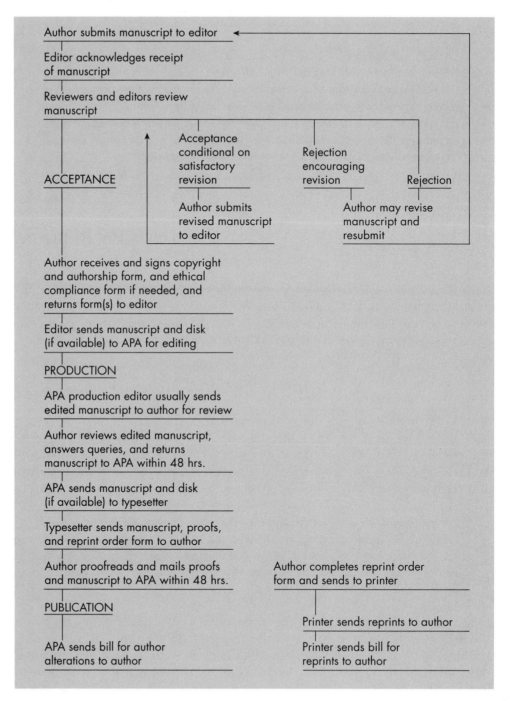

**FIGURE 13–1** The APA publication process. Copyright © 1994 by the American Psychological Association. Reprinted with permission.

Other considerations when submitting an article to an APA journal for review are:

1. You should keep a hard copy and an electronic version of your manuscript on diskette.
2. The data on which the report is based should be available throughout the review process and for at least 5 years after publication.
3. The authors(s) should state in writing that they have complied with APA ethical standards (see Chapter 4) in the treatment of their participants.

These agreements between authors and publishers facilitate the review process, minimize errors, and ensure that the research has been conducted ethically and responsibly.

## *Editor Acknowledges Receipt of Manuscript*

Shortly after submitting the manuscript to the journal editor for review, you will receive a letter of acknowledgment. This letter from the editor or the editorial staff confirms receipt of your manuscript and may indicate which associate editor will handle the manuscript, how long it will take to obtain reviews, and so forth. As a guideline (and this really varies), allow about 2 or 3 months for the review of an experimental paper, and possibly even longer for theoretical pieces or major literature reviews.

The letter acknowledging the receipt of our manuscript might take the form shown in Figure 13–2. We should keep this letter on file in case we need to inquire about the status of the review process or to communicate with the editor.

## *Reviewers and Editors Review the Manuscript*

Once the editor acknowledges receipt of our manuscript and judges the topic appropriate for the journal, she or he will submit the manuscript to specialists in the field for evaluation. These reviewers, typically two or three, are asked to comment on the perceived importance of the report, the adequacy of the methodology, the strength of the findings, the appropriateness of the writing style, and most importantly, the suitability of the manuscript for publication in the journal.

Occasionally a journal may have standing reviewers who serve as members of the editorial board of the journal, or the journal may select reviewers on an

*A Publication of the American Psychological Association*

Larry E. Beutler, Editor
Graduate School of Education
University of California, Santa Barbara
Santa Barbara, California 93106-9490
(805) 893-2923
E-mail beutler@edstar.gse.ucsb.edu
FAX (805) 893-7264

| Barbara L. Andersen, Associate Editor | Enrico E. Jones, Associate Editor | Philip C. Kendall, Associate Editor | Frederick L. Newman, Associate Editor |
|---|---|---|---|
| Department of Psychology | Department of Psychology | Division of Clinical Psychology | Health Services Administration |
| Ohio State University | University of California, Berkeley | Temple University | FIU North Miami Campus |
| 1885 Neil Avenue | Berkeley, California 94720 | Philadelphia, PA 19122 | North Miami, FL 33181 |
| Columbus, Ohio 43210 | (510) 642-5427 | (215) 204-1558 | (305) 940-5895 |
| (614) 292-4236 | | | |

June 30, 1996

Dr. Jack R. Nation
Department of Psychology
Texas A&M University
College Station, TX 77843

Dear Dr. Nation:

Your submission to Journal of Consulting and Clinical Psychology has been received and copies have been sent out for review. I will contact you as soon as the evaluation process is completed. If your address should change at any time during the review or production process, please let us know immediately.

Please sign and return the enclosed Certificate of Compliance with APA Ethical Principles.

Sincerely,

Larry E. Beutler, Ph.D.
Editor

LEB:do
enclosures

FIGURE 13–2 Acknowledgment letter from *JCCP* regarding receipt of our "model" manuscript. Copyright © 1996 by the American Psychological Association. Reprinted with permission.

*ad hoc* basis. Either way, the reviewers make their recommendations to the editor of the journal or to an associate "action" editor who has the ultimate authority regarding the acceptability of a manuscript for publication. Although some reviewers choose to sign their reviews, the understanding that prevails between editors and reviewers is that the reviewers remain anonymous. With the identity of the reviewers concealed, a more honest and straightforward appraisal of the scientific credibility of the article is likely. This may sound as if the basic rights of the author(s) are being compromised, but it has been and continues to be a workable system and one that everyone knows about and accepts going in.

## *Acceptance or Rejection*

The guarantees in research are essentially those in life—none. Simply submitting a manuscript for editorial consideration in no way ensures publication. The scientific community seemingly is awash with manuscripts based on poorly conceived ideas, flawed collection procedures, inappropriate statistical assays, and overly ambitious assertions. Embedded in these are jewels, however, and it is the reviewers' responsibility to serve as referees or gatekeepers—to see that quality gains visibility. This requires that the reviewers think not only in terms of what is acceptable, but also in terms of what may eventually be acceptable.

There are basically four possible outcomes in the review process. One is that the reviewers will uniformly agree that the manuscript is ready for publication and recommend it for acceptance. Understand that is rare, and you should not be disappointed if it never happens to you. Reviewers unavoidably read the manuscript with their own biases and preferences in style, focus, and so on. Even with the most objective reviewers some dissatisfaction with some aspect of the article is likely to be expressed. You are not going to please everyone. You may even find two reviewers who make diametrically opposing recommendations. Because the chances for immediate acceptance are so remote, you should not expect your paper to be accepted in its original form.

A second possibility, which is favorable and more probable than immediate acceptance, is an acceptance conditional on the completion of a satisfactory revision. As just mentioned, based on their prejudices, reviewers will usually want some minor stylistic changes, and they may also request more substantive, major changes. This may take the form of including coverage of missing literature, reanalyzing data sets, or even conducting additional experiments. The reviewers send copies of their detailed recommendations to the editor, and they agree that the article will be acceptable for publication when the changes they indicated are made. As the author, you will receive copies of the review comments when the editor returns the manuscript.

The author's task is to address each of the points the reviewers raised. As an author you are not obligated to honor every request a reviewer makes. If you have sound reasons for disagreeing with a reviewer's recommendations, state them in a cover letter to the editor when you resubmit your revised manuscript for another round of reviews (usually the reviewers on the initial submission are used again). The article should reflect your interests, not those of an anonymous reviewer. At the same time, when a legitimate issue is raised or an oversight is identified, address it. The objective is to publish the best version of the report possible, and this is most likely to be accomplished by working within the review system.

Once the revised version of the manuscript is resubmitted and rereviewed, it is returned to the editor for final determination regarding its suitability for publication. If you have dealt satisfactorily with the issues the reviewers raised, the manuscript should be deemed acceptable for publication.

A third possible outcome of the review process is that the manuscript may receive a recommendation of rejection encouraging revision. This means that the reviewers and the editor view the topic as important and that the research may eventually merit publication in the journal, but until a more compelling case can be made, no further attention can be given the project. This outcome does not commit the editorial staff in any manner. Even if the manuscript is revised and a substantially modified version of the report is resubmitted for editorial consideration, the article may never be judged acceptable for publication in the journal. In all probability, the review process will start over with a new set of reviewers and a new time frame for evaluation. All the editorial staff express with a rejection encouraging revision is that the journal sees potential in the work, but it is not possible to recommend publishing it in its present form.

A fourth outcome of the review process is an outright rejection. Essentially, a rejection indicates that the journal editor and reviewers are not interested in your manuscript. Here another important point regarding the publication process must be made: Just because one journal does not want to publish your article doesn't mean another won't. Indeed, psychology lore is rife with examples of famous experiments that were turned down by one journal only to be picked up by a second and given widespread distribution. One example is the now-classic study by Garcia and Koelling (1966). This simple but elegantly designed study on conditioned taste aversion in rats challenged contemporary thinking in animal learning and behavior so strongly that it was labeled a maverick finding and was summarily rejected by the popular *Journal of Comparative and Physiological Psychology (JCPP)*. The manuscript was resubmitted to a lesser quality and now defunct journal, *Psychonomic Science*. The Garcia and Koelling report gained immediate currency in scientific circles and became extremely influential in learning theory.

Therefore, don't be too discouraged if you receive a recommendation of rejection for your first submission. But don't be inappropriately stubborn and persistent either. If the reaction to your report is consistently negative and similar valuative themes are expressed by several editorial offices, it may be time to move to another project.

## *Author Receives Copyright and Authorship Form, Signs It, and Returns It to the Editor*

When a manuscript is accepted for publication in an APA journal, the editor forwards a copyright and authorship form to the author(s). Figure 13–3 shows the transfer form (front and back) the editor of *JCCP* would send, which is the journal to which we submitted our report from our model experiment. The APA retains the copyright for the published material for 75 years from the time of publication, and when the material is reproduced in part or in its entirety, permissions must be obtained from the appropriate APA office.

In addition, to transfer the copyright to APA the author(s) must sign a part of the form which indicates he or she/they accept responsibility for the contents of the article and verify agreement on the order of authorship. As a safeguard, each author must sign the form. Finally, when the research was conducted under the authority of the U.S. Government or some other organization where authority for transferring the copyright may reside elsewhere, the authors are asked to obtain the appropriate signatures.

Because some published articles will attract considerable attention over a period of years, the transfer of the copyright to the publisher is an important legal step. Figures, excerpts from the text, and other information in the article may show up in review papers or books and understandably the journal will want to control the distribution of material it essentially owns. In most cases, APA grants authors permission to use their material elsewhere for free.

## *Editor Sends Manuscript to APA for Editing*

Once the copyright transfer is received, the journal editor forwards the hard copy and electronic versions of the final manuscript to the production office of APA for copyediting. Copyediting is done by trained professionals who change grammar and style and prepare the manuscript for the printer. Copyeditors check for omitted references, spelling errors, inappropriate word use, and other technical matters. The copyeditors do not judge content, so the basic text of the manuscript remains largely unchanged. When the copyeditor finishes the manuscript, as far as the publisher is concerned the article is ready for publication. The author(s), however, must make this final determination.

**APA PUBLICATION RIGHTS FORM**

Accepted manuscripts cannot be published unless this form is completed, signed, and returned to the appropriate editor.
FOR INFORMATION ON APA COPYRIGHT POLICIES, READ REVERSE OF THIS FORM.

Title of manuscript: _____

Author(s): _____

Corresponding author's name: _____   PHONE NUMBER: _____

APA publication: _____

*For office use only*

Year: _____   Volume: _____   Issue: _____   Pages: _____

**SECTION I - AUTHORSHIP CERTIFICATION**

(NOTE: **All authors must sign.** The senior/corresponding author must provide an original signature; original or faxed signatures for the other authors will be acceptable.)

Through signature below, the undersigned author(s) agrees to accept responsibility for the contents of the manuscripts and to approve the order of authorship as listed at the top of this form.

_____         _____
Date                           Date

_____         _____
Date                           Date

_____         _____
Date                           Date

CORRESPONDING AUTHOR: Proceed to Section II and sign.

**SECTION II - COPYRIGHT TRANSFER**

(NOTE: **Do not substitute company or other forms for this form.**)

A. The undersigned, desiring to publish the above manuscript in a print publication or electronic information service of the American Psychological Association (APA), hereby transfers on behalf of all authors, copyright of the above manuscript to the APA.

In return for copyright, the APA hereby grants to the above authors, and the employers for whom the work was performed, royalty-free permission to

1.  Retain all proprietary rights other than copyright, such as patent rights.
2.  Reproduce, or have reproduced, the above paper for the author's personal use or for company use provided that (a) the source and APA copyright are indicated, (b) the copies are not used in a way that implies APA endorsement of a product or service of an employer, and (c) the copies per se are not offered for sale.
3.  Make limited distribution of all or portions of the above paper prior to publication.
4.  In the case of work performed under U.S. Government contract, the APA grants the U.S. Government royalty-free permission to reproduce all or portions of the above paper, and to authorize others to do so, for U.S. Government purposes.

Through signature below, the undersigned author (1) signifies acceptance of the terms and conditions listed above, (2) affirms that written permission has been obtained for all previously published and/or copyrighted material contained in this manuscript, and (3) affirms that he/she is empowered to sign this form on behalf of all authors.

**Authors of work done for hire,** in addition to signing here in Section A, must obtain in Section B the signature of an authorized representative of the employer.

**U.S. Government employees** whose work is not subject to copyright may so certify by signing Section C.

_____   _____
Authorized Signature and Title                  Date

B. **Work Created Within The Scope Of Employment**

_____   _____
Authorized Signature and Title                  Date

_____
Name of employer for whom work was performed

C. **Government Employee Certification**

(If your work was performed under Government contract but you are not a Government employee, see item 4 above. Do not sign below.)

I certify that the majority of the authors or the primary authors of the above manuscript are employees of the U.S. Government and performed this work as part of their employment and that the paper is therefore not subject to U.S. copyright protection.

_____   _____
Authorized signature                    Signer's title if not author

_____   _____
Name of government organization         Date

**FIGURE 13–3** Copyright and authorship form for *JCCP.* Copyright © 1996 by the American Psychological Association. Reprinted with permission.

## INFORMATION TO AUTHORS

The new United States copyright law requires that the transfer of copyrights in each contribution from the author to the APA be confirmed in writing. It is therefore necessary that you execute either Part A, B, or C of the form on the reverse side of this sheet and return it to the Editor.

If your paper was prepared as a part of your job, the rights to your paper initially rest with your employer; therefore Part B of the copyright transfer form also must be signed by an authorized agent of your employer.

Authors who are U.S. Government employees are not required to sign Part A of the copyright transfer form, but any co-authors outside the Government are required to sign Part A. However, if the majority of the authors or the primary authors are U.S. Government employees and the work was done as a part of their job, then the primary author should sign Part C of the transfer form.

## APA PERMISSION POLICY GOVERNING THE SECONDARY USE OF COPYRIGHTED MATERIAL

It is the policy of the APA to own the copyrights to its publications, and to the contributions contained therein, in order to protect the interests of the Association, its authors and their employers, and at the same time to facilitate the appropriate reuse of this material by others.

In exercising its rights under copyright, the APA makes all reasonable effort to act in the interests of the authors and employers as well as in its own interest. In order to do so, the APA requires the following:

1. The consent of author(s) be a condition to granting most republication permissions to others. In the case of a work made for hire, the employers' permissions will also be sought.
2. The consent of author(s) or employers as a condition to granting permission to others to reuse all or portions of the paper for promotion or marketing purposes.

Permission and fees are waived for authors who wish to reproduce their own material for personal use; fees only are waived for authors who wish to use their own material commercially (but in the case of edited books, only for the book editor).

Permission is not required for the photocopying of **isolated** articles for nonprofit classroom or library reserve use. There may be a fee if students are charged for the material, multiple articles are copied, or large scale copying is involved (e.g., for course packs).

A fee of $20 per page, table, or figure is normally charged to all commercial organizations that secure permission to reprint APA copyrighted material. This fee, after an appropriate deduction to APA to cover the costs associated with administering the permission function, is turned over to the American Psychological Foundation, a charitable nonprofit 501(c)(3) organization, incorporated independently of the American Psychological Association.

The American Psychological Foundation was established in 1953 to promote psychology and to help extend its benefits to the public through donations of journals to libraries in underdeveloped nations, awards for achievements, and grants to promising young investigators of psychology.

**FIGURE 13–3 continued**

## *APA Sends Manuscript to Author(s) for Final Review*

After the copyediting is completed at the APA publication office, the manuscript is returned to the author(s) for final approval. It is the responsibility of the author(s) to ensure that the manuscript is ready for publication. When editing changes have been made, the author(s) must ensure that such changes do not blemish the scientific expression of the report. Because copyeditors are not typically specialists in experimental psychology, they may inadvertently suggest modifications that render new meaning to sentences, omit a key point, or otherwise corrupt the text. Although problems along these lines seldom occur, when they do the author(s) must step forward and correct the final manuscript.

After copyediting, there will be numerous editorial marks and queries on the manuscript. With the manuscript will be a code sheet which explains the editorial marks and helps the author(s) better understand what changes are being made. The copyeditor may request page numbers of published chapters in the reference list, question a figure caption or the placement of a table in the text, or bring up other minor matters that need resolution. The review by the author(s) at this stage in the publication process is a matter of routine and should not take more than a day or two to complete. It should be understood, however, that this is the last chance for the author(s) to make substantive changes in the report. Once the manuscript is returned to APA, future changes are discouraged and may prove very expensive.

## APA Sends Manuscript to Printer for Typesetting

Assuming that the author(s) have satisfactorily handled the copyeditor's queries and approved the manuscript for publication, APA will send the final version of the report to the printer for typesetting upon receipt. Technology in the printing industry is changing so rapidly that today's techniques may well be replaced by this time next year. Whatever the contemporary mechanism for setting type, the result is a throwback to literary antiquity——the wording is written in stone. This means that at this point it is difficult to accomplish anything other than the slightest changes in the article. You can correct typographical errors and the like, but other changes are not permitted.

## Printer Sends Manuscript, Proofs, and Reprint Order Forms to Author(s)

When the final report is typeset, the printer communicates directly with the author(s). APA is temporarily out of the loop, and the article becomes the joint task of the independent printing agency and those who submitted the manuscript for publication—the authors.

The final article that is to appear in the journal is sent to the author(s) in the form of "page proofs." At one time, "galley proofs" were sent as a preliminary step to the final "page proofs," but the more recent practice is to go straight to page proofs. The proofs appear pretty much as the published article will appear in the journal. The title and abstract begin the article, the format is fixed, the figures are placed properly, and so forth. The authors once again look over every detail of the report as it appears in proofs. By this time, of course, you can recite your entire article by memory, and you may be so tired of seeing it that you are inclined to just return it as soon as possible. But then you realize that after the months or even years of work you have put into this project you have this last opportunity to make sure everything is right with the article—everything rests on these final efforts.

As a rule, with the manuscript and proofs the printer sends a reprint order form. Reprints are bound or unbound copies (your choice) of the article that may be sent to other investigators as a professional courtesy. Some journals provide a limited number of reprints *gratis,* but in most cases the author(s) incur the costs of reprinting the article. You are not required to order reprints from the printer, but even if you choose not to, you should complete the order form and return it.

## *Proofs and Manuscript Are Returned to APA within 48 Hours*

Although the reprint order form is returned directly to the printer, the proofs and manuscript are returned to the production editor of the journal (*JCPP* in this case, American Psychological Association, 750 First Street, Washington, DC 20002-4242). Because the volume in which your article will appear has an established publication date, you must return the proofs and manuscript within 48 hours of their receipt. This may seem too short a period to review the proofs, but keep in mind that at this point all you are doing is reading for typographical errors and such. In this light, the 48-hour turnaround time is quite reasonable.

Once you ship the proofs and manuscript to APA, the situation is a *fait accompli*—it's over. The next time you will see your article is when everyone will see it published in the journal. The journey that commenced with the opening chapter of this book is now near completion.

## *Publication*

Within a few months from the time of the final return of your proofs and manuscript to APA, the journal containing your published article will appear. There is justifiably a great sense of accomplishment in seeing an article you authored in print. The reader, of course, sees only an economical, methodologically sound text that is relatively free of flaws. As the author, however, you can recall the countless hours spent on pilot investigations, data collection and analysis, revisions, and the rest of the publication process. From your point of view it is sometimes difficult to believe that so much of your effort could be condensed to 8 to 10 printed pages, but that is the reality of scientific communication.

Often, before you receive reprints from the printer, you will begin to receive reprint requests from other researchers who are interested in your article. Many of these requests will come from subscribers to the journal in which the article is published or from people who have access to library copies of the journal. Then, in a couple of weeks or so, there will be a second wave of reprint requests from people who monitor one of the several computer packages that search by topic or by author (see the discussion of computer software in Chapter 2). Finally, the international community will respond and you will begin receiving requests from all over the world. In some sense, the latter seem most gratifying because many researchers in certain countries have limited access to published information.

After a while, the flow of requests becomes a trickle, and after a couple of months it virtually stops. However, don't misinterpret this as a lack of interest. A good article that is properly placed in the reference literature will have an impact for years, maybe even decades. Other investigators will cite your work and weave a story, as you did, and the process is recapitulated.

The important aspect to publishing and sharing your ideas and findings is that you have participated. Perhaps you have only added a small piece to the puzzle, but it is a piece nonetheless, and our awareness and the scientific information base is enhanced accordingly. You have been a part of a venture into the unknown. You have risked a precious commodity—your time—so that we may all better understand the world of which we are a part.

# THE PUBLICATION TIMETABLE

As you can see, the publication process is complex. A relevant question, now that we have waded through the sequence of submitting, reviewing, revising, resubmitting, reviewing, proofing, and publishing, is "How long does all this take? From the date I send the article to the editor for evaluation, how long before I can expect to see my paper in print?"

Sommer and Sommer (1991) have provided a reasonable estimate of the timetable for publishing in a scientific journal (see Figure 13–4). You can see that

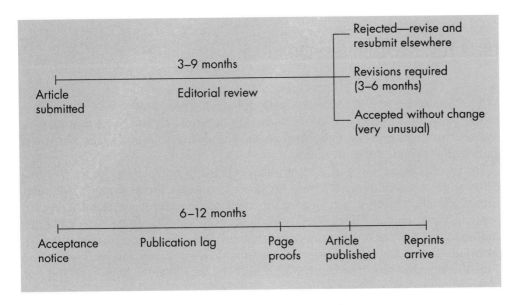

**FIGURE 13–4** Timetable for publication of a scientific report. (Adapted from Sommer and Sommer, 1991.)

generally we are looking at a minimum of one year from submission to publication. When there is a backlog of articles awaiting publication, the lag may extend to two years. This may seem frightfully long, and you may worry that your findings will be obsolete by the time they finally make it to press. As discussed earlier, however, truly valuable reports which make lasting contributions will have an impact for years, so you needn't be so concerned. Of course, in some disciplines technology changes so rapidly and the knowledge base shifts so sharply that it may be necessary to publish the information quickly. To allow for these special situations, many journals now include "Rapid Communications" sections that permit authors to quickly publish brief reports that convey novel findings which may alter the way other scientists approach a problem, either conceptually or technically.

# LOOKING BACK: OUR MODEL EXPERIMENT

As I reflect on this text in research methodology, I sense that we have completed a mission. It is a mission that people who are intrigued by the order that may be wrested from uncertainty must undertake. The desire to know—just know—is the singular driving force in research.

For us, "knowing" initially meant formulating a hypothesis about the relative efficacy of a cognitively oriented treatment strategy for younger and older chronically ill children. We reviewed the available literature, selected the appropriate independent and dependent variables, designed the experiment, collected and analyzed the data, and confirmed that cognitive therapies that may be appropriate for one age group may not be suitable for another. Finally, we drafted a manuscript that reported our findings and shared these findings with the rest of the scientific community.

It was an ambitious project. I know of no other textbooks of this kind in any academic area. We have collaborated as architects of a model experiment that emerged systematically, piece by piece, layer upon layer. And this is as it must be in any form of construction. First you establish the foundation, and then you build according to a logical scheme which ensures the structure will last. Once completed, the project takes on added meaning—it offers continuity.

The model experiment that was our common objective in this book may never be conducted, but from a purely parochial standpoint, it need not be. Our model instructed each of us in the excitement of the research enterprise, and that is sufficient.

# The Next Step

Now that the final report on the model experiment in this book (see Appendix for final version) has been published, what comes next? Are we truly finished, or are we just beginning?

The research process is expansive. In our efforts to supply answers to one question, we spawn numerous other questions that merit our attention. Perhaps some aspect of the data raises concerns about the generality of the findings, or an unexpected result may stimulate interest in a secondary topic or even provide the essential intellectual base that leads to a completely different line of reasoning. And, of course, there is always the issue of reliability. Just how robust are the data we have presented to the research community?

# THE EXPANDING STORY

There are several examples of the mushrooming effects associated with psychological experimentation in the report on our model experiment. For instance, consider the finding relating to the enhanced therapeutic effectiveness of the "sensory information strategy" for the younger chronically ill children (ages 4 to 6). This result was not critical to the rationale that formed the basis for conducting the experiment, but it does pose some interesting questions. Why would a simple descriptive approach, where you merely tell children what will happen to them, be more effective with younger than older age children? As was alluded to in our discussion section of the report, the cognitive apparatus of the younger child may be sufficiently constrained such that elaborate attempts at intervention serve only to confuse. Moreover, the limited range of coping mechanisms in the younger child may mandate including only those techniques that can be implemented in strictly behavioral formats. Attempts to incorporate mental components into the treatment scheme may compromise simpler operations that would be better presented in basic form. Here, then, we have an observation from our experiment that was not anticipated, and yet may reveal something about the relevance of a variety of treatment packages for younger patients. Chronically ill children, children with Conduct Disorder (CD) or Attention Deficit Hyperactivity Disorder (ADHD) cases, and a host of other populations of younger children with psychological disorders may be more suitably treated within a nonmentalistic framework. Of course, this position requires empirical documentation. In any event, our unexpected finding regarding the differential effectiveness of the sensory information strategy as a treatment for younger and older age children illustrates how an incidental result can promote further investigation.

Another piece of the data obtained in our model experiment that invites investigation is the fact that differences were only observed on the dependent measure of heart rate. Neither the behavioral scale (the OSBD) or the self-report measure (the fear thermometer) yielded evidence of group differences. It may be the case, of course, that such a finding may be specific to our project, involving only our narrowly defined subject population and experimental design. But it also needs to be considered that a more fundamental issue must be addressed. Perhaps autonomic reactions define a more sensitive index of anxiety among children and therein provide a more credible measure of treatment effectiveness. If so, future experiments with children examining the therapeutic effectiveness of different intervention strategies would benefit by incorporating such measures into their overall designs. At the very least, autonomic reactivity would need to be monitored over the course of treatment, if for no other reason than to gauge the children's overall stress levels.

Therefore, we see that even in a comparatively brief and straightforward study such as our model experiment, questions as well as answers are the substance of research. It could even be argued that a good experiment raises more questions than it answers. So now what? After generating so many novel ideas, which path do we follow?

# THE LOGICAL PATHWAY

By building on results from one's laboratory as well as the findings other investigators report in the literature, the research enterprise abides by a logical flow of ideas. The supposition is that the experimenter will work within a cohesive informational framework that contributes to the knowledge pool in some systematic way. To accomplish this, future research efforts should proceed according to an established script. More often than not, this means taking small steps.

## *Science Meets Art: The Role of Creativity in Research*

Scientific lore is rife with documented episodes of insight in which sudden avalanches of creative ideas led to breakthroughs or major reformulations of existing dogmas. With the aid of a ripening apple, Sir Isaac Newton provided us with an account of the physical character of the universe that survived 200 years. A bathtub of water helped the Greek mathmetician Archimedes develop a method for determining the purity of gold. But is this how science normally happens? Are "eureka experiences" the rule in scientific advancement? Probably not, for a couple of reasons.

First, the notion of isolated intellectual innovation is probably a myth. New-ton had considered the role of gravity in the movement of physical objects long before using the apple falling from a tree to illustrate this principle. It is equally implausible to believe that Archimedes had never considered the concept of dis-placement of equal volumes before his celebrated immersion in the bathtub. This is not to say that these concepts were not facilitated by these legendary events, but rather that the giant steps were made possible by many earlier and smaller steps.

Also keep in mind that along with prominent leaps in scientific awareness come unavoidable holes in our understanding. In the field of psychopharmacol-ogy, the discovery of naturally occurring pain-killers in the human body (beta-endorphins) in the mid-1970s (see Kow & Pfaff, 1988) was a tremendous breakthrough and confirmed expectancies of how the human system works, but 20 years later we are still filling in pieces of the puzzle. Opiates can be short act-ing or long acting, they may be released from different areas in the body, they interact with other molecular substrates to determine how we think and feel, and on it goes. The point is that if scientists relied on major departures from the pre-vailing sentiment or large jumps in our understanding of how the world is struc-tured, incompleteness would result. Therefore, we must be careful not to overlook more modest contributions. The thundering home run is an exciting part of the game and a real crowd pleaser, but slap singles up the middle are likely to be productive when they are strung together.

This raises a question of what constitutes a genuinely artistic talent in science. Is it not a creative accomplishment to polish the details of a masterpiece? Imag-ine Mark Twain's *Mysterious Stranger* without the last chapter, or Michelangelo's painting of the Vatican's Sistine Chapel without the *Creation of Adam* panel. The poet Kahlil Gibran walked in the mountains of Lebanon with the manuscript *The Prophet* for four years, continuing to change it and making sure every word was right. Is the craft of science less significant? No, there is much to be said for those who are willing to do the small things and refine our understanding of the events that take place around us.

## Following Directions

Advancement by small steps, or large steps, must be accomplished according to a specified plan. A logical approach to research requires that we progress using cues from available guidelines. In the absence of such guidelines, the investiga-tor risks simply gathering unrelated facts, the ultimate consequence of which is that at the end of the journey there is no story to tell. It is true that individual descriptive accounts of the conditions that promote behavioral change add to the general knowledge store, but an awareness of the relations between and among the data is essential if we ever hope to gain a genuine understanding of our world.

What is needed, then, is a map that provides directions about where to go to find such relations. As noted in the opening chapter of this book, more often than not this map takes the form of a carefully formulated theory. Based on existing empirical findings, the theoretician sets forth fundamental principles that lead researchers along a clearly marked path. Of course, the path may broaden or narrow depending on what is found along the way. An unexpected finding that questions the validity of a principle, a new piece of technology, or a timely confluence of novel ideas may necessitate redirection and the charting of a new course. But you still proceed systematically, from point to point, toward some greater appreciation of an orderly world.

Even in the absence of global theory, it makes sense to ask for direction. Look for clues that may be embedded in earlier reports or hidden in large data sets used for another purpose. You may want to ask, "What are the applied implications of my basic research findings?" "Are there other populations that would show parallel effects?" "Will my findings using an animal model hold true with human participants?" In all cases, there is a logical rationale for progressing to the next experiment. Because you have a *reason* to conduct the research, it is more likely to yield something meaningful.

# WISHING YOU WELL

As this book closes, we see that we are involved in an ongoing process of asking questions that ultimately lead to even more questions. In a way, we have completed a circle. At the beginning of this book, we began to gather information related to a specified topic. Based on this information, we formulated a hypothesis that we evaluated within an experimental framework. Now we see that our findings have brought us to the essential condition that existed before: more information is needed.

Research of any kind offers excitement, and behavioral research is especially stimulating because of its relevance. Inherent curiosity, a need to comprehend, a recognition of what is not known, and the "irrepressible desire to gather data" (p. 2) are all human qualities integral to a meaningful research experience. Behavioral research in any topic area offers exhilaration through discovery. It may be exasperating at times, but it will never be boring.

I have made a life of conducting research. Transmitting my enthusiasm for it to others has been a most gratifying dimension of my professional link with psychology and the behavioral sciences. I wish you the same good fortune as you take "the next step."

# References

Abramson, L. Y., Seligman, M. E. P., & Teasdale, J. D. (1978). Learned helplessness in humans: Critique and reformulation. *Journal of Abnormal Psychology, 87,* 49–74.

American Psychological Association (1973). *Ethical principles in the conduct of research with human participants.* Washington, DC: Author.

American Psychological Association (1982). *Ethical principles in the conduct of research with human participants.* Washington, DC: Author.

American Psychological Association (1994). *Publication Manual of the American Psychological Association.* Washington, DC: American Psychological Association.

Anastasi, A. (1988). *Psychological testing* (6th ed.). New York: Macmillan.

Anderson, C. A., & Anderson, D. C. (1984). Ambient temperature and violent crime: Tests of the linear and curvilinear hypotheses. *Journal of Personality and Social Psychology, 46,* 91–97.

Armstong, B. (1995). Study design for exposure assessment in epidemiological studies. *Science of the Total Environment, 168,* 187–194.

Asch, S. E. (1956). Studies of independence and submission to group pressure: I. A minority of one against a unanimous majority. *Psychological Monographs, 70* (9, Whole No. 416).

Atkinson, J. W., & Birch, D. (1978). *An introduction to motivation.* New York: Van Nostrand-Reinhold.

Baddeley, A. (1993). *Human memory: Theory and practice.* Boston: Allyn and Bacon.

Badia, P., & Runyon, R. P. (1982). *Fundamentals of behavioral research.* Reading, MA: Sage Publications.

Ballieux, R. E. (1995). The mind and the immune system. *Theoretical Medicine, 15,* 387–395.

Bandura, A., O'Leary, A., Taylor, C. B., Gauthier, J., & Gossard, D. (1988). Perceived self-efficacy and pain control: Opioid and non-opioid mechanisms. *Journal of Personality and Social Psychology, 53,* 563–571.

Bandura, A., Ross, D. M., & Ross, S. A. (1963). Imitation of film-mediated aggressive models. *Journal of Abnormal and Social Psychology, 66,* 3–11.

Baumrind, D. (1964). Some thoughts on ethics of research: After reading Milgram's "behavorial study of obedience." *American Psychologist, 19,* 421–423.

Bayer, R., & Toomey, K. E. (1992). HIV prevention and the two faces of partner notification: Policies, politics, and ethics. *American Journal of Public Health, 82,* 1158–1164.

Benjamin. L. T. (1988). *A history of psychology: Original sources and contemporary research.* New York: McGraw-Hill.

Benjamin, L. T., Hopkins, J. R., & Nation, J. R. (1994). *Psychology.* New York: Macmillan.

Bergin, A. E., & Strupp, H. H. (1970). New directions in psychotherapy research. *Journal of Abnormal Psychology, 76,* 13–26.

Beutler, L. E., Crago, M., & Arizmendi, T. G. (1986). Research on therapists variables in psychotherapy. In S. L. Garfield & A. E. Bergin (Eds.), *Handbook of psychotherapy and behavioral change.* New York: Wiley

Binder, A., McConnell, D., & Sjoholm, R. (1957). Verbal conditioning as a function of experimenter characteristics. *Journal of Abnormal Social Psychology, 55,* 309–314.

Blanck, P. D., Bellack, A. S., Rosnow, R. L., Rotheram-Borus, M. J., & Schooler, N. R. (1992). Scientific rewards and conflicts of ethical choices in human subject research. *American Psychologist, 47,* 959–965.

Bok, S. (1978). *Lying: Moral choice in public and private life.* New York: Pantheon Books.

Bordens, K. S., & Abbott, B. B. (1988). *Research design and methods.* Mountain View, CA: Mayfield Publishing Company.

Boring, E. G. (1950). *A history of experimental psychology.* New York: Appleton-Century-Crofts.

Bower, G. H. (1981). Mood and memory. *American Psychologist, 36,* 129–148.

Bronstein, P., & Quina, K. (1991). *Teaching psychology of people: Resources for gender and socio-cultural awareness.* Washington, D.C.: American Psychological Association.

Brown, J., O'Keeffe, J., Sanders, S. F., & Baker, B. (1986). Developmental changes in children's cognition to stressful and painful situations. *Journal of Pediatric Psychology, 11,* 3–7.

Burkey, R. T., Nation, J. R., & Bratton, G. R. (1994). Chronic lead exposure attenuates ethanol-induced hypoalgesia. *Pharmacology, Biochemistry, and Behavior, 47,* 227–231.

Burt, C. (1940). *The factors of the mind.* London: London University Press.

Campbell, D. T., & Stanley, J. C. (1963). *Experimental and quasi-experimental designs for research.* Chicago: Rand McNally.

Campbell, K. E., and Jackson, T. T. (1979). The role of and need for replication research in social psychology. *Replications in Social Psychology, 1,* 3–14.

Canli, T., Detmer, W. M., & Donegan, N. H. (1992). Potentiation or diminution of discrete motor unconditioned responses (rabbit eyeblink) to an aversive Pavlovian unconditioned stimulus by two associative processes: Conditioned fear and a conditioned diminution of unconditioned stimulus processing. *Behavioral Neuroscience, 106,* 498–508.

Cannon, W. B., & Washburn, A. L. (1912). An explanation of hunger. *American Psychologist, 29,* 441–454.

Carlson, N. R. (1991). *Physiology and behavior.* Boston: Allyn & Bacon.

Carson, R. C., Butcher, J. N., & Mineka, S. (1996). *Abnormal psychology and modern life.* New York: HarperCollins.

Centers for Disease Control (CDC). (1991). *Preventing lead poisoning in young children: A statement by the Centers for Disease Control.* Atlanta, CDC.

Church, R. M. (1964). Systematic effect of random errors in the yoked control design. *Psychological Bulletin, 62,* 122–131.

Cohen, M., & Nagel, E. (1934). *An introduction to logic and scientific method.* New York: Harcourt.

Conrad, E., & Maul, T. (1981). *Introduction to experimental psychology.* New York: Wiley.

Cook, M., Mineka, S., & Trumble, D. (1987). The role of response-produced exteroceptive feedback in attenuation of fear over the course of avoidance learning. *Journal of Experimental Psychology: Animal Behavior Processes, 13,* 239–249.

Corte, H. E., Wolf, M. M., & Locke, B. J. (1971). A comparison of procedures for eliminating self-injurious behavior of retarded adolescents. *Journal of Applied Behavior Analysis, 4,* 201–213.

Cowles, M. F. (1974). N = 35: A rule of thumb for psychological researchers. *Perceptual and Motor Skills, 38,* 1135–1138.

Cronbach, L. J., & Meehl, P. E. (1955). Construct validity in psychological tests. *Psychological Bulletin, 52,* 281–300.

Curry, S. L., & Russ, S. W. (1985). Identifying coping strategies in children. *Journal of Clinical Child Psychology, 14,* 61–69.

Damasio, H., Grabowski, T., Frank, R., Galaburda, A. M., & Damasio, A. R. (1994). The return of Phineas Gage: Clues about the brain from the skull of a famous patient. *Science, 264,* 1102–1105.

Danzinger, K. (1990). *Constructing the subject: Historical origins of psychological research.* New York: Cambridge University Press.

Davis, J. D., & Smith, G. P. (1992). Analysis of the microstructure of the rhythmic tongue movements of rats ingesting maltose and sucrose solutions. *Behavioral Neuroscience, 106,* 217–228.

Davis, S. F., Nation, J. R., & Mayleben, M. A. (1993). The effects of chronic lead exposure on reactivity to frustrative nonreward in rats. *Toxicology Letters, 66,* 237–246.

Deese, J. (1972). *Psychology as science and art.* New York: Harcourt, Brace, Jovanovich.

Deni, R. (1986). *Programming microcomputers for psychology experiments.* Belmont, CA: Wadsworth.

Dethier, V. (1962). *To know a fly.* San Francisco: Holden-Day.

Diggle, P. (1990). *Time series: A biostatistical approach.* New York: Oxford University Press.

Dillman, D. A. (1978). *Mail and telephone surveys: The total design method.* New York: John Wiley & Sons.

Domjan, M. (1996). *The essentials of conditioning and learning.* Pacific Grove, CA: Brooks/Cole.

Doring, K., Schneider, J., & Koenig, W. (1995). Estimating psychomental strain—circulatory and neurohormonal indicators of strain in patients with coronal heart disease and under physical and psychomental stress. *Herz Kreislauf, 27,* 244–255.

Dyck, D. G., Greenberg, A. H., & Osachuck, T. A. G. (1986). Tolerance to drug-induced (POLY:IC) natural killer cell activation: Congruence with a Pavlovian conditioning model. *Journal of Experimental Psychology: Animal Behavior Processes, 12,* 25–31.

Ebbinghaus, H. (1954). Retention of nonsense syllable lists learned by Ebbinghaus as measured by the methods of "savings." In *Memory: A contribution to experimental psychology.* New York: Dover. (Original work published in 1885.)

Ehrlich, J. S., & Riesman, D. (1961). Experimenter effects as a function of age. *Public Opinion Quarterly, 25,* 39–56.

Eiseley, L. (1957). *The immense journey.* New York: Random House.

Emerson, R. W. (1968). Intellect. In B. Atkinson (Ed.), *The selected writings of Ralph Waldo Emerson.* New York: The Modern Library.

Emerson, R. W. (1968). Self-reliance. In B. Atkinson (Ed.), *The selected writings of Ralph Waldo Emerson.* New York: The Modern Library.

Esposito, J. L., Agard, E., & Rosnow, R. L. (1984). Can confidentiality of data pay off? *Personality and Individual Differences, 5,* 477–480.

Evans, R. L., & Connis, R. T. (1995). Comparison of brief group therapies for depressed cancer patients receiving radiation treatment. *Public Health Reports, 11,* 306–311.

Fantz, R. L., & Nevis, S. (1967). Pattern preferences and perceptual-cognitive development in early infancy. *Mirrill-Palmer Quarterly, 13,* 88–108.

Feild, H. S., & Barnett, N. J. (1978). Students versus "real" people as jurors. *Journal of Social Psychology, 104,* 287–293.

Gallup, G. (1993). *The Gallup Poll: Public Opinion 1992.* Wilmington, DE: Scholarly Resources, Inc.

Garcia, J., & Koelling, R. A. (1966). Relation of cue to consequences of avoidance learning. *Psychonomic Science, 4,* 123–124.

George, F. R. (1987). Genetic and environmental factors in ethanol self-administration. *Pharmacology, Biochemistry, and Behavior, 27,* 379–384.

Gerber, L. E., & McFadden, M. (1990). *Loren Eisley.* New York: Ungar.

Gerralda, M. E., Kim, S., & Klein, S. (1994). Psychiatric adjustment in children with chronic physical illness. *British Journal of Hospital Medicine, 52,* 230–234.

Goldstein, E. B. (1988). *Sensation and perception.* Belmont, CA: Wadsworth.

Goodall, J. (1971). *In the shadow of man.* Boston: Houghton-Mifflin.

Gould, S. J. (1991) *The mismeasurement of man.* New York: Norton.

Gravetter, F. J., & Wallnau, L. B. (1995). *Essentials of statistics for the behavioral sciences.* St. Paul, MN: West Publishing Company.

Grover, C. A., Nation, J. R., Burkey, R. T., McClure, M. C., & Bratton, G. R. (1993). Lead/ethanol interactions I: Rate-depressant effects. *Alcohol, 10,* 355–361.

Groves, P. M., & Thompson, R. F. (1970). Habituation: A dual process theory. *Psychological Review, 77,* 419–450.

Guilford, J. P., & Fruchter, B. (1973). *Fundamental statistics in psychology and education* (5th ed.). New York: McGraw-Hill.

Hamilton, E. W., & Abramson, L. Y. (1983). Cognitive patterns and major depression disorder: A longitudinal study in a hospital setting. *Journal of Personality and Social Psychology, 29,* 856-864.

Hamilton, J. O. (1974). Motivation and risk-taking behavior: A test of Atkinsson's theory. *Journal of Personality and Social Psychology, 29,* 856–864.

Hanfling, O. (1981). *Logical positivism.* New York: Columbia University Press.

Harford, T. C., Parker, D. A., Grant, B. F., & Dawson, D. A. (1992). Alcohol use and dependence among employed men and women in the United States in 1988. *Alcoholism: Clinical and Experimental Research, 16,* 146–148.

Harlow, J. M. (1868). *Publication of the Massachusetts Medical Society, 2,* 327.

Harris, B. (1988). Key words: A history of debriefing in social psychology. In J. Morawski (Ed.), *The rise of experimentation in American psychology.* New Haven, CT: Yale University Press.

Hart, B. M., Allen, K. E., Buell, J. S., Harris, F. R., & Wolf, M. M. (1964). Effects of social reinforcement on operant crying. *Journal of Experimental Child Psychology, 1,* 145–153.

Hawkins, R. P., & Dotson, V. A. (1975). Reliability scores that delude: An Alice in Wonderland trip through the misleading characteristics of interobserver agreement scores in interval recording. In E. Ramp & G. Semp (Eds.), *Behavior analysis: Areas of research and application* (pp. 359–376). Englewood Cliffs, NJ: Prentice-Hall.

Helmstadter, G. C. (1970). *Research concepts in human behavior.* New York: Appleton-Century-Crofts.

Hiroto, D. S., & Seligman, M. E. P. (1975). Generality of learned helplessness in man. *Journal of Personality and Social Psychology, 31,* 311–327.

Hirvonen, J., & Huttunen, P. (1995). Hypothermia markers—serum, urine, and adrenal gland catecholamines in hypothermic rats given ethanol. *Forensic Service International, 72,* 125–133.

Holloway, F. A. (1978). State-dependent retrieval based on time of day. In B. T. Ho, D. W. Richards, & D. L. Chute (Eds.), *Drug discrimination and state-dependent learning.* (pp 319–344). New York: Academic Press.

Hopkins, R. (1974). *Curvature as a dimension in infant visual perception.* Unpublished doctoral dissertation, Harvard University, Cambridge, MA.

Hopkins, R., Kagan, J., Brachfeld, S., & Linn, S. (1976). Infant responsivity to curvature. *Child Development, 47,* 1166–1171.

Howell, D. C. (1995). *Fundamental statistics for the behavioral sciences.* Belmont, CA: Duxbury Press.

Hughes, R. (1992 May 25). Really Rembrandt? *Time,* 60–61.

Hull, C. L. (1943). *Principles of Behavior.* New York: Appleton-Century.

Hurlburt, R. T. (1994). *Comprehending behavioral statistics.* Pacific Grove, CA: Brooks/Cole.

Hyman, H. H., Cobb, W. J., Feldman, J. J., Hart, C. W., & Stember, C. H. (1954). *Interviewing in social research.* Chicago: University of Chicago Press.

Jay, S. M., Elliott, C. H., Ozolins, M., Olson, R. A., & Pruitt, S. D. (1985). Behavioral management of children's distress during painful medical treatment. *Behavior Research and Therapy, 23,* 513–520.

Jones, J. (1981). *Bad blood: The Tuskegee syphilis experiment—A tragedy of race and medicine.* New York: Free Press.

Jones, S. L., Nation, J. R., & Massad, P. (1977). Immunization against learned helplessness in man. *Journal of Abnormal Psychology, 86,* 75–83.

Joynson, R. B. (1990). *The Burt affair.* London: Routledge.

Kalivas, P. W. (1995). Interactions between dopamine and excitatory amino acids in behavioral sensitization to psychostimulants. *Drug and Alcohol Dependence, 37,* 95–100.

Kamin, L. J. (1957). The retention of an incompletely learned avoidance response. *Journal of Comparative and Physiological Psychology, 50,* 457–460.

Kamin. L. J. (1974). *The science and politics of IQ.* New York: Wiley.

Kasof, G. M., Mandelzyz, A., Maika, S. D., Hammer, R. E., Curren, T., & Morgan, J. I. (1995). Kainic acid-induced neuronal death is associated with DNA damage and a unique immediate-early gene response in C-FOS-LACZ transgenic mice. *Journal of Neuroscience, 15,* 4238–4269.

Katz, E. R., Kellerman, J., & Siegel, S. E. (1982). *Self-report and observational measurement of acute pain, fear, and behavioral distress in children with leukemia.* Paper presented at the meeting of the Society of Behavior Medicine, Chicago.

Katz, I., Robinson, J. M., Epps, E., & Waly, P. (1964). The influence of race of the experimenter and instructions upon the expression of hostility by Negro boys. *Journal of Social Issues, 20,* 54–59.

Kendall, G., Hrycaiko, D., Martin, G. L., & Kendall, T. (1990). The effects of imagery, rehearsal, relaxation, and self-talk package on basketball game performance. *Journal of Sport and Exercise Psychology, 12,* 457–466.

Kendler, T. S., & Kendler, H. H. (1967). Experimental analysis of inferential behavior in children. In L. Lipsitt & C. Spiker (Eds.), *Advances in child development and behavior.* (vol. 3). (pp. 157–190). New York: Academic Press.

Kerlinger. F. N. (1973). *Foundations of behavioral research.* New York: Holt, Rinehart, and Winston.

King, D. W., & King, L. A. (1991). Validity issues in research on Vietnam veteran adjustment. *Psychological Bulletin, 109,* 107–124.

Klein, S. B. (1991). *Learning: Principles and applications.* New York: McGraw-Hill.

Knight, J. A. (1984). Exploring the compromise of ethical principles in science. *Principles in Biology and Medicine, 27,* 432–441.

Kolata, G. (1986). New drug counters alcohol intoxication. *Science, 234,* 1198–1199.

Kow, L. M., & Pfaff, D. W. (1988). Neuromodulator actions of peptides. *Annual Review of Pharmacology and Toxicology, 28,* 163–188.

La Greca, A. M., Siegel, L. J., Wallander, J. L., & Walker, C. E. (1992). *Stress and coping in child health.* New York: The Guilford Press.

Lancaster, F. E., & Spiegel, K. S. (1992). Sex differences in patterns of drinking. *Alcohol, 9,* 415–420.

Lawrence, D. H., & DeRivera, J. (1954). Evidence for relational transposition. *Journal of Comparative and Physiological Psychology, 47,* 465–471.

Lazarus, R. S. (1983). Thoughts on the relation between emotion and cognition. *American Psychologist, 37,* 1019–1024.

Leahey, T. H. (1987). *A history of psychology: Main currents in psychological thought.* Englewood Cliffs, NJ: Prentice-Hall.

Leahey, T. H., & Harris, R. J. (1993). *Learning and cognition.* Englewood Cliffs, NJ: Prentice-Hall.

LeUnes, A. D., & Nation, J. R. (1982). Saturday's heroes: A psychological portrait of college football players. *Journal of Sport Behavior, 5,* 139–149.

LeUnes, A. D., & Nation, J. R. (1996). *Sport psychology.* Chicago: Nelson-Hall.

LeVay, S. (1991). A difference in hypothalamic structure between heterosexual and homosexual men. *Science, 253,* 1034–1037.

LeVay, S., & Hamer, D. H. (1994). Evidence for a biological influence in male homosexuality. *Scientific American, 270,* 44–49.

Likert, R. (1932). A technique for the measurement of attitudes. *Archives of Psychology, 19,* 44–53.

Loft, A. (1989). A quasi-experimental design based on regional variations: Discussion of a method for evaluating outcomes of medical practice. *Social Science & Medicine, 28,* 147–154.

MacCorquodale, K., & Meehl, P. E. (1948). On a distinction between hypothetical constructs and intervening variables. *Psychological Review, 60,* 55–63.

Majors, R. (1992). *Cool pose. The dilemmas of black manhood in America.* New York: Macmillan.

Maritz, J. S. (1995). *Distribution-free statistical methods.* New York: Chapman and Hall.

Martin, G., & Pear, J. (1988). *Behavior modification: What it is and how to use it.* Englewood Cliffs, NJ: Prentice-Hall.

McClelland, D. C. (1985). *Human motivation*. Glenview, IL: Scott-Foresman.

McMichael, A. J., Baghurst, P. A., Wigg, N. R., Vimpani, G. V., Robertson, E. F., Roberts, R. J., & Tong, S. (1992). Lifelong exposure to environmental lead and children's intelligence at age seven: The Port Pirie cohort study. *New England Journal of Medicine, 327,* 1279–1284.

McNamara, C. G., Davidson, E. S., & Schenk, S. (1993). A comparison of the motor activating effects of acute and chronic exposure to amphetamine and methylphenidate. *Pharmacology, Biochemistry, & Behavior, 45,* 729–732.

McVaugh, M., & Mauskopf, S. H. (1976). J. B. Rhine's extrasensory perception and its background in psychical research. *ISIS, 67,* 161–189.

Mellgren, R. L. (1972). Positive and negative contrast effects using delayed reinforcement. *Learning and Motivation, 3,* 185–193.

Melzack, R., & Wall, P. D. (1988). *The challenge of pain*. New York: Penguin.

Merchant, D. A. (1990). *Treating abused adolescents*. Holmes Beach, FL: Learning Publications.

Metalsky, G. I., Abramson, L. Y., Seligman, M. E. P., Semmel, A., & Peterson, C. (1982). Attributional styles and life events in the classroom: Vulnerability and invulnerability to depressive mood reactions. *Journal of Personality and Social Psychology, 43,* 612–617.

Meyers, M. C., Bourgeois, A. E., & LeUnes, A. D. (1991). *Sports Inventory for Pain (SIP)*.

Milgram, S. (1963). Behavioral study of obedience. *Journal of Abnormal and Social Psychology, 67,* 371–378.

Milgram, S. (1974). *Obedience to authority*. New York: Harper & Row.

Miller, M. M., Sherman, H., Combs, C., & Kruus, L. (1992). Patterns of children's coping with medical and dental stressors: Nature, implications, and future directions. In L. Siegel, G. Walker, J. Wallander., & A. La Greca (Eds.), *Advances in pediatric psychology: Stress and coping in child health*. New York: Guilford Press.

Miller, P. (1995). Jane Goodall. *National Geographic, 188* (Dec.), 102–128.

Milner, P. M. (1991). Brain stimulation reward: A review. *Canadian Journal of Psychology, 45,* 1–36.

Mower, O. H. (1960). *Learning theory and behavior*. New York: Wiley.

Myers, J. L. (1991). *Research design and statistical analysis*. New York: HarperCollins.

Nation, J. R., Baker, D. M., Taylor, B., & Clark, D. E. (1986). Dietary lead increases ethanol consumption in the rat. *Behavioral Neuroscience, 100,* 525–530.

Nation, J. R., & Burkey, R. T. (1994). Attenuation of cocaine-induced elevation of nucleus accumbens dopamine in lead-exposed rats. *Brain Research Bulletin, 35,* 101–105.

Nation, J. R., Burkey, R. T., & Grover, C. A. (1993). Lead/ethanol interactions II: Pharmacokinetics. *Alcohol, 10,* 363–367.

Nation, J. R., & Cooney, J. B. (1982). The time course of extinction-induced aggressive behavior in humans: Evidence for a stage model of extinction. *Learning and Motivation, 13,* 95–112.

Nation, J.R., Cooney, J.B., & Gartrell, K.E. (1979). Durability and generalizability of persistence training. *Journal of Abnormal Psychology, 88,* 121-136.

Nation, J. R., Dugger, L. M., Dwyer, K. K., Bratton, G. R., & Grover, C. A. (1991). The effects of dietary lead on ethanol-reinforced responding. *Alcohol and Alcoholism, 26,* 473–480.

Nation, J. R., & LeUnes, A. D. (1983). Personality characteristics of intercollegiate football players as determined by position, classification, and redshirt status. *Journal of Sport Behavior, 6,* 92–102.

Nation, J. R., Livermore, C. L., & Bratton, G. R. (1995). Cadmium exposure attenuates the initiation of behavioral sensitization to cocaine. *Brain Research, 702,* 223–232.

Nation, J. R., Roop, S. S., & Dickinson, R. W. (1976). Positive contrast following gradual and abrupt shifts in reward magnitude using delay of reinforcement. *Learning and Motivation, 7,* 571–579.

Nation, J. R., & Woods, D. J. (1980). Persistence: The role of partial reinforcement in psychotherapy. *Journal of Experimental Psychology: General, 109,* 175–204.

Nation, J. R., Wrather, D. M., & Mellgren, R. L. (1974). Contrast effects in escape conditioning with rats. *Journal of Comparative and Physiological Psychology, 86,* 47–61.

Needleman, H. L., Gunnoe, C., Levition, A., Reed, R., Peresie, H., Maher, C., & Barrett, P. (1979). Deficits in psychologic and classroom performance of children with elevated dentine levels. *New England Journal of Medicine, 300,* 689–695.

Nehas, G., Trouve, R., Demus, E. F., & Von Sitbon, A. (1985). A calcium channel blocker as antidote to the cardiac effects of cocaine intoxication. *New England Journal of Medicine, 313,* 520–521.

Nurss, S. (1989). Rough-and-tumble play. *Parents, 64* (November 89), 243–244.

Ollendick, T. H. (1995). Cognitive behavioral treatment of panic disorder with agoraphobia in adolescents—A multiple baseline design analysis. *Behavior Therapy, 26,* 517–531.

Orne, M. T. (1962). On the social psychological experiment: With particular reference to demand characteristics and their implications. *American Psychologist, 17,* 776–783.

Overmier, J. B., & Seligman, M. E. P. (1967). Effects of inescapable shock upon subsequent escape and avoidance learning. *Journal of Comparative and Physiological Psychology, 63,* 28-33.

Parsons, J. E., & Ruble, D. N. (1977). The development of achievement-related expectancies. *Child Development, 48,* 1075–1079.

Patel, J. K. (1982). *Handbook of the normal distribution.* New York: M. Dekker.

Peterson, L., & Shigetomi, C. (1981). The use of coping techniques to minimize anxiety in hospitalized children. *Behavior Therapy, 12,* 1–14.

Petri, H. L. (1981). *Motivation: Theory and research.* Belmont, CA: Wadsworth.

Pillard, R. C., & Bailey, J. M. (1995). A biologic perspective on sexual orientation. *Psychiatric Clinics of North America, 18,* 71–84.

Popper, K. R. (1968). *The logic of scientific discovery.* London: Hutchinson and Company.

Powell, J. (1975). An evaluation of time-sample measures of behavior. *Journal of Applied Behavior Analysis, 8,* 463–469.

Putka, G. (1992). Research on lead poisoning is questioned. (1992, March 6). *The Wall Street Journal.*

Reamer, F. G. (1979). Protecting research subjects and unintended consequences: The effects of guarantees of confidentiality. *Public Opinion Quarterly, 43,* 497–506.

Reese, H. W., & Lipsitt, L. P. (1970). *Experimental child psychology.* New York: Academic Press.

Rholes, W. S., Blackwell, J., Jordan, C., & Walters, C. (1980). A developmental study of learned helplessness. *Developmental Psychology, 16,* 616–624.

Roberts, F. S. (1979). *Measurement theory with applications to decision making utility and the social sciences.* Reading, MA: Addison-Wesley.

Roethlisberger, F. J., & Dickson, N. M. (1939). *Management and the worker.* Cambridge, MA: Harvard University Press.

Rosenthal, R. (1976). *Experimenter effects in behavioral research.* New York: Irvington.

Rosenthal, R. (1994). Parametric measures of effect size. In H. M. Cooper & L. V. Hedges (Eds.), *Handbook of research synthesis.* (pp. 231–244). New York: Russell Sage Foundation.

Rosenthal, R., Friedman, N., & Kurland, D. (1965, April). *Instruction reading behavior of the experimenter as an unintended determinant of experimental results.* Paper presented at the annual meeting of the Eastern Psychological Association, Atlantic City, NJ.

Rosenthal. R., & Rosnow, R. L. (1975). *The volunteer subject.* New York: Wiley.

Rotheram-Borus, M., Koopman, C., & Bradley, J. (1989). Barriers to successful AIDS prevention programs and runaway youth. In J. O. Woodruff, D. Doherty, & J. G. Athey (Eds.), *Troubled adolescents and HIV infection: Issues in prevention and treatment.* Washington, DC: Janis Press.

Samuelson, F. (1992). Rescuing the reputation of Sir Cyril Burt. *Journal of the History of the Behavioral Sciences, 28,* 221–233.

Sargent, J., & Liebman, R. (1985). Childhood chronic illness: Issues for psychotherapists. *Community Mental Health Journal, 21,* 294–311.

Scavio, M. J., Clift, P., & Wills, J. C. (1992). Post-training effects of amphetamine, ketamine, and scoplamine on the acquisition and extinction of the rabbit's conditioned nictitating membrane response. *Behavioral Neuroscience, 106,* 900–908.

Schachter, S. (1959). *Psychology of affiliation.* Stanford, CA: Stanford University Press.

Schaie, K. W. (1983). The Seattle longitudinal study: A 21-year exploration of psychometric intelligence in adulthood. In K. W. Schaie (Ed.), *Longitudinal studies of adult psychological development.* New York: Guilford Press.

Schenk, S., Snow, S., & Horger, B. A. (1991). Pre-exposure to amphetamine but not nicotine sensitizes rats to the motor activating effects of cocaine. *Psychopharmacology, 103,* 62–66.

Seligman, M. E. P. (1975). *Helplessness: On depression, development, and death.* San Francisco: Freeman.

Sewell, T. E., Chandler, M. E., & Smith, R. (1983). Self-regulation and external reinforcement in problem-solving strategies of black adolescents. *Journal of Clinical Psychology, 39,* 39–45.

Shavit, Y., Terman, G. W., Martin, F. C., Lewis, J. W., Liebeskind, J. C., & Gale, R. P. (1985). Stress, opioid peptides, the immune system, and cancer. *The Journal of Immunology, 135,* 834-837.

Shepard, S., & Metzger, D. (1988). Mental rotation: Effects of dimensionality of objects and type of task. *Journal of Experimental Psychology: Human Perception and Performance, 14,* 3–11.

Sieber, J. E. (1992). *Planning ethically responsible research.* Newbury Park, CA: Sage.

Sieber, J. E., & Sorensen, J. L. (1991). Ethical issues in community-based research and intervention. In J. Edwards, R. S. Tindale, L. Heath, and E. J. Prosavac (Eds.), *Social applications to social issues: Vol. 2. Methodological issues in applied social psychology.* New York: Plenum Press.

Siegel, L. J., & Peterson, L. (1980). Stress reduction in young dental patients through coping skills and sensory information. *Journal of Consulting and Clinical Psychology, 48,* 785–787.

Simpson, D. D. (1980). Leisure patterns of opioid addicts: A six-year follow-up of clients. U.S. Dept. of Health and Human Services, Public Health Service, Alcohol, Drug Abuse, and Mental Health Administration. Rockville, MD: U.S. GPO.

Skinner, B. F. (1974). *About behaviorism.* New York: Knopf.

Smith, S. M. (1986). Environmental context-dependent recognition memory using a short-term memory task for input. *Memory & Cognition, 14,* 347–354.

Smith, S. M. (1988). Experimental context dependent memory. In G. Davies & D. Thompson (Eds.), *Aspects of memory: Theoretical aspects.* New York: Wiley.

Snyder, D. K., Wills, R. M., & Grady-Fletcher, A. (1991). Longterm effectiveness of behavioral versus insight-oriented marital therapy: A 4-year follow-up. *Journal of Consulting and Clinical Psychology, 59,* 138–141.

Sokolov, E. N. (1960). Neuronal models of the orienting reflex. In M. Brazier (Ed.), *The central nervous system and behavior.* New York: J. Macy.

Sommer, B., & Sommer, R. (1991). *The practical guide to behavioral research: Tools and techniques.* New York: Oxford University Press.

Sonnert, G. (1995). *Gender differences in science careers: The project access study.* New Brunswick, NJ: Rutgers University Press.

Spatz, C. (1993). *Basic statistics: Tales of distributions.* Pacific Grove, CA: Brooks/Cole.

Spatz, C. & Johnston, J. O. (1976). *Basic statistics: Tales of distributions.* Monterey, CA: Brooks/Cole.

Spiegler, M. D., & Guevremont, D. C. (1993). *Contemporary behavior therapy.* Pacific Grove, CA: Brooks/Cole.

Squire, L. R., Amaral, D. G., & Press, G. A. (1990). Magnetic resonance imaging of the hippocampus and mammillary nuclei distinguish medial temporal lobe and diencephalic amnesia. *Journal of Neuroscience, 10,* 3106–3117.

Sternberg, R. J. (1992, September). How to win acceptances by psychology journals: 21 tips for better writing. *APS Observer,* 12–15.

Stevenson, H. W., & Odum, R. O. (1963). *Visual reinforcement with children.* Unpublished manuscript. University of Minnesota, Minneapolis, MN.

Strowmetz, D. B., Alterman, A. I., & Walter, D. (1990). Subject selection bias in alcoholics volunteering for a treatment study. *Alcoholism: Clinical and Experimental Research, 14,* 736–738.

Stunkard, A. J., Sorensen, T., Hanis, C., Teasdale, T. W., Chakraborty, R., Schull, W. J., & Schulsinger, F. (1986). An adoption study of human obesity. *The New England Journal of Medicine, 314,* 193–197.

Sue, S., & Zane, N. (1987). The role of culture and cultural techniques in psychotherapy: A critique and reformulation. *American Psychologist, 42,* 37–45.

Suinn, R. (1972). Behavior rehearsal training for ski racers. Brief report. *Behavior Therapy, 3,* 210–212.

Suinn, R. (1983). Imagery and sports. In A. Sheikh (Ed.), *Imagery: Current theory, research, and application.* New York: Wiley.

Summers, G. F., & Hammonds, A. D. (1965). Toward a paradigm of respondent bias in survey research. Unpublished paper, University of Wisconsin, Madison, WI.

Tanford, S. L. (1984). Decision making processes in joined criminal trials. Unpublished doctoral dissertation, University of Wisconsin, Madison, WI.

Thomas, S. B. (1991). The Tuskegee syphilis study, 1932-1972: Implications for HIV education and AIDS risk education programs in the black community. *American Journal of Public Health, 81,* 1498–1505.

Thoreau, H. D. (1887). Autumn. In H. G. O. Blake (Ed.), *From the journal of Henry David Thoreau.* New York: Houghton-Mifflin.

Thoreau, H. D. (1887). Winter. In H. G. O. Blake (Ed.), *From the journal of Henry David Thoreau.* New York: Houghton-Mifflin.

Thorndike, E. L. (1898). Animal intelligence: An experimental study of the association processes in animals. *Psychology Review Monograph, 2* (Whole No. 8).

Tuckwell, H. C. (1995). *Elementary applications of probability theory.* New York: Chapman and Hall.

Tulving, E. (1962). Subjective organization in free recall of unrelated words. *Psychological Review, 69,* 344–354.

Vedlitz, A. (1988). *Conservative mythology and public policy in America.* New York: Prager.

Warwick, D. P., & Lininger, R. (1975). *The sample survey: Theory and practice.* New York: McGraw-Hill.

Watson, J. B. (1913). Psychology as the behaviorist views it. *Psychological Review, 20,* 158–177.

Webb, E. J., Campbell, D. T., Schwartz, R. D., & Sechrest, L. (1966). *Unobtrusive measures.* Chicago: Rand McNally.

Webster's Ninth New Collegiate Dictionary. (1991). Springfield, MA: Meriam-Webster Inc.

Weekes, D. P. (1995). Adolescents growing up chronically ill: A life-span development view. *Family & Community Health, 17,* 22–34.

Wispe, L. (1991). *The psychology of sympathy.* New York: Plenum.

Worchel, F. F., Copeland, D. R., & Barker, D. G. (1987). Control-related coping strategies in pediatric oncology patients. *Journal of Pediatric Psychology, 12,* 25–38.

Zajonc, R. B. (1965). Social facilitation. *Science, 149,* 269–274.

# The Model Experiment

Psychotherapy      1

PSYCHOTHERAPY AND AGE DIFFERENCES


The Effectiveness of Psychotherapy

for Chronically Ill Children

as a Function of Age

Jack R. Nation                    You A. Student

Texas A&M University        Your College or University

## Abstract

This study examined the relationship between age and the effectiveness of a cognitively oriented therapeutic intervention in pediatric oncology patients.  Forty-eight patients from ages 4 to 6 and 48 patients from ages 10 to 12, received treatment with a (a) cognitive coping, (b) sensory information, or (c) contact control treatment before receiving medical treatment. Behavioral observations, self-reports, and heart rate recordings were taken immediately before treatment and compared to baseline records. On the heart rate measure, the cognitive coping intervention was effective only in alleviating the older children's anxiety. Conversely, the sensory information treatment reduced only the younger children's fear. The contact control had no ameliorative effects. These data suggest that further investigations of the effect developmental parameters have on various therapeutic strategies are needed.

The Effectiveness of Psychotherapy for Chronically Ill Children

as a Function of Age

The developmental aspects of human cognition have long been recognized as important determinants of performance in laboratory settings. It has been demonstrated, for instance, that younger children (5- or 6-year-olds) perform better on extradimensional discrimination tasks than on intradimensional discrimination tasks, while the opposite is true for older children (11- or 12-year-olds) (see Baddeley, 1993; Kendler & Kendler, 1967). One reason rests with the respective cognitive capacities of younger versus older children (Reese & Lipsitt, 1970). Because older children are able to invoke problem-solving strategies and to use abstract decision rules, concepts such as "opposite," which facilitate performance in an intradimensional situation, are immediately available. Conversely, younger children must rely more on their conditioning histories, so they would be expected to perform better on an extradimensional task (refer to Reese & Lipsitt, 1970, for a detailed discussion of this line of reasoning).

Recently, the notion that developmental differences in the cognitive apparatus may affect clinical phenomena has received attention (Gerralda, Kim, & Klein, 1994; Sargent & Liebman, 1985; Weekes, 1995). As a result, it is now clear that learned helplessness that results in the laboratory, which many believe to parallel clinical depression (Abramson, Seligman, & Teasdale,

1978), is more likely to occur in older rather than younger children. Parsons and Ruble (1977) showed that experiences with success and failure has more impact on 11-year-olds than on 3-year olds. That is, the older children's past performances were more likely to affect their future behavior, either positively or negatively. Rholes, Blackwell, Jordan, and Walters (1980) were able to demonstrate that younger children are less susceptible than are older children to helplessness due to age-related differences in casual attributions. Apparently, when younger children deal with failure, their diminished cognitive levels act as a buffer against the negative attributional styles that would emerge with a more elaborate mental network.

As further evidence of the importance of developmental parameters to clinical issues, several papers point to the fact that age differences are responsible for substantially different approaches in dealing with stress. Specifically, Brown, O'Keeffe, Sanders, and Baker (1986) assessed children's ability to cope with a dental injection and found that in the 8 to 18 age range the variety and total number of cognitive coping strategies increased as age increased. Similarly, Curry and Russ (1985) reported coping methods as a function of increasing age. It seems that as the overall cognitive and intellectual ability increases, the reliance on cognitive responses to cope with stressors increases as well. Even in instances of severe medical problems involving chronic, life-threatening illness, coping strategies shift in a more cognitive direction as a child matures. Along these lines, Worchel, Copeland, and Barker (1987) observed that chronically ill pediatric oncology patients in adolescence were more likely to use spontaneous cognitive interventions to help them cope with such painful procedures as spinal taps and bone marrow tests.

Findings like these and numerous others in this expanding pool of literature raise serious questions about the efficacy of certain types of therapeutic interventions which currently are being recommended for children facing stressful life situations. To date, virtually everything that has been attempted in the area of the interaction between age and coping strategies focuses on indexing the coping techniques children invoke under chronic or acute stress conditions. Perhaps an even more important issue rests with the general suitability of therapeutic interventions that are so solidly tied to events we now suspect are more appropriate for one age group rather than another. Insofar as commonly recommended treatment approaches like the coping program Peterson and Shigetomi (1981) advanced depend on the patient's cognitive sophistication, and given the aforementioned data revealing the disinclination (indeed, the inability) of younger children to use cognitive coping strategies, it follows that such techniques may be comparatively ineffective with this age range. In simple terms, it is likely to do very little good to invite a child to deploy elaborate mental images to combat stress when that child possesses marginal imaging skills.

Accordingly, this study was designed principally to show that a cognitively oriented strategy that is patterned after that by Peterson and Shigetomi (1981) would more effectively alleviate stress in 10- to 12-year-old children diagnosed with cancer than in 4- to 6-year-old children with the same illness. By demonstrating the age-related limitations of a cognitively oriented therapeutic regimen, the need to examine the scope of other treatment procedures would be enhanced.

An additional, adjunctive concern of this study was the role information played during the coping period. Information is known to produce beneficial results in dealing with stressful situations (Miller, Sherman, Combs, & Kruus, 1992), but it appears more true for younger children than for older children (Curry & Russ, 1985). For some reason, younger children seek more information about the source of their stress than do older children. Therefore, we predicted that a technique like sensory information (see Siegel & Peterson, 1980) would be more effective with 4- to 6-year-olds than for 10- to 12-year-olds. The expected interaction between age and therapeutic style would underscore the need to incorporate developmental parameters into studies of treatment efficacy.

Method

## Participants

The participants in this study were 96 English-speaking pediatric patients (48 male and 48 female) who were undergoing

cancer treatment at the University of Texas M.D. Anderson
Hospital and Tumor Institute in Houston, Texas. Of the 48 male
participants, 29 were Caucasian, 15 were Mexican-American, and 4
were African-American. Of the 48 females who participated in the
experiment, 31 were Caucasian, 12 were Mexican-American, and 5
were African-American. Half of the male and female participants
were from each of the two age ranges included in the experiment
(4- to 6-year-olds and 10- to 12-year-olds).

Participants were selected randomly from all medical
services (i.e., leukemia, lymphoma, solid tumors, rare solid
tumors) except brain tumors. Eligibility criteria included (a)
age 4 to 6 or age 10 to 12, (b) English speaking, (c) in
sufficiently good health to respond to the various points of
intervention (see following), and (d) experienced as both an
inpatient and outpatient. All patients were receiving treatment
that required a series of at least four bone marrow aspirations
(BMAs) and lumbar punctures (LPs).

## Materials

A behavioral rating scale and a self-report scale were used
in this experiment. The behavioral rating scale was the
observational Scale of Behavioral Distress (OSBD) (reproduced in
Smith, Ackerson, & Blotcky, 1989); the self-report scale was the
"fear thermometer," which is easily constructed in house (see
Katz, Kellerman, & Seigel, 1982). In addition, heart rate was
measured using an electrocardiograph (EKG) [model 69-2204]

manufactured by Carolina Biological Supply Company (Burlington, NC).

<u>Procedure</u>

   <u>Demographic data.</u> Each child's age, gender, type and date of diagnosis, maternal educational level, primary provider's occupation, and family income were obtained from family members and hospital staff.

   <u>Design and assignment to treatments.</u> This study employed a 2 age range (4 to 6, 10 to 12) x 3 treatment conditions (cognitive coping strategy, sensory information, and contact control) equal Ns design. Eight male and eight female participants from each age range were randomly assigned to receive one of the three interventions. (Note: Because of ethical considerations, after the research was completed all participants were offered the most beneficial program as defined by the results of this study, but these results are not presented here.) The same physicians and nursing staff were present throughout the study.

   <u>Experimenters.</u> The experimenters (therapists) included graduate students and postdoctoral students who had received extensive training in psychotherapeutic intervention. All personnel had a minimum of 100 practica (therapy) hours of supervised experience with children.

   Each experimenter involved in the treatment phase of the proposed project was supervised by a licensed clinical psychologist, certified by the State Board of Examiners of

Psychologists as a health service provider in the State of Texas. During the data collection phase of the experiment, it was the responsibility of each experimenter to monitor the psychological welfare of the participant (patient) and determine whether or not the participant was at risk.

Medical treatment (stressor). The study was explained to both patient and parent, and the parent signed an informed consent form. All data collectors were blind to the interventions used in the study, and data were collected in the same manner across four scheduled medical procedures. The first two procedures were used to gather baseline data, and the respective interventions were performed before the last two procedures. Parents accompanied children during the procedures in all cases.

After the child was placed in a treatment room and examined by a physician, a research assistant entered the room, attached a heart rate monitor, and had the child complete a self-report (see following) regarding his or her fear or expected pain. Subsequently, behavioral observations were recorded and heart rate was measured. At this point, the intervention was introduced. When the nurse actually brought the medical procedure instruments into the room, behavioral records and heart rate recordings were again taken, for 2 minutes. The data collected for the 2-minute period immediately before the four BMA or LP medical procedures (two baseline and two post-intervention) were used for the analyses.

Interventions. Depending on treatment assignment, one of the three following intervention strategies was used.

In the cognitive coping condition (see Peterson & Shigetomi, 1981), a research assistant pointed out to the children how good the children felt when they were safely in their homes and that sometimes, when children are hospitalized, they wish to feel those same feelings. The research assistant had already taught these children three techniques to achieve such feelings: (1) cue-controlled, deep-muscle relaxation; (2) mental imagery; and (3) comforting self-talk.

Participants were trained in deep-muscle relaxation by stretching and tensing their muscles, then relaxing completely. After the children had practiced this technique several times, the cue word calm and slow deep-breathing exercises were introduced. The participants practiced each of the components until each was able to demonstrate that relaxation could be achieved quickly using these cognitive-behavioral techniques.

The imaginal distraction technique was then introduced. Participants were asked to imagine a scene that made them quite happy. Scenes such as playing outdoors, lying at the beach, or walking in the mountains were common. The children were encouraged to make the scene as vivid and as positive as possible.

Finally, participants receiving the cognitive coping intervention were given two comforting self-talk phrases: "I will be better in a little while," and "Everything is going to be all right." The children were encouraged to say these phrases out loud and to then repeat them silently to themselves.

As a result, the participants who were assigned to the cognitive coping strategy intervention were adept at these tasks before actually being asked to use the intervention during the last two of the four scheduled medical procedures.

In the sensory information intervention, participants were told that one way of learning to cope with the medical procedures was to know exactly what to expect, including what they might think and feel (see Siegel & Peterson, 1980; Smith, Ackerson, & Blotcky, 1989). When the last two of the four medical treatments were conducted, it was explained that the nurse was going to provide this type of detailed information, telling them step by step what she was going to do. An example of what the nurse told the participants is, "I am about to put the numbing medicine in the place I just washed. I'll count to three and then put it in so that you won't feel the needle. You may feel a pinprick as I put the numbing medicine in and, sometimes the medicine stings as it starts to work. OK, one, two, three."

In the contact control condition, a research assistant simply read the children a chapter from <u>Winnie the Pooh</u> or <u>The Never Ending Story</u>. While there was an attempt to keep the intervention times uniform across the cognitive coping strategy, the sensory information approach, and the contact control condition, the inherently shorter time associated with the sensory information intervention could not be avoided.

Dependent Measures. As mentioned earlier in the Materials subsection, a behavioral rating scale, a self-report measure, and an EKG were available for this study. Accordingly, the dependent measures used to index the patients' levels of apprehension before treatment, and thereby determine the relative effectiveness of each intervention with the different age groups, were:

1.  Observational Scale of Behavioral Distress (OSBD). This scale (refer to Smith, Ackerson, & Blotcky, 1989) required that two trained observers record behaviors in 11 categories (e.g., crying, nervous behavior, and verbal resistance) in 15-second intervals for 2 minutes to obtain a total distress score. The scale has good reliability and validity and has been described in detail (Jay, Elliot, Ozolins, Olson, & Pruitt, 1985).

2.  Self-Report Measure of Fear and Pain. Three visual analog thermometers were used to assess the children's perceptions of fear and expectancies of pain. With this procedure the participant simply points to a location on the thermometer that best describes how he or she feels (0 = no fear; 100 = as afraid as much as possible). This instrument has also been shown to be reliable in studies similar to the one reported here

(Katz, Kellerman, & Siegel, 1982).

3.   Heart Rate. Heart Rate (HR) was monitored using the EKG
     device discussed previously. Chest electrodes were
     attached to the participants. The HR value was averaged
     over five beats and appeared as digital beats per
     minute.

Following the data collection phase, all participants were
debriefed and, as indicated earlier, each was given the option of
using the intervention technique that produced the most favorable
results.

### Results

The results of this study showed that the cognitive coping
strategy diminished the anxiety associated with medical treatment
only in the older participants (10- to 12-year-olds). The levels
of the 4- to 6-year-old children did not differ from baseline
when this intervention strategy was used. A quite different
pattern of results was evident when the sensory information
approach was used, however. With this intervention, fear and
apprehension concerning scheduled medical treatments was reduced
more in the younger age range than in the older age range. The
contact control procedure did not alter fear reactions. Finally,
regardless of the intervention used, only the heart rate measure
showed any evidence that fear and anxiety levels were affected in
this study.

Because neither the observational scale data nor the self-

report data showed significant differences due to type of
intervention or age of the participant, only the statistical
findings on the heart rate measure are presented in this report.
The physiological measure of heart beats per minute was totaled
over each of the 2 minute recording periods for both the 4- to 6-
year-old range and the 10- to 12-year-old range, and behavior
(heart rate) during the final two post intervention periods is
presented as percent of baseline in Figure 1. A 2 age ranges x 3
interventions ANOVA test showed that the cognitive coping
strategy significantly reduced heart rate relative to the other
two forms of treatment among the older children, and that the
sensory information regimen resulted in significantly greater
declines over the remaining two interventions in the younger
children $(F(2,90) = 4.13$, $p < .05)$.

Additional analysis of the heart rate measure showed that
there were no overall differences between the two age groups
$(F(1,90) = 1.48$. $p < .05)$. This means that when you compare the
two age ranges over all three types of intervention, there is no
real difference. Of course, what differs is that one type of
intervention worked better with one age range and another type
worked better with the other. From the overall pattern of the
findings reported here, it seems clear that a given intervention
is not uniformly effective for younger and older children.

Discussion

The findings from this study generally agree with the

rationale that formed the basis for the research. Specifically, it was shown that an intervention technique based on cognitive principles (the cognitive coping strategy suggested by Peterson & Shigetomi, 1981) was more effective in reducing fear of medical treatment when it was used with older children (10- to 12-year-olds). Conversely, younger children (4- to 6-year-olds) benefitted more than older children from a treatment that relied on information concerning the sensory events that were about to take place during medical treatment.

The finding which showed that the older participants were more responsive to the cognitive therapy regimen than were the younger participants is consistent with a large pool of literature which shows that developmental stage determines a person's behavioral orientation in a problem-solving situation. Discrimination learning (Baddeley, 1993; Kendler & Kendler, 1967) and reactions to failure and reward (Rholes, Blackwell, Jordan, & Walters, 1980) are psychological phenomena that depend heavily on a person's cognitive capacity. It seems that this cognitive capability is linked to age, with older children demonstrating greater cognitive capability than younger children. In this context, it is understandable that a therapeutic approach based on verbal cues, imagery, and comforting self-commentary might be appropriate for children ages 10 to 12 but would be contraindicated for children ages 4 to 6.

Similarly, the greater effects observed with the sensory information strategy in the younger children may be explained in terms of cognitive development. As noted previously, the older a child becomes, the more reliant he or she is likely to be on cognitive coping strategies (e.g., Brown, O'Keeffe, Sanders, & Baker, 1986; Worchel, Copeland, & Barker, 1987). In fact, older children seem to prefer spontaneous cognitive methods for dealing with stress, and this may obscure more rudimentary attempts at fear reduction. In contrast, in the absence of a more elaborate mental framework, younger children may rely exclusively on simple descriptive approaches, such as being told what is happening next. Along these lines, the greater effectiveness of the sensory information intervention in the younger children is interpreted as a special case involving distraction: The greater cognitive tendencies of older children interfere with simple information benefits. Because younger children are not distracted by such mental processes, they experience the fear-reducing effects of knowing just how bad the pain of medical treatment is likely to be.

Regardless of theoretical issues, the findings from this study permit one very important conclusion. A given intervention is not likely to be the most effective treatment across all age ranges. Greater attention should be given to the impact of developmental parameters on the efficacy of various therapeutic techniques.

References

Abramson, L. Y., Seligman, M. E. P., & Teasdale, J. D. (1978). Learned helplessness in humans: Critique and reformulation. Journal of Abnormal Psychology, 87, 49-74.

Baddeley, A. (1993). Human memory: Theory and practice. Boston: Allyn and Bacon.

Brown, J., O'Keefe, J., Sanders, S. F., & Baker, B. (1986). Developmental changes in children's cognition to stressful and painful situations. Journal of Pediatric Psychology, 11, 343-357.

Curry, S. L., & Russ, S. W. (1985). Identifying coping strategies in children. Journal of Clinical Child Psychology, 14, 61-69.

Gerralda, M. E., Kim, S., & Klein, S. (1994). Psychiatric adjustment in children with chronic physical illness. British Journal of Hospital Medicine, 52, 230-234.

Jay, S. M., Elliott, C. H., Ozolins, M., Olson, R. A., & Pruitt, S. D. (1985). Behavioral management of children's distress during painful medical treatment. Behavioral Research and Therapy, 23, 513-520.

Katz, E. R., Kellerman, J., & Siegel, S. E. (1982, March). Self-report and observational measurement of acute pain, fear, and behavioral distress in children with leukemia. Paper presented at the meeting of the Society of Behavioral Medicine, Chicago, IL.

Kendler, T. S., & Kendler, H. H. (1967). Experimental

analysis of inferential behavior in children. In L. P. Lipsitt & C. C. Spiker (Eds.), Advances in child development and behavior. New York: Academic Press.

Miller, M. M., Sherman, H., Combs, C., & Kruus, L. (1992). Patterns of children's coping with medical and dental stressors: Nature, implications, and future directions. In L. Siegel, G. Walker, J. Wallander, & A. La Greca (Eds.), Advances in pediatric psychology: Stress and coping in child health. New York: Guilford Press.

Parsons, J. E., & Ruble, D. N. (1977). The development of achievement-related expectancies. Child Development, 48, 1075-1079.

Peterson, L., & Shigetomi, C. (1981). The use of coping techniques to minimize anxiety in hospitalized children. Behavior Therapy, 12, 1-14.

Reese, H. W., & Lipsitt, L. P. (1970). Experimental child psychology. New York: Academic Press.

Rholes, W. S., Blackwell, J., Jordan, C., & Walters, C. (1980). A developmental study of learned helplessness. Developmental Psychology, 16, 616-624.

Sargent, J., & Liebman, R. (1985). Childhood chronic illness: Issues for psychotherapists. Community Mental Health Journal, 21, 294-311.

Siegel, L. J., & Peterson, L. (1980). Stress reduction in young dental patients through coping skills and sensory information. Journal of Consulting and Clinical Psychology, 48, 785-787.

Smith, K. E., Ackerson, J. D., & Blotcky, A. D. (1989). Reducing distress during invasive medical procedures: Relating behavioral interventions to preferred coping styles in pediatric cancer patients. Journal of Pediatric Psychology, 14, 405-419.

Weekes, D. P. (1995). Adolescents growing up chronically ill: A life-span development view. Family & Community Health, 17, 22-34.

Worchel, F. F., Copeland, D. R., & Barker, D. G. (1987). Control-related coping strategies in pediatric oncology patients. Journal of Pediatric Psychology, 12, 25-38.

Author Note

The original idea for this experiment came from Patricia L. Nation, Department of Educational Psychology, Texas A&M University, College Station, TX  77843.

Jack R. Nation is currently with an academic institution that offers a course this text supports.

Requests for reprints should be sent to Jack R. Nation, Department of Psychology, Texas A&M University, College Station, TX 77843.

Figure Caption

<u>Figure 1.</u> Percent of baseline heart rate for the 4- to 6-year old range participants and the 10- to 12-year-old range participants following intervention with the cognitive coping strategy, sensory information, or contact control. A value of 100% indicates no change from baseline.

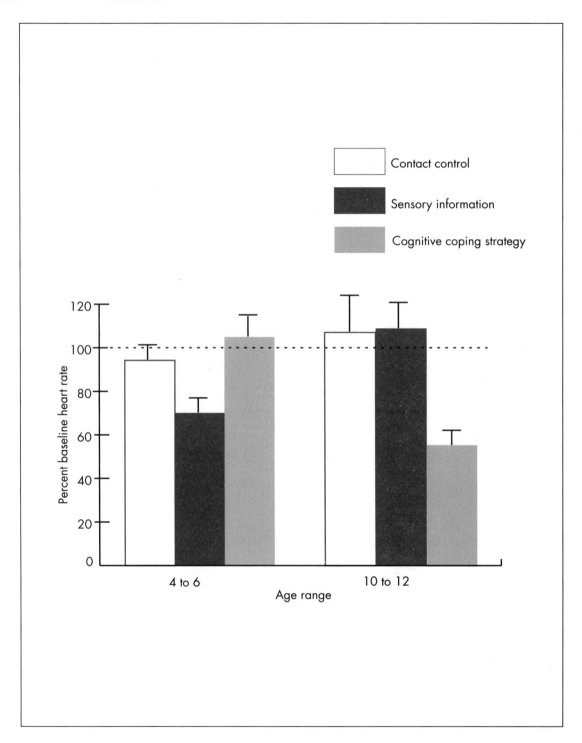

# Index

Note: Page numbers followed by an *f* indicate figures; those with a *t* indicate tables; page numbers in bold type indicate definitions.